THEORIES OF COMPARATIVE
POLITICAL ECONOMY

Other Books by Ronald H. Chilcote

Imperialism: Theoretical Directions (editor, 2000)

*Comparative Inquiry in Politics and Political Economy:
Theories and Issues* (1999)

*Political Economy of Imperialism:
Critical Appraisals* (editor, 1999)

*Theories of Comparative Politics:
The Search for a Paradigm Reconsidered* (1981, 1994)

*Amilcar Cabral's Revolutionary Theory and Practice:
A Critical Guide* (1991)

*Power and the Ruling Classes in Northeast Brazil:
Juazeiro and Petrolina in Transition* (1990)

*Latin America: Capitalist and Socialist Perspectives of
Development and Underdevelopment* (with Joel C. Edelstein, 1986)

Theories of Development and Underdevelopment (1984)

*Dependency and Marxism: Toward a Resolution of
the Debate* (editor, 1982)

*The Brazilian Communist Party:
Conflict and Integration, 1922–1972* (1974)

Latin America: The Struggle with Dependency and Beyond
(edited with Joel C. Edelstein, 1974)

*Protest and Resistance in Angola and Brazil:
Comparative Studies* (editor, 1972)

THEORIES OF
COMPARATIVE
POLITICAL
ECONOMY

Ronald H. Chilcote
University of California at Riverside

Westview Press
A Member of the Perseus Books Group

Copyright © 2000 by Westview Press, A Member of the Perseus Books Group

Published in 2000 in the United States of America by Westview Press, 5500 Central Avenue, Boulder, Colorado 80301-2877, and in the United Kingdom by Westview Press, 12 Hid's Copse Road, Cumnor Hill, Oxford OX2 9JJ

Find us on the World Wide Web at www.westviewpress.com

Library of Congress Cataloging-in-Publication Data
Chilcote, Ronald H.
    Theories of comparative political economy / Ronald H. Chilcote.
        p.   cm.
    Includes bibliographical references and index.
    ISBN 0-8133-1018-0 (hc.)—ISBN 0-8133-1019-9 (pbk.)
    1. Comparative government.   I. Title.
JF51.C44   2000
320.3—dc21
                                                                99-088513
                                                                    CIP

The paper used in this publication meets the requirements of the American National Standard for Permanence of Paper for Printed Library Materials Z39.48-1984.

10   9   8   7   6   5   4   3   2   1

To
FRANCES,
STEPHEN, AND EDWARD

CONTENTS

TABLES AND FIGURES

PREFACE

Nearly two decades ago, I began assembling a critical overview of the field of comparative politics. I hoped to bring order to a diverse field and to overcome my dissatisfaction with the literature, which at the introductory level tended to emphasize configurative and formal-legal studies of dominant European countries such as England, France, Germany, and the Soviet Union, whereas the advanced level offered general and often poorly informed understandings of the historical experience, often devoid of any theoretical considerations. This effort resulted in the publication in 1981 of a book, *Theories of Comparative Politics: The Search for a Paradigm,* in which I argued that political science and political economy are deeply influenced by ideology. No matter what our concern for science and objectivity, politics has an impact on the profession, and any pretense of value-free inquiry is imbued with conservative and antipolitical biases. Additionally, I argued that comparative politics embraces all levels of politics: The study of politics everywhere is comparative. I set forth the proposition that the study of politics has been largely shaped by the reproduction of traditional ideas and approaches, the result being the prevalence of an orthodox mainstream and a reluctance to seek radical alternatives. I traced this notion to inquiry emanating from the nineteenth century in order to reveal at least two patterns of thought, one around the ideas of Max Weber, which today influence the mainstream, and the other around the ideas of Karl Marx, which have influenced the pursuit of alternative explanations.

Theories of the political system were contrasted with those of the state; both conservative and progressive ideas were associated with a politics of culture; distinctions were drawn between theories of development and theories of underdevelopment; and theories of class were assessed in light of pluralism, instrumentalism, and structuralism. Recognition of differences in thought stimulates critical thinking, opens up dialogue to more than a prevailing mode of explanation, and provides choice in the formulation and reinforcement of individual perspectives. In short, in comparative inquiry the reader is challenged to weigh arguments, find positions, and defend ideas.

My book concluded with a plea for adopting a political-economic approach in the search for a paradigm. I traced the origins and evolution of political economy in its Marxist and non-Marxist forms since the nineteenth century and identified some of the prevailing schools of thought, leaving the reader with guidelines, theories, concepts, and methods that might be useful in pursuing this direction.

This present book builds on the proposition that the study of politics and economics has evolved into political economy in a number of significant ways and that the new issues and ideas that became prominent in the 1980s and 1990s will carry on into the new millennium. The book is organized around six chapters. The first examines significant comparative historical themes and case studies that emphasize theoretically oriented analysis. Among the important issues emanating from this work are the agrarian transition to capitalism and the rise of the absolute state, and the role of revolution. The second chapter explores the transitions from feudalism to capitalism and capitalism to socialism. The third chapter turns to theories of class. The fourth chapter examines theories of the state, tracing the origins and evolution of the state in formulations from Hegel through Marx and Engels to Lenin, Gramsci, Poulantzas, and Miliband. The fifth chapter on the theories of imperialism looks at capitalist and socialist development, with attention to capital accumulation, relations of production, and forces of production. The final chapter examines democracy from the perspective of political economy, describing its representative, indirect, and bourgeois as opposed to its direct participatory forms and recognizing the many socialisms—social democratic, democratic socialist, orthodox socialist, and revolutionary socialist—and considers new and old themes in the struggle for a progressive democratic socialism.

I would like to express my gratitude to persons who read portions or all the manuscript at various stages. Students in my seminar "Political Economy of Imperialism," in particular Matt Cowell, Katie Ghost, Stan Mallison, Monica Martins, Pamela Stricker, Michele Weber, and Bassam Y. Yousif, provided suggestions and input for Chapter 5. Early drafts of these chapters were shared with graduate students in the advanced seminar "Comparative Political Economy" that I taught jointly with my colleague Victor Lippit, and I am grateful to Victor and the students for their generous feedback and suggestions. Barbara Metzger read, extensively edited, and immeasurably improved the entire manuscript. Krista Eissfeldt incorporated the editing and pulled together many details during revision of my manuscript. Frances Chilcote carefully proofed the revision, and Sean Dillingham prepared the final manuscript for the press. Howard Sherman offered constructive suggestions for further revision. At Westview Press, Stephanie Hoppe undertook final copyediting, and Kay Mariea gently pushed the project ahead. Leo Wiegman patiently encouraged me to finish this work over five years of writing and facilitated its editing and revision.

Finally, I am especially appreciative of the support of my wife, Frances, and my sons, Stephen and Edward. This project has been many years in preparation and frequently interfered with our precious time together, and I wish to dedicate this book to them.

Ronald H. Chilcote

1

POLITICAL ECONOMY AND THE COMPARATIVE UNDERSTANDING OF HISTORY

The present generation of political scientists wrestles with the question of what is political and what is political science. Economists debate the prospects of development under equilibrium or inegalitarian conditions. Many acknowledge the contributions of Marx to these questions, yet most tend to steer clear of Marxism, preferring instead to distinguish politics from economics and to avoid issues of state, power, class, and class struggle. Addressing these issues constructively will require critical attention to political economy and to the contributions of comparative analysis.

This book is a sequel to my 1981 *Theories of Comparative Politics: The Search for a Paradigm,* which was substantially revised and published in a second edition in 1994. Its mission was to assess the prospects for a paradigm in political science and comparative politics in general and in political economy in particular and to encourage students and academics to reexamine issues that appeared to be settled, challenge established theories and concepts, and probe new areas of inquiry. It focused on Marx and Weber as precursor thinkers on system and state, culture, development and underdevelopment, and class. Its conclusion, dedicated to the concepts and theory of political economy, serves here as a point of departure.

The themes that emerge from this earlier book are fundamental to comparative political economy: transitions to capitalism and from capitalism to socialism; class; the state; imperialism; and the links between theories of imperialism and development, and democracy.

My work differs somewhat from another recent effort to synthesize an understanding of political economy. In *Theories of Political Economy,* James Caporaso and David Levine (1992) examine a multitude of approaches to political economy, identify and briefly develop principal concepts, and reflect on contrasting perspectives. Their emphasis, however, is on mainstream rather than alternative approaches. Their treatment of questions of the state, democracy, and other themes would benefit from more detailed attention to class analysis and its methodological possibilities for the study of political economy; it is this concern, among others, that characterizes the radical political economy that this book seeks to promote.

In search of a new formulation, I begin this chapter with a historical overview of how political economy has been envisaged by various thinkers over time. The chapter describes the impact of debates and positioning with regard to political economy on the social sciences in general and political science and economics in particular and goes on to discuss a number of ideas that shape our thinking about important issues and problems in the contemporary world. It turns next to the methods employed by a comparative political economy and finally to the results of important comparative studies in a variety of theoretical frameworks.

ORIGINS AND EVOLUTION OF POLITICAL ECONOMY

The origins of political economy date to the late eighteenth century and to the writings of the important classical political economists, including not only Marx but also David Ricardo and Adam Smith. These thinkers focused on capitalism and its evolution mainly in rapidly developing Europe, and especially in England. The major schools of thought that have shaped the theory of political economy from ancient to modern times are

Petty commodityism
Mercantilism
Classical liberalism
Utopian socialism
Marxism
Marginalism
Neoclassicalism
Keynesianism
Post-Keynesianism
Neo-Marxism

My summary of these schools, which is necessarily sketchy, borrows from the useful overviews of Ronald Meek (1956) and Ernest Mandel (1968); it will serve as a guide for understanding political economy today.

Most historians of political economy date its origins to petty commodity production, under which money appeared, prices fluctuated, some producers fell into debt, and primitive communal relations began to dissolve. Mang-tsze in China and Plato and Aristotle in Greece first attempted to explain the instability that accompanied petty commodity production and to find ways to overcome it on behalf of the communal society. They recognized the impact of the division of labor on commodity production, and Aristotle in particular distinguished between use value and exchange value. Mang-tsze considered agricultural labor the source of value, and Plato came close to offering a similar theory. The expansion of petty commodity production in the European Middle Ages stimulated the scholastic theologians Albertus Magnus and Thomas Aquinas to address the problem of value. Aquinas, for instance, sought a fair price, thereby justifying the merchant's profit and defending the established commercial order. Eventually, this medieval conception of a just price lost its significance in the face of international trade. Duns Scotus, another scholastic thinker, worked with a theory of exchange value based on labor, and Abd-al-Rahman-Ibn-Khaldun, an Islamic philosopher, elaborated a historical-materialist view of history.

The principal concern of political economy between the fourteenth and seventeenth centuries was the nature of wealth in an impersonal system of markets. This was a period marked by the discovery and conquest of new geographical areas, new flows of capital to and from the New World, and the rise of monarchs and merchants who promoted nationalism, undermined local barriers to commerce, and benefited from foreign trade and the erosion of the power of the old order of church and nobility. Mercantilist writings of the period pragmatically analyzed how nations produced wealth, pointing to the importance of a credit balance of payments, a favorable trade balance, manufacturing, and fertile soil. The early mercantilists described economic life in terms of a circulation of commodities, whereas writers in the late seventeenth and eighteenth centuries addressed questions about the social surplus product that became evident with the growth in manufacturing and technology in agriculture. Two strains of political economy appeared. One, the British school, was represented by William Petty, who in *Political Arithmetic* (1651) analyzed the agricultural origins of surplus value. The French Physiocrats constituted the other. In *Détail de la France* (1695), Pierre Boisguillebert concentrated on agricultural labor as the only source of value. François Quesnay argued in his *Economic Table* (1758) against the mercantilist assumption that wealth sprang from trade and stressed the surplus produced in agriculture. He advocated that taxes be paid by the landowners, not the small farmers, merchants, and manufacturers, whom he considered productive. Finally, Nicholas Barbon, in *A Discourse of Trade* (1690), related the value of a commodity to the cost of making goods and emphasized communal profit, which according to Ronald Meek (1956) represented a transition from mercantilism to the classical approach of Adam Smith and others.

The classical liberals believed that private property should be protected and that the production of wealth was based on the incentive to work instilled in the individual by the right to property. Individual initiative therefore had to be free of mercantilist constraints. These ideas emanated from English thought, in particular the advocacy of free trade in the writings of Dudley North and the notion in John Locke that production was the consequence of individual effort to satisfy human needs and that workers should be able to use or consume their own products.

Adam Smith consolidated these ideas in classical political economy. In his *Inquiry into the Nature and Causes of the Wealth of Nations* (1776), he brought together the major themes of commodity, capital and value, and simple and complex labor. He was the first to formulate a labor theory of value, making it possible to identify the amount of labor in the value of commodities. He identified laws of the market to explain the drive of individual self-interest in competition and envisaged a competitive market equilibrium.

David Ricardo, in *Principles of Political Economy and Taxation* (1817), was both a disciple and a critic of Smith, and he contributed refinements to political economy. Ricardo advocated the accumulation of capital as the basis for economic expansion. He believed that governments should not intervene in the economy and argued that a division of labor and free trade policies would benefit all nations. He related Smith's ideas of orderly growth and market equilibrium to the international economic system. He also noted the conflict between the interests of landlords (opposed to the community) and capitalists (favorable to the community). His interpretation influenced socialist interpretations of political economy, in particular his propositions that the value of any commodity was purely and solely determined by the quantity of labor necessary for its production and that social labor was divided among three classes, landowners, capitalists, and workers.

Among other classical liberals were Thomas R. Malthus and Jeremy Bentham. In *Principles of Political Economy* (1820), Malthus contributed a theory of population to political economy, arguing that population reproduced faster than food production and therefore unchecked population growth would mean mass starvation and death. In *Introduction to the Principles of Morals and Legislation* (1789), Bentham viewed man's selfishness as natural and desirable but believed that individual and public interests should coincide. Government action was acceptable as long as it was not a response to the narrow interests of special groups, and individuals should be allowed freedom within a framework of moral and legal constraint.

The insights of Ricardo into labor and production and the gloomy prognosis of Malthus stimulated a group of utopian socialists in their criticism of capitalism. Robert Owen pushed for labor reforms, including a shorter workday and the ending of child labor, and promoted village cooperatives. Claude-Henri de Rouvroy, Comte de Saint-Simon, an aristocrat later relegated to poverty, believed that the workers deserved the highest rewards of society and advocated the reorganization of society. John Stuart Mill manifested socialist leanings in his *Principles of Political Economy* (1848), in which he retraced the path of Smith and Ricardo but placed emphasis on production rather than on distribution. Pierre-Joseph Proudhon, another utopian socialist, was a critic of the orthodox economics of his time.

Transcending the theory of the utopian socialists as well as that of the classical liberals, Karl Marx worked out a theory of surplus value and a synthesis that allowed for an explanation of class struggle. He developed theories on the prices of production and the tendency of the rate of profit to fall. His early work attacked the utopian socialists and his later work the classical liberal economists, Ricardo and Smith in particular. For example, in *The Poverty of Philosophy* (1847) he exposed the "metaphysics" of Proudhon's political economy and argued that one should examine the historical movement of production relations and that the production relations of a society formed a whole.

The marginalist theory of value and neoclassical political economy were developed in response to all three of these schools. The marginalists looked for "marginal" qualities in their analysis of equilibrium. The neoclassicists attempted to be rigorous, detailed, and abstract. They emphasized equilibrium and thus were often criticized for not accounting for the disturbances that affected equilibrium and structural crises.

In the midst of the great depression, John Maynard Keynes, in *The General Theory of Employment, Interest, and Money* (1936), moved political economy from an apologetic stance on capitalism to a pragmatic one. Rather than justify capitalism in theory, it was now essential to preserve it in practice by mitigating the extent of periodic fluctuations. One of Keynes's followers, Paul Samuelson, and others have persisted in this macroeconomic tradition to this day.

The post-Keynesians stressed explanation rather than prediction, focused on history and institutions, and argued that a free market economic process was fundamentally unstable, production rather than exchange was at the base of analysis, and disequilibrium and change over time rather than equilibrium and stability were essential. Post-Keynesianism drew its intellectual inspiration from Keynes and M. Kalecki.

The neo-Marxists carried on in the Marxist tradition. Frederick Engels edited and published the second and third volumes of Marx's *Capital*, followed by Karl Kautsky's editing of Marx's *History of Economic Doctrine*.

Later efforts to expand on Marx's earlier contributions included Kautsky's treatment of capitalism in agriculture, Rudolf Hilferding's *Das Finanzkapital* (1910), Rosa Luxemburg's *Accumulation of Capital* (1913), and V. I. Lenin's *Imperialism: The Last Phase of Capitalism* (1917). The Stalinist period dampened interest in Marxist theories of political economy, but after about 1960 there was a revival of interest promoted by the work of Paul Baran, Leo Huberman, Harry Magdoff, and Paul Sweezy and that of hundreds of other Marxists throughout the world.

Both Marxist and non-Marxist approaches may be useful to the study of political economy. For example, the influence of the classical political economists is apparent in recent debates such as Robert Brenner's (1976; see annotated reference in Chapter 2) challenge to the world systems approach of Immanuel Wallerstein and the ideas about underdevelopment of the early André Gunder Frank.

The study of capitalist accumulation with emphasis on precapitalist and capitalist formations and modes of production makes possible an integration of the inquiries of economists with regard to the material base of society and those of political scientists with regard to the political superstructure. Theories of imperialism and dependency and of the state and class should all become part of the armamentarium of the political economist.

SORTING THEORIES

The intellectual divisions inherent in political economy, especially during the twentieth century, reflect currents in Western philosophy that Pauline Rosenau (1988) has synthesized as romanticism, empiricism, and rationalism.

Romanticism implies idealism associated with our perception of ideas. It assumes that human beings are qualitatively different from nature and that human values are based on individual freedom and personal consciousness. Knowledge is premised on totality and is opposed to positivism and empiricism. Facts and values are seen as related. Methodologically, nominal rather than real concepts and teleological rather than causal explanations are preferred. This current is represented by critical theorists such as Jürgen Habermas and Michael Löwy, neo-Hegelians such as Georg Lukács, existentialists such as Jean-Paul Sartre, and Freudians such as Herbert Marcuse.

In contrast, empiricism is positivist, with an emphasis on quantification and materialism. It assumes that humans are part of nature and therefore their behavior can be studied scientifically. Rationalism represents a compromise between empiricism and romanticism. It is neither determinist nor voluntarist, and its methodology is postpositivist. Its proponents in-

TABLE 1.1   Patterns of Thought and Schools of Marxism

Major Patterns of Thought	Related Schools of Marxism
Romanticism	Philosophical
Knowledge as totality	Critical theorists
Emphasis on human-centered philosophy	Yugoslav praxists
Stress on individual freedom, experiences	Frankfort philosophers
Differentiation of humans from nature	Phenomenological Marxists
Nominal rather than real concepts	Neo-Hegelians
Rejection of fact-value distinction	Freudians
Teleological rather than causal explanation	Existentialists
	Some Trotskyists
Empiricism	Materialist
Positivist methodology based on observation	Soviet (prior to 1920, late 1950s)
Humans part of nature	Frankfort school up to 1930
Social scientific study of human behavior	2nd and 3rd International Marxists
	Contemporary materialists
Rationalism	Structuralist
Deductive	Progressive non-Marxists
Neither determinist nor voluntarist	Althusserian Marxists
Postpositivist	Non-Althusserian Marxists
Theory rather than data	Analytical Marxists

SOURCE: Adapted from Rosenau 1988: 423–454.

clude Austro-Marxists such as Rudolf Hilferding, Karl Kautsky, and Edward Bernstein of the Second International and Nicolai Bukharin of the Third International, along with contemporary theorists such as Ralph Miliband, Paul Baran, and Paul Sweezy.

Rationalism pursues both causal and structural explanation; relies more on theory than data; and is objective and usually deductive in drawing knowledge from reason, proof, and intellectual reflection. Allied with this current are structuralists influenced by Louis Althusser such as Nicos Poulantzas and Göran Therborn, other structuralists such as Claus Offe, and analytical Marxists such as Jon Elster and John Roemer.

These thought patterns and schools of thinking reflect divisions and differences. Within Marxism, despite assertions to the contrary, it is also evident that consensus rarely exists and many currents persist (see Tables 1.1 and 1.2). Distinctive trends can be noted within particular national traditions, and the ideas of individual consciousness and alienation, embod-

TABLE 1.2   Trends in the Crisis of Marxism

	Western Marxism			Eastern Marxism
Major Countries	Germany	Italy	France	Russia
Precursor Pioneers	Lukács (Hungary)	Gramsci		Lenin Trotsky Stalin
Non-Marxist Influences	Weber	Croce	Heidegger Lacan	Consolidation of Stalinism
Contemporary Marxists	Marcuse	Della Volpe	Sartre Althusser	
Critical Theory	From Marx and his early writings Frankfort school Horkheimer Habermas Lukács			

ied in the early writings of Marx and Lukács, are juxtaposed with the materialist collective vision in the thinking of revolutionaries such as Lenin and Leon Trotsky, who spawned distinctive ideological international movements and eventually the sectarian and dogmatic doctrines of Stalin.

Along the way, Louis Althusser, a French philosopher and communist, provoked a generation of intellectuals to reconsider their allegiance to Stalinism and the Soviet path to socialism. Althusser attempted to rescue Marxism while trying to transcend economism, or technological determinism, and humanism and historicism. In *For Marx* (1970; see annotated reference in Chapter 3) he launched his own brand of Marxism with powerful and pertinent criticisms. One of his followers, Nicos Poulantzas, moved in a new theoretical direction that led to the contemporary focus on the new social movements and postmodernism. Although these writers challenged the old orthodoxy, they nevertheless adhered to a structural approach and used Marxism as Marx had, as a framework for deep analysis of societal problems. The ensuing decade represented a revitalization and an awakening of Marxism, but this soon succumbed to a crisis proclaimed by Althusser himself in a dramatic announcement in November 1977 and eventually evidenced in the fall of so-called communist regimes in Eastern Europe and the Soviet Union. Gregory Elliott (1987: 331–335, notes 9–15) has balanced the theoretical advances of Althusserianism against its problems and identified a long list of scholars influenced in their research and writing by Althusser. In an appraisal of structural Marxism in the thought of Althusser, Nancy Hartsock argues that his work constituted a first step along the path later taken by the poststructuralist thinkers whom she criticizes in a review of three themes in his work: the last instance and the concept of overdetermination, science and ideology, and theoretical antihumanism. She sets out to balance the emphases on intellectual work and political practice in Marxism (1991: 14) and to rectify what she characterizes as Althusser's undermining of the dialectical unity of theory and practice.

A parallel resurgence of Marxism and new theories took place in the Third World. It too was manifested in the discontent of intellectuals with the orthodoxy of Stalinism and the traditional communist movements, especially in Latin America, where progressive intellectuals of Marxist, Christian Socialist, Democratic Socialist, and Trotskyist persuasions began to work out ideas on why capitalism had not brought about the bourgeois revolution that had occurred in Western Europe and the United States. One of its precursors, Caio Prado Jr., like Althusser a respected Marxist historian and communist, turned against the old ideas of his party in the search for understandings that reflected the backwardness and limited capitalist development of his native Brazil.

Throughout the twentieth century, there were waves of popular resurgence and defeat. Although the Russian Revolution of 1917 remained intact, the proletarian insurgencies in Austria, Germany, Hungary, and Italy from 1918 to 1922 eventually succumbed to fascism. Likewise, the popular governments in France and Spain fell by the late 1930s. Resistance movements led by communist and socialist parties during World War II had evaporated by 1945 and 1946. After the war, old Western and Eastern Marxism rejected reformism, and their mass communist parties and rigid Stalinized structures became intransigent foes of capitalism. But these movements also declined with the death of Stalin in 1953, the end of the Communist International, the intransigence of bureaucratic elites, and attempts to open up politically and economically and eventually collapsed with the fall of the Berlin Wall and the popular insurrection in 1989 and thereafter.

No single ideology or doctrine is necessarily correct. Ideas may spawn many perspectives, and those that dominate may or may not be helpful in comparative analysis. When a single perspective prevails, for instance, it may crowd out competing or alternative understandings. Pauline Rosenau has categorized major Marxist thinkers in terms of four themes.

TABLE 1.3   Marxist Directions

Criticalism	Analytical Individualism	Materialism	Structuralism
Early Marx		Mature Marx	
Lukács	Sartre	Lenin Stalin Trotsky	Althusser Poulantzas
Frankfort school (humanist, alienation)	Cohen Elster (methodological individualism)	Cohen (functionalist)	Resnick and Wolff (neostructuralism)
Laclau and Mouffe (post-Marxist)	Roemmer (rational choice)		
Habermas Bowles and Gintis (postliberalist)	Przeworski (individual choice)		
	Wright	Wright (contradictory locations)	

She argues, "Marxism is not an independent ideology or doctrine, separate and qualitatively different from Western political thought when it comes to inquiry. The perspective advanced by each Marxist orientation parallels major trends in Western, non-Marxist philosophy" (1988: 445). The logic of inquiry that underlies Marxist research should be of interest to non-Marxists, and Marxists should recognize influences from the non-Marxist side (Perry Anderson 1983 has mentioned Laclau's influence on Althusser, Weber's on Lukács, and Heidegger's on Sartre). "Marxism lacks a unified view of philosophy, method, and research, separate and distinguishable from that held by non-Marxists" (424).

The terms of the dialogue among progressive thinkers are set out in Tables 1.3 and 1.4. The content of different schools of thought usually reveals a preference for one or another theorist. For example, those influenced especially by the economic foundations of society commonly build their formulations around the idea of the material base and the forces of production, whereas those interested in political questions may emphasize the ideological superstructure—the state and its agencies or apparatuses. Material base and ideological superstructure appear as diametrically opposite or as a dichotomy, and an effective analysis would attempt

TABLE 1.4   Terms of the Progressive Dialogue

Economic	Political
Economism	Voluntarism
Material base	Ideological superstructure
Class	Group
Vanguard	Coalition
Hegemony	Counterhegemony
Democratic centralism	Pluralism
Central planning	Market

to integrate them dialectically. Many other distinctions appear in political discourse and in social science terminology: economism in contrast to voluntarism, class rather than group, the vanguard rather than a coalition of forces, democratic centralism rather than a pluralism of varied views, central planning rather than the free market. Marx went to some lengths to demonstrate his method in dialectical fashion, but many of his followers have emphasized one point of view over another.

Reference has been made to the crisis of Marxism and the fall of the regimes in Eastern Europe and the Soviet Union. What was at the root of this apparent exhaustion of Marxism in those situations? As for the failed experiences, clearly entrenched bureaucracies had much to do with the disenchantment. The ruling communist parties with their vanguard pretensions had lost touch with the people. Furthermore, Marxism everywhere had been assimilated into academia, which clearly contributed to the tendency to hang on to sectarian slogans and models and push discourse into confusion and obscurity. In a serious probe into the crisis, the historian Perry Anderson (1983) showed that since 1974 Western Marxist thought and its methodology have been shaped in large measure by the contemporary international capitalist order. He argued that with the passing of its elders, such as Lukács, Marcuse, and Sartre, Western Marxism began to run its course. The turn to empirical and concrete studies by some Marxists was significant, however, and produced contributions that are influential even today, such as the writing of Ernest Mandel on late capitalism, Harry Braverman on labor and monopoly, Michel Aglietta on the theory of capitalist regulation, and Ralph Miliband and Nicos Poulantzas on capitalism and the state, along with contributions to English historiography by Christopher Hill, Eric Hobsbawm, Edward Thompson, and Rodney Hilton and the North American contributions of Erik Olin Wright, Eugene Genovese, Eric Foner, and Robert Brenner. Anderson believed that the crisis was provoked by Latin Marxism in France, Italy, and Spain, signified by a renunciation of Marxism by the older generation on the left (represented by the Italian philosopher Lucio Colletti) and skepticism of the idea of a revolutionary rupture with capital (Poulantzas in his final interview shifted his view on dual power and proclaimed the virtues of parliamentary democracy). Anderson considered the decline of Marxism in the Latin societies and the ascent of Marxism in the English-speaking world "an uncanny paradox." The English revitalization of Marxism was eventually corrected by the post-Marxist currents in England and the United States and the retreat of intellectuals from the impact of Thatcherism and Reaganism (Anderson 1983: 18–20, 30).

In her more recent chronology of the new left, past and present, Ellen Meiksins Wood (1995) has also reviewed the rise of the Western (new) left and the subsequent retreat of left intellectuals and decline of the labor movement. This brief history begins with Nikita Khrushchev's denunciation of Stalin in 1956 and the subsequent rise of a new left in Britain, culminating with the founding of *The New Reasoner* by the communist dissidents John Saville and E. P. Thompson in 1956–1957 and its merger with *University and Left Review* into *New Left Review* in 1957 and the ascendance of Perry Anderson, Robin Blackburn, Tom Nairn, and others to its editorial board. Wood characterizes this as a transition from a first to a second new left and goes on to examine the divisions and currents of this left.

In the view of Anderson, Western Marxism in its old form was unlikely to produce any new significant theory. Theory and practice could combine in Western countries to refocus attention on the world economy, structures of the capitalist state, social classes, and the nation. Although he acknowledged the turn to the concrete and toward a "strategic discussion of ways in which a revolutionary movement could break past the barriers of the bourgeois-democratic state to a real socialist democracy beyond it" (1983: 19), Anderson believed that Marxist culture would evolve in the United States and Britain—the bastions of capitalism—with the push of the campus revolts and the new left after 1968. In the end, historical materialism would have to reexamine the historical thinkers but also the gains of Marxist historiography, especially Anglo-American: "The grand Western Marxist tradition . . . has effectively come to an end, and in its stead there has emerged, with remarkable celerity and confidence, another kind of Marxist culture, primarily oriented towards just those questions of an economic, social or political order that had been lacking from its predecessor" (20).

This analysis suggests that Marxism evolves through cycles of interest and creativity. From the time of Marx and Engels to the present, Marxism can be understood in terms of interaction with revolutionary movements and shifts in thinking from orthodoxy to open and eclectic formulations. The latest cycle began with the surge of mass movements of the late

1960s, followed by the isolation of Marxism from mass struggles and an orientation toward reformism and mainstream politics. History shows that Marxism becomes vital at moments of crisis and that its vitality and exhaustion are linked to conjunctural conditions. On a note of optimism, Al Szymanski argued that when orthodoxy prevails, critical theoretical ideas also appear, whereas when reformism dominates Marxism tends to be less imaginative and insightful: "It can, thus, be predicted that the current predominance of open and reformist Marxism will be reversed with either protracted economic depression or warfare" (1985: 331).

THE COMPARATIVE APPROACH

How do we approach comparisons in the study of political economy, and in what ways can comparison be useful to the social sciences? Scholars have debated these questions throughout the twentieth century (see Table 1.5). In the first half of the twentieth century, the major controversy in the study of international politics was between idealists in the mold of Woodrow Wilson, who believed in a unified global society moderated by international mechanisms such as the League of Nations and later the United Nations, and realists like Hans Morgenthau and Henry Kissinger, who adopted a statist, power-centered conception of global politics. Inquiry in comparative politics focused on such themes as the formation of the nation-state, constitutions, and governmental activities in Europe and the United States. Investigation in both fields initially tended toward description and later incorporated theory and methods that sought to provide a more systematic basis for understanding. With the rise of behaviorism in the 1950s, attention focused on the choice of scientific method and value-free research, a dominant movement that was challenged by the postbehavioral revolution of historicism and normative theory that accompanied dissent during the 1960s. From the 1980s to the present, the search for a paradigm has evolved through a third controversy, involving, on the one side, the refinement of the positivist approach and attention to rational choice models and, on the other, the formulation of a postpositivist approach and incorporation of critical theory.

Comparative inquiry in the social sciences, especially in the United States, has also considered whether our comparisons must be based on field research that incorporates the history and culture of particular situations or on formal or abstract models in which data are manipulated and hypotheses tested. Sometimes, this debate is cast in terms of normative or empirical theory. The analysis may be subjective or objective. The main issue in these distinctions is whether social science is really scientific—whether it is possible to predict human behavior. During the 1950s and 1960s, behavioral science attempted to answer this question in the affir-

TABLE 1.5   Major Debates and Turning Points

	International Politics	Comparative Politics
First debate (1920s to 1950s)	Management of global conflict (idealism) vs. international relations of states (realism)	Euro-American configurative traditional studies vs. structural-functional and system comparisons
Second debate (1960s to 1980s)	Behavioralist, scientific, and positivist neorealism vs. intellectual pluralism and critical assessment of paradigms	Behavioral, scientific, and positivist attention to aggregate data vs. post-behavioral normative and historical comparisons in a theoretical context
Third debate (1980s to 1990s)	Positivist, including rational choice, conceptions vs. postpositivism and break with earlier ideas through reflexive theorizing	Positivist, including rational choice, vs. historical single- and multiple-case and postpositivist studies in a theoretical context

SOURCE: Adapted from Sjolander and Cox 1994.

mative with survey data on individual preferences. That tradition carried on in the 1980s and 1990s with so much emphasis on formal theory and rational choice as to make it unclear in political science and sociology, for example, that one needed to be an area specialist as well as a scientist.

In a useful summary of this dispute, Robert Bates (1997) reflects on the differences between an older generation of scholars who had studied particular national and cultural situations abroad and a younger generation caught up in statistical data and abstract theoretical models. Charles Lindblom (1997), reviewing the trends of the 1940s and 1950s, criticizes the belief that the study of politics is largely scientific and points out that its tendency to be subjective and ideological persists today. Rogers M. Smith (1997) warns of the need to open up social science theoretically to ensure pluralism and democratic outcomes among the warring factions. Frances Rothstein (1986) earlier confronted the limitations and ethnocentric biases inherent in the prevailing patterns of social science research by describing theoretical currents among Third World intellectuals.

One example of a study that illustrates these limitations is Noam Chomsky's (1990) effort to show the continuing devastating impact of capitalism and its consequences and the ongoing resistance of peoples of the Americas. Another is Eric Hobsbawm's (1996) historical synthesis of the world from 1914 to 1991. Hobsbawm's book is divided into three parts, covering the time from the outbreak of World War I to the defeat of Hitler, the period of growth from 1950 to the mid-1970s, and the history of the past two decades. A third example is Alex Callinicos's effort in *The Revenge of History: Marxism and the East European Revolutions* (1991) to provide a balanced understanding of the need for the upheavals in Eastern Europe in 1989 and the ongoing optimism for Marxism in the region. His perspective reveals not only the strengths of Marxism but the weaknesses of Stalinism and social democracy.

There is also the view that somehow we have transcended capitalist modernism and the need for state control and regulation of economies, by turning either to the free market or to some post formulation. In their introductory essay on this question, Frederick Cooper and Randall Packard (1997) trace the evolution of the concept of modernist development in social science and identify two schools of thought that reject it: the ultramodernists, who argue that the market solves all problems, and the postmodernists, who argue that development implies controlling practices.

Examples of the qualitative and quantitative approaches to case comparison abound, but there is a dearth of material that contributes to a theoretical framework. Exceptions are Gabriel Almond, G. Bingham Powell Jr., and Robert J. Mundt's *Comparative Politics: A Theoretical Framework* (1993); James A. Bill and Robert L. Hardgrave Jr.'s *Comparative Politics: The Quest for Theory* (1973); and Mark Irvine Lichbach and Alan S. Zuckerman's *Comparative Politics: Rationality, Culture, and Structure* (1997).

The success of some mainstream political scientists in combining a quantitative approach with rational choice and formal modeling allowed them to go on to comparative work. An early attempt at a quantitative-oriented text for empirical theory and statistical analysis is Philip Burgess, James Harf, and Lawrence Peterson's *International and Comparative Politics: A Handbook* (1979). Russell Dalton, in *Citizen Politics in Western Democracy* (1988), combined survey data with a traditional comparison of selected countries (United States, Britain, West Germany, France). In contrast, Mark Kesselman and Joel Krieger focused on a broader range of countries and regions in their *European Politics in Transition* (1992) while framing discussion and analysis in terms of themes such as state formation and constitutional order, the new political economy after World War II, institutions of representation, institutions of policy implementation, and political transition.

Pure textbook treatments of political economy are few, but there is an abundant literature on specific themes and case studies. James A. Caporaso and David P. Levine (1992) presented an overview of political economy that distinguishes between politics and economics and argues for a balanced understanding; a critical assessment of the classical orientation; attention to Marxist, neoclassical, and Keynesian political economy; focus on economic approaches to politics; and analysis of power-centered, state-centered, and justice-centered approaches and theories of political economy. Their study examines the multitude of approaches to political economy, identifies and elaborates briefly on principal concepts, and describes contrasting perspectives. Texts on international political economy include *Globalisation and Interdependence in the International Political Economy* by R. J. Barry Jones (1995) and *States and Markets: An Introduction to International Political Economy* by Susan Strange (1994). Within economics, there is Victor Lippit's *Radical Political Economy* (1996).

My approach combines comparative inquiry, incorporating both field-work and case studies, with theoretical frameworks that draw on the origins and evolution of particular experiences. I wish to move beyond the debates about whether inquiry is driven by area specialization or social science, formal or normal theory, and so on that are pointed to by Robert Bates (1997) in explaining his preference for rational choice theory over area study. As Chalmers Johnson has put it, "Neither neoclassical economics nor rational choice theory provides a mechanical alternative to genuine social science analysis" (1997: 173). Although Rogers Smith assumes that political science will become more rigorously empirical and responsive to political problems, he argues that it would probably do so "in ways that are more self-consciously historical, with both deductivist formal theory and abstract normative theory playing less prominent roles" (1997: 254). Smith predicts a trend toward historical and interpretive new institutionalism (see Thelan 1999) in contrast to rational choice forms. His criticism of rational choice theory focuses on its emphasis on building universal theory rather than relying on careful empirical testing. Many of the useful sources on theory, method, and themes in the use of historical cases and qualitative-oriented analysis include attention to quantitative work (see Bonnell 1980; Chirot 1976; Lijphardt 1971, 1975; Przeworski and Teune 1970; Ragin and Zaret 1983; Skocpol 1984).

The dichotomy between qualitative and quantitative study was a principal concern of Charles C. Ragin (1987). The comparative social sciences have a tradition of qualitative work and tend to be case oriented and historical, but their goal, Ragin argued, should be "to identify the unique strengths of case-oriented methods and to formalize these as a general method of qualitative comparison using Boolean algebra" (x). Cross-national studies tend to be vague and abstract and to treat each case separately rather than synthesize across an array of cases, but they have their advantages. They tend to be holistic, and therefore the parts may be understood in the context of the whole case. Furthermore, their causation may be understood conjuncturally: "Outcomes are analyzed in terms of intersections of conditions, and it is usually assumed that any of several combinations of conditions might produce a certain outcome." Thus, case studies "are sensitive to complexity and historical specificity; they are well-suited for addressing empirically defined historical outcomes, and they are often used to generate new conceptual schemes, as well" (ix–x).

The case-oriented approach is a way of interpreting common historical outcomes or processes across a number of examples. Although complexity, diversity, and uniqueness may be identifiable and a solid basis for comparing cases historically is possible, the investigator must limit the number of cases so as to avoid allowing the analysis to succumb to description. In contrast, the variable-oriented approach of mainstream social science breaks down cases into variables and patterns. This approach tends to yield broad statements about large bodies of data. Ragin combined these two strategies in the examination of several case studies, none of which transcended the split between qualitative and quantitative analysis in comparative social science. He illustrated the comparative method with Alexis de Tocqueville's examination of American, English, and French customs. Although the method has its limitations, in particular application to a small number of cases and often to a single case, it can be used to analyze not only similarities and differences but different sets of conditions in relation to particular processes or outcomes. It is also helpful in understanding complex causal relationships that are impossible to measure through statistical methods.

In their approaches to the comparison of cases, most researchers do not concern themselves with formal method. Rather, they employ historical chronology and description in their analyses. Those influenced by Weber may make use of "ideal types" and other typologies as a context in which to examine various cases. Others may employ "causal mechanisms" across comparable cases. Yet others may draw on "universalizing" or "encompassing" strategies in their comparisons (Ragin 1987: 34).

The qualitative comparative method contrasts sharply with variable-oriented comparative research, which focuses on features of social structure identifiable as variables. Investigators may limit the number of variables employed, but they cast their net widely for the largest possible population. Usually, they specify a hypothesis to be tested. Multivariate statistical techniques, especially multiple regression, have helped social science in a number of ways, according to Ragin. They permit study of more than a handful of cases; they do not demand the high level of familiarity of case-oriented comparisons; they allow researchers to refer to and reject alternative explanations as a means of demonstrating a preferred explanation; and they make cross-national data available to all investigators and allow for statistical control.

Ragin suggested a strategy of combining the two approaches:

> The case-oriented strategy, because it is holistic, becomes more difficult to use as the number of cases increases. The volume of comparison explodes as

the number of empirical and hypothetical cases is expanded. The method simply becomes unwieldy. A morphologically parallel problem incapacitates the variable-oriented strategy. As the complexity of the causal argument to be tested increases, intractable methodological problems are introduced. Complex conjunctural arguments cannot be tested, nor can subtypes be differentiated, in the absence of sufficient cases to permit statistical manipulation. (1987: 28)

He argued that the two strategies can be complementary: The case-oriented strategy is best for analyzing general patterns among a few cases, and the variable-oriented strategy allows for looking at probabilistic relationships between variables over a large population. He illustrated this synthetic approach by reference to Edward Shorter and Charles Tilly's *Strikes in France 1830–1968* (1974), Jeffrey Paige's *Agrarian Revolution: Social Movements and Export Agriculture in the Underdeveloped World* (1975), and John Stephens's *The Transition from Capitalism to Socialism* (1979). Shorter and Tilly, for example, use statistical analysis to support their general discussion of the era when Marx was interpreting the impact of industrial transformation and strikes in France. In this way, the quantitative basis complements the use of basic Marxist concepts to facilitate historical analysis. Paige also uses a combined strategy in testing a theory of agrarian unrest with data from agricultural export categories in seventy countries. Stephens combines strategies to include both quantitative cross-national data analysis and detailed analysis of individual cases in a comparative study of the possibilities of the transition from capitalism to socialism. His quantitative data are drawn from seventeen cases, and his comparative detailed analysis focuses on France, Britain, Sweden, and the United States. Max Kaase and Kenneth Newton's *Beliefs in Government* (1995) combines qualitative analysis with quantitative data in a five-volume series on mass political life. An eclectic approach with quantitative data drawn from the biannual Eurobarometer surveys, it attempts to move beyond earlier work by David Easton, Gabriel Almond, and Sidney Verba in its attention to the attitudes of individual citizens.

CASE STUDIES THROUGH HISTORY

Charles Tilly has focused on collective action in Europe and the United States (1978) and also has looked at European social history, concentrating on reconstructing the experience with change of ordinary people: "Its writers rail against histories of kings and generals, insist on the intrinsic value of knowing how relatively powerless people lived in the past, claim that synthetic histories commonly misconstrue the character of the masses, and argue for a significant cumulative effect of ordinary people's action on national events, such as revolutions and onsets of economic growth" (1990: 692). He illustrated the differences between humanistic and social-scientific practices in this social history through four case studies. The first, by Carlo Ginzburg, *The Cheese and the Worms* (1980), exemplified small-scale humanistic inquiry into Italian popular culture in the sixteenth century, focusing on an individual tried and convicted by the Roman Inquisition. Ginzburg used the text of the interrogation as a prism for depicting a worldview. His method was based on "patient, subtle glossing of the texts concerning the village miller [which] eventually expands a reader's awareness of popular creativity and of intellectual traditions that moved in partial independence of elite culture" (Tilly 1990: 699).

The second case was E. P. Thompson's *The Making of the English Working Class* (1963), which looked at the English working class between 1790 to 1832, a period in which working people came to identify their interests as opposed to those of their rulers and employers. The method was not chronological but topical, organized around movements, experiences with industrialization, popular radicalism, and class and politics. He incorporated in his account stories, quotations, poems, songs, slogans, visual symbols, and ritual acts, using these fragmentary sources to show how workers expressed their ideas and popular traditions. Juxtaposing important texts with these working-class fragments of the day, Thompson determined "which thinkers and activists came closest to the genuine temper of workers" (Tilly 1990: 701).

A third case was E. A. Wrigley and R. S. Schofield's *The Population History of England, 1541–1871: A Reconstruction* (1981), which used extensive study of household composition, genealogies, and estimates of national vital rates compiled from parish registers to portray English population dynamics. This massive research produced surprising results, demonstrating that during the sixteenth and seventeenth centuries large numbers of people, for example, did not marry or suffer from waves of death due to periodical harvest failures.

Finally, Olivier Zunz's *The Changing Face of Inequality* (1982) looked at Detroit's changing conditions from 1880 to 1920 to show how a city of small machine shops and mixed trades evolved into the factory-dominated center of the automobile industry. Zunz's method involved systematically sampling the household manuscript records of the 1880, 1890, and 1920 censuses, focusing on defined blocks to show uniform and comparable observations in different parts of the city at different points in time.

What Tilly has shown in this masterful synthesis of four exhaustive case studies is how a skilled researcher can move from the individual to the group to the nation without losing sight of the historical problem under study. Thus, both small- and large-scale approaches and emphasis on human or social science themes are possible with useful results.

These examples show how a single case may yield insights, interpretations, analyses, and even comparisons of some significance, and they are illustrative of a massive literature that is historically grounded and theoretically significant. The ensuing discussion briefly identifies some of these studies in terms of their themes—institutional development, transitional experiences, authority and power, the capitalist world system, and class and experiences of workers.

Institutional Development

Throughout the twentieth century, the social sciences have addressed questions about institutions. Initially, the concept "state" was central to studies of political life. For a time the concept was supplanted by that of "system," but when it once again became prominent in the middle 1980s attention turned to the possibility of a theory of institutional life. The linking of institutions to the state was an effort to move away from rigid premises and ideological assumptions about what to study in society.

In *Structure and Change in Economic History* (1981), Douglass C. North proposed a theory of institutional change in an effort to reveal the assumptions and weaknesses of neoclassical theory. His institutional approach involved theory on property rights, the state, and ideology. His comparative overview of history focused on two economic revolutions, the first occurring 10,000 years ago and involving the development of settled agriculture in herding and breeding animals and cultivating plants for food, and the second involving industrialization and technological advances that "created an elastic supply curve of new knowledge which builds economic growth into the system" (171). Both revolutions involved extensive reorganization of institutional life.

Institutions and institutional change also were of concern to Alex Callinicos (1988), but he concentrated on the theoretical work of progressive thinkers such as Eric J. Hobsbawm, E. P. Thompson, G. A. Cohen, Louis Althusser, Anthony Giddens, Jon Elster, and Jürgen Habermas and focused on the mechanisms and institutions through which human beings transformed their societies.

Transitions

Several extraordinary works analyze the complicated process of transition from precapitalist social formations to capitalism and the dilemmas of achieving an effective transition to socialism. A point of departure is Rodney Hilton's *Class Conflict and the Crisis of Feudalism* (1990 [1985]). Arguing that the conflict between landlords and peasants was essential to the evolution of medieval society, Hilton observed that both peasant and

landlord economies were consequences of the commercialization of peasant production. He suggested that peasant labor was organized by peasants within the household unit of production, which the family effectively possessed but did not actually own; that peasant holdings were
able to produce sufficiently for subsistence and some surplus; and that
peasant households sought cooperation while developing resilience and
capacities for resistance. By demonstrating that the power of feudal society was decentralized through the local mobilization of landlord power,
Hilton was able to explore the extent of social conflict in medieval towns
in the form of antagonisms between peasants and landlords, peasant revolts, urban resistance, and factional struggles within oligarchies.

Complementing these insights are the findings of Perry Anderson in
two comparative surveys of historical developments. In *Passages from
Antiquity to Feudalism* (1974b), Anderson synthesized and reinterpreted
the work of modern historians. The first part of this work examined classical antiquity, the slave mode of production, and the Greek and Roman
experiences: "Slavery represented the most radical rural degradation of
labour imaginable . . . and the most drastic urban commercialization of
labour conceivable" (24–25). The second looked at Western and Eastern
Europe and discussed the feudal mode of production, "a juridical amal-
gamation of economic exploitation with political authority: with the peasant subject to the jurisdiction of his lord" (148). In *Lineages of the Absolute
State* (1974a), Anderson compared cases of the absolutist state in the
postmedieval monarchies of both Western and Eastern Europe during the
transition to capitalism. He attempted to strike a balance between history
from below, with attention to the economic base and development of the
forces of production, and history from above, with emphasis on the political apparatuses of the state that influence the relations of production and
class forces. Examining whether the absolute state was a mediator between the ascendant bourgeoisie and the declining feudal aristocracy, he
asserted that absolutism was

> a redeployed and recharged apparatus of feudal domination designed to
> clamp the peasant masses back into their traditional social position—despite
> and against the gains they had won by the widespread commutation of
> dues. . . . The Absolutist State was never an arbiter between the aristocracy
> and the bourgeoisie, still less an instrument of the nascent bourgeoisies
> against the aristocracy: it was the new political carapace of a threatened no-
> bility. (1974a: 18)

Anderson pointed to two traits of Eastern Europe that distinguished it
from Western Europe: a state apparatus that was a by-product of the military machine of the ruling class (a prominent example being Prussia) and
the functional relationship between feudal landowners and the absolutist

monarchies wherein purchase of bureaucratic office by nobles was widely practiced (see Tibebu 1990).

In his now classic synthesis *Social Origins of Dictatorship and Democracy: Lord and Peasant in the Making of the Modern World* (1966), Barrington Moore Jr. studied the transition from agrarian to modern industrial societies and identified three paths: the bourgeois revolution, combining capitalism and parliamentary democracy, in the English Civil War, the French Revolution, and the American Civil War; the conservative revolution in capitalism, culminating in fascism in Germany and Japan; and the peasant revolution, culminating in communism in China and Russia. In working through these cases, Moore criticized earlier interpretations, among them Lenin's. Lenin believed that the abolition of capitalism and its replacement by socialism would end the exploitation and rivalries that fed modern war in contemporary industrial societies, but just "how and why socialism would end these rivalries Lenin never paused to make clear" (Moore 1987: 106). Moore argued that "authority, especially bureaucratic authority, and inequality are likely to be prominent features of the social landscape for the foreseeable future" (120) and concluded that "the prospects for a free and rational society seem bleak in the world's leading societies" (122). He set forth a prescription for the possible attainment of a free form of socialism or socially controlled capitalism:

> To maintain the system some sectors have to remain sufficiently profitable to support the social and welfare costs generated elsewhere in the economy. A central feature of such a society would be a two-sector economy. In one sector the government would control prices. Presumably this sector would turn out goods and services that were to have overriding social importance or could not yield a profit. In the other sector prices would be freely negotiated between sellers and buyers. Food products and goods that can be manufactured in small shops requiring little capital are among probable candidates. Planning would exist. State, social, and cooperative prorate would replace largest private ownership of the means of production. (121–122)

In the tradition of Moore, her mentor, Theda Skocpol also compared the revolutionary experiences of France, Russia, and China, in *States and Social Revolutions* (1979). Skocpol argued that the social revolutions in the three countries were "rapid, basic transformations of a society's state and class structures . . . accompanied and in part carried through by class-based revolts from below" and distinguished by "the coincidence of societal structural change with class struggle" (4). Adopting a comparative approach with a perspective on the state that was both "organizational" and "realist," Skocpol stressed that the state is central to comparative historical analysis: "In short, the causes and outcomes of the great social revolutions of the past could hardly be recapitulated in future democratic socialist revolutions in advanced industrial societies. Still, the past does have something to teach us about the future" (293).

The central thesis of Skocpol's work was that bureaucracies ruled over relatively wealthy and successful agrarian societies in France, Russia, and China. All three regimes evolved independent of the colonization that had swept much of the world, but all were ultimately threatened and challenged by an international disorder that provoked collapse. Revolutionary leaders and movements supported by popular uprisings were able to step into the space left by the old regimes. The revolutionary regimes had in common staying power and the ability to resist foreign intervention and counterrevolutionary forces.

Ernest Mandel, in *Late Capitalism* (1972), set out "to explain the postwar history of the capitalist mode of production in terms of the basic laws of motion of capitalism discovered by Marx in *Capital*" (10). He built on, updated, and revised earlier classical writing and Marxist theory in an examination of the recent concentration and internationalization of capital brought about by multinational capital. Pointing to the "long waves" of expansion identified by Nikolai Kondratieff, Mandel argued that although the conditions of capitalism changed over time, its essence had not changed since Marx's *Capital* and Lenin's *Imperialism:* "The era of late capitalism is not a new epoch of capitalist development. It is merely a further development of the imperialist, monopoly-capitalist epoch. By implication, the characteristics of the imperialist epoch enumerated by Lenin thus remain fully valid for late capitalism" (9).

Examining the problem of unequal exchange, Mandel agreed with thinkers like Samir Amin that the disadvantageous conditions for the accumulation of capital in these countries had to be ascribed to social causes and the impact of imperialism. He also concurred with André Gunder Frank that capitalism caused overdevelopment in metropolitan countries and underdevelopment in the less developed areas. He differed with Frank, however, in suggesting that the less developed areas should be understood in terms of precapitalist, semicapitalist, and capitalist relations of production, arguing that Frank confused them with subordination to the world market. The value of Mandel's work lies in its attention to a specific historical period and phase of capitalism, its analysis of contemporary conditions in the light of classical Marxist theory, and its reference to national and practical experiences.

Charles Bettelheim, in *Class Struggles in the USSR* (1976–1978), argued that Russia continued to be characterized by class struggle and uneven relations of production. He acknowledged the economic achievements of the Soviet experience but also noted its contradictions and the inability of its leadership to assess reality without using Marxism as a tool of analysis. The persistence of class struggle "concentrated economic and political power in the hands of a minority, so that the contradictions engendered by these class relations, far from diminishing, were actually deepened" (1976: 11). Bettelheim traced this class struggle to the period from the inception of the Russian Revolution in 1917 to 1930 to unravel the contradictions that precipitated the eventual failure of this great socialist experiment.

In *Transition and Development* (1986; see annotated reference in Chapter 2) Richard Fagen, Carmen Diana Deere, and José Luis Coraggio focused on socialist revolutionary movements in the Third World both successful and failed. The failure of socialist transitions in many countries has stimulated thinking about ways of transcending contemporary capitalism and modernism. In a provocative synthesis, Boaventura de Sousa Santos (1995) looks to a "paradigmatic transition." He argues that the paradigm of modernity has exhausted its possibilities. His perception of epistemological and societal transitions in process today is drawn from an argument in favor of the oppressed and their struggles against oppression.

In his comparative study of European social history, Charles Tilly (1990) has shown the need to focus on the impact of capitalism on ordinary people (692). Other comparative studies that cut across historical periods and geographical regions include *The Rebellious Century, 1830–1930* by Charles Tilly, Louise Tilly, and Richard Tilly (1975); and Reinhard Bendix's *Nation-Building and Citizenship* (1964).

Authority and Power

Harold Lasswell once compared power to the lubricant in the engine of an automobile, implying that each of us has a stake and influence in the system in which we live. This abstraction diffuses the more commonly understood connotation of power as associated with international conglomerates, national states, or blocs that exercise hegemony over society.

Power may be exercised through established and legitimate authority, as it was by the Great Powers during the era of the world wars and in the first half and the cold war in the last half of the twentieth century. Power has also been exercised by authoritarian regimes, as in the case of dictatorship. In *The Crisis of the Dictatorships* (1976), Nicos Poulantzas offered a comparison of dictatorships in Portugal, Spain, and Greece in terms of state apparatuses and dominant and popular classes, and the themes of power and authority run through much of Poulantzas's work, including *Political Power and Social Classes* (1973) and *State, Power, Socialism* (1978). In *Transitions from Authoritarian Rule* (1986; see annotated reference in Chapter 6), Guillermo O'Donnell, Philippe C. Schmitter, and Laurence Whitehead consider comparatively the shift from dictatorship to representative democracy in Southern Europe and in the Southern Cone of South America.

Reinhard Bendix, in *Kings or People* (1978), looked at structures of authority in medieval history, the transformation of these structures in the sixteenth century, and the problems of state building in the twentieth century. Case studies of Japan, Russia, Germany and Prussia, England, and France show that the authority of kings depended on religious sanctions as well as on internal and external struggles for power, that monarchs governed with the aid of notables to whom they delegated authority, that popular sovereignty only gradually became an alternative to monarchical authority, and that its institutionalization reflected the way in which the authority of kings was left behind. Michael Mann (1986) set forth a theory of power relations in human societies with a focus on Europe up to the year 1760. He argued that "societies are constituted of multiple overlapping and intersecting sociospatial networks of power"(1) and examined the structure and history of European societies in terms of four sources of social power: ideological, economic, military, and political. John A. Hall (1986) considered power and liberty in the rise of the West, discussing imperial China, the Brahmans, Islam, and Christian Europe and later liberal polities in capitalism, the Soviet model, and the Third World. Asking how people deal with domination, James Scott, in *Weapons of the Weak* (1985), argued that peasants may engage in everyday forms of resistance (sabotage, arson, defiance, and so on) that may lead to collective protest, and many examples suggest that economically subordinate groups may challenge the dominant classes or government through coordinated direct efforts (strikes, demonstrations, land seizures, riots, rebellions, and so on). Finally, Peter Evans, Dietrich Rueschemeyer, and Evelyne Huber Stephens, in *States Versus Markets in the World-System* (1985), identified tensions between international markets and state strategies and discussed how hegemonic power shaped commodity and capital markets at the international and local levels. In *Strong Societies and Weak States: State-Society Relations and State Capabilities in the Third World,* Joel Migdal (1988) developed a theory that explains the varying capabilities of weak states such as Egypt, India, Israel, Mexico, and Sierra Leone and argued for a shift from state-centered analysis to critical examination of power at the top.

The Capitalist World System

The experience of capitalism pervades our thinking about the world, past and present. In *Civilization and Capitalism* (1981), the French historian Fernand Braudel outlined the origins and evolution of capitalism from the fifteenth century to the twentieth in a now-classic account that served as the foundation for Immanuel Wallerstein's *The Modern World System* (1974). Wallerstein identified two types of world systems: world empires or great civilizations such as those of China, Egypt, and Rome and world economies dominated by nation-states and their colonial networks such as those of Britain and France. He conceptualized the modern world system as having a core in northwestern Europe, a periphery in Eastern Europe, and a semiperiphery in Mediterranean Europe. This framework allowed him to reinterpret the European experience from the breakup of feudalism through the rise of capitalist agriculture and mercantilism and the development of centralized bureaucracies. Wallerstein and his school caused social scientists to rethink history—to break from traditional understandings and seek new interpretations. (For conceptualization and a typology useful for comparative purposes, see Chase-Dunn and Hall 1993; for a comparative review of the Braudelian and Marxian conceptions of history, see Aguirre Rojas 1992; and for a thoughtful piece on recent changes in the world system, see Arrighi, Hopkins, and Wallerstein 1992; and Wallerstein 1992).

In his provocative *The Rise and Fall of the Great Powers* (1989), Paul Kennedy offered an interpretive historical overview in three parts, covering strategy and economics in the preindustrial world, with attention to the rise of Ming China, the Muslim world, Japan and Russia, and Europe; the industrial era of shifting balances from 1815 to 1885 and the rise of a bipolar world from 1885 to 1942; and the period of stability and change since 1943. His emphasis was on how large powers, especially Britain and the United States, the Soviet Union, China, Japan, and the European Union, grapple with the historical dilemma of rise and fall, shifting productive growth, technological innovation, and international change.

In a revision of this approach, Giovanni Arrighi (1994) focuses on world hegemonies and modern capitalism. World hegemony, in the sense suggested by Antonio Gramsci with regard to class and political groups, refers to the power of a state over a system of sovereign states. In the historical context of financial capital, Arrighi analyzes the cyclical rise and decline of capitalist states, beginning with late medieval Europe with the northern Italian capitalist city-states and going on to Genoese, Dutch, British, and U.S. instances of capitalist expansion. His analysis of the earlier cases, although interpretive, is deeper than his more tentative assessment of the United States. He is principally indebted, however, to Braudel's view that finance capital was not simply a phenomenon of the early twentieth century but was associated with earlier capitalist developments.

To some extent, these interesting studies on capitalism in Europe are assimilated into a Eurocentric understanding that extends to all the world order. An interesting example is the assertion of David Landes (1998) that northwestern Europe with its natural environment and culture is superior to other regions in the world, its imperialist expansion and colonialism were natural and good, and its production and life represented an example for the rest of the world to follow. Thus, the poverty of much of the world is attributable to the tropics and climatic conditions that make these areas ripe for exploitation by the West.

Class

The cases identifiable thus far have been concerned with authority, power, dominance, transition, capitalism, and the world system, but useful comparative study has also turned to the less privileged, suppressed, and exploited. Combining interpretive and analytical history with anthropology and the other social sciences, Eric Wolf, in *Europe and the People Without History* (1982), asked why we persist in making dynamic and interconnected phenomena static and disconnected. Part of the problem, he believed, was the particular concerns of the various disciplines. Influenced by the holism of Marx's thought, the questioning of modernization in the writing of Frank, and Wallerstein's historical account of the origins and evolution of European capitalism, Wolf argued for the need for a theory of growth and development that included people. Using the experience of Europe as a case study, he began with the fifteenth century and examined European mercantile expansion and its global impact. He then turned to the industrial revolution, examined its impact on areas of the world supplying resources to the industrial centers, and sketched the formation of working classes and their migrations within and between continents. In his account, "Both the people who claim history as their own and the people to whom history has been denied emerge as participants in the same historical trajectory" (1982: 23). His approach consciously turned away from dominant elites to focus on primitives, peasants, workers, immigrants, and minorities, "the people without history."

Wolf's analysis was grounded in the various modes of production identified by Marx and others, which he took to ensure essential distinctions among humans that generated contrasting ideologies. For example, the kin-order mode is characterized by descent and affinity (through blood ties) and the capitalist mode by opposition between owners of means of production and workers. Wolf believed that although ideologies mediated contradictions, they could not resolve them. He concluded that we cannot think of societies as isolated and self-sustaining or of cultures as integrated totalities.

There is a great deal to be learned from study of peasant labor in medieval times. We have seen Hilton's (1990 [1985]) case study of conflict in medieval towns. Other exceptions to the rule that social scientists tend to shy away from study of workers are Harry Braverman's classic *Labor and Monopoly Capital* (1974), E. P. Thompson's *The Making of the English Working Class* (1963), and Philip Sheldon Foner's *History of the Labor*

Movement in the United States (1947). Concerned that class, especially the working class, and socialism are not really on the agenda in writings on the United States, Foner (1990) reminded us that Marx and Engels were unable to solve the riddle of the United States, which they believed had developed its capitalism "shamelessly." The failure of socialism to prevail is usually explained in terms of the absence of a large social democratic party, but Foner argued that in the United States it was due to the success of American capitalism, the superior economic conditions of American workers, and the ability to acquire property. Furthermore, the consensus of American historiography, as expressed in Louis Hartz's *The Liberal Tradition in America* (1955), is that the ethos of American life is inherently hostile to class consciousness, socialism, and radicalism and favors liberal sentiments. No consensus has yet emerged in the new social and labor history, sensitive to the experience of blacks, women, and classes. Also, there is the school of intellectual history that posits the theory of the hegemony of middle-class or capitalist values in the United States and assumes that state regulation of the economy mitigates capitalist exploitation and may even lead to socialism. Finally, there is the view that emphasizes culture rather than political ideology and sees mass culture and the mass media as shaping American culture in capitalist society.

Another exception is Michael Burawoy, a political sociologist whose research emanated from personal experiences in the Zambian Copper Industry Service Bureau, as a machine operator in the engine division of a multinational corporation located in Chicago, and in several factories in Hungary. His approach was to combine working-class experiences in the factory with academic research and writing. He argued that the industrial working class had self-consciously intervened at important historical moments. His fascinating study (1985) was concerned with "bringing workers back in" and theorizing "a politics of production." It attempted to "reconstruct" Marxism by examining "how the process of production shapes the industrial working class not only objectively—that is, the type of labor it carries out—but also subjectively—that is, the struggles engendered by a specific experience or interpretation of that labor . . . it must examine the political and ideological as well as the purely economic moment of production" (8). Following closely the significant work of Braverman but also influenced by the more abstract work of Gramsci, Althusser, and Poulantzas, Burawoy argued that class was at the root of the organization of contemporary society—that it explained capitalist development and shaped racial and gender domination. Although he distinguished a production politics from a state politics, he examined the similarities as well as the differences between workplace and state apparatuses and their interrelationship. He looked at state intervention in four types of factory regimes: bureaucratic, despotic, collective, and self-management. His alternative understanding of politics "refuses to accept the reduction of politics to state politics and of state politics to the reproduction of class relations" and "challenges the reduction of production to economics" (254).

Case studies that are historical in scope but incorporate in-depth analysis of class with implications for the comparison of capitalism, imperialism, and revolution elsewhere include Charles Bettelheim's study of class struggles in Russia (1976–1978) and Richard Curt Kraus's study of class conflict within Chinese socialism (1981). David Abraham, in *The Collapse of the Weimar Republic: Political Economy and Crisis* (1986), has analyzed the position of the state and the relations among classes during the Weimar Republic and its fall to dictatorship in Germany during the 1920s, including conflicts between industrial capital and agricultural interests and the struggles between capital and labor. In *The Question of Class Struggle: Social Foundations of Popular Radicalism* (1982), Craig Calhoun uses the case of Britain to offer a reassessment of theories of community, class, collective action, revolution, and popular protest.

In *False Promises: The Shaping of American Working Class Consciousness* (1973), Stanley Aronowitz examined the history of American workers, with particular attention to the rise and decline of labor unions. Maurice Zeitlin's *Revolutionary Politics and the Cuban Working Class* (1967) is an intriguing study of the Cuban working class at the outset of its revolutionary experience. Among other studies on the popular classes are Samuel Kline Cohn Jr.'s *The Laboring Classes in Renaissance Florence* (1980); David M. Gordon, Richard Edwards, and Michael Reich's *Segmented Work, Divided Workers: The Historical Transformation of Labor in the United States* (1982); Elie Halévy's *Imperialism and the Rise of Labour* (1951); Roland Mousnier's *Peasant Uprisings in Seventeenth-Century France, Russia, and China* (1970); Gwyn A. Williams's *Proletarian Order: Antonio Gramsci, Factory Councils, and the Origins of Communism in Italy, 1911–1921* (1975); and Peter Winn's *Weavers of Revolution: The Yarur Workers and Chile's Road to Socialism* (1986).

HISTORICAL STUDIES

Case studies demonstrate the strength and potential of combining historical context and theoretical framework. Representative regional, two-nation, and single-case studies of this kind include the following:

Regional Studies

In addition to the comparative and monographic studies of Moore and Skocpol discussed above, there are edited collections of essays on different countries, such as Robert Bates's *Toward a Political Economy of*

Development (1988; see annotated reference in Chapter 5), adopting a rational choice perspective and concerned with the political economy of international markets and the state in Taiwan, Argentina, and Central America. Andrei S. Markovits and Mark Silverstein's *The Politics of Scandal: Power and Process in Liberal Democracies* (1988) compares cases drawn from the political experience of the United States, Canada, Britain, France, Italy, Western Germany, Austria, Japan, and Israel.

Among the more useful strictly regional studies, Dieter Senghass's *The European Experience: A Historical Critique of Development Theory* (1985) critically examined various theories of development in European history (see Senghass 1988) with attention to autocentric and export-led development through capitalism, peripheral capitalism, and socialism. Senghass described various types of development in the periphery, contrasting growth with equity, as in Scandinavia, with the alternative paths of export economics found in Uruguay, Cuba, Hungary, Thailand, and Argentina. Peter Katzenstein, in *Small States in World Markets: Industrial Policy in Europe* (1985), compared the industrial policies and relations with the world market of small European countries. Other studies of Europe are Alex Callinicos's (1991) comparison (mentioned above) of the fallen regimes in East Europe and Heiko Augustinus Oberman's *Masters of the Reformation: The Emergence of a New Intellectual Climate in Europe* (1981), which looks at the intellectual world during the Reformation. R. R. Palmer, in *The Age of the Democratic Revolution: A Political History of Europe and America, 1760–1800* (1959), offers a comparative historical overview and interpretation of "Western civilization" during the "democratic" period of the last four decades of the eighteenth century and argues that a single revolutionary movement manifested in different ways and with varying success in different countries and that the two real revolutions were the American and the French. Finally, the multivolume work edited by Kaase and Newton (1995) examined political beliefs and ideologies across European nations.

Thematic studies that compare countries across the Third World include Joan M. Nelson's *Access to Power: Politics and the Urban Poor in Developing Nations* (1979), which stresses migration and the political participation of the urban poor through patron-client relations, ethnic ties, neighborhood and occupational associations, and political parties. Nelson attempted to understand a variety of participatory practices, including individual action to placate traditional leaders; collective mobilization to improve conditions within a broader ethnic political framework; special interest group participation based on neighborhood, occupation, or other shared concerns; and populist movements or reformist political parties that seek to win sustained support from the poor. In another comparison of the developing nations, *The Weak in the World of the Strong: The Developing Countries in the International System* (1977), Robert L. Rothstein argued that the relationship between the advanced and less developed world had led to tension and conflict, in part because of the failure of import substitution, which benefited entrenched elites and left the less developed countries more dependent. He advocated a new strategy of development based on external support and rejected the radicals' assumption that the underdeveloped countries lacked choices. Finally, in *Reluctant Rebels: Comparative Studies of Revolution and Underdevelopment* (1984), John Walton argued that in the light of the literature on dependency and underdevelopment in the Third World, revolts against authority could be compared through case studies on the Huk rebellion in the Philippines, La Violencia in Colombia, and the Mau Mau revolt in Kenya.

In *State, Capitalism, and Democracy in Latin America* (1995) Atilio Borón has suggested guidelines for understanding the complex and obscure problem of the contradictory relationship between capitalism and democracy. The relevance of this problem became particularly clear in the mid-1960s, when military dictatorships proved necessary to ensure the deepening of capitalist development, thereby exposing the myth that through capitalist development the region's chronic authoritarianism could be eradicated and bourgeois democracy secured. He describes the different perceptions of classical and contemporary theorists of democracy as the earlier revolutionary and liberating substance of democratic ideas has gradually given way to a convergence of democracy and capitalism in the twentieth century: "When bourgeois hegemony succeeded in introducing into the consciousness of the subordinated classes the ideological justification of its class domination, the democratic state could coexist without force," yet when "bourgeois hegemony was not achieved, the faulty constitution of democratic capitalism rapidly gave way to fascism or dictatorship" (8). Given this paradox, Borón shows that although bourgeois revolutions established a liberal state, they did not establish bourgeois democracy: "It was the prolonged contestation and rebellion of the laboring classes . . . that democratized the capitalist state" (11). The democratization of the capitalist state in Latin America will be "the people's victory," and rather than serving to accommodate "the authoritarian edges of bourgeois domination . . . it should accelerate toward superior forms of political organization, the integral and substantive democracy of socialism" (27). He also shows that liberal conceptions of the market misrepresent and distort the role of the state in shaping and reproducing capitalism. The state not only ensures the hegemony of ruling-class interests but also shapes a new model of accumulation and capitalist development in which it actively intervenes to mitigate the periodic crises inherent in capitalism. Therefore, he argues, the proposition of neoliberals that one must choose between market and the state is false, for the dilemma is choice between the market and democracy. For neoliberals, "democracy is the real enemy, lying at the bottom of the antistate criticism of neoliberalism" (64).

In *The State and Capital Accumulation in Latin America* Christian Anglade and Carlos Fortín (1985 and 1990) set forth a theoretical framework for critical examination of the role of capitalist accumulation and then test their theory against the experience of state development in Brazil, Chile, and Mexico. They suggest the state can serve as the guarantor for the maximization of the extraction of surplus value by capital as a whole, as an intervenor in the sharing of surplus value among various capitals, and as an accumulator itself, given involvement in direct productive activities that benefit private capital (1985: 22). Their study identifies the connections between the power bloc and its hegemony in relation to the state and which fractions of the dominant class are promoted by the state to ensure continuing class hegemony.

In *Mobile Capital and Latin American Development* (1996), James E. Mahon Jr. analyzes the movement of capital in Latin America, looking first at changes in international finance; the regional patterns of industrialization; and financial integration, wealth distribution, and asset preference. In particular, he examines capital flight in six countries after the economic crisis of 1980 to 1983 and emphasizes structural influences on policy decisions. Critical of dependency theory and superficial analysis that sees international forces as the cause of problems, he seeks to understand causal relations by comparing situations over time.

Although the agrarian question has not been adequately addressed for Latin America, several comparisons are useful. In a seminal work, Alain de Janvry developed an important analysis of the uneven capitalist development and the role and limits of the state in implementing agricultural reforms. He argued that whereas accumulation occurred through periods of expansion and stagnation, capitalist development was combined and uneven—"combined because capitalism forms a system on a world scale . . . uneven because development is not linear, homogeneous, and continuous" (1981: 1). He saw uneven development as a consequence of capitalism, reflecting both class society and unplanned economy. He examined the agrarian crisis and debates on the agrarian question, the mode and class position of peasants, contradictions in agriculture (between rents and profits, cheap labor and balance-of-payment requirements, cheap food and development of productive forces, use and reproduction of peasantry as a source of cheap food), state and reformism, and the history of land reform in the area. In *From Peasant to Proletarian: Capitalist Development and Agrarian Transitions* (1982; see annotated reference in Chapter 2) by David Goodman and Michael Redclift, the experiences of Brazil, Chile, and Mexico are compared with capitalism in rural agricultural areas.

As an agricultural commodity of significance to the advance of capitalism in Latin America, coffee has attracted the attention of scholars. In *Coffee, Contention, and Change in the Making of Modern Brazil* (1990), Mauricio Font analyzes its role among planters in the state of São Paulo. Jeffrey Paige traces its influence on powerful families in Central America. In *Coffee and Power: Revolution and the Rise of Democracy in Central America* (1997), he is concerned with the agrarian transition, also the focus of an earlier work, *Agrarian Revolution* (1975). Paige draws his framework from Moore's (1966) influential comparative study and notes that the paths of El Salvador, Costa Rica, and Nicaragua up to the crisis of the 1980s roughly parallel the transforming experiences of other nations through conservative authoritarianism (fascism), revolutionary socialism, and bourgeois democracy. In his description of the origins of the coffee families and their class relations from the late nineteenth to early twentieth centuries, he distinguishes between the traditional agrarian and the more recent agro-industrial fractions and their relationships to the state and to subordinate classes. He argues that comprehension of the crisis of the 1930s, the failure of revolutionary socialism in El Salvador, the rise of communism in Costa Rica, and unsuccessful revolutionary nationalism in Nicaragua is crucial for understanding the crisis of the dominant elites in the 1980s and how the coffee families came to support conservative authoritarianism in El Salvador, revolutionary socialism in Nicaragua, and social democracy in Costa Rica. He concludes that socialist revolution from below profoundly changed the political and economic institutions of Central America. The research here shows that the rise of the agro-industrial bourgeoisie alone was not sufficient to bring about a full transformation of Central American society. The armed actions of the revolutionary left destroyed the old order and opened the way for the bourgeoisie to triumph economically and politically: "The old liberalism of the authoritarian state intervention has been replaced by the new liberalism of democratic deregulation" (360). With the defeat of the left, the fundamental contradiction between the bourgeoisie and the poor and semiproletariat persisted alongside the expansion of the agro-export economy.

The strengths of Paige's study are threefold. First, it depicts the historical threads of political and economic life in the three Central American countries. Second, it departs from theoretical premises drawn from the work of others but modified and molded around real-life experiences in this particular region. Family life is linked to class interests, fractional differences within the dominant social structure are noted, and tensions are tied to intrinsic economic and political interests and motives. Third, it uses in-depth interviewing to elicit family history and varying perspectives on the role of the coffee rulers and their retrenchment or break with tradition or alliance with transforming causes. Interpretative, subjective, and qualitative analyses are based on sound historical understanding.

Other comparative writings that help us to understand the potential for analysis of case studies in other regions include the work of Bruce Cumings (1984), who has traced the origins and development of the regional political economy in Japan, Taiwan, and South Korea and argued that despite their different traditional politics, these countries have adopted similar political models and roles for the state. Their industrial development commenced early in the twentieth century and was premised on a hegemonic system in the form of unilateral colonialism until 1945 and U.S. hegemony thereafter. James C. Scott, in *The Moral Economy of the Peasant: Rebellion and Subsistence in Southeast Asia* (1976), has also provided a basis for understanding rebellion and subsistence among the poor of Southeast Asia.

Two-Nation Comparisons

Successful comparisons of two nations are rare, but three studies help us to understand their potential. First, in *Political Economy and the Rise of Capitalism* (1988), David McNally compared the rise of agrarian capitalism in England and France and argued that classical political economy prior to Ricardo did not represent the interests of industrial capitalism and that classical political economists up to and including Adam Smith were critics of values and practices associated with merchants and manufacturers. The political movements favored agrarian, not commercial and industrial, capitalism. In England, political-economic thought emphasized the self-government of landed gentlemen, whereas in France political economy stressed a centralized absolute monarchy. Second, William G. Rosenberg and Marilyn B. Young, in *Transforming Russia and China: Revolutionary Struggle in the Twentieth Century* (1982), analyzed similarities and differences and aimed "to lay bare the principal historical features determining the development and outcome of these two great twentieth-century revolutions, and to analyze parallel developments within the specificity of Russian and Chinese historical contexts" (x). Third, in *Crafting the Third World: Theorizing Underdevelopment in Rumania and Brazil* (1996), Joseph Love has compared two once-backward but now-developing countries, Romania (1880–1945) and Brazil (1930–1980). He employs concepts dating to the early twentieth century to reveal some of the underlying premises of contemporary development theory and analyze the contributions of major Romanian and Brazilian developmental theorists. This work successfully synthesizes well-known history around the developmental currents and theories that have guided us for the past half century, but it also breaks new ground in its effort to identify the origins of underdevelopment theory. Its comparative perspective and the search for parallel ideas and influences have opened up an interesting and provocative area for inquiry.

Single-Nation Studies

Comparative research often draws on monographs of particular countries. Studies that look at mercantilism and early capitalism include Bernard Bailyn's *The New England Merchants in the Seventeenth Century* (1979), a social and business history of the seventeenth-century interests that emerged with the merchants in the rise and fall of the New England fur trade and the beginning and end of experiments in the production of iron and the merchant sea trade. In *The English Cotton Industry and the World Market 1815–1896* (1979), D. A. Farnie looked at the English cotton industry centered in Lancashire as a "barren and isolated region erupted suddenly into a fury of productive power of which its previous history had given but faint promise and of which its later history showed little trace" (324). He examined this industry's "dependence upon free trade, free ports, and universal peace and its essentially, nomadic, and ephemeral nature" (325) by showing connections to the international market. In *The Century of Revolution, 1603–1714* (1961), Christopher Hill argued that this period was decisive for modern English society and state, and in *The World Turned Upside Down: Radical Ideas* (1972) he examined the role of small groups of activists and radical theorists who challenged the dominant class and authority in the English Revolution of the 1640s. Of contemporary interest is Leo Panitch's *Social Democracy and Industrial Militancy: The Labour Party, the Trade Unions and Incomes Policy, 1945–1974* (1976), which argued that Labour had never been exclusively a working class party and that despite its internal conflict it played an integrative role.

Studies of revolution include Paul Avrich's *Russian Rebels, 1600–1800* (1972), which examined the four great rebellions that disrupted Russia during the seventeenth and eighteenth centuries. Teodor Shanin's historical treatment, in *The Roots of Otherness: Russia's Turn of the Century* (1986), of the subsequent revolutionary struggles of the peasantry for land and freedom represents an interpretive breakthrough and is interestingly complemented by Boris Kagarlitsky's systematic analysis, in *The Thinking Reed: Intellectuals and the Soviet State, 1917 to the Present* (1988), of the enthusiasm for socialism and disillusionment of the Russian intelligentsia during the twentieth century. Other useful studies include *Leninism and the Agrarian and Peasant Question* (1976), by S. P. Trapeznikov, who assessed the applicability of Lenin's views to the Soviet experience. In *Roots of Revolution: A History of the Populist and Socialist Movements in Nineteenth-Century Russia* (1966), Franco Venturi focused on revolutionary populism and its connections with the socialist movements of nineteenth-century Europe. In *Workers Control and Socialist Democracy: The Soviet Experience* (1982), Carmen Sirianni argued in the tradition of Marx that the future of socialism depended on popular democracy.

In *Rebellion and Democracy in Meiji Japan: A Study of Commoners in the Popular Rights Movement* (1980), Roger Bowen examined the origins of modern popular protest. Two relevant studies of China include John W. Dardess's *Confucianism and Autocracy: Professional Elites in the Founding of the Ming Dynasty* (1983), which examines conditions in the last half of the fourteenth century that enhanced political centralization through the involvement of Confucian public service professionals. Richard Curt Kraus's *Class Conflict in Chinese Socialism* (1981) grapples with the theoretical problem that the Chinese term for "class" has a variety of meanings emanating from historical changes and developments. This study focuses on the character of class relationships in socialist society and the linkage of Marxist social theory to Chinese conditions, particularly during the Maoist period. Kraus argued that class was used periodically by central bureaucrats against their old class enemies and, furthermore, that Maoist application of Marxism to processes of social change also coincided with bureaucratic interests.

Interesting studies of Southern Europe include Jerome R. Mintz's *The Anarchists of Casas Viejas* (1982), an ethnohistory that analyzes the uprising of 1933 and recounts the personal experiences of survivors. In *Proletarian Order: Antonio Gramsci, Factory Councils, and the Origins of Italian Communism, 1911–1921* (1975), Gwyn Williams argued that communism was "central to the historical patrimony of workers and revolutionary socialists—in Europe generally and in the British Isles in particular" (7).

Particularly influential studies of Latin America include Adolfo Gilly's *The Mexican Revolution* (1983), a case study of the impact of U.S. capitalist expansion and imperialism on Mexico with a focus on the particular capitalist contradictions that led to social unrest and upheaval, and Peter Evans's *Dependent Development: The Alliance of Multinational, State, and Local Capital in Brazil* (1979; see annotated reference in Chapter 2), which analyzes how a combination of capitalist forms permits development under conditions of dependency.

The themes and issues identified in this review provide the framework for the remainder of the book. The ensuing chapters deal with theories of transition, class, the state, imperialism, and democracy. This chapter has reviewed various schools of thinking, looked at divergent theories, and identified relevant monographic literature and sensitive case studies in comparative political economy. A focus on political economy allows us to transcend disciplinary distinctions, but it does not necessarily bring closure to debate.

Political economy seeks to answer questions around the origins, reproduction, and accumulation of capital and about prices, wages, and surplus value. Referring to Marx and the thinkers who followed him, such as Luxemburg, Hilferding, and Bukharin, Ernest Mandel suggests that the study of political economy may eventually lead to its own extinction: "Political economy withers away together with the economic categories it tries to explain" (1968, 2: 729). Alluding to two lines of inquiry, one being positivist and the other socialist political economy, Mandel suggests that in reality once the categories have withered away, there will be no room for economic doctrine. It will serve only to evaluate the past as a means of avoiding future crises: "There will be nothing more to 'explain.' All economic relations will have become transparent. . . . As a 'positivist science,' political economy 'will have little in common with past or present economic theory, with bourgeois political economy, or with the Marxist criticism of it. Marxist economists can claim the honor of being the first category of men learning to work consciously toward the abolition of their own profession" (2: 730).

REFERENCES

Aguirre Rojas, Carlos Antonio. 1992. "Between Marx and Braudel: Making History, Knowing History." *Review* 15 (Spring):175–219. A comparative review of the Marxian and Braudelian conceptions of history, beginning with Marx's observation that there is only one science, the science of history.

Anderson, Perry. 1974a. *Lineages of the Absolute State.* London: New Left Books. An effort to combine Marxist theory with empirical study of cases of the absolutist state in Europe during the transition to capitalism.

_____. 1974b. *Passages from Antiquity to Feudalism.* London: New Left Books. A "prologue" to his study of the absolute state in Europe (1974a).

_____. 1983. *In the Tracks of Historical Materialism.* London: Verso. Explores the crisis of Marxism and shows its need for a revitalization. Argues for new thinking that takes us into the heart of Marxist thought and its method in an effort to relate theory to the real and evolving conditions shaped by the contemporary international capitalist order.

Arrighi, Giovanni. 1994. *The Long Twentieth Century.* London: Verso. An important overview of the rise and fall of major capitalist states. Explores the contradictions of capitalism by identifying their roots in the historical rise and decline of dominant capitalist experiences reaching back before the sixteenth century.

Arrighi, Giovanni, Terrence K. Hopkins, and Immanuel Wallerstein. 1992. "1989, the Continuation of 1968." *Review* 15 (Spring):221–242. An assessment of the breakup of the Soviet Union and the countries of Eastern Europe and implications for comparison with the events of the 1960s.

Bates, Robert H. 1997. "Area Studies and the Discipline: A Useful Controversy?" *PS: Political Science and Politics* 30 (June):166–174. Draws out the criticisms of area studies and regional specialists in political science, suggesting differences between scholars of different generations and theoretical perspectives. Seeks a synthesis between "context-specific knowledge and formal theory as developed in the study of choice" (168).

Bendix, Reinhard. 1978. *Kings or People: Power and the Mandate to Rule.* Berkeley: University of California Press. Historical case studies on struggles for power.

Bettelheim, Charles. 1976–1978. *Class Struggles in the USSR.* New York: Monthly Review Press. Translated by Brian Pearce.

Bonnell, Victoria. 1980. "The Uses of Theory, Concepts, and Comparison in Historical Sociology." *Comparative Studies in Society and History* 22 (2):156–173. Useful for understanding the qualitative approach to comparative inquiry.

Braudel, Fernand. 1981. *Civilization and Capitalism, 15th–18th Century.* Vol. 1, *The Structures of Everyday Life.* Vol. 2, *The Wheels of Commerce.* Vol. 3, *The Perspective of the World.* New York: Harper and Row. A celebrated reinterpretation of early European capitalism conceived in the context of a world system.

Burawoy, Michael. 1985. *The Politics of Production: Factory Regimes Under Capitalism and Socialism.* London: Verso. Theoretical and empirical study that focuses on how surplus is obscured and secured within the workplace.

Callinicos, Alex. 1988. *Making History: Agency, Structure, and Change in Social History.* Ithaca, N.Y.: Cornell University Press. Looks at both Marxist and non-Marxist positions in the debate over institutions and institutional change.

Caporaso, James A., and David P. Levine. 1992. *Theories of Political Economy.* Cambridge, England: Cambridge University Press. Examines the distinction between politics and economics and stresses the need for a balanced understanding; critically assesses the classical orientation; compares Marxian, neoclassical, and Keynesian political economy; focuses on economic approaches to politics; and analyzes power-centered, state-centered, and justice-centered approaches to political economy.

Chase-Dunn, Christopher, and Thomas D. Hall. 1993. "Comparing World-Systems: Concepts and Working Hypotheses." *Social Forces* 72 (June):851–886. Includes a typology of world systems based on mode of accumulation (kin based, tributary, capitalist).

Chirot, Daniel. 1976. "Introduction: Thematic Controversies and New Developments in the Uses of Historical Materials by Sociologists." *Social Forces* 55 (December):232–241. A review of debates relevant to comparison through historical cases.

Chomsky, Noam. 1990. *Year 501: The Conquest Continues.* Boston: South End Press. Examines the history of discovery, conquest, and imperialism, adopting the premise that the interests of the ruling classes drive the foreign policies of nations toward domination and exploitation.

Cooper, Frederick, and Randall Packard, eds. 1997. *International Development and the Social Sciences: Essays on the History and Politics of Knowledge.* Berkeley: University of California Press. A collection of original articles on various subjects related to the concept of development.

Cumings, Bruce. 1984. "The Origins and Development of the Northeast Asian Political Economy: Industrial Sectors, Product Cycles, and Political Consequences." *International Organization* 38 (Winter):1–40. Emphasizes the role of the state in the economic development of successful Asian economies.

de Janvry, Alain, 1981. *The Agrarian Question and Reformism in Latin America.* Baltimore: Johns Hopkins University Press. A classic analysis of the agrarian question.

Elliott, Gregory. 1987. *Althusser: The Detour of Theory.* London: Verso. An important synthesis and critical analysis of the rise and decline of the thought of Louis Althusser during the 1960s and 1970s.

Farnie, D. A. 1979. *The English Cotton Industry and the World Market 1815–1896.* Oxford, England: Clarendon Press. Case study of the dynamics of cotton in nineteenth-century England.

Foner, Eric. 1990. "Why Is There No Socialism in the United States?" pp. 249–277 in William K. Tabb, ed., *The Future of Socialism.* New York: Monthly Review Press. Reviews various interpretations of the American experience.

Hall, John A. 1986. *Powers and Liberties: The Causes and Consequences of the Rise of the West.* Berkeley: University of California Press. Strives "to offer an account of the rise of the West in comparative perspective, to characterize our own world, and to reflect upon certain options that face the modern world" (2).

Hartsock, Nancy C. M. 1991. "Louis Althusser's Structural Marxism: Political Clarity and Theoretical Distortions." *Rethinking Marxism* 4 (Winter):1040. Seeks to analyze "how the defeats of Marxism in the West have come to be inscribed in its theories, and to expose the ways in which some theoretical moves foreclose new possibilities, both intellectually and politically" (11).

Hilton, Rodney. 1990 (1985). *Class Conflict and the Crisis of Feudalism: Essays in Medieval Social History.* London: Verso. Examines commercialization of agricultural production as a factor in the decline of feudalism in England.

Hobsbawm, Eric. 1996. *The Age of Extremes: A History of the World, 1914–1991.* New York: Pantheon. An extraordinary historical synthesis of "the short twentieth century," a continuation and complement of his history of the "long nineteenth century." For a review of this and other work by Hobsbawm, see Tony Judt, "Downhill All the Way." *New York Review of Books* 42 (May 25, 1995):20–25.

Johnson, Chalmers. 1997. "Preconception vs. Observation, or The Contributions of Rational Choice Theory and Area Studies to Contemporary Political Science." *Political Science and Politics* 30 (June):170–174. Favors the work of comparative area specialists and attacks the rational choice model, which "not only does not transcend culture and may itself be an expression of contemporary American culture, it also fails even to understand the concept of culture that it repeatedly attacks" (171–172).

Kennedy, Paul. 1989. *The Rise and Fall of the Great Powers.* New York: Vintage Books. Examines cycles of prosperity and decline, especially in Britain and the United States.

Landes, David. 1998. *The Wealth and Poverty of Nations: Why Some Are So Rich and Some So Poor.* New York: W. W. Norton. Argues that the history of the world emanates from the experience of the West and that the West exemplifies a road toward "the ideal growth-and-development society" (216). Sees capitalism and imperialism as natural and "the expression of a deep human drive" (63).

Lichbach, Mark Irving, and Alan S. Zuckerman, eds. 1997. *Comparative Politics: Rationality, Culture, and Structure.* Cambridge, England: Cambridge University Press. Overviews on theoretical possibilities in comparative politics.

Lijphardt, Arend. 1971. "Comparative Politics and the Comparative Method." *American Political Science Review* 65 (September):682–693. An important overview of methods in comparative politics, with attention to multiple cases and databases.

_____. 1975. "The Comparative-Cases Strategy in Comparative Research." *Comparative Political Studies* 8 (2):158–177. Emphasis on multiple cases and use of variables for comparison.

Lindblom, Charles E. 1997. "Political Scientists in the 1940s and 1950s." *Daedalus* 126 (Winter):225–251. Takes issue with the proposition that political science research after 1930 has been largely quantitative, in contrast with earlier work. Argues that political science is a continuing debate rather than a field of scientific inquiry.

Mandel, Ernest. 1968. *Marxist Economic Theory.* 2 vols. New York: Monthly Review Press. A major synthesis of economic theory drawn from the writings of Marx.

_____. 1972. *Late Capitalism.* London: Verso. Translated by Joris De Bres. Builds on classical writing and Marxist theory in examining the recent concentration and internationalization brought about by multinational capital.

Mann, Michael. 1986. *The Sources of Power.* Vol. 1, *A History of Power from the Beginning to A.D. 1760.* Cambridge, England: Cambridge University Press. The first of a projected three-volume work on the history and theory of power relations in human societies.

Meek, Ronald. 1956. *Studies in the Labor Theory of Value.* New York: Monthly Review Press. An ambitious and interpretive historical overview of major economists who have focused on the labor theory of value.

Mintz, Jerome, R. 1982. *The Anarchists of Casas Viejas.* Chicago: University of Chicago Press. Case study in Spain.

Moore, Barrington, Jr. 1966. *Social Origins of Dictatorship and Democracy: Lord and Peasant in the Making of the Modern World.* Boston: Beacon Press. A classic comparative study.

_____. 1987. *Authority and Inequality Under Capitalism and Socialism.* Oxford, England: Clarendon Press. An interpretive and comparative synthesis focusing on the United States, Soviet Union, and China.

Nelson, Joan M. 1979. *Access to Power: Politics and the Urban Poor in Developing Nations.* Princeton: Princeton University Press.

North, Douglass C. 1981. *Structure and Change in Economic History.* New York: W. W. Norton. Presents an institutional framework and contends with traditional economic theory.

Paige, Jeffrey. 1997. *Coffee and Power: Revolution and the Rise of Democracy in Central America.* New York: Cambridge University Press. Comparative study of coffee and its influence on power and economy.

Poulantzas, Nicos. 1976. *Crisis of the Dictatorships.* London: New Left Books. Delves into the coups in Spain, Portugal, and Greece in the mid-1970s and subsequent transitions from authoritarian to representative democratic regimes. Concludes that the state can be penetrated through revolutionary organization and confrontation.

———. 1978. *State, Power, Socialism.* London: New Left Books. Suggests that socialism can evolve through the reform and transformation of capitalism by manipulation of the state and its agencies.

Przeworski, A., and H. Teune. 1970. *The Logic of Comparative Inquiry.* New York: John Wiley. An early effort to develop a systematic approach to comparison in the social sciences.

Ragin, Charles. 1987. *The Comparative Method: Moving Beyond Qualitative and Quantitative Strategies.* Los Angeles: University of California Press. A critical assessment of qualitative versus quantitative analysis in comparative inquiry.

Ragin, Charles, and David Zaret. 1983. "Theory and Method in Comparative Research: Two Strategies." *Social Forces* 61 (March):731–756. A synthesis of the argument in Ragin (1987).

Rosenau, Pauline. 1988. "Philosophy, Methodology, and Research: Marxist Assumptions About Inquiry." *Comparative Political Studies* 20 (January):423–454. An incisive synthesis on theoretical schools and directions; dissects past and present trends in Marxist thinking.

Rosenberg, William G., and Marilyn B. Young. 1982. *Transforming Russia and China: Revolutionary Struggle in the Twentieth Century.* New York: Oxford University Press. Comparative analysis of different revolutionary experiences.

Rothstein, Frances. 1986. "The New Proletarians: Third World Reality and First World Categories." *Comparative Studies in Society and History* 28 (April):217–238. A critical review of the literature on peasant work and the relationship to the peasant and industrial worlds. Argues on the basis of a case study of San Cosme Mazataechochco, a community in central Mexico, that to view Third World industrial wage workers as stuck in a prolonged transitional stage is "oversimplified, ahistorical, and ethnocentric" and that proletarianization in both the advanced capitalist and the developing world is part of the same process of capital accumulation.

Santos, Boaventura de Sousa. 1995. *Toward a New Common Sense: Law, Science and Politics in the Paradigmatic Transition.* New York: Routledge. Argues that the paradigm of modernity is exhausted, illustrating with field research, case studies, and personal experience in favelas in Rio de Janeiro and Recife, Brazil. A related piece on this theme is in his "Discourse on the Sciences," *Review* 15 (Winter 1992): 9–47.

Senghass, Dieter. 1988. "European Development and the Third World: An Assessment." *Review* 9 (Winter):3–54. Departing from the debates on developmental theory during the 1970s, focuses on export-oriented growth and its implications for Europe and the Third World. Offers a typology of "socio-political constellations" as a basis for comparisons of a range of case studies. A sympathetic but engaging assessment is in Samir Amin, "Comment on Senghass" *Review* 11 (Winter 1988):55–66.

Sjolander, Claire Turenne, and Wayne S. Cox, eds. 1994. *Beyond Positivism: Critical Reflections on International Relations.* Boulder: Lynne Rienner.

Skocpol, Theda. 1979. *States and Social Revolutions: A Comparative Analysis of France, Russia, and China.* Cambridge, England: Cambridge University Press. Historical cases are the foundation for comparative analysis.

Skocpol, Theda, ed. 1984. *Vision and Method in Historical Sociology.* Cambridge, England: Cambridge University Press. A collection of essays on historical method and how to approach cases comparatively.

Smith, Rogers M. 1997. "Still Blowing in the Wind: The American Quest for a Democratic, Scientific Political Science." *Daedalus* 126 (Winter):253–287. Argues that American political science has not resolved the conflict emanating from the dual purpose of serving American democracy and being a true science.

Szymanski, Al. 1985. "Crisis and Vitalization in Marxist Theory." *Science and Society* 49 (Fall):315–331. Argues that Marxist theory tends to evolve through periods of vitality and stagnation, in line with world developments.

Thelen, Kathleen. 1999. "Historical Institutionalism in Comparative Politics." *Annual Review of Political Science* 2:369–404. An overview of recent trends in historical institutionalism.

Thompson, E. P. 1963. *The Making of the English Working Class.* New York: Vintage Books. A reinterpretation of English history in response to the neglect of workers as well as a polemic against economistic interpretations and a too-rigid application of Marxist categories.

Tibebu, Teshale. 1990. "On the Question of Feudalism, Absolutism, and the Bourgeois Revolution." *Review* 13 (Winter):49–152. A lengthy overview of the theory and historical practice of feudalism and the consequences of absolutism and the rise of the bourgeoisie in some parts of Europe and continuing feudalism in other parts.

Tilly, Charles. 1978. *From Mobilization to Revolution.* Reading, Mass.: Addison-Wesley. An imaginative study of collective action, based on European and American examples. Examines competing theories of collective action; presents a set of concepts and models for analysis; focuses on forms of conflict, repression, and struggles for power; assesses rebellions and revolutions.

_____. 1990. "How (and What) Are Historians Doing?" *American Behavioral Scientist* 33 (July-August):685–711. Identifies the basic characteristics of the study of history, including its comparative prospects and necessary variation depending on time and place, and the peculiarities of social and economic history.

Tilly, Charles, Louise Tilly, and Richard Tilly. 1975. *The Rebellious Century, 1830–1930.* Cambridge, Mass.: Harvard University Press. Applies a sociological model to many national experiences in the course of a century.

Wallerstein, Immanuel. 1974. *The Modern World System.* 4 vols. New York: Academic Press. Offers a reinterpretation of Braudel that serves as the basis for world systems theory.

_____. 1992. "Post-America and the Collapse of Leninism." *Rethinking Marxism* 5 (Spring):93–100. A thoughtful piece on political trends based on events in 1968 and 1989. Predicts the development of two North bipolarities, with the South increasingly becoming marginalized.

Williams, Gwyn A. 1975. *Proletarian Order: Antonio Gramsci, Factory Councils and the Origins of Italian Communism, 1911–1921.* London: Pluto Press. Examines Gramsci and the working class in early-twentieth-century Italy.

Wolf, Eric K. 1982. *Europe and the People Without History.* Berkeley: University of California Press. An effort to bring analytical history to anthropology, in particular examining the forces of commercial expansion and industrial capitalism and the experiences of primitives, peasants, workers, immigrants, and minorities.

Wood, Ellen Meiksins. 1995. "A Chronology of the New Left and Its Successors, or: Who's Old-Fashioned Now?" pp. 22–49 in Leo Panitch, ed., *Why Not Capitalism: Socialist Register.* London: Merlin Press. A review of the rise of the Western (new) left and the subsequent retreat of left intellectuals and decline of the labor movement.

2

THEORIES OF TRANSITION

In prehistoric classless societies, most people participated in decisions affecting life in the community and relations between the community and the outside world. Living conditions were poor in this collective society, and people struggled to survive in the face of the forces of nature. One of the first divisions of labor occurred in ancient times with the appearance of towns and professional artisans who produced commodities and exchanged them freely and more or less equally for products they immediately needed. Another division of labor took place with the introduction of money and the emergence of usurers or merchants specializing in international commerce. Merchant capitalism was an elementary form of capitalism, in which owners of capital appropriated the surplus produced by workers, and it was especially conspicuous in Western Europe from the fourteenth to the sixteenth centuries. Modern capitalism was characterized by a clear separation of producers from their means of production and subsistence—the formation of a class (the bourgeoisie) that owned and controlled these means of production and a class (the proletariat) that owned only its labor and had to sell this to the owners of the means of production in order to survive.

Until the late nineteenth century, capitalism was thought of as free competition. As technology spawned new industries, however, capitalists began to form cartels, trusts, and holding companies, and there was a concentration of finance capital (the bank capital that penetrates and dominates industry). In his *Imperialism* Lenin (1917) considered this the latest and most highly developed form of capitalism. In *Late Capitalism* (1975; see annotated reference in Chapter 5), Ernest Mandel focused on the concentration of production in the large industrial monopolies and the export of capital from advanced nations to less developed parts of the world. He classified the imperialist era into a classical phase of monopoly, from the late nineteenth century to the end of World War II, and a phase of the multinational firm thereafter.

Socialism implies collective rather than private ownership of the major means of production and appropriation of the social surplus product (the production of workers beyond their requirements for subsistence). In the transition from capitalism to socialism, labor power continues to be sold for wages, some surplus product is appropriated as individual privileges, and a money economy prevails. The transitional economy may be managed by bureaucrats uncommitted to the principle of political and economic participation by all the people, and private rather than public interest may be a motivating force. The shift from a capitalist mode of production to a collective one can occur only when these tendencies have been overcome. The transition to socialism therefore involves the replacing of the capitalist state with the workers' state—the substitution of proletarian democracy for bourgeois democracy. The provision for the basic needs of all the people, usually under a planned economy, becomes a priority. The goal of the socialist society is communism, characterized by the creative use of work and leisure and the elimination of a commodity and money economy, inequality, classes, the state, and alienated labor.

PRECAPITALISM AND CAPITALISM

A mode of production is composed of the mix of productive forces and relations of production in a given society. Samir Amin (1976 and 1985) has distinguished five different modes of production in order of their appearance: primitive-communal, tribute paying, slave owning, simple petty commodity, and capitalist. The early indigenous community is organized partly on an individual basis and partly collectively, with land as the fundamental means of production owned by the clan or village and used by all; the community lacks commodity exchange and distributes its product collectively. Some communities exhibit class distinctions based on a hierarchy of religious and political authority. The tribute-paying mode distinguishes two classes, the peasantry and the ruling class that extracts tribute from it. When this ruling class denies the peasantry access to land, this mode is known as feudalism. The lords appropriate the surplus through land, and there are no commodity relations. When a lord frees his peasant tenants, they become proletarianized, but their right of access to land can potentially undermine the system. Under the slave-owning mode of production, the worker as slave may be involved in the essential means of production, either in the circuit of noncommodity transfers, as in patriarchal slavery, or in commodity circuits, as in Greco-Roman slavery. Under the simple petty commodity mode of production, technically there is equality among free petty producers, for example, in handicraft production that is distinguishable from agricultural production.

None of these modes has ever existed in a pure state, says Amin, and societies at particular historical moments are best understood in terms of social formations, "organized structures that are marked by a dominant mode of production and the articulation around this of a complex group of modes of production that are subordinate to it" (1976: 16). Precapitalist societies, for example, are social formations marked by the dominance of a communal or tribute-paying mode of production, evidence of simple commodity relations, and long-distance trade. This trade links independent formations where certain scarce goods or low-cost commodities permit local dominant classes to profit both in trade abroad and in extracting surplus from local producers. Examples include the rich tribute-paying social formations, based on a large internal surplus, generated in Egypt and China; the poorer tribute-paying formations characteristic of most of the civilizations of antiquity and the European Middle Ages; and the tribute-paying and trading formations found in ancient Greece, the Arab world at the height of its power, and some states of black Africa. The slave-owning mode was conspicuous in the social formations of ancient Greece and Rome, and it was followed by a new tribute-paying mode in the form of European feudalism; later it had an impact of a different kind on Africa (Meillassoux 1992). The simple petty commodity mode evolved among small farmers and free craftspeople in New England between 1600 and 1750 and in South Africa between 1600 and 1880 as well as in Australia and New Zealand from the beginning of white settlement to the rise of capitalism. (For elaboration on mode of production, see Heller 1985; Hindess and Hirst 1975; Ingham 1988; Laibman 1984, 1987; McLennan 1986; and Ward 1985.)

The social formation is based on historical and technological progress through the development of the forces of production:

> The principal, most common line of development shows us first a series of communal formations, then a series of tribute-paying ones. . . . A secondary, marginal line of development shows a succession of communal formations, and then of feudal formations (which are a borderline variety of the tribute-paying family) with a strong commodity element in them (slave-owning commodity and/or nonslave-owning simple commodity), which testifies to the original or, in other words, peripheral character of this line. Along this line, the development of the productive forces comes once more into conflict with social relations, and the formations of capitalism are the result. (Amin 1976: 21–22)

Capitalist social formations are all characterized by capitalist production; all products are commodities and all commodities are exchanged. In the precapitalist modes, in contrast, the means of subsistence are not involved in exchange, and the surplus usually takes the form of tribute or rent in kind. Although a single mode of production may appear to be dominant in a particular social formation, identification of that mode may be difficult. Before the rise of towns in continental Europe, feudalism may have been the single mode, but the social order of late feudalism was "characterized by two exploitative modes of production, one based on feudal rent and the other based on wage labour, and two non-exploitative modes of production, petty bourgeois simple commodity production and subsistence farming of free peasantry" (Stephens 1986: 5). Whereas in the precapitalist formations different modes are linked and arranged hierarchically, the capitalist mode supplants all other modes. Finally, dominant and dominated classes appear in each mode of production: "state-class and peasants in the tribute-paying mode, slave owners and slaves in the slaveowning mode, feudal lords and serfs in the feudal mode, bourgeois and proletarians in the capitalist mode" (Amin 1976: 23).

THE TRANSITION
FROM FEUDALISM TO CAPITALISM

During the Middle Ages, people lived clustered in what the English called manors and the French called seigneuries, the local economic domains of feudal lords. According to Max Weber, three types of elites prospered under feudalism: monarchs; hereditary nobility, whose income was generated independently on the basis of fiefs; and staffs with income-producing offices held for life, such as the Catholic clergy. Most people were peasants living in individual households, usually clustered in villages, with access to and control over some agricultural land.

Politically, the manorial system involved mutual obligations between lords and their vassals. The vassal would swear fidelity to the lord and would often be given a fief, usually a piece of land, in exchange for his services (usually military). Feudal property, widespread in medieval Europe, is given two meanings: feudal as derived from the *feudum*, or fief, to distinguish feudal law from Roman and other kinds of law (feudal involved divided or shared ownership of property, whereas in Roman law property was indivisible); and feudal in the sense of service owed by the holder of the fief. A very elaborate discussion of these terms of law and property and of services rendered is developed by John Critchley (1978), who examined the relationship between lord and vassal. He showed that the fief was in fact conditional and that in later medieval England personal loyalty was separated from feudal tenure and aristocrats made contractual arrangements for indentured service.

Peasants worked their own fields and the common fields of the village. Wage labor was uncommon, work in the lord's fields being supervised by his representatives. A low level of technology was characteristic of medieval agriculture. The lords and the church sustained themselves through collection of feudal rents from all serf households in the form of direct labor in the household or fields of the lord; a portion of their production; and in-kind payments for the use of production facilities, such as mills belonging to the lord. Commerce between villages and between peasants within villages was uncommon because products were consumed within households or paid to the lord in rent. By the tenth and eleventh centuries, some commodities had begun to circulate through informal networks of traders, markets, and fairs, and eventually these networks served as the foundation for emerging cities that absorbed rural industry and trade (Bloch 1961).

The transition to capitalism was depicted by Marx and Engels in the *Manifesto of the Communist Party* as a transformation of production and social conditions that swept away all past relations and practices: "Constant revolutionizing of production, uninterrupted disturbance of all social conditions, everlasting uncertainty and agitation distinguish the bourgeois epoch from all earlier ones. All fixed, fast-frozen relations, with their train of ancient and venerable prejudices and opinions are swept away, all new-formed ones become antiquated before they can ossify" (1976 [1848]: 487). Marx and Engels viewed the transition as progressive in the sense that it would facilitate the eventual development of a free and more humane society. Although the shift from an agrarian to a specialized industrial society and the adoption of the capitalist mode of production were accompanied by an improvement in the material conditions of society, the deteriorating conditions of workers produced contradictions that he believed would foster movement toward socialism.

Many Marxists who have discussed the nature of the transition insist that Marx believed that it would vary with the historical circumstances and socioeconomic conditions of the particular society. Marx did not provide a comprehensive theory of the transition; although he saw the class struggle as the motor force of historical development, he did not explain why a stagnant and entrenched feudal mode of production would foster conditions leading to its decline and eventual demise. He examined petty commodity production, in which small-scale producers are attached to large feudal estates, and surplus extraction in the relationship between rulers and peasants. In advanced feudalism, peasants are evicted from their land and become wandering wage laborers and part of the new rural proletariat. Some peasants fare well and exploit less fortunate others, whereas many of the rural proletariat migrate to the cities for seasonal work. These conditions provide the labor forces necessary for industrialization. Thus, the countryside provides the resources for the transition to capitalism: increases in agricultural products as a result of technological advances on larger and more efficient farms and a large pool of migrating rural laborers seeking work for wages.

The Timing of Transition

Where and when the transition to capitalism took place must be considered in a historical context (see Table 2.1). The experience from about 800 until the early nineteenth century serves as the backdrop for historians, but the robust capitalist stirrings in England in the early 1800s must be contrasted with the capitalist development in France, Germany, and the United States later in the century. Western Europe, and especially England, caught the attention of Marx and other nineteenth-century scholars. Clearly, there were later dramatic changes in Eastern Europe as well, but as Perry Anderson and others have noted, sharp distinctions were evident between the two Europes. Immanuel Wallerstein (1974b), however, suggests that distinctions between Western and Eastern Europe become more difficult to maintain as the two regions are gradually unified in a single economy of reciprocal and unequal exchange of commodities. With the European explorations, conquests, and colonial projects of the fifteenth and sixteenth centuries, this economic system expanded well beyond the two Europes and the United States, and thus eventually the problematic of the transition also became relevant for backward countries such as prerevolutionary Russia and the less developed and late capitalist countries of twentieth-century Africa, Asia, and Latin America.

The Breakup of Feudalism

Another major question is how competitive capitalism developed out of Western European feudalism. Three changes are identifiable. The effort of feudal lords to increase revenues without augmenting productivity led to a decline in agricultural resources and provoked peasant resistance; the decentralized political structure of feudalism permitted the emergence of incipient capitalist urban centers; and the international commercial and colonial system stimulated financial resources and markets for capitalist development. Roger Gottlieb has argued that

> class relations involve not only those groups which confront each other directly in production and expropriation (lords and peasants), but also geographically distant groups connected by a world trade network and/or various forms of colonialism. . . . Historical change in feudal society is very much the indeterminate outcome of political struggles, not the predictable product of a mechanical economy. (1987: 189)

TABLE 2.1   The Transition from Feudalism to Capitalism

850 to 1000	Consolidation of feudalism in Europe
1000 to 1300	Feudal expansion and emergence of centralized states
1300 to 1450	Crisis: Population growth, signs of decline, peasant rebellions and warfare
1450 to 1650	Transition: Explorations, emergence of world economy, enclosure
1650 to 1800	Early mercantile capitalism: Proletarianization of the peasantry, industrial revolution
1800 to 1900	Consolidation of capitalism: Monopoly and imperialism

Gottlieb believes that viewing the shift to capitalism as the product of objective laws of historical development obscures the pursuit by oppressed groups of a political agenda oriented to the alteration of the socialization processes, including those affected by gender, that result in passivity and subordination and to the building of cooperation among different segments of an organizationally divided working class (198).

Political economists such as Samir Amin, Arghiri Emmanuel, André Gunder Frank, and Ernest Mandel have argued that the transition to capitalism involves an unequal and uneven process of capital accumulation. For Marx, it was surplus value and its conversion to capital that was the basis of accumulation. Absolute surplus value was produced by extension of the workday, and relative surplus value was created through reductions in necessary labor time as a result of, for example, the reorganization of labor and new technology. Capitalist accumulation was usually linked to a free labor force. Marx, in *Pre-Capitalist Economic Formations* (1967 [1857–1858]), spoke of primitive accumulation based on precapitalist relations of production and their transformation to capitalist relations of production, but Frank (1978) showed that both forms of relations may be in evidence at the same time. Frank also suggested that primitive accumulation might accompany both precapitalist and noncapitalist relations of production but that noncapitalist production might be associated with primary, as distinct from primitive, accumulation. Before the industrial revolution, within and outside Europe a variety of noncapitalist and precapitalist relations of production existed, including colonial, slave, serf, and feudal.

The Motive Force

Two general views dominate the extensive debate on the primary motive force underlying the transition. One of these is that forces within feudalism led to the change. In the *Manifesto,* Marx and Engels said that the

"means of production and of exchange, on whose foundation the bourgeoisie built itself up, were generated in feudal society" (1976 [1848]: 489),
and most of the contributors to the early debates adopted this view. The
increasing monetary needs of the landowning aristocracy, coupled with
inefficiencies in the manorial system of production, resulted in exploitation of the peasant producers. Accompanying this process was a shift
from a system of feudal rents and peasant labor on manorial land to one
of monetary payment or remuneration in kind. This shift, according to
Maurice Dobb (1947) produced widespread flight of the peasantry from
the land and the transformation of the feudal mode of production. Two
paths toward capitalism were possible: Direct producers such as peasants
might become capitalists (as Lenin illustrated with the case of the Russian
kulaks), or merchants might become capitalists, that is, take control of the
process of industrial production (see van Zanden 1993 and van Zanden et
al. 1997 on the origin, development, and disappearance of the merchant
capitalist labor market system in Holland).

An alternative perspective understands capitalism as having emerged
relatively independent of feudalism: Paul Sweezy, for instance, believed
that "the feudal system contains no internal prime mover and when it un-
dergoes genuine development—as distinct from mere oscillations and
crises which do not affect its basic structure—the driving force is to be
sought outside the system" (in Hilton 1978: 106; see also Sweezy 1971 and
1986). Sweezy questioned Dobb's idea of an increase in the monetary
needs of landlords due to an increase in their numbers and their extrava-
gance and in the cost of wars. Sweezy argued that there was a corresponding increase in the size of the peasantry but that the transition to
capitalism was largely attributable to the rise of merchant traders and international trade in the eleventh century. He believed that feudalism was
an immobile social formation and therefore the catalyst for transition was
the establishment of a system for exchange.

There is dispute over the origin of towns. Dobb argued that feudalism
remained the predominant mode of production until at least the bourgeois revolution in seventeenth-century England. Sweezy held that neither feudalism nor capitalism was dominant and the transition period
was more accurately described as one of a "precapitalist mode of production" as a distinct intermediate mode between feudalism and capitalism.
Kohachiro Takahashi noted, however, that neither Dobb nor Sweezy had
correctly explained the transition in all cases and that different countries
experienced different paths (quoted in Hilton 1978: 96).

Critical of the debate for not yet yielding a theory of capitalist development in the West and being of little relevance elsewhere, Ashok Rudra
(1987) pointed out that the original Dobb-Sweezy exchange was focused

on causes of the decline of feudalism and not the transition itself. He assessed the early debate over feudalism as

> a futile and wasteful exchange involving errors not of Marxian method but of elementary logic: failure to distinguish between necessary and sufficient conditions, between generative and contributory factors. . . . Sweezy made the initial mistake of describing as external long distance trade and towns. . . . The results have been disastrous for three decades of Marxian historiography in the English language. In their burning zeal to defend "the general Marxist law of development that economic societies are moved by their own contradictions" (Dobb) and yet not being able to demonstrate the working of the law, his opponents ended up by taking the absurd position that the opening up of the world did not have any effect whatsoever either on the decline of feudalism or on the emergence of capitalism. (175)

Labor and Class Struggle

An important condition in the evolving capitalist mode of production was the appearance of free wage labor. Marx (1975 [1857–1858]) elaborated the preconditions for capital, free wage labor, and its exchange against money: The worker had to be separated from the land and to be allowed ownership of his productive capacities. The transformation process had two phases: the dissolution of the servile relationship of worker to land and the dissolution of relations of property that make a worker a free peasant. The transformation of the peasant farmer into a free wage laborer accompanied the transformation of money into capital and established an accumulation process.

A parallel issue was the potential intervention of groups and individuals in the shaping of the emerging capitalism. Most traditional Marxists, following Marx and Engels, in the *Manifesto,* see the struggle between classes as decisive in the process: "Freeman and slave, patrician and plebeian, lord and serf, guild-master and journeyman, in a word, oppressor and oppressed, stood in constant opposition to one another, carried on an uninterrupted, now hidden, now open fight, a fight that each time ended, either in a revolutionary reconstitution of society at large, or in the common ruin of the contending classes" (1976 [1848]: 482). Some contemporary Marxists have questioned this emphasis on class and on the working class as an agent of change in the transformation process. If the proletariat has not yet fulfilled its historical role of defeating the bourgeoisie and initiating the transition to socialism, is it likely that the serfs and peasants were responsible for the transition from feudalism to capitalism?

Lenin showed that capitalism emerged from such conditions as "competition, the struggle for economic independence, the snatching up of land . . . the concentration of production in the hands of the minority, the forcing of the majority into the ranks of the proletariat, their exploitation by a minority . . . and the hiring of farm workers" (1956 [1899]: 172–173). He saw a rural petty bourgeoisie, a rural proletariat, and even a tenuous middle class as having replaced the peasantry in Russia. This depeasantization led, in his view, to a home market for capitalism, with the result that with the creation of a new rural bourgeoisie a market of personal consumption developed. He noted that this dissolution of the peasantry was accompanied by migration from agricultural areas to more densely populated areas and an increase in usurer capital in the countryside. Commerce and usury were manifestations of the disintegration of the old mode of production and its replacement by the capitalist mode.

Several perspectives on the transition from feudalism to capitalism are discernible in the English case. Richard Lachmann (1985) leaned toward a view, illustrated in the work of Robert Brenner (1977), that attributed the origins of capitalism in England to the crisis of feudalism in the fourteenth and fifteenth centuries, but he conceded that this view did not explain why the feudal crisis led to capitalism rather than some other different social formation and suggested that this was because of a focus on agrarian class relations. From another perspective, capitalism evolved from the urban market as an economic activity separate from an undynamic feudal sector. Lachmann set out to provide an alternative explanation that located "the feudal dynamic in elite relations beyond the point of production" (350). He illustrated this approach with a reinterpretation of English history from the fourteenth-century crisis of feudalism to the establishment of agrarian capitalism in the early seventeenth century. Here, he argued that

> opportunities for agency were doubly constrained within manors: by the equilibrium of class forces between landlords and peasants, and by the balance of power among the three elites—crown, clergy, and lay landlords—which constituted the feudal ruling class. As long as each class and each elite retained their capacities to institutionalize their political power within the manor, that structure could not become the site of transformative conflicts. Only after the relative strengths of the three sites had been altered in conflicts beyond the manor, conflicts in which the peasant class played no role, was the structural space opened within manors for those struggles that upset the feudal organization of production. (350)

Some scholars argue that the market, removed from feudal social relations in urban enclaves, was more profitable and productive than the precapitalist modes of production. Sweezy argued this position in his critique of Dobb, and the line of argument also runs through Wallerstein's history of the world system and Douglass C. North and R. P. Thomas's

(1973) analysis of the modernization of economic organization. It was the competitive advantage of markets over manors rather than the political strength of classes, the lure of city life for workers, and the greater efficiency of more highly specialized production that Sweezy stressed. Similarly, Wallerstein argued that it was England's core position in the world economy that permitted the development of a unique state and productive system: "Class power and relations of production, in Wallerstein's history, flow from world market position, not from political struggle" (Lachmann 1985: 351). North and Thomas suggested that feudal society was stagnant and English entrepreneurs sought a higher level of economic activity that led to insistence on private property rights. Lachmann considered these efforts evidence of the circularity of market in that they overlooked the feudal crises (352).

Brenner (1976), in contrast, examined these crises and showed how landlords intensified their demands on peasants after the Black Death of 1348 to 1350 had eliminated a third to half of the population. Their efforts to reimpose seigneurial constraints succeeded, however, only in Eastern Europe. Elsewhere, peasants resisted through communal institutions. English and French peasants were able to win freedoms, a share of agrarian income, and control over land through collective organization at the point of production. The evidence of internal class conflict and its results revealed the weakness of interpretations of the transition in terms of feudal stagnation. Brenner showed that it was fourteenth-century class struggle that propelled Eastern and Western Europe along different paths to state formation and economic development. Lachmann, although recognizing the strengths of the crisis approach in explaining the varying trajectories of class and state formation as consequences differing possibilities for class agency within different social formations, argued that it was incapable of accounting for either "the unique emergence of capitalism in England" or for "the specific character of postfeudal English social structure" (1985: 355).

Elites possessed the capacity to regulate production and extract surplus within the manors. The struggle among them was over protecting their access to and control over the surplus:

> Elites found the greatest room for agency away from the level of production, where they could confront elite opponents without also having to guard their individual and collective domination over the peasant class. As a result, elite conflict was initially more efficacious than class struggle in altering feudal social structure. . . . The ability of the elites to effect such considerations was limited by peasant resistance. Thus, while elite conflict beyond, and class conflict at, the point of production were endemic to feudalism, only rarely did an elite or class achieve a double victory that could be institutionalized within the structure of the manor. (357)

Lachman believed that before the profound realignment of elites during the sixteenth century, class conflict around production generally took place within narrow structural confines: "The reconstitution of the feudal ruling class through internal conflict made possible new forms of class struggle that were resolved with a new market organization of production" (357). The crown, the clergy, and the lay landlords possessed their own institutional mechanisms for extracting surplus from the peasantry, but they were unable to act in unison as a ruling class, and this allowed the peasantry some mobility and freedom.

Adam Smith emphasized industrialization and the invisible hand of the market as the way out of feudalism in the direction of individual land tenure, capital-intensive land use, division of labor, and increased efficiency in production. Marx stressed the exploitation in the transformation of serfs to a proletariat, the rise of moneylenders and merchants, competition among capitalists, and the division of labor. Brenner (1993; see Callinicos 1994) examines the role of London merchants during the English Revolution of the 1640s and 1650s, a decisive moment in the rise of the bourgeoisie in England. The new overseas traders, breaking with then-traditional patterns of mercantile development, controlled particular lines of trade through crown charters granting them monopolies in the colonies, and thus they represented a shift in power and wealth during that period.

Diverse Paths Toward Capitalist Development

In a clear summary of the capitalist transition and various interpretations, Ellen Meiksens Wood (1999) elaborates on "the commercialization model" and then offers two alternative histories. The model reveals the emergence of a class of merchants in the cities of Europe who foster the early roots of capitalism. First, the Roman invasions and later the Muslim invasions served to undermine and break down the early trade routes of Mediterranean commercial civilization, but with the expulsion of the Muslims and the growth of urban areas, commerce revived. According to the model, commerce accompanied a major transformation and a rupture with feudalism and its institutions. Wood goes on to describe refinements of this classical commercialization model in thinking ranging from Max Weber to Fernand Braudel. She identifies both "a demographic model" based on economic development being spurred on by autonomous cycles of population growth and decline and also a new sociological explanation, grounded in the notion that industrial capitalism was already implanted in medieval society. She delves into Karl Polanyi's *The Great Transformation* (1944) to demonstrate an alternative interpretation based on how technological improvements inevitably impacted on the capitalist market. Her analysis of the origin of capitalism also draws heavily on the transition debates between Dobb and Sweezy as well as Anderson's seminal studies of feudalism and absolutism and the attack by Brenner on both the comercialization and demographic models.

The patterns of capitalist development identified by Smith and Marx were not, however, reproduced everywhere in the world. Relatively late development in Germany was a response to innovative institutional arrangements and bank capital, and in Russia it took place under the aegis of the state. In much of the Third World, theorists have focused on the role of the state, large landowners, and small producers in world markets in their analysis of the transition to capitalism. Although Marx was primarily interested in the origins and evolution of capitalism in Europe, in his writings on India and Ireland he showed that nations existed at different levels of development and that capitalism did not necessarily affect them in the same ways. He envisaged "a double mission in India: one destructive, the other regenerating—the annihilation of the old Asiatic society, and the laying of the material foundations of Western society in Asia" (Marx 1943: 154–155). The British had brought destruction to India "by breaking up the native communities, by uprooting the native industry, and by leveling all that was great and elevated in the native society. . . . The work of regeneration hardly transpires through a heap of ruins. Nevertheless it has begun" (13). Marx was implying that capitalism was creating the material conditions for the capitalist advance. His later writing on the Irish question approximated some contemporary thinking on unequal development throughout the world: "A new and international division of labor, a division suited to the requirements of its chief centers on modern industry, springs up and converts one part of the globe into a chiefly agricultural field of production, for supplying the other part which remains a chiefly industrial field" (Marx 1967, 1: 451). This line of thinking essentially served Bill Warren (1980) in his argument that underdevelopment was associated with the elimination of noncapitalist modes of production through imperialism and the building of the capitalist forces of production. Marx also argued that the Irish needed self-government and independence, agrarian revolution, and protective tariffs against the dominance of England.

The early work of Lenin on Russia emanated from debates about the necessity and possibility of capitalist development in that country. During the late nineteenth century, the Narodniks argued that capitalist development was neither viable nor necessary for Russia's evolution toward socialism. Lenin responded that although Russia was backward in contrast to other capitalist countries, it was indeed capitalist: "There are three main stages in this development: small commodity production (mainly peasant industries); capitalist manufacture; and the factory.

... The facts quite clearly show that the main trend of small commodity production is towards the development of capitalism, and, in particular, towards the rise of manufacture" (Lenin 1956 [1899]: 594–595).

J. M. Blaut has rejected the idea of European historical superiority or priority in the development of the world, arguing that the origins of the industrial revolution are found outside Europe as well: "The evolutionary processes that were going on in Europe during and before the Middle Ages were essentially like the processes taking place elsewhere in the world in terms of rate and direction of development" (1994: 51). After 1492, he suggests, the ascendancy of Europe was based not on any special inherent quality but on the immense wealth produced by European colonialism.

In an effort to transcend the limitations of Eurocentrism and to identify various paths toward development, Peter Gran has contended with the conventional historical view that a single power center, Europe or the West, is hegemonic and distinguishable from the rest of the world. He proposes four distinctive state formations, each with unique characteristics: first, the "Russian Road," which shares characteristics of a weak middle class and an inclination to shift between phases of liberal and autocratic rule similar to that in Turkey, Iraq, and some other states; second, the "Italian Road," which reflects regional conflict, weak integration, and an underdeveloped southern population, with characteristics reminiscent of state formation in India and Mexico; third, the "Tribal-Ethnic Road," exemplified by Albania and followed in Africa by the example of Zaire; and finally, the "Bourgeois Democracy Road" as experienced in Great Britain and the United States. Gran argued that the world as a whole became "a decentered totality comprising a large number of countries conforming to these four hegemonies" (1996: 337). He felt that his framework allowed for innovative comparative study while permitting understanding of world history as the confrontation of different hegemonies, the recognition that comparative approaches will mitigate the attention to Eurocentrism, and the possibility of rethinking assumptions: "If we find that most of the world in this, the age of modern capitalist nation state, is still outside capitalism and barely a part of the nation state, does this not have theoretical implications for the analysis of both and, by extension, for our definition of modernity?" (350).

The transition to capitalism in Brazil has often been explained in terms of the autonomy of the state—its capacity to conceive and act on large-scale development initiatives and thus to contend with collective and individual demands of the society. The date of 1930 is taken as a turning point in the replacement of the agricultural oligarchy by a new agricultural and industrial bourgeoisie. The power base of the oligarchy was centered in coffee production and exports that served as a basis for agrarian capitalist accumulation and industrialization. Some writers see the state as instrumentally facilitating the emergence of an industrial bourgeoisie and changes in the relations of production as leading to conflict between the agrarian and industrial dominant classes. Others interpret the change in 1930 as a reflection of decline in the coffee oligarchy in the face of the worldwide depression, so that no social group exercised hegemony, allowing the state greater autonomy over fragmented interests. Still others suggest that the state had taken an interventionist role since the late nineteenth century. Finally, it has been suggested that the hegemonic class position of large coffee planters had eroded well before 1930 and that small and medium-sized producers also had a role in the advance toward industrial capitalism.

Adopting this latter view, Mauricio Font (1990) suggested that the expansion of export or commercial agriculture did not always generate capitalist development. The classical European experience indicated that expanded production for trade led to a transition from a stable agrarian social order to capitalism and industrialization. The failure of enclave or export economies in Latin America to produce the anticipated economic changes domestically or establish a progressive link with the global capitalist economy stimulated Latin American intellectuals to suggest the dependency model, which posited either underdevelopment (Frank 1967) or a triad of domestic, state, and international interests that could produce progressive dependent capitalism in contrast to the traditional model of dependency (Evans 1979) or associated dependent capitalism (Cardoso and Faletto 1979).

The traditional view posited political dominance and hegemony by export producers until the 1930 revolution that aimed to undermine their position in Brazilian and other Latin American societies. Font (1990) contended with this instrumental view of ruling class dominance over the state. He was interested in how the cohesiveness of export producers or intraclass conflicts affected their demands and in the nature of their internal social organization. He dissected the "monistic view of the link between capitalist development and export economy expansion in São Paulo which has emphasized not only the coherence and effectiveness in planters' actions, but also the integration of coffee and industrial capital and planter dominance and hegemony over industrialists, incumbents of the state apparatus, and other groups" (5). This view appears in works by Cano (1977), Mello (1982), Mello and Tavares (1985), and Silva (1976). Font saw this process of accumulation as unitary or holistic, with the coffee export elites concentrating processes of capitalist accumulation under their own control and exercising hegemony over the rest of society. This expansion of coffee capital determined the crisis of the bourgeoisie and ushered in the bourgeois revolution. The change in regime marked by the

1930 revolution, however, may be explained by an alternative hypothesis—that intraelite difficulties and cleavages had undermined the Paulista planters during the 1920s.

Font attacked revisionist interpretations of "dualistic models of social change" in the work of Frank, Caio Prado Jr., Rodolfo Stavenhagen, and others who questioned the fact that industrialists, especially the advanced wing in São Paulo, did not support the revolution and that the Vargas government at its outset adopted policies favoring the agrarian elites. Luciano Martins (1982) explicitly denied the revolution any "structural" significance and rejected class analysis for political or exogenous factors. Although questioning this approach, Font also emphasized the political dimension.

Font's book examined the rise and decline of São Paulo coffee planters and associated their decadence with the growing strength of the state as well as the emergence of various forms of independent agriculture, a process he characterized as "structural differentiation in the state" (11). At the outset, he considered "the extent to which the Big Coffee economy of large coffee producers and merchants was being challenged by an alternative economy based on independent agrarian producers and their urban allies" (13). Drawing on considerable data to demonstrate the role of an independent commercial agriculture in São Paulo, he suggested that *colono* mobility was a path to independent farming of coffee and other crops: "The displacement of the economic center of gravity in the state generated tensions between producers and merchants. But, for Big Coffee elites the more insidious reality was that all major functional areas within the export sector—production, commerce, financing, even transportation—were becoming internally differentiated into competing subgroups" (30). Politics, he believed, was becoming important in determining the competing models of social organization and change, and the state was playing a major role in this process.

Font addressed the major issues that faced the Paulista elite and looked at the claims of coffee associations and congresses during the period 1920 to 1926, concluding, "In matters as diverse as taxation, immigration and colonization, monetary and fiscal policies, and even the regulation of the coffee sector, the state had shown a capacity to sustain autonomous impulses which, rather than merely reflecting those of planters, expressed its own interests and bore directly on the dynamics of civil society" (77). He showed that relations between the planters and government reached a low in 1926 and that "the climate of intra-elite confrontation could be found over the entire texture of associational life in the state" (78). The state, in the form of the São Paulo bureaucracy, thus boldly assumed leadership of the coffee industry and in the process deepened cleavages and conflict.

The family enterprise has traditionally been understood, in Europe and in the United States, in particular, as a means of modernizing agrarian structure. Large numbers of European peasant farmers migrated to Latin America at the turn of the century in what was assumed would result in a middle-sized farming sector that would meet the growing needs of the emerging agricultural industries and provide food for the expanding urban markets. These immigrants settled in Argentina, Brazil, Chile, Uruguay, Venezuela, and elsewhere, but the promise of a dynamic rural middle class was often undermined by lack of access to land despite reformist and revolutionary efforts at agrarian reform and strategies of international lending agencies oriented toward transforming peasant sectors into an agrarian petty bourgeoisie.

Most analysis understands agrarian development in Latin America as centered on large-scale and small-scale units, with the agrarian petty bourgeoisie considered largely absent. In Brazil and Mexico, for example, some debate has focused on whether the modern peasant farmer who hires wage labor is capitalist or simply subordinated economically to large agro-industrial enterprise (Goodman and Redclift 1982 and 1988). Property rights that define the social relations of production as rights to disposal of land, labor, capital, technology, and produce served Spencer Wellhofer (1990) in his study of five forms of production in agrarian capitalist enterprises in Argentina (family enterprise; tenancy property relations, including cash tenancy and sharecropping; farmer capitalist and ranch enterprise; plantation and capitalist farm systems; and manorial or latifundium enterprise). In Nicaragua after the revolution of 1979, government planners worked with two competing models, one based on exports emanating from large export-oriented capitalist farms and a semi-proletarian rural population and the other on a peasant capitalist model that stressed the activity of small and medium-sized independent agricultural producers and fully proletarianized workers. From the outset, a strategy of socialist transition and rapid growth in the socialized sector through a balance of planning and state production could not be sustained, either economically or politically, and state policy turned to reliance on market and decentralization. In his assessment of these models and the Nicaraguan experience, David Kaimowitz argued for a new approach to the transition to socialism that took into account a strategic alliance between government and peasantry, a survival economy, and localized territorial planning: "Peripheral countries in transition have few alternatives to this type of model" (1988: 132).

Arguing that conceptions of family farms merge the images of peasant and capitalist, Luis Llambi concluded that "the capitalized family farm is . . . no more than a phenomenal category of petty capitalist production in agriculture" (1989: 749). He showed that in many parts of Latin America petty capitalist production appeared in a period of growth shaped by an industrialization strategy of import substitution, stimulated both by national governments and agribusiness seeking the domestic supply of agricultural inputs to the emerging agro-industrial complexes. Thus, many paths of transition to a fully capitalist agriculture have appeared in Latin America. The importance of the landlord road to capitalism may have been exaggerated and that of petty capitalist farming overlooked. Capitalized family farms in Latin America may not have been the social and economic panacea assumed by some reformers, but their presence has been important:

> More often than not, these farms have emerged through the combined effects of induced market and technical changes and by the joint efforts of agribusiness and state agencies. In contrast to some ideological expectations, however, market inducements have been far more effective than a whole variety of direct national and international interventions. (771)

World System and Regulation

The transition to capitalism suggested by Immanuel Wallerstein in his *The Modern World System* (1974a) is distinguished by a division of labor over a period of two centuries (from about 1450 to 1640) in which free labor, pastoral production, and industry appeared in agriculture in the core states of Western Europe, forced labor (slave or coerced cash crop) in the peripheries of Latin America and Eastern Europe, and sharecropping as an intermediate form of labor in the semiperiphery of Southern Europe. Wallerstein's analysis of the breakup of feudalism, the rise of the centralized state bureaucracies, and the social organization of agriculture was especially influenced by the methodology of the French historian Fernand Braudel. Wallerstein was concerned with the world economies dominated by nation-states such as Britain and France and their colonial networks. His attention to the transition from feudalism to capitalism tended to support the positions of André Gunder Frank and Paul Sweezy, who, although not always faithfully following the arguments of Marx, nevertheless captured "an understanding of what actually happened" (Wallerstein 1974a: 393).

Departing from this formulation in a criticism and evaluation of Wallerstein, Steve Stern (1988) outlined four perspectives intended to transcend the simplistic dichotomy between a feudal and a capitalist characterization of backwardness in the Third World. One view understands the features of the colonial economy in terms of mode-of-production categories, for example, the colonial and the colonial slavery that originated outside Europe. Another position emphasizes the primacy of feudalism but links colonial feudalism to mercantilism, capital accumulation, and so on. A third perspective stresses the dominance of commercial capital in the relations of production, and a fourth points to the capitalist character of the colonial economy. Stern argues that Wallerstein's depiction of development since the fifteenth century is misleading—that

> the world-system constituted only one of several great "motor forces" that shaped patterns of labor and economy in the periphery; it did not always constitute the decisive causal force even in sectors of high priority; and the various limitations on the world-system's power help to explain the chasm, on a descriptive level, between the world-system and the reality it purports to illuminate. (857)

Stern showed that there were three major influences: world system, popular strategies of resistance within the periphery, and mercantile interests. Other criticisms of this world system interpretation can be found in Aston and Phippin (1985), Brenner (1977), DuPlessis (1977 and 1987), Sella (1977), and Skocpol (1977).

An alternative theoretical perspective on the transition and the evolution of capitalism emanates from the French school of regulation. Initially, this school was concerned with ways of regulating advanced capitalist economies and the discrepancies between North and South. At the same time, it attempted to work out a theory of capitalist development as an effort to complete Marx's project on international trade and the world market (Ruccio 1989). In their incisive historical overview and detailed dissection of this school, Robert Brenner and Mark Glick (1991) show that these theorists sought to provide an intermediate model that allowed theory to be more historically concrete and empirically testable. The theory, as developed by its founder, Michel Aglietta, in *A Theory of Capitalist Regulation* (1979), and carried on in the work of Robert Boyer (1986) and Alain Lipietz (1983), understands capitalism in terms of a succession of phases, each structurally related to distinctive economic patterns. Its concepts include mode of regulation, regime of accumulation, and mode of development, which can be seen as analogous to the Marxist modes of production, social relations of production, and forces of production. The *regime of accumulation* is a relatively stable series of regularities (organization of production within firms that identifies the work of wage workers with the means of production; timing of decisions about capital formation; distribution of income among wages, profits, and taxes; volume and composition of effective demand; and link between noncapitalist and capitalist modes of production). The *mode of regulation* is

> a historically developed relatively integrated network of institutions that reproduces the fundamental capitalist property relationships, guides the prevailing regime of accumulation, and helps make compatible the myriad de-

centralized decisions, potentially contradictory and conflictual, taken by the economy's individual units: In particular, it determines the relationship of capital to wage labor. The *mode of development* arises from the combining of the mode of regulation with accumulation and the experience of cyclical and self-regulating crises. As the mode of development reproduces itself, the outcome is a structural crisis accompanied by conflict of classes, firms, political groups, and governments. Out of this evolves a new mode of regulation and eventually a new mode of development. (Brenner and Glick 1991: 48)

Regulation theory contains a typology of two modes of accumulation (extensive and intensive) and two modes of regulation (competitive and the monopoly). In Western capitalism over the past 150 years, three modes have appeared: a competitive mode of regulation during the nineteenth century, a new mode of development allowing for intensive accumulation at the turn of the century up to the structural crisis of depression in 1930, and a new monopoly mode of regulation that serves as the basis for a new, Fordist mode of development.

Capitalism can also be envisaged theoretically in terms of a historical process of modernity. The Mexican philosopher Bolívar Echeverría (1991) argues that capitalism is a mode of production in human life and in the historical construction of modernity, perhaps "the last great affirmation of a spontaneous historical materialism" (475). Modernity is no longer external to us. It evolves from different levels of possibility and implementation and works through various phases, from the Middle Ages through the industrial revolution. Capitalist modernity is ambivalent in its arming of Europe to discover and exploit the New World; the reproduction of social wealth in the capitalist mode is inconsistent with the satisfaction of social needs. Five distinctive phenomena characterize modernity: humanism, progressivism, urbanism, individualism, and economism. Furthermore, the capitalist process of reproduction evolves from repolarization and recomposition through various stages. Capitalism is diversified by its pervasiveness throughout the economy of a society, its intensity in subsuming the process of reproducing the social, and its differentiation relative to the economy of a society within the world economy.

Echeverría believed that modernity emerged out of the building of European civilization, the subordination of wealth to the mercantile form, and Catholic consolidation of a Christian cultural revolution. Europe was not naturally modern, but modernity was naturally European. Marx, he argued, understood modernity through his critique of capitalism, in particular its dual and contradictory form, leading to a formal process of production and accumulation and a process of subsumption and subordination of the social body, and in its mercantile thrust, resulting in the market as an instrument of expansion and consolidation (but here a distinction is noted between simple commodity exchange and mercantile capitalism). In contrast, political democracy did not evolve at any particular time but was tied to the mixed (state) process of reproduction that initially emphasized commercial activity. Commercial capitalist socialization or commodification is an aspect of modernity that prevails alongside religious expansion. Peace and violence are evident in social life, but peace is impossible in conditions of scarcity. Additionally, language, codes, and discourse are largely determined by modernity. Furthermore, postmodernity appears within modernity as it begins to exhaust itself. Modernity is the civilizing totality. Modernization builds on both endogenous and exogenous influences, with its European form resulting in less conflict than its non-Western one in adapting to the cultural traces of capitalism. Finally, what was distinctive about Soviet modernity was not its partial or total absence of capitalism but its peripheral relation to Europe and its dependence on state capitalism; it thus became a deformed version of the capitalist world economy. Echeverría associated modernity with the pursuit of a technological utopia, whether within the capitalist or a left socialist vision, but considered modernity to have lost its progressive socialist inspiration and adopted a capitalist path. He proclaimed that this outline of theses would move us toward a noncapitalist modernity.

A different sort of transition within capitalism and actually existing socialism is suggested by Mário Murteira (1996) in a look at the Portuguese experience after the revolutionary period of 1974–1975 and the revolutionary regimes in Angola, Mozambique, and Guinea-Bissau after long wars of liberation. Murteira analyzes the shift from central planning under socialism and capitalism to the market economy. Departing from Karl Polanyi, who in *The Great Transformation* (1944) argued that the "transformation" would occur with the end of the self-regulating market economy, and Joseph Schumpeter, who in *Democracy, Capitalism, Socialism* (1942) observed that capitalism was evolving to socialism not because of its failure but because of its success, Murteira outlines how the planned economies in the former Portuguese colonies in Africa turned to the market economy because of their inadequate performance under a planned system, the inability of the world socialist system to assimilate these peripheral economies, and their dependence on external aid from the Western countries. His conclusion suggests the end of a historical alternative to the present capitalist world system and the tendency of marginal countries to improve their economic situation within the existing world system.

Other schools focus on crises within capitalism. For example, the social-structures-of-accumulation approach looks at the postwar crisis of capitalism in the United States and such issues as conflict between labor and capital, national struggles for citizenship rights, and so on, as represented in the work of Samuel Bowles, David Gordon, and Thomas

Weisskopf (1983). Skeptical of the conjunctural crisis theories of the early 1970s, which lacked useful analytical frameworks, John Willoughby criticized both the regulation and social-structures-of-accumulation schools for failing to consider "how global accumulation and domestic class struggle have organized each other during the postwar period" (1989: 84). He concluded that advanced capitalism in the United States had not reached crisis because economic repression can stabilize capitalism and mitigate its contradictions and the political order tends to sustain the dominance of international capitalism.

The idea of a new stage in the era of advanced capitalism has been incorporated in interpretations developed since World War II in response to the long-term crisis of accumulation manifested as stagnation and financial speculation and growth in the center and as imperialist underdevelopment in the periphery. This crisis has involved a global restructuring of classes, corporations, and nations, the essence of which is captured by Joyce Kolko, who in *Restructuring the World Economy* (1988) examines the restructuring of international organizations and the impasse and conjunctural contradictions of the world system (Foster 1989). Arthur McEwan and William K. Tabb (1989), however, contend with the proposition that a new stage of capitalism will develop around the unification of much of the world in a single market.

THE TRANSITION
FROM CAPITALISM TO SOCIALISM

In his significant synthesis of Marxist thought, Hal Draper assessed the major socialist views and theories criticized by Marx and Engels. His analysis revealed many varieties of socialism, past and present, that emerged in particular national contexts. These included the critical-utopian socialism and communism that Engels confronted in his *Socialism Utopian and Scientific* (1880). Draper showed that Marx and Engels were respectful of this form of "French" thought, in particular the contributions of Fourier and Saint-Simon that influenced their own work, although they were critical of the retrogressive role of the followers: "While Marx and Engels paid homage to the 'critical' (social-analytical) element in these great innovators, it was the utopian element that was subsequently hardened into sects as socialism took organized form" (1990: 6). Counterposed to this tendency was scientific socialism, which, Draper argued, led to the claim that Marx believed that socialism had to be scientific. In fact, this was a notion advocated by Mikhail Bakunin and "refuted by Marx when he ran across it" (9). Marx saw the use of scientific socialism as a means of opposing utopian socialism rather than employing socialism to analyze social relations and the forces generated through government social change. Sentimental socialism implied "substituting sentiment for revolutionary ideas and action" (22) and was associated with "free socialism" or "German socialism" in the *Manifesto* and notions of morality, humanism, and love that usually lack real content. State socialism, sometimes called "Bismarckian socialism" or "monarchical socialism" during Marx's lifetime, implied that the state would gain control of production, exercise a complete monopoly over the economy, and become the only producer. This form of socialism was sometimes based on a demand for state aid to establish socialist institutions. Marx referred to it as "Bonapartist socialism" or "imperial socialism," to suggest something engineered from above by the state. The *Manifesto* also referred to reactionary socialism as an ideology hostile to the bourgeoisie and to the proletariat and representing a pattern "in which an upper class under pressure from commercial classes stretched out its hand to the plebes, over the heads or behind the backs of its moneyed rivals, in order to mobilize in its own support the lower classes threatening those rivals" (177). Reactionary socialism could be similar to feudal socialism, a manifestation of the aristocracy against the bourgeoisie; petty bourgeois socialism; and true or German socialism.

In the transition from capitalism to socialism, the working class that was subordinated in the capitalist system emerges in the socialist system but owns no new force of production and does not exploit another class. The transition, according to Charles Bettelheim, is "nothing other than the increasing domination by the immediate producers over their conditions of existence and therefore, in the first instance, over their means of production and their products" (1970: 2).

The transition from capitalism to socialism and the evolution of the proletarian state in place of bourgeois society is synthesized by Frank Parkin (1979) in terms, on the one hand, of an organic theory of political and social change premised on an orthodox interpretation of Marxism, principally in the thinking of Karl Kautsky, and on the other, of an alternative theory of socialist transition premised on the role of the vanguard party. Marx's conception of a socialist transition was rooted partly in the rise of forms of property and productive relations that might conflict with and eventually replace bourgeois property relations, such as the joint stock company (a separation of ownership implied a negative impact on capital) and the workers' cooperative movement (the contradiction between labor and capital might be overcome). These forms exemplified how a new mode of production evolved out of an old one. Thus, if new property relations could be found within capitalism, bourgeois relations of production might eventually be replaced by socialist relations.

This organic theory of the socialist transition was premised on the notion that far greater obstacles confronted the bourgeois revolution than the socialist revolution and that the transition from capitalism to socialism would be relatively peaceful. Kautsky and the school of social democracy that evolved from his thinking believed that the socialist transition would be clearly different from previous forms of transition. The transition from feudalism to absolutism and from absolutism to capitalism was usually felt to be more violent than a transition from capitalism to socialism. Whereas feudal institutions persist within the bourgeois revolution and change is marked by violence, the liberal organizations of bourgeois society are perceived as flexible and can be further developed rather than destroyed en route to socialism.

Lukács, however, shared the pessimism of Lenin in asserting that the representatives of capital could become hegemonic without experiencing a bourgeois revolution. Bourgeois ascendancy was influenced largely by latent economic forces rather than political organization and struggle. Lukács believed that the proletariat had no special conditions for rising to power. The proletariat could only succeed if it were politically conscious of its historic goal. Lukács and Luxemburg also referred to the tendency of capitalism not only to follow a bourgeois democratic path to parliamentarism but also to turn to the "new barbarism," or military dictatorship or fascism: "Whereas the passage from feudalism to absolutism, and from absolutism to capitalism, allowed of no exception or alternatives, the passage from capitalism led to more than one possible destination" (Parkin 1979: 169). Nicos Poulantzas echoed this theme in his recognition that contradictions in capitalism could lead to fascism or socialism, suggesting that the particular conjuncture of class struggle and the position of a particular country in the imperialist chain accounted for the different outcomes. This notion of contradictions in the transition to socialism was also explained theoretically by Louis Althusser, who related contradictions at the base to the legal, political, and ideological apparatuses of the superstructure to show that the economic crisis alone was insufficient to bring about a transition and that the state apparatuses tended to mesmerize and mitigate the revolutionary tendencies of the proletariat.

Although recognizing these constraints in the transition, James Petras envisaged a way out:

> Collectively, these and related policy measures allow for the market and profit motive to operate but within political and social parameters consciously determined by the socialist forces. This pattern of socialist "encirclement" and market freedom provides a framework within which to encourage capitalist cooperation and from which to gradually build up the capacity for a socialist transformation. (1983: 17)

Petras described the transition to socialism as a complex process involving attention to both developing productive forces and changes in social relations.

Considering ways of implementing the transition to socialism, Adam Przeworski suggested three: seize the means of production from capitalists and reorganize the system of production in line with the interests of the citizens rather than the owners of capital or their representatives; seize the means of production or part of them without reorganizing the system of production; or gain control over the means of production but allow capitalists to use part of it for profit. The first option moved toward socialism, the second was an economist strategy, and the third involved class compromise and cooperation with capitalists (1980: 130). Przeworski looked at the question of compromise and the prospects for socialism but was inclined to believe that whenever a conflict or crisis appeared, capitalism remained intact. A transition, he believed, would not succeed if socialism were assumed to be a superior means of satisfying basic material needs. He argued that socialist democracy involved individual autonomy and more than a democratization of capitalist institutions. He pessimistically concluded that "capitalism will continue to offer an opportunity to improve material conditions and . . . will be defended by force where and when it does not, while conditions for socialism continue to rot" (153).

The implications of a third line of socialist development—one that is neither capitalist nor socialist but eventually leads to socialism—were explored by Harry Magdoff (1978). This line involves democratic reforms opposed to feudalism, capitalism, and imperialism and is usually undertaken by nations in a transitional stage between national liberation and socialist revolution. It assumes the possibility of bypassing some stages of capitalism, especially advanced capitalism, and the shift from dependency on capitalism and imperialism to socialism takes considerable time. Also advocating a third position, but under differing conditions in the periphery, Barry Munslow argued that the world system is "gradually being transformed by a whole range of struggles among which those of the peripheral states fighting to build socialism are centrally important" (1983: 27). He considered the taking of power by a revolutionary movement essential to the transition to socialism and believed that revolutionary movements had to account for both internal and external class forces.

The Agrarian Question

The transition to socialism may depend in large measure on changes in the countryside, but development usually involves markets and trade at the international level as well. In the Cuban Revolution, for example, the drive toward socialism was initially associated with industrialization as a panacea, but attention soon turned to exploitation of agricultural resources as the basis of development. At issue were questions such as how to work with and organize (through cooperatives and state farms) the peasant farmers and agricultural workers who supplied a good share of foodstuffs to urban areas, how to reorganize the large estates and unused lands through agrarian reform, and how to diversify agricultural commodities for export to international markets. In the case of Europe, David Goodman and Michael Redclift argued that "capital has the capacity to both transform and retain the labour process in agriculture" (1988: 791) and that this process is dependent on the level of profitability, especially in stages of the food system where value is created. They opposed rigid Marxist theories in which analysis was directly tied to modes of production, suggesting that changes in the transforming process are due in part to political mediation, social policies, and even government policies. Furthermore, they argued that an understanding of the progressive role of capital in agriculture and the food system must extend beyond categories of class such as peasant, worker, or farmer and recognize that technology in agro-industry, food processing, and marketing have been instrumental in transforming agriculture. Goodman and Redclift focused on Western European agriculture since the end of World War II, which has become more specialized and capital intensive, and therefore held that an understanding of the agrarian transition should recognize "historically and geographically specific differences as well as provide for a general theory that acknowledges the systematic, transformational nature of capitalism" (791).

Agricultural reforms may not eliminate large landowners from the countryside and merchants and rich farmers who rule in rural villages. Even cooperatives may become institutions of exploitation if there has been no fundamental change in social life and in the economy. Reforms oriented to investment must find ways of appropriating surplus, usually by eliminating accumulation in the private sector and regulating prices and wages. This may come through state-owned industries that are not profitable or through industries that keep prices low to compete with exports of their goods and services in world markets. The major source of development, taxation, may be undermined by tax evasion or the paucity of income among the masses. Given this problem, a country might turn to foreign investment and loans that increase dependency on imperialist countries if there has been no basic restructuring of the economy.

The Vanguard Party

Lenin opposed the organic model of an evolutionary socialist transition and instead advocated violence and seizure of the state. He derived from Kautsky the thesis that workers could not by themselves become fully conscious of their destiny and that the party as vanguard and agent of the transition would serve this purpose. For the party to lower itself to the level of the masses would undermine organization and leadership and lead to reformism; thus, Lenin recognized inevitable tensions between the proletariat and its organized agent of political expression.

Lenin also stressed stages of development and considered what might constitute the opportune revolutionary moment for a transition to socialism. Capitalism in its final phase of imperialism was vulnerable to explosive tensions. Capitalism was like a chain with strong and weak links, and Russia, a backward nation, was one of the weak ones. Even informed segments of the bourgeoisie believed that capitalism in Russia was in trouble, thus reinforcing Lenin's rejection of the social democrats' view that revolution was impossible. Analysis of failures in the transition to socialism in Europe often allude to the Kautskyian view that the favorable conditions for the working class there militated against revolution. Frank Parkin (1979: 162–163) argued that Lenin underestimated the determination of social democratic leaders to deter revolutionary tendencies in favor of reformism and misjudged Kautsky because he was skillful at using the language and concepts of revolutionary Marxism in advocating parliamentary socialism. Parkin believed, in fact, that there were not two Kautskyian positions, but one consistent preference for a peaceful transition, despite references to class struggle and revolution. Trotsky in particular felt strongly that the vanguard party should reflect the leadership: "If Leninism signifies a shift away from Marx's emphasis on social class to a greater emphasis on the role of party, Trotskyism signifies a further shift from the role of party to the role of leader" (Parkin 1979: 166).

Control over the Means of Production

The modes-of-production school evolved from efforts to link the global relationship of metropole to satellite in the work of André Gunder Frank, in particular his *Capitalism and Underdevelopment in Latin America* (1967), to more empirical fieldwork, for the most part undertaken by anthropologists concerned with peasant production. The attention to modes of production may also have been inspired by criticism (especially by Laclau 1971) of the emphasis Frank gave to trade and markets in his conception of how capitalism persistently developed underdevelopment. Ernesto Laclau showed the need to understand underdevelopment in terms of noncapitalist modes and relations of production as well as capitalist ones emphasized in Frank's work. Three approaches are identifiable in the modes-of-production school, according to David Ruccio and Lawrence Simon (1986: 213): articulation of modes of production, allowing explanations of relations between capitalist and noncapitalist modes (Rey 1975); the colonial mode of production, relevant especially to Africa (Alavi 1975; Banaji 1972; Meillassoux 1980); and the internationalization of capital, focusing on the laws of motion in the capitalist mode of production that dominates the world economy (Barkin 1981; Palloix,1975). Rey outlined three stages of articulation in the development process. At the outset, the traditional or precapitalist mode remains dominant; capitalism may draw raw materials from it, but this exchange tends to reinforce the precapitalist mode rather than promote capitalist relations of production. Capitalism becomes dominant as peasant agriculture and handicrafts are partially transformed and then completely eliminated with the emergence of a labor force. Finally, as capitalism is able to nurture its own labor supply, it enters a stage not yet known to much of the Third World.

In a structuralist view of history that drew on the modes-of-production approach, John Taylor (1979) focused on a reinterpretation of the Latin American experience by arguing that different modes of production can be intertwined in social formations so as to obstruct capitalism and imperialism. Merchant capital under the control of a feudal oligarchy, for example, prevented the spread of capitalism into agriculture.

Market Socialism and Socialist Planning

In an exchange of views with Paul Sweezy, Charles Bettelheim took issue with the two "stages" of plan and market emphasized by Sweezy and suggested that the transition to socialism should be understood in terms of contradictions. A focus on plan or market may obscure the contradictions—that is, planning may keep producers from dominating the conditions of their production. Identification of a market with capitalism and a plan with socialism may overlook that planning can be an instrument of bourgeois politics, whether under a state bureaucracy or in a capitalist country. Bettelheim argued that one must look closely at the political conditions, that is, class relations, to find the real meaning of development: "We know that the advance toward socialism requires that commodity relations disappear and give way to socialist relations" (1970: 7).

The socialist vision of Alec Nove (1983) assumed a "dual" economy dominated by directives from planning offices and subordinated through markets. In contrast to a mixed economy, the economy Nove envisaged consists of state enterprise, cooperatives, and individually owned businesses but without large-scale private ownership of the means of production. In this system, choice depends on market and planners accountable to an elected assembly. In the case of a Third World economy, Nove insisted on a mixed economy with some large state enterprises and many private and cooperative ones. If there were few or no big capitalists or landowners, then the state would have to be cautiously involved.

Nove's conception of markets was vague, however, and he did not elaborate how they functioned in capitalism or socialism. Furthermore, a self-regulating market does not necessarily provide for a stable or desirable social order and leads to devastation in the developing world (Bienefeld 1989). The principal problem, according to Diane Elson, was

> some concern for the transformation of the social and material relations of production, but not of exchange, distribution and consumption. There is not much focus on the reorganization of the labour process beyond an advocacy of small firms, and none on the reorganization of the relations between the production of goods and services and the production and reproduction of labour power. (1988: 5)

This "idealized" and "utopian" scheme fails to account for popular participation in planning, for example, through organizations of producers and households that consume their products.

In contrast to those calling for attention to market and central planning, Ernest Mandel proposed a form of "articulated workers' self-management" that encouraged decentralization. Although agreeing that a socialist market had to go beyond market coordination and that decentralization was helpful, Elson rejected this approach: "The central weakness of Mandel's approach is that he not only rejects markets, he also rejects prices. I shall argue that a decentralized socialist economy needs a decentralized price mechanism, but that this does not imply price formation through private markets" (1988: 11). Mandel advocated reducing the role of money and buying and selling to a minimum by freely distributing the goods required to satisfy basic needs. Councils of workers in each industry would make decisions on allocation of resources. This self-management approach, however, would not allow for a response to unexpected problems. Elson argued that even Marx recognized the progressive nature of market coordination, for markets are inclined not simply to decentralize decisionmaking but to atomize it: "In the fundamental market relation, the cash nexus, each decision-making unit is disconnected from other decision-making units and is connected only to quantities and prices of goods" (13).

A third approach involved socializing the market. A socialized market, according to Elson, is

> made by public bodies, which are financed out of taxation of enterprises and households, rather than out of sales. It is also one in which the "invisible handshakes," the relations of good will and reciprocity, which market economies have found it necessary to construct at least to some degree, are made into public information networks with open access. . . . Such networks would have secretariats financed by taxation, rather than by sale of their services. (32)

Elson envisaged public market-makers or price and wage commissions that would facilitate the interchange of information about terms of sales and purchases between enterprises and between enterprises and households, expose for public scrutiny the relations between costs and prices, and guide the establishment of prices and wages. Her approach thus involved coordination and conscious control of the economy through open access to information.

A similar emphasis on decentralized and popularly based planning and control of accumulation was suggested by Maureen Mackintosh and Marc Wuyts (1988), who linked investment in social services and in rural production with intervention in the market, drawing on the experience of Mozambique after independence in 1975.

The Fall of Existing State Socialism and Prospects for Socialism

Paul Sweezy has argued that the Russian Revolution and the others that followed it were genuine socialist revolutions led for the most part by Marxists whose goal was to replace exploitative capitalism with socialism. He believed that these revolutions occurred under extremely unfavorable conditions and consequently produced neither a capitalist nor a socialist society but an authoritarian class society with state ownership of the main means of production and central planning.

In agreement with this view, Ralph Miliband has acknowledged that despite crises and serious social deficiencies and injustices, capitalism remains strong and resilient: "The Communist regimes presided over thorough social revolutions, indigenous or imposed. But what they made of these revolutions was a system of power which cannot legitimately be called socialist" (1991: 19). Miliband considered semidirect democracy, with popular rule at all levels and representatives subject to the dictates of their constituents, impossible for the moment and argued that socialism had to build on liberal democracy instead. Socialism and Marxism are not dying, however, because "socialism does represent the only rational and humane alternative to capitalism" (26).

Samir Amin, speculating on the future of socialism, began by criticizing three premises of liberalism: economic rationality requires the market, democracy requires capitalism, and development requires free trade (in Anderson 1990: 16). Assessing the "postcapitalist" societies of Russia and the East (see also Raskin et al. 1991), he noted that a capitalist expansion encouraged by the local bourgeoisie would be challenged by the masses, a contradiction not envisaged by Marx in his classical conception of a socialist transition (18). He understood the transition as part of a lengthy process imposed by the unequal development of capitalism and associated with tendencies counterposed to liberal practices, specifically "bureaucratic planning (rationality without the market); anti-democratic political monopoly of a ruling party-state (no democracy to go with no capitalism); and a total delinking from the capitalist world system" (18). Given these contradictory tendencies, he considered the future of socialism in terms of North-South relations and the new globalization of capital. He advocated a "polycentric" world for progressive forces on a world scale. The peoples of different parts of the world must be permitted autonomy to pursue their own interests, a balance between interdependence and autonomy must be established, and the productive forces must be organized with emphasis on the agricultural revolution.

Somewhat pessimistically, Carlos Vilas (in Anderson 1990) argues that socialism is the only possible alternative for countries desiring both economic development and effective democracy but that their choice is between socialist independence and capitalist peripheralization.

Culture and Socialism

Much impressed with the analysis of Rudolf Bahro in *The Alternative in Eastern Europe* (1978), Raymond Williams (1980) noted that the left, which had once dismissed the use of culture in the analysis of change, had been surprised by the "cultural revolution" of the Chinese experience and now had to contend with Bahro's notion of cultural revolution in the path to communism. In particular, Bahro saw consciousness not as the mere product of social being but as a condition of practical existence, in fact a central productive force. He argued that social relations can be revolutionized through knowledge and conscious decision rather than necessarily by change in the relations of production. Bahro alluded to the concept of "surplus consciousness" to suggest that mental capacity need not be directed solely to immediate needs but should be oriented to problems of greater scope: "What was then already outlined in communications, in education and in communal self-management is radically strengthened by proposals in economic planning, in factory organization and in the 'problem-solving collectives' of technical and scientific work" (Williams 1980: 11).

Socialism and Democracy

Socialism, in the view of Robin Blackburn (1991), can contribute to a gradual improvement of the situation of the backward nations in a global market system. Democratic institutions must be combined with socialist market economies to ensure more egalitarianism in the market. Massive global poverty and the global threat to the environment imply the need to rely on public enterprise and planning on a global scale but not to the point of a global command economy. Blackburn argues that the logic of capitalism will not necessarily be replaced by the approaches that permeate the socialist discourse, including the "new concepts of trade unions, of self-management, of cooperative and municipal enterprise, of contract compliance and basic income, of market socialism and socialized market, and of egalitarian and ecological responsibility" (66).

The evolution of capitalism has usually been understood in economic terms, with questions of power and politics being of less concern, but Samuel Bowles and Herbert Gintis (1990) have attempted to fill this gap in their search for the "contested exchange" in relations emanating from command over goods, services, and agents. They set forth a series of propositions on how power functions in the political economy, arguing, for example, that "contested exchanges may allocate power to agents on the short side of nonclearing markets"; "those in positions of decision-making authority in capitalist firms occupy locations on the short side of the labor market and exercise power over employees"; "the competitive equilibrium of contested exchange economy may exhibit racial, gender, and other forms of labor market discrimination among otherwise identical workers" (207–208). They propose an economic theory that recognizes the cultural and political aspects of the economy and moves away from economistic thinking as a step toward "building an egalitarian and democratic postcapitalist economy" (203).

This search for democracy in the economy transcends traditional treatments of political democracy, whether in its bourgeois, liberal, social democratic, or representative form under capitalism or its democratic socialist or revolutionary socialist form under socialism. Works that address the question of democracy in political economies and the possibilities of popular participation in economies include Albert and Hahnel (1990), Bowles and Gintis (1986), Cohen and Rogers (1983), and Carnoy and Shearer (1980), all of which concentrate on the experience of the United States; Laclau and Mouffe (1985), which draws on the failures of European socialism; and Harris (1988) and Fagen, Deere, and Corragio (1986), which describe the difficulties of socialist transition in revolutionary situations throughout the developing world since the end of World War II.

This narrative of theories about transitions has concentrated on social formations, economic modes of production, and the possibilities for involvement of people in political decisions that affect their everyday lives. The transition to capitalism is not much in dispute today, although traces of precapitalism are found everywhere. The fact is that capitalism has become deeply entrenched in national societies and the whole world is integrated into the international capitalist order. Capitalism has persisted in the face of inherent contradictions. Yet, the world has also experimented with various forms of socialism, sometimes through evolutionary means, by electing socialist and democratic governments to power, and sometimes through revolution. The great revolutions of the twentieth century, in China, Cuba, and Russia, in particular, involved significant movements and individuals seeking a socialist outcome. Although today socialism may be in doubt in all three of those situations, we have learned a great deal from them about the transition, and from that experience it is possible to project a conceptualization, even possible models, of how socialism can evolve.

REFERENCES

Aglietta, M. 1979. *A Theory of Capitalist Regulation.* London: New Left Books. Sets forth the basic theoretical framework for the French regulation school.

Alavi, Hamza. 1975. "India and the Colonial Mode of Production," pp. 169–197 in *Socialist Register.* London: Merlin Press. Exemplifies one approach in the modes-of-production school.

Albert, Michael, and Robin Hahnel. 1990. *Quiet Revolution in Welfare Economics.* Princeton: Princeton University Press. Explores alternatives for participatory democracy in advanced industrial economies.

Amin, Samir. 1976. "The Precapitalist Formations," pp. 13–37 in his *Unequal Development.* New York: Monthly Review Press. Distinguishes five successive modes of production: primitive-communal, tribute paying, slave owning, simple petty commodity, and capitalist.

_____. 1985. "Modes of Production: History and Unequal Development." *Science and Society* 49 (Summer):194–207. Reviews modes of production identified in his earlier work.

Anderson, W. H. Locke, ed. 1990. *The Future of Socialism. Monthly Review* 42 (July-August). Contains articles by Paul M. Sweezy, Samir Amin, Peter Marcuse, John Saul, Daniel Singer, and Carlos M. Vilas.

Aston, T. H., and C. H. E. Phippin, eds. 1985. *The Brenner Debate: Agrarian Class Structure and Economic Development in Pre-Industrial Europe.* New York: Cambridge University Press. Reviews the debate on the emergence of capitalism out of feudal Europe.

Banaji, Jaairus. 1972. "For a Theory of Colonial Modes of Production." *Economic and Political Weekly* 7 (December). Exemplifies one dominant approach in the modes-of-production school.

Barkin, David. 1981. "Internationalization of Capital: An Alternative Approach." *Latin American Perspectives* 8 (Summer and Fall):156–161. Exemplifies one approach in the modes-of-production school.

Bettelheim, Charles. 1970. "More on the Society of Transition." *Monthly Review* 22 (December):1–21. A response to Paul Sweezy on the question of the transition, with Sweezy's reply. (Reprinted with earlier exchanges of views in Sweezy and Bettelheim 1971.)

Bienefeld, Manfred. 1989. "The Lessons of History and the Developing World." *Monthly Review* 40 (July-August):9–41. Drawing on the work of Karl Polanyi, argues that despite the market's advancing of the material forces of production, a self-regulating market does not produce a stable or desirable social order.

Blackburn, Robin. 1991. "Fin de Siècle: Socialism After the Crash." *New Left Review* 185 (January-February):5–66. An overview of trends, strengths, and weaknesses in the socialist world, past and present.

Blaut, J. M. 1994. *The Colonizer's Model of the World: Geographical Diffusionism and Eurocentric History.* New York: Guilford Press. Argues that Europe was not distinctive in its contribution to the industrial revolution—that similar developments were taking place outside Europe before 1492—but had an advantage due to its imposition of a colonial model and extraction of wealth elsewhere.

Bloch, Marc. 1961. *Feudal Society.* 2 vols. Chicago: University of Chicago Press. A major source on the history, dynamics, conflicts, and evolution of feudalism in Western Europe.

Bowles, Samuel, and Herbert Gintis. 1986. *Democracy and Capitalism: Property, Community, and the Contradictions of Modern Social Thought.* New York: Basic Books. Identifies forms of representative and political democracy in advanced political economies.

_____. 1990. "Contested Exchange: New Microfoundations for the Political Economy of Capitalism." *Politics and Society* 18 (June):165–222. Argues that the left in advanced capitalist countries seeks to make power compatible with democracy, but its demand for collective involvement in economic life is undermined by the market's opportunity for individual choice. Differentiates between exogenous and endogenous claim enforcement and focuses on the latter, which produces "a well-defined set of power relations among voluntarily participating agents" (167). Followed by critical comment by John Roemer, Michael Burawoy, Erik Olin Wright, and others.

Bowles, Samuel, David Gordon, and Thomas Weisskopf. 1983. *Beyond the Wasteland.* Garden City, N.Y.: Anchor Press, Doubleday. Examines the crises of capitalism in the late twentieth century.

Boyer, Robert. 1986. *La théorie de la régulation: Une analyse critique.* Paris: La Découverte. A basic study of regulation theory by a leading contemporary proponent. Useful in understanding long-cycle theory.

Brenner, Robert. 1976. "Agrarian Class Structure and Economic Development in Pre-Industrial Europe." *Past and Present* 70:30–75. An important critical review of ideas and literature on precapitalist times in Europe.

_____. 1977. "The Origins of Capitalist Development: A Critique of Neo-Smithian Marxism." *New Left Review* 104 (July-August):25–92. Emphasizes class struggle and relations of production rather than the market in criticisms of Wallerstein and others.

_____. 1982. "The Agrarian Roots of European Capitalism." *Past and Present* 76: 16–113. An assessment of theories on the agrarian question and the transition to capitalism in Europe.

_____. 1993. *Merchants and Revolution: Commercial Change, Political Conflict, and London's Overseas Traders, 1550–1633.* Cambridge, England: Cambridge University Press.

Brenner, Robert, and Mark Glick. 1991. "The Regulation Approach: Theory and History." *New Left Review* 188 (July-August):45–119. A systematic review of the French regulation school and its analysis of capitalist crisis through historical phases.

Callinicos, Alex. 1994. "England's Transition to Capitalism." *New Left Review* 207 (September-October):124–133. Review of Brenner (1993). See other reviews by Ian Gentles and John Morrill in the same issue.

Cano, Wilson. 1977. *Raizes da concentração industrial de São Paulo.* Rio de Janeiro: Difel. Discusses the concentration of industrial capital and the shift from agrarian to industrial base in São Paulo.

Cardoso, Fernando Henrique, and Enzo Faletto.1979. *Dependency and Development in Latin America.* Berkeley: University of California Press. Shows how capital can be mobilized to effect development in dependent situations.

Carnoy, Martin, and Derek Shearer. 1980. *Economic Democracy.* White Plains, N.Y.: M. E. Sharpe. A study of democratic practices that can lead to egalitarian economy.

Cohen, Joshua, and Joel Rogers. 1983. *On Democracy: Towards a Transformation of American Society.* New York: Penguin. Considers democratic tendencies, practices, and ideals in the experience of the United States.

Critchley, John. 1978. *Feudalism.* London: George Allen and Unwin. Chapters on fiefs and on lords and vassals provide extensive detail on historical understandings, legal traditions, customs, and practices of medieval society.

Davis, Mike. 1978. "Fordism in Crisis: A Review of Michel Aglietta's *Régulation et crises: L'experience des Etats Unis.*" *Review* 2 (Fall):207–269. A review article (see Aglietta 1979).

Draper, Hal. 1990. *Karl Marx's Theory of Revolution.* Vol. 4, *Critique of Other Socialisms.* New York: Monthly Review Press. An overview and synthesis of socialist ideas in the thinking of Marx and their strengths and weaknesses.

DuPlessis, Robert S. 1977. "From Demesne to World-System: A Critical Review of the Literature on the Transition from Feudalism to Capitalism." *Radical History Review* 4 (Winter 1977):3–41. A critical review of the literature on the transition.

_____. 1987. "The Partial Transition to World-Systems Analysis in Early Modern History." *Radical History Review* 39:11–27. Further criticism of world system theory and analysis.

Echeverría, Bolívar. 1991. "Modernidad y capitalismo: Quince Tesis." *Review* 14 (Fall):471–515. Advances fifteen theses on the transition from precapitalism to capitalism and modernity and proposes that a noncapitalist modernity is possible.

Elson, Diane. 1988. "Market Socialism or Socialization of the Market?" *New Left Review* 172 (November-December):3–44. Reviews the debate between Ernest Mandel and Alec Nove and supports a position similar to Mandel's that sees an alternative between the market and bureaucratic planning. Agrees with Nove that the price mechanism is an important means of coordinating the socialist economy but argues that it must be socialized to work for socialism. In her view, the "guiding thread" of a socialist economy is "neither the market nor the plan, but the production and reproduction of labour power" (4), at the heart of which are unpaid labor processes in the household and the community.

Evans, Peter. 1979. *Dependent Development: The Alliance of Multinational, State, and Local Capital in Brazil.* Princeton: Princeton University Press. An important study on how the triad of local, state, and international capital can promote capitalist development in a dependent situation.

Fagen, Richard, Carmen Diana Deere, and José Corragio, eds. 1986. *Transitions and Development: Problems of Third World Socialism.* New York: Monthly Review Press. Essays on the transition to socialism and prospects for development based on revolutions of the past half century.

Font, Mauricio A. 1987. "Coffee Planters, Politics, and Development in Brazil." *Latin American Research Review* 22 (3):69–90. Argues against the thesis that large Paulista coffee planters of the 1920s were cohesive, economically homogeneous, economically dominant, monolithic, or politically hegemonic.

_____. 1989. "Perspectives on Social Change and Development in São Paulo: A Reply." *Latin American Research Review* 24 (3):143–157. A rejoinder to the criticisms of his 1987 article by Love (1989) and Stolcke (1989).

_____. 1990. *Coffee, Contention, and Change: In the Making of Modern Brazil.* Cambridge, Mass., and Oxford, England: Basil Blackwell. A monograph on coffee planters in Brazil in the early twentieth century showing the various ways in which capital was formed there.

Foster, John Bellamy. 1989. "Restructuring the World Economy in a Time of Lasting Crisis." *Monthly Review* 41 (May):46–55. Favorable review of Kolko (1988).

Foster-Carter, Aiden. 1978. "The Modes of Production Controversy." *New Left Review* 107 (January-February):47–77. A useful synthesis of the origins and evolution of the modes-of-production school, with attention to the contributions of English and French anthropologists.

Frank, André Gunder. 1967. *Capitalism and Underdevelopment in Latin America: Historical Studies of Chile and Brazil.* New York: Monthly Review Press. Application of the thesis of capitalist development of underdevelopment to the case of Brazil.

_____. 1978. "Conclusions: On So-Called Primitive Accumulation," pp. 238–271 in his *World Accumulation, 1492–1789.* New York: Monthly Review Press. Summary of his thesis that "the process of accumulation is a, if not the, principal motor of modern history" (238), examining four themes: primitive, primary, and capitalist accumulation; the unequal structure and relations of production and circulation in capitalist accumulation; uneven transformation through stages, cycles, and crises of capital accumulation; and class struggle in capitalist accumulation.

Goodman, David E., and Michael R. Redclift. 1982. *From Peasant to Proletarian: Capitalist Development and Agrarian Transitions.* New York: St. Martin's Press. Theoretical essays on the transition and case studies of Brazil and Mexico.

_____. 1988. "Problems in Analyzing the Agrarian Transition in Europe." *Comparative Studies in Society and History* 30 (October):784–791. Extends the authors' thinking on the agrarian transition in Latin America to the debates on the agrarian transition in Europe.

Gottlieb, Roger S. 1984. "Feudalism and Historical Materialism: A Critique and a Synthesis." *Science and Society* 48 (Spring):1–37. A major contribution to the discussion of feudalism and the transition to capitalism.

_____. 1987. "Historical Materialism, Historical Laws, and Social Primacy: Further Discussion of the Transition Debate." *Science and Society* 51 (Summer):188–199. A rejoinder to critics of his 1984 piece.

Gran, Peter. 1996. *Beyond Eurocentrism: A New View of Modern World History.* Syracuse, N.Y.: Syracuse University Press. A revisionist interpretation that identifies four paths to state formation and provides a comparative basis for understanding the historical origins and evolution of different countries, past and present.

Harris, Richard L. 1988. "Marxism and the Transition to Socialism in Latin America." *Latin American Perspectives* 15 (1):7–54. An introduction to the literature on the socialist transition.

Heller, Henry. 1985. "The Transition Debate in Historical Perspective." *Science and Society* 49 (Summer):208–213. A synthesis of recent debates on the transition.

Hilton, R. H, ed. 1978. *The Transition from Feudalism to Capitalism.* London: New Left Books. Essays on the transition, including the prominent views of Maurice Dobb (pp. 57–67, 165–169) and Paul Sweezy (pp. 33–56).

Hindess, Barry, and Paul Hirst. 1975. *Pre-Capitalist Modes of Production.* London: Routledge and Kegan Paul.

Ingham, Geoffrey. 1988. "Commercial Capital and British Development: A Reply to Michael Barratt Brown." *New Left Review* 172 (November-December):45–65. Followed by reply by Barratt Brown. Focuses on debates on capitalist development in England and the characterization of Britain as exceptional in Marxist theory. Differs with Perry Anderson with regard to the latter's belief that Marx and Engels moved from the position that the industrial bourgeoisie was dominant in Victorian society to a view that it was subordinate to the aristocracy but in general agrees with Anderson's historical interpretations.

Kaimowitz, David. 1988. "Nicaragua's Experience with Agricultural Planning: From State-Centered Accumulation to the Strategic Alliance with the Peasantry." *Journal of Development Studies* 24 (July):114–135. Argues for an approach to accelerated accumulation and advanced socialism oriented to a strategic alliance between revolutionary state and peasantry and local territorial planning. Shows that the revolutionary Sandinista government in Nicaragua had to shift from rapid growth and centralized planning of the socialized state sector to a model based on market mechanisms and economic decentralization and regionalization.

Kolko, Joyce. 1988. *Restructuring the World Economy.* New York: Pantheon. Particularly useful for identifying the global restructuring that characterized the long period of accumulation, stagnation, and financial speculation from World War II to the 1980s.

Lachmann, Richard. 1985. "Feudal Elite Conflict and the Origins of English Capitalism." *Politics and Society* 14 (3):349–378. Examines two strands in the debate on the transition from feudalism to capitalism by looking, in particular, at the English case and suggests an alternative explanation in terms of the market.

Laclau, Ernesto. 1971. "Feudalism and Capitalism in Latin America." *New Left Review* 67 (May-June):19–38. Emphasis on the primacy of production in a critique of the attention to exchange and circulation in the work of André Gunder Frank.

Laclau, Ernesto, and Chantal Mouffe. 1985. *Hegemony and Socialist Strategy: Towards a Radical Democratic Politics.* London: Verso. A theoretical exposition of how representative politics can be turned toward social democracy and socialism.

Laibman, David. 1984. "Modes of Production and Theories of Transition." *Science and Society* 49 (Winter):257–294. Offers a model for understanding the transition to capitalism, with attention to forces and relations of production.

_____. 1987. "Modes and Transitions: Replies to the Discussion and Further Comments." *Science and Society* 51 (Summer):179–188. Examines whether laws of motion exist in modes of production other than capitalism; whether the post-communal and precapitalist period can be theorized in terms of one (Amin), two (Laibman), or three (Marx) subperiods; and whether the theory of the abstract social totality or the productive-forces productive-relations model is teleological.

Lenin, V. I. 1956 (1899). *The Development of Capitalism in Russia: The Process of the Formation of a Home Market for Large-Scale Industry.* Moscow: Foreign Language Publishing House. A major theoretical and empirical study of the transition from precapitalist to capitalist social formations in Russia.

Lipietz, Alain. 1983. *The Enchanted World: Inflation, Credit and the World Crisis.* London: Verso. A major contribution to the French regulation school.

Llambi, Luis. 1989. "Emergence of Capitalized Family Farms in Latin America." *Comparative Studies in Society and History* (October):745–775. Focuses on the role of the "modern" farmer and how the labor of owner and hired workers has combined with technology to shape new forms of agrarian production in Latin America.

Love, Joseph L. 1989. "Of Planters, Politics, and Development." *Latin American Research Review* 24 (3):127–135. Agrees with Font (1987) that coffee planters were dissatisfied with government policy but questions Font's insistence that the coffee economy was not fully capitalist and suggests that he exaggerates the role of the small farm.

Mackintosh, Maureen, and Marc Wuyts. 1988. "Accumulation, Social Services, and Socialist Transition in the Third World: Reflections on Decentralized Planning Based on the Mozambican Experience." *Journal of Development Studies* 24 (June):136–179. Suggests an approach to the socialist transition that ties investment in social services and rural production to intervention in the market.

Magdoff, Harry. 1978. "Is There a Noncapitalist Road?" *Monthly Review* 30 (December):1–10. Explores the implications of a third line of socialist development, one that is neither capitalist nor socialist but leads eventually to socialism.

Mandel, Ernest. 1986. "A Critique of Market Socialism." *New Left Review* 159 (September-October):5–37. Reviews and critiques Nove (1983) and suggests an alternative to Nove's market socialism in the form of a decentralized system of workers' self-management.

Martins, Luciano. 1982. "A revolução de 1930 e seu significado político," in *A revolução de 30: Seminário internacional.* Brasília: Fundação Getúlio Vargas. Relates the important political changes of 1930 to the rise of capitalism in Brazil.

Marx, Karl. 1943. *Articles on India.* Bombay: People's Publishing House.

_____. 1967 (1867, 1885, 1894). *Capital: A Critique of Political Economy.* 3 vols. New York: International Publishers.

_____. 1975 (1857–1858). *Pre-Capitalist Economic Formations*. Edited by Eric Hobsbawm. New York: International Publishers.

Marx, Karl, and Frederick Engels. 1976 (1848). *Manifesto of the Communist Party (Collected Works*, Vol. 6). New York: International Publishers.

McEwan, Arthur, and William K. Tabb. 1989. "A New Stage of Capitalism Ahead." *Monthly Review* 41 (May):1–5. Points to stagnation and lack of productivity along with slow growth and mass unemployment as reasons the projected new stage is not achievable under capitalism.

McLennan, Gregor. 1986. "Marxist Theory and Historical Research: Between the Hard and Soft Options." *Science and Society* 50 (Spring):85–95. An interpretive and critical assessment of theories and perspectives on the transition from feudalism to capitalism.

Meillassoux, Claude. 1980. "From Production to Reproduction: A Marxist Approach to Economic Anthropology," pp. 189–210 in Harold Wolpe, ed., *The Articulation of Modes of Production*. London: Routledge and Kegan Paul. An example of anthropological work and theory in the modes-of-production school.

_____. 1992. *The Anthropology of Slavery: The Womb of Iron and Gold*. Chicago: University of Chicago Press. A neo-Marxist study of the Sudanese empires of western Africa, offering generalizations about slavery and the socioeconomic world in which it existed and arguing that the slave as a fundamental form of property converted to a commodity is incapable of reproducing itself either culturally or biologically. Includes a glossary that is helpful in dealing with a difficult, sometimes obscure, and jargon-filled text.

Mello, João Manoel Cardoso de. 1982. *O capitalismo tardio*. São Paulo, Brazil: Editora Brasiliense. Describes late capitalism in Brazil.

Mello, João Manoel Cardoso de, and Maria da Conceição Tavares. 1985. "The Capitalist Export Economy in Brazil, 1884–1930," pp. 82–136 in Roberto Cortés Conde and Shane J. Hunt, eds., *Latin American Economies: Growth and the Export Sector, 1880–1930*. New York: Holmes and Meier. Argues for a direct relationship between coffee capital and industrialization.

Miliband, Ralph. 1991. "Socialism in Question." *Monthly Review* 42 (March):16–26. Responds to the skepticism on right and left about the future of socialism, emphasizing the persistence of capitalism and the deficiencies of communist regimes but concluding that socialism will emerge as an alternative.

Munslow, Barry. 1983. "Is Socialism Possible on the Periphery?" *Monthly Review* 25 (May):25–39. Focuses on the African experience to examine socialist development in the periphery in terms of both world systems theory and various tendencies in the Trotskyist tradition. Favors revolution as a means of bringing about the socialist transition. Argues that world systems theory does not give sufficient attention to class struggle and that Trotskyist positions tend either to overestimate the power of the working class in the periphery or to dismiss it on account of its weaknesses.

Murteira, Mário. 1996. "The Transition from Central Planning to Market Economy: An International Comparison." *Review* 19 (Winter):79–98. A comparative overview of transitions from central planning to market-oriented societies, with attention to Portuguese-speaking African nations and Macau. Suggests that the notion of development as progress is now questionable and that either development is not altogether necessary or different "economic cultures" are emerging in the traditional world economy.

North, Douglass C., and R. P. Thomas. 1973. *The Rise of the Western World: A New Economic History.* Cambridge, England: Cambridge University Press. Suggests that a stagnant feudalism was transcended through political institutionalization and capitalist markets external to feudalism.

Nove, Alec. 1983. *The Economics of Feasible Socialism.* London: George Allen and Unwin. Advances a vision of market socialism. For debate on this theme see Ernest Mandel (1986); Jay Mandel, "Feasible Socialism and Economic Development," *Socialist Review* 91 (January-February 1987):96–110; and Alec Nove, "Markets and Socialism," *New Left Review* 161 (January-February 1987): 98–104. See also John B. Judis, "Market Socialism: The Makings for Practical Politics—Particularly in U.S.," *In These Times* 14 (May 9–15, 1990):8–9.

Palloix, Christian. 1975. "The Internationalization of Capital and the Circuit of Social Capital," pp. 63–88 in Hugo Radice, ed., *International Firms and Modern Imperialism.* New York: Penguin. Represents an alternative current in theory on development, related to dominant approaches in the modes-of-production school.

Parkin, Frank. 1979. "The Transition to Socialism," pp. 145–175 in his *Marxism and Class Theory: A Bourgeois Critique.* London: Tavistock. A brilliant exposition of the ideas of classical Marxism, with particular attention to the thought of Marx, Kautsky, Lenin, and Trotsky and reference to Althusser and Poulantzas.

Petras, James. 1983. "Problems in the Transition to Socialism." *Monthly Review* 35 (May):14–24. Examines the transition as a mixed economy driven by a socialist regime mediating the struggle between capital and labor. Argues that capital tends to seek security through collaboration with the state and to align itself with business and the formal aspects of democracy. In contrast, a socialist regime finds support in other classes, especially wage and petty commodity producers, but seeks the cooperation of capital without alienating labor.

Przeworski, Adam. 1980. "Material Interests, Class Compromise, and the Transition to Socialism." *Politics and Society* 10 (2):155–203. Assesses the question whether workers in pursuit of their material interests will opt for socialism.

Raskin, Marcus G., et al. 1991. "The Road to Reconstruction." *The Nation* (April 22):512–525. Reflects on the need for reconstruction and institutional transformation in the wake of the collapse of the Soviet bloc and upheavals in Eastern Europe and the Soviet Union.

Reich, Robert B. 1991. *The Work of Nations: Preparing Ourselves for 21st Century Capitalism.* New York: Alfred A. Knopf. Argues that national products, technologies, industries, and corporations are disappearing as each nation turns to citizen skills and insights as its major assets in contending with the dominant global economy.

Rey, Pierre-Philippe. 1975. "The Lineage Mode of Production." *Critique of Anthropology* 3 (Spring):27–79. Exemplifies the modes-of-production school, in particular the approach to the articulation of modes. Argues that history is not necessarily unilinear and that old and new modes are evident in the transition from feudalism to capitalism.

Ruccio, David F. 1989. "Fordism on a World Scale: International Dimensions of Regulation." *Review of Radical Political Economics* 21 (Winter):33–53. A review of the regulation school, especially the work of Lipietz. Examines global Fordism and peripheral Fordism in terms of the Marxist agenda for theorizing capitalist development.

Ruccio, David F., and Lawrence H. Simon. 1986. "Methodological Aspects of a Marxian Approach to Development: An Analysis of the Modes of Production School." *World Development* 14 (February):211–222. An update to an important earlier work by Foster-Carter (1978). Examines three basic positions in the Marxist modes-of-production school in terms of theory, concept formation, and the relationship between theory and conceptualization. Concludes that this school suffers from economic determinism and a theory-fact dichotomy.

Rudra, Ashok. 1987. "The Transition Debate: Lessons for Third World Marxists." *Science and Society* 51 (Summer):170–178. Examines the role of Third World countries in the transformation process and ways of analyzing problems of transition. Concludes that except for the work of Samir Amin, the debate has been Eurocentric in emphasis.

Sella, Domenico. 1977. "The World-System and Its Dangers." *Peasant Studies* 6 (January):29–32. Criticizes world system interpretations and theories.

Silva, Sergio. 1976. *Expansão cafeeira e origens da indústria no Brasil.* São Paulo, Brazil: Alfa-Omega. Examines coffee expansion and the origins of industry and capitalism in Brazil.

Skocpol, Theda. 1977. "Wallerstein's World Capitalist System: A Theoretical and Historical Critique." *American Journal of Sociology* 82:1075–1090. A detailed assessment.

Stephens, John D. 1986. *The Transition from Capitalism to Socialism.* Urbana: University of Illinois Press. Departs from a critique of Marx's theory of the transition from capitalism to socialism in theory and practice. Argues that historical changes in capitalist society support rather than contradict Marx's view of the transition and that working class organization is the key to the transition—that democracy and the welfare state were responses to the growing strength of labor.

Stern, Steve J. 1988. "Feudalism, Capitalism and the World-System in the Perspective of Latin America and the Caribbean." *American Historical Review* 93 (October):829–897. An exhaustive survey of feudalism, capitalism, and the world system that departs from a critical review of the work of Immanuel Wallerstein.

Stolcke, Verena. 1989. "Coffee Planters, Politics, and Development in Brazil: A Comment on Mauricio Font's Analysis." *Latin American Research Review* 24 (3):136–142. Criticizes Font (1987), arguing that "competition and contradictions were not generated by an emerging 'alternative economy' but inhered in the coffee production system itself, just as they inhere in capitalism per se, governed as it is by the market principle" (141). Recognizes the value of Font's analysis of political tensions and alignments among the São Paulo elite.

Sweezy, Paul M. 1971. "Modern Capitalism." *Monthly Review* 23 (June):1–10. Suggests that capitalism as a world system originated in the fifteenth and sixteenth centuries with the discoveries and explorations of the Europeans, resulting in a handful of dominant exploiting countries and a majority of dominated and exploited countries. Points out that despite their differences the two parts of the world system have always been linked. Traces processes and stages in capitalism from primary accumulation of capital and mercantile capitalism to manufacture, the earliest form of capitalism; the development of machinery and technologies in industry, transport, and communication in the eighteenth and nineteenth centuries; and the concentration of corporate capital from the last third of the nineteenth century until the present.

_____. 1986. "Feudalism-to-Capitalism Revisited." *Science and Society* 50 (Spring):81–84. Reflections and update of views expressed in Hilton (1978).

Sweezy, Paul, and Charles Bettelheim. 1971. *On the Transition to Socialism.* New York: Monthly Review Press. A compilation of articles and letters previously published (see, for example, Bettelheim [1970]).

Taylor, John G. 1979. *From Modernization to Modes of Production: A Critique of the Sociologies of Development and Underdevelopment.* London: Macmillan. A critical overview of modernization and other approaches to a theory of development and underdevelopment, with special attention to the modes-of-production school.

van Zanden, Jan Luiten. 1993. *The Rise and Decline of Holland's Economy: Merchant Capitalism and the Labour Market.* Manchester: Manchester University Press.

van Zanden, Jan Luiten, et al. 1997. "Merchant Capital." *Review* 20 (Spring):189–270. Reviews debate around van Zanden's theory of merchant capital in the early period of Dutch capitalism. Interprets merchant capitalism in the theoretical framework of Marxist historiography.

Wallerstein, Immanuel. 1974a, 1980, 1989. *The Modern World System.* New York: Academic Press. Influenced by Fernand Braudel, elaborates a theory of the world system with a reinterpretation of European history since the fifteenth century.

_____. 1974b. "The Rise and Decline and Future Demise of the World Capitalist System: Concepts for Comparative Analysis." *Comparative Studies in Society and History* 16 (September):387–415. Sets forth the basic concepts of world systems theory.

Ward, John O. 1985. "Feudalism: Interpretative Category or Framework of Life in the Medieval West?" in Edmund Leach, S. N. Mukherjee, and John Ward, eds., *Feudalism: Comparative Studies.* Sydney: Sydney Association for Studies in Society and Culture. Reviews ten different meanings of "feudalism."

Warren, Bill. 1980. *Imperialism: Pioneer of Capitalism.* London: New Left Books. Argues that underdevelopment is associated with the persistence of noncapitalist modes of production and can be overcome through the expansion of imperialism and the implantation of the forces of production.

Wellhofer, E. Spencer. 1990. "Agrarian Capitalism, Property Rights, and Rural Class Behavior." *Comparative Political Studies* 22 (January):355–396. Identifies the property rights that define the social relations of production as rights to disposal of land, labor, capital, technology, and produce. Compares the new institutional economics (emphasizing rational choice and market forces) with traditional Marxian and Weberian approaches. Identifies five forms of production in agrarian capitalist enterprises: family enterprise; tenancy property relations, in-

cluding cash tenancy and sharecropping; farmer capitalist and ranch enterprise; plantation and capitalist farm systems; and manorial or latifundium enterprise. Uses Argentina to illustrate these concepts and ideas.

Williams, Raymond. 1980. "Beyond Actually Existing Socialism." *New Left Review*
120 (March-April):3–19. Examines the noncapitalist path to industrialization,
analyzes the weaknesses of "actually existing" socialist societies, and offers an
outline of possible communist society drawing on utopian thought.

Willoughby, John. 1989. "Is Global Capitalism in Crisis? A Critique of Postwar
Crisis Theories." *Rethinking Marxism* 2 (Summer):84–101. Criticizes the conjunctural crisis theories of the early 1970s for lacking useful analytical frameworks
and the regulation and social-structures-of-accumulation schools for overlooking the relationship between global accumulation and domestic class struggle.
Reviews four other postwar theories of crisis. Concludes that advanced capitalism in the United States has not reached crisis because economic repression can
stabilize capitalism and mitigate its contradictions and the political order tends
to sustain the dominance of international capitalism.

Wood, Ellen Meiksins. 1999. *The Origin of Capitalism.* New York: Monthly Review
Press. A succinct and clear critical review of various historical approaches to
analysis of capitalism and to understanding the transition to capitalism.

3

THEORIES OF CLASS

Social scientists of various persuasions use the concept of class, and it has been central to analyses of political experiences and possible strategies for mobilization, both reformist and revolutionary. Class has been important in the official Marxism of "socialist" states (the Soviet Union and other countries in Eastern Europe in the past and China, Cuba, North Korea, Vietnam, and other socialist states today). Historically, class was part of the more open theory and discourse of social democrats and democratic socialists everywhere (especially in Western Europe), and it has been significant in the analysis of the major revolutionary experiences of the Third World (Angola, Mozambique, Nicaragua, and others).

ORIGINS

The concept of class originated not with Marx but with Saint-Simon and others who preceded him. The earliest conception of class structure appears to date to eighteenth-century political economy and, in particular, to the work of Adam Smith and David Ricardo. In *Inquiry into the Nature and Causes of the Wealth of Nations* (1776), Smith classified society in three classes—landlords, capitalists, and workers—and argued that an invisible hand would evolve in a self-regulating economic order in place of the self-interest of individuals; he also distinguished between productive and unproductive workers and their relationships to capitalism. In *Principles of Political Economy and Taxation* (1817), Ricardo emphasized owners of land, owners of capital, and workers and demonstrated that rent was unearned income and that the high rents of the landowning class undermined capitalism and impeded the possibility for capitalist profit. Marx showed that not only landowners but capitalists acted in their own interests. He demonstrated that profit was also a form of unearned income and focused on class in his critical analysis of issues of growth, accumulation, distribution, stagnation, and crisis that affect capitalist societies. He believed that labor power as a commodity applied to the process of production created value and surplus beyond the equipment and raw materials necessary to reproduce capital and sustain workers. The followers of Marx were to establish a tradition of radical political economy that incorporated class into economic analysis (Clegg, Boreham, and Dow 1985: 13).

Richard Wolff and Stephen Resnick identified three usages of "class" since the eighteenth century and argued that analysis yielded different results depending on the usage. According to the first, classes are groups of persons defined by the amount of property they own. According to the second, class is a group of persons who exercise or do not exercise power and authority. According to the third, classes are identifiable in "groups of persons who share the common social position of performing surplus labor or of appropriating it" (1986: 98–99). They suggest that class can be conceived in terms of a combination of these three ideas—property, power, and surplus.

Although Marx did not elaborate any definitive conception or theory of class, those who have interpreted and adopted his ideas have engaged in extensive debate over what constitutes class and its relevance to the study of politics and society. Jean L. Cohen, for example, asserts that "Marxian class theory is in crisis . . . the dogma of the industrial proletariat as the revolutionary class and the one and only revolutionary subject has, accordingly, been more or less abandoned" (1982: 1). Frank Parkin (1979) criticizes "professorial Marxism" and argues that although classical Marxism, including the applied and vulgar versions, was counterposed to bourgeois social theory, the intellectual variety is in fact entrenched in bourgeois Western universities. In contrast, Erik Olin Wright offers a defense of the Marxist tradition and commitment to class analysis, arguing that a Marxist approach allows for "the most comprehensive and compelling theoretical framework within which to understand the possibilities for and obstacles to emancipatory social change" (1991: 31). Uwe Becker argues that class structure is important in analysis of society and that the starting point of the analysis must be the class structure of capitalist society. He refers to the objective interests of capitalists and workers: "Capitalists have an objective interest in a mode of production resembling 'actually existing socialism,' which Wright calls 'statism,' and the working class has an objective interest in what Marxism traditionally describes as full communism" (1989: 82). Jon Elster (1985) believes that Marx never defined class but had a theory of class related to relations of class, consciousness, class struggle, and so on. In an attempt to revise Marxist thought and make it more useful and coherent, Elster focuses on four definitions of class, in terms of property, exploitation, market behavior, and power. Although criticizing Marxists for their vague and inadequate understandings of class, especially their emphasis on a two-class model around labor and capital, Resnick and Wolff argue that Marx himself developed "a complex, carefully specified concept of classes" (1982: 1).

Because the evolution of capitalism has been accompanied by shifts and changes in the bourgeoisie and the proletariat, the behavior of these classes is not easily predicable. Stewart Clegg, Paul Boreham, and Geoff Dow (1985) point to various class models in Marx's work: First, in *The Poverty of Philosophy* (1847) Marx identified the proletariat as a class "in itself" (in the sense of a working class organized against capital) that would eventually become a class "for itself" (in the sense of becoming conscious of and struggling against the conditions that dominate it). Second, in the simple abstract model of Marx's early writings, including the *Manifesto of the Communist Party* (coauthored with Engels, 1848), the antagonistic bourgeoisie and proletariat appear distinguishable by property ownership or lack of it. On the one side were capitalists and owners of the means of production, and on the other side were the wage workers who sold their labor to live. Third, in the complex descriptive model evident in *The Class Struggles in France, 1849–1850* (1850) and *The Eighteenth Brumaire of Louis Bonaparte* (1852), Marx attributed the defeat of the 1848 revolutionary movements to the diffusion of class interests and the subsequent rise of an exceptional state based on the personal power of Bonapartism. Here, Marx delineated the role and actions of the commercial, financial, and industrial fractions of the bourgeoisie, a petty bourgeoisie, a peasantry, and an incipient working class and argued that the republic was lost to an alliance of the industrial bourgeoisie, the small peasant owners, and the petty bourgeoisie. Given the internal strife among bourgeois fractions, the state itself had achieved a degree of autonomy: "Politics was not organized around abstract programmes, pitting labour against capital, so much as a battle for command and control of the state and its resources, between factions of the bourgeoisie" (Clegg, Boreham, and Dow 1985: 35). Fourth, the complex abstract model found in the incomplete last chapter of the third volume of *Capital* identifies wage laborers, capitalists, and landowners as constituting the three main classes of capitalist society. Here, Marx also identified middle strata, and later, in *Theories of Surplus Value,* he explored their complexity. Indeed, as capitalism advanced, theorists devoted increasing attention to the "new middle class" and the "new petty bourgeoisie."

Alvin So and Suwarsono (1990) suggest that the *Manifesto* presents a structural class theory of testable propositions and predictions, whereas the *Eighteenth Brumaire* offers an interpretive historically oriented scheme relevant to changing political events. They demonstrate that contemporary thinkers simplify and distort Marx with a cut-and-paste approach to class. In the *Manifesto,* they argue, Marx and Engels focused on a simplistic model of two classes so as to demonstrate how modern capitalism would evolve and assumed that intermediate classes would gradually meld with the proletariat. In his historical writing on mid-nineteenth-century France, however, Marx developed a multiclass approach and envisaged the state as attaining autonomy and dominance over civil society when bourgeois power was undermined by working-class insurgency and the strength of the proletariat was weakened by bourgeois repression. A comparison of the two approaches, as adapted from So and Suwarsono (1990: 52), is suggested in Table 3.1.

Max Weber's view of class diverged from Marx's in that class was a product of interests in the market. Weber identified four essential social classes: the working class, the petty bourgeoisie, the propertyless intelligentsia and specialists, and the educated privileged classes that control property. He also conceived of status groups within economic classes, stratified and hierarchically ranked according to the demands of the market and reflecting a diversity of interests and preferences. As markets changed, status groups were rearranged within classes, some achieving a higher level and others dropping in rank. Status groups and the individuals within them were mobile and in flux; individual talent and initiative might bring about change in individual and group position in society (Weber 1958: especially 181–187).

Erik Olin Wright (1991), comparing the Marxian and Weberian concepts of class, shows that for Weberians the concept of class structure does not have to be tied to the concept of mode of production; instead categories of stratification are linked to market societies. Furthermore, the concept is not based on polarized antagonistic relations and does not deal with problems of material interests, experiences, and possibilities for collective action. Weberians therefore face fewer constraints than Marxists in applying occupational categories to their analysis and have less difficulty in forming a concept of the middle class.

Val Burris also offers distinctions between classical Marxian and Weberian theories of class:

> Marx conceptualizes class as an objective structure of social positions, whereas Weber's analysis of class is constructed in the form of a theory of social action. Marx holds to a unidimensional conception of social stratification and cleavage, with class relations being paramount, whereas Weber holds to a multidimensional view in which class relations intersect with and are often outweighed by other (nonclass) bases of association, notably status and party. In Marx's theory, the essential logic of class relations and class conflict is one of exploitation, where political and ideological domination are interpreted as merely the means by which exploitation is secured, whereas for Weber domination is conceived as an end in itself, with its own independent force and logic. For Marx, classes are an expression of the social relations of production, whereas Weber conceptualizes classes as common positions within the market. (1987b: 68)

TABLE 3.1   Marxist Theories of Class

Structural Theory of Class	Historical Theory of Class
Abstract	Concrete
Two-class model	Multiclass model
Class polarization and struggle	Class alliances and fractions
State as instrument of ruling class	State as autonomous
Outcome of proletarian revolution	Unpredictable outcome and classless society

SOURCE: Adapted from So and Suwarsono 1990: 52.

Reminding us that Weber argued that the market is decisive in individual outcomes and that economic interests in the market lead to the creation of class, Clegg, Boreham, and Dow emphasize that property and capital today have "increasingly assumed institutional forms so that policy issues acquire a different character in a society no longer dominated by a two-class structure but by a complex structure of classes and parties, historically grounded in class" (1985: 3). The rise of a new middle class and the diminishing importance of the petty bourgeoisie are associated with the possibility of economic growth in an era of postcapitalist development in which "the central arena . . . is the political class struggle in and through the state" (4).

Claus Offe (1972) explores the implications for late capitalist societies of conflict theory, which distinguishes between ruler and ruled and between dominant and repressed classes and groups, and of integration theory, which views political power as integrated by a legitimate system of political institutions that neutralize the power advantages of particular groups or classes. He argues, therefore, that both orthodox Marxian and traditional Weberian perspectives should be abandoned in favor of "analysis of systems of political administrative action" to confront "three fundamental system problems": economic stability, foreign trade and military policy, and mass loyalty. He goes on to emphasize the need for an institutionalized pattern of priorities and preventive crisis management through "a new technocratic concept of politics," suggesting that "under state-regulated capitalism, all-out class conflict is no longer the driving force of social change" (97–102). He believes that technological rationality will prevail, especially if political parties, parliament, and universal suffrage continue as "the most important state instruments for maintaining the mass loyalty necessary for stability" (105).

From ancient times to the present, comparative studies of politics have examined the relationship of rulers to ruled. The theoretical contributions of Marx and Weber on this subject have produced polemical discourse. Divisions among intellectuals in this regard were evident in the dichotomy of perspectives that evolved in the twentieth century, one around pluralism and individual choice and the other departing from a structuralist position.

CLASS AND THE PARADOX OF
PLURALISM AND INDIVIDUAL CHOICE

North American political scientists tend to emphasize the pluralist character of Anglo-American politics—its diversity of interests and dispersion of power. They draw their theory from liberal economic and political thought, especially that of John Locke and Jeremy Bentham, who focused on property rights and individual initiative; of James Madison, who stressed competing interests in the struggle for power; of Arthur F. Bentley and David Truman, who devised theories of interest groups; and of pluralists such as Seymour Martin Lipset. In his *Process of Government*, Bentley argued that class was not a viable category of scientific analysis: "Indeed, despite what the socialists say, there are no real classes in great modern nations . . . Compromise—not in the merely logical sense, but in practical life—is the very process itself of the criss-cross groups in action . . . groups are freely combining, dissolving, and recombining in accordance with their interest lines" (quoted in Ross 1991: 335). In their attention to groups and interests, these thinkers tended to defend capitalism as the economic base for a pluralistic society. Since class implies a division of labor between owners and producers in capitalist society, class distinctions are inevitable even though the pluralist literature largely ignores them.

Gabriel Almond and Sidney Verba, in *The Civic Culture* (1963), suggested that people become involved in political life in a variety of ways and offered a typology of parochial, subject, and participant political cultures. Their notion of participation is tied to representative democratic political systems, of which the Anglo-American model is a prototype, involving political parties, interest groups, and individuals rather than classes. E. P. Thompson, in *The Making of the English Working Class* (1963), argued in contrast that history can be rescued from "below" through a focus on class consciousness and the creativity and initiative of the mass of people. Thompson examined subjective aspects of class and in the process rejected structural interpretations of history. Critics, such as Perry Anderson (1980), have accused Thompson of "subjectivism" and "voluntarism," but Ellen Meiksins Wood (1982) believes that instead he resurrected the concept of class and used it against bourgeois social "by insisting upon class as a *relationship* and a *process*, to be observed over time as a pattern in social relations, institutions, and values" (50).

The following discussion elaborates on this paradox, first through the writing of two Italian political sociologists, Vilfredo Pareto and Gaetano

Mosca, who developed what is known as the elitist theory of democracy, the central premise, attributed to Plato, being that in every society a minority makes the major decisions. Pareto (1966) emphasized distinctions between elites and nonelites and projected the idea of *circulation of elites,* with one elite taking the place of another and individuals moving from lower to higher strata of society. Pareto divided the high stratum into governing and nongoverning elites. He drew examples of the rise and decline of elites from the Italian experience, but his theory has been criticized as general, sometimes polemical, and not well grounded in historical examples. Mosca (1939) preferred the terms "ruling class," "governing class," and "political class," but his conception did not differ radically from that of Pareto: "In all societies . . . two classes of people appear—a class that rules and a class that is ruled" (50). Mosca believed that the small ruling class monopolized power and benefits from its position but also that the majority, once discontented, could influence the ruling class and even depose it and assume its functions. In emphasizing this circulation of ruling classes, Mosca assigned importance to the rise of new interests, a position closer to Weber than to Marx.

Robert Dahl acknowledged his intellectual debt to James Madison in the formulation of a theory of democratic order with a wide dispersion of power and authority among government officials, groups, and individuals. Dahl understood the structure of power as segmented, not organized hierarchically. He envisaged society as made up of "polyarchies," characterized by subsystem autonomy and organizational pluralism, in which barriers to political opposition were not substantial. The theory suggests consensus and order, constraints on violence, and a society in equilibrium. Critics of Dahl's work observed that the challenge to the politics of a class or group was often obscured by abstract pluralistic explanations or models so that politics functioned to mitigate conflict and pacify competing interests. Dahl later elaborated on his theory, arguing that pluralism "is no longer limited to Western bourgeois thought" (1978: 192) and distinguishing between organizational pluralism (the increase in autonomy relative to the increase in organizations) and conflictive pluralism (the cleavages that characterize conflicts in a collective of persons). He argued that socialist economies can be highly decentralized and pluralistic and that a decentralized socialist order may generate as much organizational pluralism as a capitalist one. Although he acknowledged conflictive pluralism, Dahl deemphasized the importance of orthodox interpretations of class as tending "vastly to underestimate the extent to which ideological diversity among elites leads to fragmentation rather than solidarity. . . . 'class' in its various manifestations is only an element, albeit nearly always a significant one, in a fragmented pattern of cleavages and conflicts that is persistently pluralistic" (193).

Some of these concerns appear in the Hegelian-Marxist tradition that draws from the early Marx's criticisms of Hegel's distinction between the institutions of civil or private society and the state. In the *Economic and Philosophical Manuscripts of 1844*, Marx showed that work is external to the workers, who cannot satisfy themselves because under capitalism they produce for someone else. Marx desired to expose the false consciousness that accompanies capitalism and reflects the nature of the state that the bourgeoisie adopts for the protection of its property and interests. This concern with consciousness and alienation is found in the seminal work of Georg Lukács in *History and Class Consciousness* (1923) and in writings of the Frankfurt school, including Erich Fromm, Herbert Marcuse, and Jürgen Habermas. Isaac Balbus, for example, demonstrates "the critical dependence" of the Marxist concept of "interest" and hence of "class" on the overarching concept of alienation (1972: 53). Alienation is therefore "neither purely empirical nor purely normative but rather critical" (55).

Ralf Dahrendorf's (1959) synthesis of Marxist class theory confirmed the difficulty of incorporating a Marxist view in a theory of pluralism. He resolved the problem by constructing ideal types of class in a "post-capitalist society" in which authority does not necessarily depend on wealth and prestige, conflict between classes and groups is mitigated, and pluralism of institutions and interests allows for broad participation in decisions.

Since the late 1950s, with Daniel Bell's advocacy of an end of ideology, intellectuals have blurred traditional notions of bourgeois order, the dilemmas of capitalism and socialism, and class struggle with futuristic thought (Frankel 1987). The thesis of a postindustrial society envisioned an improvement of living standards and a reduction of class differences and ethnic, linguistic, regional, and religious loyalties. This notion has been criticized as idealistic or apologetic, provoking Samuel Bowles and Herbert Gintis to advocate a "postliberalism," a synthesis in which democratic personal rights displace property rights because "neither the Jeffersonian universalization of individual property nor the Marxian collectivization of private property is acceptable" (1986: 178). Their synthesis rejects many ideas of Marxism, in particular that of class consciousness and direct democracy (ignoring Marx's advocacy of representative democracy in certain instances and his association of democracy with direct participatory activities). Their argument that Marxism reduces institutions to class terms leads to an emphasis on conflictual pluralism while obscuring class interests, diminishing the role of the state, and playing down the internal contradictions of capitalism that affect relations of production and often lead to class struggle (see Wright 1987 for a sympathetic review).

An explicitly post-Marxist framework is evident in the recent work of Ernesto Laclau, an Argentine political sociologist now teaching in England and influential in left circles. Together with Chantal Mouffe, he argues that "it is no longer possible to maintain the conception of subjectivity and classes elaborated by Marxism, nor its vision of the historical course of capitalist development" (Laclau and Mouffe 1985: 4). Their ideas relate to the British experience, in particular the moderation of a Marxist position among some intellectuals. Although these intellectuals differ in many respects, they appear to agree that the working class in capitalist countries has failed to live up to its revolutionary expectations and the model of struggle should now incorporate a multitude of interests emanating from various strata, groups, and social movements. Laclau and Mouffe outline a new politics for the left based on a project of radical democracy. Their retreat from class with regard to the socialist project can be summarized as follows: The working class has not evolved into a revolutionary movement; economic class interests are relatively autonomous of ideology and politics; the working class holds no basic position in socialism; a socialist movement may evolve independent of class; a political force may form out of "popular" political and ideological elements, independent of class ties; the objectives of socialism transcend class interests; and the struggle for socialism comprises a plurality of resistances to inequality and oppression (Wood, 1986: 3–4). (For the continuing debate, see Geras 1987, 1988; Laclau and Mouffe 1987.)

The post-Marxism of Laclau and Mouffe reflects the thinking that has accompanied political discourse on social democracy and democratic socialism where socialist parties have come to power (especially France and Italy, Spain, Portugal, and Greece since the mid-1970s). This discourse has focused on the transition to socialism, the necessity of blocs of left-center political forces to ensure a political majority in a fragmented multiparty setting, popular reforms to mitigate demands of the popular classes (workers and peasants), and tolerance to promote and develop the forces of production in the present capitalist stage. Mainstream politics appears to have mitigated the revolutionary rhetoric, with the result that terms such as "class struggle," "working class," "dictatorship of the proletariat," and even "Marxism" are being dropped from left dialogue. Miliband (1985) refers to Laclau and Mouffe as "the new revisionists."

The new thinking not only excises classes from a socialist perspective but dissents from the traditional Marxist view that the working class is essential for its revolutionary potential because of its structural position as the class that produces capital. The post-Marxists generally avoid analysis of the exploitative relations between capital and labor. Furthermore, their emphasis on politics and ideology as autonomous from economics undermines the attention to political economy that has characterized classical and contemporary Marxists. The nature of capitalism loses importance, and classes and class struggle are displaced by an emphasis on political pluralism, political organizations, and interest groups. Analysis of the state may stress differences between the power bloc and the people while overlooking opposition between capital and labor. There may also be a tendency to focus on a single or a few political institutions, and the segmenting of political forces may limit prospects for a societal overview. Political movements attempting to penetrate the mainstream may be isolated, and populist strategies designed to challenge the establishment may be diffused and weakened by the separation of particular interests.

Another new tendency, similar to post-Marxism and oriented to transcending rigid Marxist formulations, is represented by intellectuals calling themselves "analytical" or "rational choice" or "subjective" Marxists. Their ranks include G. A. Cohen, Jon Elster, Adam Przeworski, John Roemer, and Erik Olin Wright. This school adopts a positivist approach to social science and tends to build on micro foundations (Roemer 1989) or behavioral assumptions relating to individual decision. For example, Elster (1985, 1986) argues that the actions of classes are reducible to the actions of individuals, and he attempts to demonstrate that Marx himself was a founder of rational choice theory. Przeworski and Wright differ from Elster in their emphasis on structurally determined positions that influence individual decisions, whereas Cohen's (1978) theory of history is based on the forces of production and is thus functionalist at its core. Roemer employs rational actor assumptions to show that capitalist exploitation is the consequence of unequally distributed property relations. In *Free to Lose* (1988), he argues that the injustices of capitalism occur in property relations that determine class, income, and welfare, not at the point of production.

In his recent work on class, Wright (1985) shifts from an earlier emphasis on structure and contradictory class locations (1978) to a more subjective realm. The central focus is no longer upon classes as they emerge out of the labor process but upon the manifestation of political power groups and the power classes wield (Chilcote and Chilcote 1992: 99). Critics (see Mayer 1989; Barbalet 1991–1992; Carling 1986, 1988; and Levine, Sober, and Wright 1987 for favorable impressions and cf. Amariglio, Callari, and Cullenberg 1989; Anderson and Thompson 1988; Burawoy 1989; Cullenberg 1991; Devine and Dymski 1989; Kirkpatrick 1994; Lebowitz 1988; Luke 1987; Ruccio 1988; and Smith 1989 for negative assessments) suggest that this rational choice approach has been unaccepting of traditional or structural Marxian conceptions of exploitation and class and is oriented to the realm of subjective social analysis. Class no longer characterizes the process whereby groups of people become differentiated through labor but has to do with the formation of groups. Ellen Meiksins Wood provides the most comprehensive and exhaustive criticism of analytical Marxism, which she sees as converging with post-Marxism, both having begun "as an effort to establish 'rigor' in Marxist theory and . . . ended for many in a general repudiation of Marxism in theory and in practice" (1989: 87).

CLASS AND STRUCTURALISM

Juxtaposed to approaches that view society as composed of pluralistic groups and classes or of individuals competing for power or pursuing particular interests is attention to the structural context of class. Who rules and the nature of power are issues of significance in political studies. Marx and Engels in the *Manifesto* referred to the modern state as a sort of committee that manages the affairs of the bourgeoisie. Marx went on to suggest that the ruling or dominant class is an economic class that rules politically. Variations of this instrumental theme appear in the political literature and are not necessarily Marxist. Jean Cohen, for example, objects to an emphasis on the contradictions of the capitalist mode of production in Marx's work and prefers the term "stratification" to "class" as a means of avoiding the problem of assimilating stratification into a dogmatic class theory (1982: 2–3). Val Burris identifies four principles that constitute the theoretical core of the structuralist method in Marx (antiempiricism, antireductionism, antihistoricism, and antihumanism) and affirms that the "basic task of Marxist theory remains, as always, to illuminate the structural bases of human exploitation and oppression" (1979: 15).

Community studies in political science and political sociology have traditionally addressed the question of who rules, usually on the basis of stratification theory with an upper class of political and civic leaders (identifiable by criteria such as income, occupation, and education) that runs the local community. This upper class is often characterized as a power elite that rules in its own interest and is separated from the lower classes. Among the important studies employing this notion of stratification was the work of Robert and Helen Lynd in the middle1920s and the 1930s in Muncie, Indiana; of Floyd Hunter, who in the early 1950s utilized panels of persons knowledgeable about community life to identify decisionmakers in Atlanta, Georgia; and of C. Wright Mills, who examined vertical and horizontal dimensions of power in the United States. Mills (1956) identified a power elite of politicians and bureaucrats, high corporate executives, and prominent military officers. Critics of Mills included liberals like Dahl, who contended that Mills exaggerated the influence of elites, which could not be measured empirically, and that the study of decisionmakers should be based on the input of interest groups, and radicals, who felt that leaders should be linked to socioeconomic classes. G. William Domhoff (1978) empirically linked members of the upper class to control of the corporate economy and argued that the concept "power elite" was a bridge between pluralist and radical positions and an extension of the concept of a ruling class. He concentrated on "networks" of institutions and groups, arguing that his notion of ruling class should be understood in a Marxist context and not as liberal instrumentalism as some left critics had alleged, although he acknowledged (1976) that his approach tended to be static and one dimensional.

In an analysis that moved away from mere positioning of powerful people in an economic power structure, Ralph Miliband (1969) contributed an explicitly Marxist theory of state and class under capitalism. The capitalist ruling class, he believed, wields economic power and used the state as its instrument of domination over society. He identified an owning class and a working class, along with two elements of a "middle class," one composed of professional people and the other of farmers and business owners in small and medium-sized enterprises. Taking issue with Miliband, Nicos Poulantzas (1969) emphasized the possibility that the ruling class might be unable to manipulate the state in its own interest. Miliband (1973) responded by reminding us that Marx had viewed the state as acting in the interests of capitalists but not necessarily at their command.

Poulantzas (1973) drew from important sources in developing his thesis that it was the structures of society rather than influential people that generally determined policy. Antonio Gramsci (1957) emphasized the hegemony or dominance of a social group or class in explaining the success or failure of a ruling class. When there is a crisis in the hegemony of the ruling class, the masses may become disenchanted and rebellious, possibly provoking the ruling class to seize control of the state by crushing its adversaries. Louis Althusser (1970) distinguished the structuralist formulations in the later writings of Marx from the humanist ideas in his early writings. Like Gramsci, he called attention to the superstructure of politico-legal and ideological apparatuses and envisaged the state as repressive in its shielding of the bourgeoisie and its allies in the class struggle against the proletariat. Thus, the whole of the political class struggle revolved around the state.

In an analysis of the crisis and fall of dictatorships in Spain, Portugal, and Greece, Poulantzas (1976) conducted a class analysis in terms of dominant and popular classes. The Portuguese experience, in particular, appears to have persuaded him to abandon a Marxist-Leninist emphasis on dual power and an assault on the state by workers and popular forces for the possibility of a bloodless revolution through penetration and occupation of key apparatuses within the state. In his last work (1978), he argued that it was struggle within the state apparatuses that would disrupt the balance of forces and bring about a transition to socialism.

This perspective may have inspired some left intellectuals in the early 1980s to move in one of two directions. On the one hand, Marxist feminists have attempted to understand the interaction of patriarchal relations to class relations in what they term "dual systems theory" (Hartman 1981). Additionally, much theorizing has been done about the relationship between race and class (Marable 1983). Rather than beginning from the individual or from abstract notions of ideology, these structuralists build their theory of contemporary society on what they perceive to be a system of class-based structures. On the other hand, in an effort to transcend structural interpretations, some scholars have turned their attention to newly emerging social movements. For example, Jean L. Cohen has pursued "a post-Marxist critical stratification theory able to come to grips with the diversity and innovations of contemporary capitalist society without ignoring the Marxian achievement" (1982: 2), exploring theories seeking a substitute for the revolutionary role of the proletariat (Herbert Marcuse) and theories of a new working class (André Gorz) and a new intellectual class (Alvin Gouldner).

In *Knowledge and Class* (1987), Stephen Resnick and Richard Wolff emphasize the class process of extraction of surplus labor through different forms ranging from primitive communist to ancient, feudal, slave, and capitalist and distinguish between fundamental classes (performers and extractors of surplus labor) and subsumed classes (persons who neither perform nor extract surplus labor but share in the distribution of extracted surplus labor). Their review of examples of subsumed classes in Marx's writings includes merchants, moneylenders, and supervisory managers of joint stock companies. Pointing out that Marx explained that these classes produced neither value nor surplus value, they suggest a distinction between productive and unproductive labor. Drawing from Althusser and Marx, they employ the term "overdetermination" to describe the situation in which "each process has no existence other than as the site of the converging influences exerted by all the other social processes . . . the class process is a condition of existence of each and every other social process" (1982: 2; also see Therborn 1976). This notion of overdetermination leads them to an understanding of class struggle that they believe is basic in Marxist theory. They argue that Marxist theory begins with the class process and contradictions that produce struggles in the social formation: "We conceive each and every class and nonclass process of the social formation to be in a process of contradictory change." In any social formation, they believe, the fundamental and subsumed class processes "define the different class positions occupied by individuals." Class processes and positions are conceptualized as "the combined effort of all other social processes," with the result that "each class position is constituted to be in tension, movement, and change." Thus, struggle or conflict occurs in "a particular moment or conjuncture in which the overdetermined contradictions embedded in social processes have fused to motivate intense collective effort to change the process in question" (1982: 14–15). They go so far as to suggest that there are different forms or types of class structure under communism: "the specifically collective ways of producing, appropriating and distributing surplus labor which distinguish communist class structures from the various forms of the capitalist, feudal, slave and other kinds of class structures" (1988: 17).

A general conception of class struggle is suggested in Harry Braverman's depiction of the working class as "that class which, possessing nothing but its power to labor, sells that power to capital in return for its subsistence." This class has a social and political life of its own: "It protests and submits, rebels or is integrated into bourgeois society, sees itself as a class or loses sight of its own existence, in accordance with the forces that act upon it and the moods, conjunctures, and conflicts of social and political life" (1974: 378).

Conflict and struggle between classes is usually associated with structural categories at the levels of state and production. Gosta Esping-Andersen, Roger Friedland, and Erik Olin Wright (1976), for example, suggest ways in which state structures are shaped by class struggle rather than simply being mechanisms that serve the process of capitalist reproduction and repression of the working class and mediate the demands of the ruling class on the state as well as the state policies that constrain the class struggle. Mark Kesselman (1982) looks at Marxist trends in political science, with considerable attention to the role of state and class struggle but without reference to class theory. French Marxists have employed the language and methodology of Althusser in the formulation of a theory of modes of production that stresses the articulation of different modes of production and the dialectical relationship between the economic base and the political superstructure (Hall 1977). The language of articulation of modes of production was explicit, for example, in Les alliances des classes (1973), by Pierre-Philippe Rey, who suggested that different modes are evident in the transition from feudalism to capitalism and that history does not necessarily advance unilinearly from one stage to another. Modes may coexist independently and in conflict in a transitional social formation. Critics of this approach have questioned the possibility of applying any single explanation to all cases at different stages of development. Göran Therborn (1978), for instance, argues that historical materialism has to break from "a traditional capitalist-centric mode of analysis" to examine capitalism in relation to other modes of production. Ira Gerstein (1989) cautions against any premature abandonment of structural Marxism and links mode of production to historical materialism employing the concepts of hierarchy and mutual determination to overcome the contradictions of a theory with the mode of production at its center. Michael Burawoy calls for bringing the workers back into analysis. In a study based on participant observation, he asserts that the industrial working class has made significant interventions in a history shaped by the process of production. In his rebuttal to the "newer left," he asserts the need to defend two central propositions in Marxism: "the privileged status of the working class, and the primacy of production" (1985: 5). Although he criticizes economic determinism, Burawoy defends the thesis that "the process of production decisively shapes the development of working-class struggles" (7). He considers the concept of class important for analyzing the development and reproduction of contemporary societies and argues that "racial and gender domination are shaped by the class in which they are embedded in more than the forms of class domination are shaped by gender and class." Thus, "any attempts to eliminate non-class forms of domination must acknowledge the limits and character of change within capitalism and state socialism, considered as class societies" (9).

Class Analysis

Pluralists and power structure instrumentalists alike have encountered conceptual difficulty with their indiscriminate use of loose categories such as "circulating elite," "power elite," "upper class," "governing class," and "ruling class." When the groups to which these terms apply are examined in isolation from other socioeconomic classes, the result is a static analysis. Whatever the conceptual difficulties, however, it is clear that class analysis is essential to understanding contemporary capitalist society (Scase 1992). Although Marx often spoke of social classes as sharing characteristics such as income, pointing to the industrial class, the ideological classes, or the unproductive classes, he differentiated classes in relation to the historical development of the forces of production and the appearance of a surplus product beyond the needs of the workers or direct producers. Thus, the ruling class was distinguished from the working class in terms of relations of production. Whereas Weber's location of class in the market and relations of circulation leads to the common ground of consensus and bargaining, Marx's notion implies struggle.

Structural Categories

Historically, classes have evolved through transformations in society. A bourgeoisie arose from the merchant class in European towns established during the feudal Middle Ages. Then manufacturing replaced production in closed guilds and a manufacturing class supplanted the guild masters. Modern industry soon took the place of this early manufacturing, accompanied by the invention of machinery, the expansion of markets, and the rise of a new bourgeoisie. In the process, serfs and peasants evolved into rural and urban wage labor.

Society is too complex, however, to be described in terms of dominant bourgeoisie and subservient proletariat. The bourgeoisie, for instance, consists of owners of capital who purchase means of production and labor, but within the bourgeoisie subcategories are distinguishable by property relations. For example, large owners of industry and banking capital may have ties with foreign capitalists and own factories, insurance companies, banks, and large commercial companies or be large landowners. Another set of subcategories is distinguishable by the type of capital or means of production possessed—for example, an agrarian bourgeoisie of modern landowners who run farms with modern machinery and pay salaries to workers; an industrial bourgeoisie; a commercial bourgeoisie; a banking bourgeoisie; and so on. Furthermore, the bourgeoisie may be subdivided by the amount of capital owned and classified as large, medium sized, or small.

Likewise, the category "petty bourgeoisie" includes small capitalists who directly or indirectly control their means of production but do not possess capital and who reside either in urban areas (as owners or tenants of small artisan industries and businesses or as independent professionals) or in rural areas (as sharecroppers, tenant farmers, and so on). The role of the petty bourgeoisie is complex in the contemporary period, however. Small petty bourgeois firms can develop into large capitalist enterprises. Some small firms are run by craftspeople. Some firms employ unskilled, low-wage workers. This potential diversity does not mitigate the ideological role of the petty bourgeoisie "in the maintenance and reproduction of a capitalist society." Key elements of its ideology are a belief in independence, a distrust of large complex organization, and a preference for tradition and continuity—"beliefs which stress the value of a passionately held, rugged, competitive individualism founded on the belief in the moral goodness of hard work and individual achievement" (Clegg, Boreham, and Dow 1985: 82).

The category "proletariat" includes workers who do not own any means of production and who sell their labor power for money; they may be either urban workers or rural farmhands who earn wages.

It is commonplace in mainstream social science to stratify society into upper, middle, and lower classes, describing each class type in terms of income, occupation, and education. This notion tends to overlook or dismiss class conflict, and the term "class" itself may eventually become blurred. The sociologist Vicente Navarro (1991) shows that in the United States class has become "an almost un-American category"; the majority of the population has been led to believe that it is in the middle, between rich and poor. Pointing out that the U.S. government collects statistics by race, gender, and region but not by class, he suggests that this reflects the dominance of a powerful capitalist class over a weak working class: "The absence of class analysis and class discourse is a victory for the capitalist class, in whose interest the myth of the 'middle-class society' is reproduced" (5). The economist Robert Reich argues, in contrast, that the occupational categories employed by the U.S. Bureau of the Census are no longer relevant to the international labor market of which U.S. workers are part. In place of the categories of "business class," "working class," and "service workers," Reich substitutes "routine production servers," "in-person servers," and "symbolic-analytic servers." These categories cover more than three-fourths of U.S. workers, he argues, the others being government employees, farmers, miners, and others. He believes that those involved in easily replicated routines are vulnerable to worldwide competition: "The only true competitive advantage lies in skill in solving, identifying, and brokering new problems" (1991: 184).

This deemphasis on class is drawn from a perspective that views the possibility of worldwide conflict as remote and sees the modern nation-state as no longer what it was: "The transformations of economies and technology are blurring the lines between nations. . . . Vanishing is a nationalism founded upon the practical necessities of economic interdependence within borders and security against foreigners outside" (Reich, 1991: 315). This view, of course, did not anticipate the breakup of the Soviet Union and Eastern Europe into a multitude of new and old nation-states. Nor did it recognize that despite growth and stability in the world capitalist system, the ranks of the poor are swelling worldwide. A United Nations survey reported that 1.1 billion people live in poverty in the Third World, whereas in the industrialized world there are more than 200 million poor people; the percentage of poor to population ranged from 51 percent in South Asia and 47 percent in sub-Saharan Africa to 31 percent in the Middle East and 19 percent in Latin America (*Los Angeles Times*, November 23, 1991).

Power and the Capitalist Class

Under capitalism, the state serves special interests and ensures unequal distribution of property favoring the bourgeoisie (Braverman 1974): "State power has everywhere been used by governments to enrich the capitalist class, and by groups or individuals to enrich themselves." The powers of the state, such as taxation, pubic lands, and other functions of public administration, serve "as an engine to siphon wealth into the hands of special groups, by both legal and illegal means" (285). This role tends to expand as the surplus generated becomes increasingly difficult to absorb under monopoly capitalism, resulting in instability, stagnation, or recession characterized by unemployment and low productivity.

Jeffrey Isaac suggests that Marxist class analysis provides a structural understanding of power with a focus on economic positions without reducing all power to the level of production relations as critics have asserted (1987: 116). He sees the new social movements (feminist, civil rights, peace, ecological) as manifesting antagonisms that arise from nonclass relations of power and argues that Marxism must address these antagonisms "without reducing them to the deprivation of class relations" (209). He believes that a critical Marxist theory must not view democracy as an illusion and must be based on "a theoretical and practical pluralism" (229).

Donald McQuarie and Marc Spalding (1989) have pointed to what they consider Marxists' uncritical acceptance of four assumptions: objective class interests, classes as social actors, classes with political consciousness, and the state as the locus of class power. They examine Poulantzas's (1973) definition of power as the capacity of a social class to realize its specific objective interests and note aspects relevant to Marx's concept of power. They find two models of power in Marx, one structural and rational, conceptualized in terms of the structural position of social classes determined by the relations of production, and one instrumental, whereby class struggle leads particular classes to seize and wield power in order to realize their own interests. Exploring the influences of Weber and Lukács and recent debates on the relevance of power and interest in Marxism, McQuarie and Spalding move toward an alternative concept of power by suggesting that power "is a structural concept appropriate to the analysis of class relations at the analytical level of the mode of production" (1989: 21).

The Middle Class

Marx acknowledged the existence of a middle class but left many questions about it unresolved. The development of a new middle class today can be analyzed "as a process which emerges from within a given structure of social relations of production . . . which are consequent upon each historical cycle of expansion and contradiction in the realization of surplus value and the accumulation of capital" (Clegg, Boreham, and Dow 1985: 145). The middle class is a product of the conflict between opposing classes, the antagonisms between labor and capital in the accumulation process, and the growth of political forces in state apparatuses.

Consideration of the role of the middle in the class struggle has led Val Burris (1987a) and Loic Wacquant (1991) to important and useful syntheses of alternative theories of class structure. They focus on thinkers who were dissatisfied with Marxist theories concentrating on two classes polarized around labor and capital. Whereas this simplistic approach had dissuaded many scholars from employing the concept of class in their analyses of society, other scholars developed new categories, including that of middle class, which was taken up by both Weberians and Marxists.

Three influential approaches represent the view of the middle class, which is generally understood to include white-collar workers, professionals, and others who fall in the middle of the statistical distribution of income and status (Wacquant 1991: 47). First, much as C. Wright Mills did in his *White Collar* (1951), David Lockwood (1958) noted differences in consciousness between clerical and manual workers and suggested that they constituted different classes. Emphasizing empirical data rather than any theory of class, he described the distinction in terms of occupation and mobility in the market, position in the division of labor, and status defined in terms of prestige. Second, Ralf Dahrendorf envisioned classes not as economic groups but as "groups in social conflict whose determining factor lies in participation in, or exclusion from, the exercise of authority within any imperatively-coordinated association" (quoted in Wacquant 1991: 49). Only two classes derive from this authority, and those in between must align themselves either with those who exercise authority (bureaucrats) or with those who are subject to it (workers). Third, Anthony Giddens referred to market capacities and a structure of three classes: an upper class, with ownership of the means of production; a working class, which holds labor power; and a middle class characterized by its technical and educational expertise (1973: 107). Wacquant reminds us that the agenda for study of the middle class should be oriented not to the search for improved theoretical maps but to "historical and comparative investigations of how agents situated at various points of the 'middle' zones of social space can or cannot be assembled . . . into a collective resembling something like one or several 'middle classes'" (1991: 58).

The major thinkers on the middle class have been influenced either by Marx or by both Marx and Weber. Their ranks include C. Wright Mills (1951), Harry Braverman (1974), Nicos Poulantzas (1977), Guglielmo Carchedi (1975, 1977), Erik Olin Wright (1978, 1984, 1985), and Barbara and John Ehrenreich (1977).

One of the early attempts to provide a comprehensive understanding of intermediate class positions was C. Wright Mills's *White Collar* (1951). As Val Burris puts it,

Although it predates the recent debate by several decades and draws upon a theoretical framework which is as much Weberian as Marxist, Mills' classic study is nevertheless an important point of reference for contemporary Marxist theorists. His conception of white collar workers as a distinctive "new middle class" anticipates many of the arguments of later, more explicitly Marxist, writers and serves as an illustration of some of the general problems involved in the identification of intermediate class positions. (1987a: 8)

Burris shows that Mills's conception was premised on a multidimensional model of stratification and points to certain problems with Mills's approach, including conflicting classifications and a failure to establish boundaries between classes, failure to identify class position in terms of domination or exploitation, and the difficulty of identifying any class conflict within the middle class.

Harry Braverman believed that the middle class would progressively erode into the working class as monopoly capitalism took hold: "While the working class in production is the result of several centuries of capitalist development, clerical labor is largely the product of the period of monopoly capitalism. Thus the early post-Marx attempts to analyze this phenomenon were severely hampered by the fact that clerical work was as yet little developed as a capitalist labor process" (1974: 348). The two types of workers, factory and office, are becoming indistinguishable because most clerical workers increasingly come from families of factory background: "The apparent trend to a large nonproletarian 'middle class' has resolved itself into the creation of a large proletariat in a new form. In its conditions of employment, this working population has lost all former superiorities over workers in industry, and in its scales of pay it has sunk almost to the very bottom" (355). This class occupies an intermediate position outside the process of capital accumulation: "Not only does it receive its petty share in the prerogatives and rewards of capital, but it also bears the mark of the proletarian condition" (407).

Guglielmo Carchedi (1975), elaborating on Braverman's view, delineated the "collective laborer," the complex coordination of workers under monopoly capitalism; the "global capital," or complex bureaucratic apparatus that controls labor to ensure accumulation; and the middle class that performs both functions of collective laborer and global capital but becomes proletarianized because of the technological changes generated by accumulation. He identified three types of dichotomous social relations: ownership relations, distinguishing the owners of the means of production from nonworkers; expropriation relations, distinguishing the expropriators from those who are expropriated of surplus labor; and functional relations, distinguishing those who function globally in the control of the labor process and those who work collectively to produce use value. Burris points to many advantages of this formulation but reminds us that it ignores forms of capitalist domination outside the direct control of the labor process (1987a: 26).

Nicos Poulantzas (1977) called the middle class "the new petty bourgeoisie," and Burris believes that much of the recent Marxist debate over the class location of salaried intermediaries has been directly inspired by this notion (1987a: 10). Poulantzas was Marxist in relating classes to class struggle rather than to static positions, assuming that classes are structurally determined rather than objectively independent of the will or consciousness of individuals and arguing that classes are determined by the relations of production rather than distribution. Problems with this theory involve his emphasis on productive labor as the basis for inclusion in the working class.

Erik Olin Wright (1978) proposed a theory of contradictory locations in which the "new middle class" contends for power in a class society through collusion with capitalists or alliances with labor. Wright's model identifies three economic controls—over investments and resource allocations, over the means of production, and over labor. It defines classes in relational terms—by the social organization of economic relations and by social relations of production rather than exchange—and recognizes three traditional classes—capitalist, labor, and the petty bourgeoisie. Other class positions are defined in terms of their contradictory class locations, including, under capitalism, managers and supervisors, semiautonomous employees, and small employers. Wright (1985: 89) applied this conception of contradictory class locations to various modes of production through history and suggested that under feudalism the bourgeoisie was in a contradictory location between lords and serfs; under capitalism managers and bureaucrats have been in a contradictory location between bourgeoisie and proletariat; and in state bureaucratic socialism the intelligentsia and experts are contradictorily located between bureaucrats and workers (see Table 3.2).

More recently, Wright (1991) has suggested that whereas at the macro level Marxists may assess the impact of private ownership of the means of production on policies of the state, at the micro level they may see class structures as determining the locations occupied by individuals. He prefers the latter, arguing that at the macro level there is a polarization of bourgeoisie and proletariat.

Reassessing his 1978 work on the new middle class and contradictory locations of class in 1984, Wright focused on two theoretical alternatives, one based on exploitation and the other on the analysis of both capitalist and postcapitalist society. The first of these alternatives relies on the work of John Roemer. Recognizing that his earlier notion of contradictory class locations failed to explain why these class locations would lead to class

TABLE 3.2   Contradictory Class Locations

Mode of Production	Major Classes	Contradictory Location
Feudalism	Lords and serfs	Bourgeosie
Capitalism	Bourgeosie and proletariat	Managers and bureaucrats
State socialism	Bureaucrats and workers	Intelligentsia and experts

SOURCE: Wright 1995: 89.

struggle, Wright showed that some positions within the middle class involved the expropriation of surplus value from workers. He envisaged
the possibility of alliances between the middle class and the working
class in the pursuit of a democratic socialist project. Thus, Wright classified the heterogeneous middle stratum of contemporary labor in such a
way as to retain a material basis for class struggle; by defining class location in terms of exploitative relationships, he provided a basis for viewing
class struggle as the impetus for a transition to socialism.

One problem with this approach was the location of semiautonomous
employees between the proletariat and the petty bourgeoisie, whereas
managers and supervisors were placed between the proletariat and the
capitalist class. In response to this and other problems, Wright, in *Classes*
(1985), revised his earlier theory, in particular expressing concern over his
incorporation of relations of domination and subordination in a Marxist
definition of class. Because this conception obscured the distinctive nature of class oppression in contrast to other forms of domination (racial,
sexual, and so on), Wright argued for a conceptualization of class in terms
of exploitation rather than in dominance relations. According to Burris,
who provides the most useful criticism of this complex theory, "Wright's
attempt to reassert the primacy of exploitation relations is accomplished
mainly by definitional fiat and by the incorporation of concepts that are
themselves at variance both with Marxism and with what we know empirically about the functioning of the class system" (1987a: 21–22; see also
1988). Carchedi considers Wright's use of game theory for conceptualizing exploitation problematic and judges his approach "ahistorical and in-
determinate." He also points to its economism and individualism (1987:
128). Brenner also is dissatisfied with Wright's revision of his earlier
work, suggesting that it depends on "an overly abstract connection between objective interests and consciousness" (1988: 86). Burris sees
Wright's focus on exploitation as appropriate but rejects his use of a
game-theoretical conception of exploitation as a point of departure (1988:

63). Becker finds his "universal thesis of the centrality of class struggle, especially with regard to periods of epochal change ... very weak. ... Wright does not provide sustained arguments for his claim" (1989: 74–75; see Wright 1988 and Wright et al. 1990 for a debate on various class issues, including a critical assessment of Wright's own efforts to evolve a Marxist conception of middle class, and Meiksins 1986 for an assessment of the prospects of the unproductive classes aligning with the working class).

Finally, Barbara and John Ehrenreich suggested that technical and cultural producers formed a distinctive professional-managerial class under monopoly capitalism, distinct from clerical and sales employees as well as the petty bourgeoisie, whose "function in the division of labor may be described broadly as the reproduction of capitalist culture and capitalist class relations" (1977: 12). Barbara Ehrenreich (1989) has since provided a critical overview and history of the middle class since the late 1950s, with attention to the experience of the United States. She identifies a central tension between the old middle-class ethos of saving and working hard and the consumerist concern with enjoying now and optimistically concludes that the democratic socialist movement should be able to appeal to some of this class and that needs can be satisfied through unlimited creative and meaningful work without being so compulsively competitive.

Theories and debates on the concept of the middle class are generally concerned with advanced industrial societies. In an effort to refocus on traditional issues of class analysis, Philippe Van Parijs (1986–1987) suggests that our search for a class concept is relevant to consciousness and action, hierarchy, distribution of material advantages, and property relations. He conceptualizes a "new class divide" in welfare state capitalism, in contrast to the traditional distinction between capitalists and workers, between those with stable jobs and the unemployed. (For further treatment of the middle class see Carter 1985.)

The new structuralists, influenced by Althusser, employ the concept of social totality as a structured process of which any single component is overdetermined by all the others. Resnick and Wolff, for example, interpret Marx's notion of class in terms of a process involving performers versus extractors in the extraction of surplus labor. Although "fundamental and subsumed processes are the critical factors to understanding the capitalist mode of production," the distribution of surplus is a fundamental process throughout society (1982: 3). These two class processes have different effects on the social totality. In the absence of a fundamental struggle over surplus extraction, a subsumed struggle may create the conditions for control over the means of production: "In any capitalist social formation at any moment of its development, the absence of any struggle

over extraction of surplus labor may coincide with the presence of significant subsumed class struggles. To ignore subsumed class struggles, theoretically or politically, is to miss this opportunity for social change" (16).

Burris (1987a) compares the various theoretical models of class structure with regard to their treatment of the middle class (Figure 3.1) and
draws the following conclusions: First, the distinction between productive and unproductive labor is irrelevant to class position; although most
salaried intermediate workers are unproductive, they occupy class positions similar to those of productive workers. Second, the distinction between manual and nonmanual worker is similarly irrelevant to class position; the expansion and rationalization of white-collar work has made
these workers part of the working class. Third, salaried managers and supervisors can be excluded from the working class.

Burris emphasizes capitalist relations of exploitation as a major crite-
rion for identifying class position. According to this model, most wage
and salaried workers, both productive and unproductive, belong to the
working class. Salaried managers and most nonsupervisory professionals
are excluded from the working class, but whether they should be labeled
an intermediate class or simply an intermediate stratum depends on
one's perspective:

> From the standpoint of social characteristics and market relations, such posi-
> tions are sufficiently similar to warrant their treatment as a single social
> class. But, from the standpoint of their location within capitalist relations of
> exploitation—the standpoint emphasized in Marxist theory—such positions
> vary considerably in the manner and extent to which they are implicated in
> the process of exploitation. As a consequence, the cohesion and political
> alignment of these intermediate class locations tends to vary according to the
> issue in question. (1987a: 42–43)

Democracy and Social Movements

In *The City and the Grassroots* (1983), Manuel Castells presented case studies of resistance to urban projects, ecological protest, and squatter movements that appeared not to be based either on class or on the traditional
labor movement and political parties and spoke of a new politics emanating from these social movements. This signified a shift from the old view
of societal change as emanating from traditional institutions to one that
envisioned the possibility of change through autonomous, spontaneous
movements and focused less on collectivities than on individual actors
(see Fuentes and Frank 1989; Luke 1989). Although some academics and
practitioners continue to emphasize the conjunctural coalescence of the
working class and other class elements to bring about transformation,
others have combined class analysis with the study of social movements

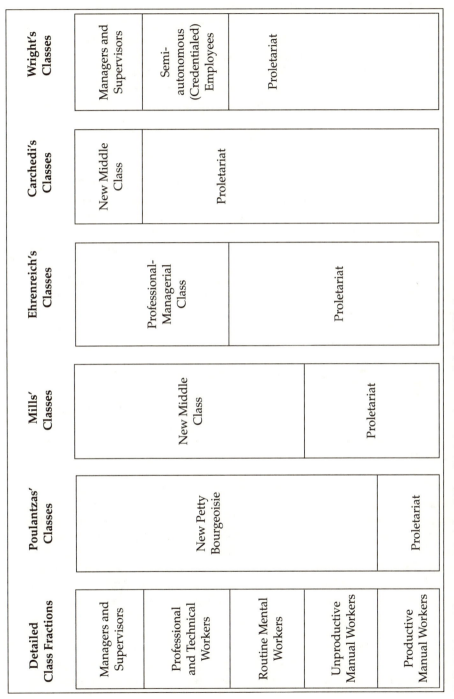

FIGURE 3.1   Alternative Models of Class Divisions Among Salaried Workers
SOURCE: Burris, 1987a: 32. Reprinted with permission of *Critical Sociology*.

and still others have turned away from the working class and political parties in search of post-Marxist explanations (Chilcote 1991). Fredric Jameson (1989) has concentrated on social movements and local struggles but within a larger international context involving class organization and class consciousness. Ralph Miliband (1985) has criticized the focus on social movements, arguing that despite a decline in organized labor in advanced industrial societies, there is still a substantial class-conscious working class. In his view, working class unity will resolve the problems of discrimination addressed by movements involving women and gays, whose position he relates to the twentieth-century history of militant activism and working-class struggles.

Post-Marxists such as Ernesto Laclau and Chantal Mouffe (1985, 1987) have pointed to the diverse interests of the new social movements in an effort to broaden Marxism's appeal. They characterize socialism as a form of participatory democracy and see the working class as only one of a number of possible agents of social transformation. They argue that society is capable of being organized in an infinite number of ways. Politics and ideology are separated from any social basis, and in their place discourse determines all action. André Gorz (1980) has questioned traditional assumptions about the role of the working class in the formation of socialist society and called attention to that of groups based on gender, race, age, and community. Barry Hindess (1987) has suggested that the application of class analysis to politics can be simplistic or misleading because of the difficulty of dealing with the problems of middle class and the position of women in class analysis. Eric Hobsbawm (1989) has continued to see the working class as the source of change but believes that in the face of "the liberalization of the bourgeois system" and the mistakes of the left, the threat to the labor movement and the left can only be overcome through "a coalition of all democrats around those mass parties of the left which still exist" (74).

A central question is whether capitalist democracy allows space for the organization of workers to pursue their own class interests. Political campaigns serve the purpose of awakening an electorate to candidates and their political platforms, but in poor areas where social movements have built networks of solidarity and collective action, political party competition for attention tends to be disruptive. Drawing from the theoretical positions of Gramsci, Lukács, Poulantzas, and Przeworski, John Sitton argues that capitalist democracy allows workers to pursue their class objectives but suggests that it also "disorganizes the working class as a class, thereby obstructing the development of working class politics" (1990: 3). Marick Masters and John Robertson extend the work of Przeworski to integrate class conflict into the broader concept of democratic stability and demonstrate that the state intervenes economically to expand resources, thus "facilitating class compromise between labor and capital through economic policies" (1988: 1183). They argue that economics is the root of class compromise and conflict and politics is relevant to the extent that parties assent to state involvement, thereby institutionalizing class relations and mitigating class conflict. Andrew Gamble (1987) explores the relationship of class to formal, indirect, and representative forms of democracy in contrast to the informal, direct participatory forms of democracy he favors.

Given the absence of class from recent post-Marxist and poststructuralist approaches, Scott McNall, Rhonda Levine, and Rick Fantasia have sought to recapture "the central elements of a Marxist class analysis and show how and why it is more efficacious than other approaches for understanding class in comparative and historical perspective" (1991: 1). They consider the Marxist model distinctive in its attention to class conflict and exploitation but observe that the contrast between Weberian and Marxian perspectives has faded with the focus on proletarianization, the role of culture in preserving class boundaries, and the independent position of bureaucracies in shaping the middle classes.

Classes persist, and the search for a theory of class continues. In an effort to justify class analysis in an era when intellectuals appear to be avoiding it, George Lafferty has worked toward a political-economic understanding of class relations. After explaining the "essentialism" of the view of the working class as engaged not in the subjective pursuit of immediate interests but in the objective pursuit of historical interests, he suggests that "so long as processes of capital accumulation pervade every aspect of our contemporary existence and systemic inequalities such as poverty, unemployment, and homelessness persist, class politics and class theory retain relevance" (1996: 64). Barry Hindess (1977) has also confronted "reductionist" and "essentialist" theoretical positions and their impact on political strategy.

Attention to gender in particular has led to questioning of the viability and effectiveness of social movements and helps us in understanding the distinction between movements and class that underlies the contemporary debate. Issues of gender include the sexual division of labor based on male and female roles in the workforce and society and the relations between the sexes. Popular interest in these and other issues about sex and gender has shaped the development of the new women's movement. Feminism implies ideological struggle against the degradation of women and male dominance from one of four principal perspectives (Giele 1988): liberal, emphasizing equality, individual rights, justice, and freedom; Marxist, stressing the exploitation and oppression of women; radical, focusing on the biological differences between the sexes as the principal cause of women's oppression; and socialist, advocating the restructuring of reproductive relations by socializing such private family activities as housework and child care. The terms "gender" and "sex" may be used interchangeably in the literature, but different meanings are apparent in relating women's liberation to class, race, and ethnicity. Gender is often conceived within institutional life, such as gender in the workplace or in the household. Gender also involves gay and lesbian movements and their struggle for the political, social, and democratic rights against sexism and homophobia.

Historians have begun to examine how powerful men have imagined masculinity in their political roles. Robert Dean argues, for example, that the career of John F. Kennedy was based on an "ideology of masculinity" drawn from America's republican heritage and employing images of courage, toughness, and youth. "An 'ideology of masculinity' amounts to a cultural system of prescription and proscription; it organizes the 'performance' of an individual's role in society and draws boundaries around the social category of manhood." An ideology of masculinity in its prescriptive aspect provides the raw material needed to imagine and construct a narrative: "Because gender is a fundamental element in the makeup of an individual's worldview, the way that powerful men have imagined masculinity is a problem worthy of study by historians" (1998: 30).

One of the problems in any new social movement is the tendency to fragment that Susan Judith Ship points to in the inclination of recent feminist theory to reject all-encompassing "totalizing" theory in favor of a "politics of identity and difference" (1994: 130). Male scholars have generally ignored issues related to women in their studies of comparative politics and political economy. Critical praxis-oriented feminist empirical research that contributes to theorizing in new and innovative directions is under way, according to Ship: "Broadening the scope of feminism to include the struggle against all forms of oppression is essential to developing critical feminist international relations theory because, for most women, specific oppression as women is inextricably linked to problems of imperialism, ethnicity, nationality, racism, and social class" (149). Mary Mellor (1992) shows how ecofeminist theory and politics evolved out of the radical feminist, peace, and environmental discourses of the early 1970s.

Elaine McCrate, interweaving feminism and Marxism, has suggested that "the key insight of Marxian class analysis—that class is a relationship, and that relationships are the foundation for explaining social structure and social change—remains intact, and extremely valuable for the analysis of inequality among women" (1999: 4–5). She notes that many younger women have entered the "female job ghetto" because of "disempowering" conditions related to globalization and the expansion of "the female-intensive informal sector" (6).

EXAMPLES OF CLASS ANALYSIS

Contemporary comparative class analyses are few. In *Social Origins of Dictatorship and Democracy: Lord and Peasant in the Making of the Modern World* (1966; see annotated reference in Chapter 1), Barrington Moore Jr. drew theoretically from both Marx and Weber in tracing three distinct developmental paths in a variety of countries: representative democracy, fascism, and communism. His analysis of bourgeois and socialist revolutions demonstrated that the political roles, interactions, and struggles of opposing classes vary with the situation. Nicos Poulantzas, in *Crisis of the Dictatorships* (1976), focused on dominant and popular classes in the transitions from authoritarian rule in Greece, Portugal, and Brazil during the middle 1970s. A follow-up study by Chilcote et al. (1990) critically examined Poulantzas's class analysis and updated it by looking at both class and institutional forces in the periods of democracy following political changes.

Specific case studies of class are included in the anthology organized by McNall, Levine, and Fantasia (1991). Commenting on the dearth of solid scholarship on the U.S. working class, Jerry Lembcke notes that class analysis has declined with the waning of Marxist and revolutionary movements abroad and that the lines between Marxism and non-Marxism have become blurred as attention focuses on studies of the middle class and the left research agenda appears to differ little from general studies of stratification (93). William G. Roy looks at the organization of the corporate segment of the U.S. capitalist class at the turn of the century and the interrelationship of productive and extraproductive aspects of class organization and extends the analysis to institutions as the sites of class relations by employing the concept of hegemony. Stephen Valocchi reports on a comparative study of the class basis of the state and the origins of welfare policy in Britain, Germany, and Sweden: "In every case, state structures mediated the effects of class forces on policy making . . . products of past struggles and compromises, and they embodied the interests of the winners of those conflicts" (179). Shelly Feldman examines the complex rural economy in Bangladesh and identifies petty commodity producers as "differentiated into a class of petty bourgeois entrepreneurs and a cadre of identified artisans and cottage industry producers forced to increasingly rely on forms of self and family exploitation to maintain reproduction" (134).

There are important studies of the peasantry as a class that resists. In his classic studies *Primitive Rebels* (1959) and *Bandits* (1969), Eric Hobsbawm analyzed relatively unorganized and sometimes anomic groupings that have resisted authority and dominance over their affairs. Several young scholars have examined the thesis of James C. Scott, in his

Weapons of the Weak: Everyday Forms of Peasant Resistance (1985), that peasant forms of struggle are found in theft, arson, sabotage, foot dragging, and other tactics. These essays, collected in Colburn (1990), focus on situations in Colombia, Zimbabwe, Nicaragua, and other countries.

Among the many works that link the experience of production to class formation and draw on specific examples and case studies, with emphasis on advanced industrial capitalist societies, are Burawoy (1985) and Thompson (1963), but also the monographs *Between Craft and Class* (1988), by Jeffrey Haydu; *Working-Class Formation* (1986), by Ira Katznelson and Aristide Zolberg; and *Work and Revolution in France* (1980), by William Sewell.

Erik Olin Wright (1985) has not only developed categories of class but applied them empirically to maps of classes in capitalist society, with Sweden and the United States as examples. Monographs focused on ruling class and bourgeois fractions in evolving capitalism in Third World situations are in Ronald H. Chilcote, *Power and the Ruling Classes in Northeast Brazil* (1990); Catherine M. Conaghan, *Restructuring Domination: Industrialists and the State in Ecuador* (1988); and Maurice Zeitlin and Richard Earl Ratcliff, *Landlords and Capitalists: The Dominant Class of Chile* (1988). This relationship of ruling class and evolving capitalism is explored by Zeitlin, Newman, and Ratcliff (1976) in a case study of Chile, where ruling-class dominance of production is decisive because the ruling class owns both large agrarian estates and large corporations. Peter Smith's case study of power in Mexico, *Labyrinths of Power* (1979), accepts the view that Mexico is an authoritarian system with limited pluralism, an idea drawn from the work of Juan Linz, and employs the concept of elite, drawing on and revising the thought of Gaetano Mosca, Vilfredo Pareto, and Robert Michels. Cynthia Enloe (1991) examines feminist issues comparatively across several diverse cases.

Janina Frentzel-Zagórska and Krzysztof Zagórski (1989) depart from an argument of Bakunin that a "new class" of bureaucrats and experts would emerge as a minority in socialist states to wield power in its own interest, a notion that appeared many years ago in Milovan Djilas's *The New Class* (1957), criticizing rule in socialist Yugoslavia. They explore this proposition in the light of recent writings by Anthony Giddens, Alvin Gouldner, and Frank Parkin and the conflict between intellectuals and the party-state apparatus in Eastern Europe. They discount theories that a "new intellectual class" is coming to power in state socialist societies and conclude that in Eastern Europe there is no third road between Soviet-type statism and market capitalism. Early work on the new middle class was carried out by Dale Johnson and his graduate students with case studies of different dependent countries (1982a, 1982b).

Asked about the nature of class in the Soviet Union and the United States, Paul Sweezy responded that in the Soviet Union the Bolshevik leaders of the revolution implemented state ownership of the means of production and economic planning but not a workers' democracy. They had to confront many outside pressures, and under Stalinism a new ruling class was organized through the Communist party. Under the reforms of Gorbachev, the privileges of this class were undermined and dispersed in many directions. Given the existence of a relatively well developed working class of wage and salary earners, constituting perhaps three-fourths of the working population, what was required was "general principles—continued public ownership of the commanding heights of the economy, overall but decentralized and flexible planning, creative use of controlled markets, and . . . genuine as distinct from merely formal democracy" (Sweezy 1991: 8). Asked about the future, Sweezy replied,

> Marxist analysis ought to have some kind of framework within which to put historical events of this kind. Marxists should be thinking in terms of classes and class struggles and they are not. . . . Every society has to be first conceived and understood as a class society. . . . If you want to understand them from a Marxist point of view, you have got to identify the class structure, the subordinate and dominant classes, the modes of extracting surpluses. (9)

He considered the working class the most clearly formed class in the Soviet Union, whereas the best examples of a monopoly class in the sense of a class for itself were found in the United States, Germany, and Japan: "You need a class analysis to understand our capitalist class, the most powerful class the world has ever seen, but one which has no thoughts, no way of understanding itself" (16).

From this brief historical overview of past and present contributions to class theory, it is clear that this theory is important to political economy, especially outside the United States, although the application of class analysis to political situations has been limited because of the complexity of such analysis. In *The Class Struggles in France, 1848–1850* and the *Eighteenth Brumaire*, Marx provides us with an extraordinary class analysis of a political situation. His examination of the finance aristocracy, industrial bourgeoisie, petty bourgeoisie, peasantry, *lumpenproletariat*, industrial proletariat, bourgeois monarchy, and big bourgeoisie in France not only yielded a host of class terms but introduced notions such as the exceptional state and relative state autonomy that have guided much contemporary political analysis.

REFERENCES

Althusser, Louis. 1970. *For Marx.* New York: Vintage Books. A collection of essays, aimed at a reinterpretation of the mature Marx.

Amariglio, Jack, Antonio Callari, and Stephen Cullenberg. 1989. "Analytical Marxism: A Critical Overview." *Review of Social Economy* 47 (Winter):415–432. A critical review of analytical Marxism, arguing that this theory is a retreat from Marxist theory.

Anderson, Perry. 1980. *Arguments Within English Marxism*. London: New Left Books. A useful delineation of debates and a critical assessment.

Anderson, W. H. Locke, and Frank Thompson. 1988. "Neoclassical Marxism." *Science and Society* 52 (Summer):215–228. A critique of Roemer's analytical Marxism on the ground that it cannot account for the class consciousness aroused by exploitation.

Balbus, Isaac. 1972. "The Negation of the Negation." *Politics and Society* 3 (Fall):49–63. In reaction to criticism of "The Concept of Interest in Pluralist and Marxian Analysis," reasserts that the central problem of Marxist class interest is the objective concept of "interest." Admits that earlier positivist ahistorical approach was limiting and that the separation of explanatory "scientific" from normative "philosophical" Marxism undermined a Marxist critical theory that must fuse the two (52).

Barbalet, J. M. 1991–1992. "Class and Rationality: Olson's Critique of Marx." *Science and Society* 55 (Winter):446–468. Shows that rational choice or analytical Marxism combines elements of rational choice theory and classical Marxism, promising "to yield methodological and research results not achievable by either alone" (447). Goes on to delineate its limitations.

Becker, Uwe. 1989. "Class Theory and the Social Sciences: Erik Olin Wright on Classes." *Politics and Society* 17 (1):67–90. Concludes that "class structure is certainly an important, and moreover, as in the case of labor and capital, a specific base of political articulation. Knowledge of it should be part of the basic knowledge of social science. The starting point of the analysis of the class structure of capitalist society should be the overlap of economic polarization and fragmentation" (85).

Bloomfield, Jon, ed. 1977. *Class, Hegemony, and Party*. London: Lawrence and Wishart. An anthology of papers on issues related to class.

Bowles, Samuel, and Herbert Gintis. 1986. *Democracy and Capitalism: Property, Community, and the Contradictions of Modern Social Thought*. New York: Basic Books. Presents a thesis of postliberalism in search of an alternative that permits both political and economic participation.

Braverman, Harry. 1974. *Labor and Monopoly Capital: The Degradation of Work in the Twentieth Century*. New York: Monthly Review Press. A seminal treatment of labor in the era of monopoly capital.

Brenner, Johanna. 1988. "Work Relations and the Formation of Class Consciousness." *Critical Sociology* 15 (Spring):83–89. Critique of Wright (1985).

Burawoy, Michael. 1985. *The Politics of Production: Factory Regimes Under Capitalism and Socialism*. London: Verso. Emphasizes the importance of production through theoretical understanding of the labor process and case studies.

――――. 1989. "Marxism Without Micro-Foundations." *Socialist Review* 14 (Summer):53–86. (With a response by Adam Przeworski, "Class, Production and Politics: A Reply to Burawoy," 87–111.) Explores two problems for Marxism, the durability of capitalism and the passivity of the working class, and criticizes the analytical Marxists' attempt to purge Marxism of its dogmatic elements with analytical philosophy and the logico-deductive models of neoclassical economics. Shows that analytical Marxists like Elster and Roemer emphasize Marx's attention to methodological individualism and stress microfoundations through the rational choice models of general equilibrium theory, game theory, and the formal modeling of neoclassical economics.

Burris, Val. 1979. "Introduction: The Structuralist Influence in Marxist Theory and Research." *Insurgent Sociologist* 9 (Summer):4–17. Examines the contemporary dialogue between Marxism and structuralism with the aim of clarifying the basic principles of structuralism as method, the issues in the debate, and the application of structuralism to Marxist research.

_____. 1987a. "Class Structure and Political Ideology." *Insurgent Sociologist* 14 (Summer):5–46. Focuses on the class position of salaried intermediaries and their role in the class struggle, considering the question of specifying the boundaries of classes, especially the distinction between intermediate class and the working class, the conceptual issue of clarifying the nature and identity of these intermediate class positions, and the political question of predicting the alignment of this group with the bourgeoisie or the proletariat in the struggle between capital and labor.

_____. 1987b. "The Neo-Marxist Synthesis of Marx and Weber on Class," pp. 67–90 in Norbert Wiley, ed., *The Marx-Weber Debate*. Newbury Park, Calif.: Sage Publications. Argues that contemporary Marxists have drawn on Weberian concepts to adapt classical Marxism to analysis of twentieth-century capitalism, a trend in recent writings on the state, bureaucracy, legitimation, and class structure. Reviews areas of convergence in Weberianism and Marxism and disagreements.

_____. 1988. "New Directions in Class Analysis." *Critical Sociology* 15 (Spring):57–66. Critique of Wright (1985). See reply by Wright (1988).

Carchedi, Guglielmo. 1975. "On the Economic Identification of the New Middle Class." *Economy and Society* 4:1–86. An early elaboration of the meaning of the new middle class.

_____. 1977. *On the Economic Identification of Social Classes*. London: Routledge and Kegan Paul. An important study of social classes with attention to the intermediate level.

_____. 1987. "Class Politics, Class Consciousness, and the New Middle Class." *Insurgent Sociologist* 14 (Fall):111–130. A review of works on the new middle class, including Clegg, Boreham, and Dow (1985), Carter (1985), and Wright (1985).

Carling, Alan. 1986. "Rational Choice Marxism." *New Left Review* 160 (November-December):24–62. A defense of Marxist rational choice theory.

_____. 1988. "Liberty, Equality, Community." *New Left Review* 171 (September-October):89–111. A favorable review of four books that stress freedom of choice, equality, and participatory democracy, including Roemer (1988). Views Roemer's work as "the textbook of contemporary Marxist theory" (91) and places emphasis on the contributions of analytical Marxism.

Carter, R. 1985. *Capitalism, Class Conflict, and the New Middle Class*. London: Routledge and Kegan Paul. Focuses on the inadequacies of orthodox Marxist approaches to understanding the class structure of capitalist societies, examines the challenge of neo-Weberian theories of social stratification, and sets forth a framework for the analysis of the new middle class.

Castells, Manuel. 1983. *The City and the Grassroots: A Cross-Cultural Theory of Urban Social Movements*. Berkeley: University of California Press; and London: Edward Arnold. Provides a framework for analysis of new urban social movements.

Chilcote, Edward B., and Ronald H. Chilcote. 1992. "The Crisis of Marxism: An Appraisal of New Directions." *Rethinking Marxism* 5 (Summer):84–106. Appraisal of new currents of Marxist thinking since the crisis in the late 1970s.

Chilcote, Ronald H. 1991. "Capitalism and Socialist Perspectives in the Search for a Class Theory of the State and Democracy," pp. 75–97 in Dankwart Rustow and Kenneth Erickson, eds., *Comparative Political Dynamics: Global Research Perspectives*. New York: Harper and Collins. A critique of "post" formulations of society and perspectives on future issues.

Chilcote, Ronald H., et al. 1990. *Transitions from Dictatorship to Democracy: Comparative Studies of Spain, Portugal and Greece*. New York: Taylor and Francis.

Clegg, Stewart, Paul Boreham, and Geoff Dow. 1985. *Class, Politics, and the Economy*. London: Routledge and Kegan Paul. A very useful overview of class theory, premised on a model for class analysis constructed so as to "integrate Marx's concerns for processes of class formation with Weber's more empirically developed categorization of class structure" (1). Examines the class structure of advanced industrial societies and the politics of macroeconomic growth and argues that ownership and control are no longer personally fused and capital has increasingly acquired institutional forms.

Cohen, Gerald Allen. 1978. *Karl Marx's Theory of History: A Defense*. Princeton: Princeton University Press.

Cohen, Jean L. 1982. *Class and Civil Society: The Limits on Marxian Critical Theory*. Amherst: University of Massachusetts Press. Sets out to create the framework for "a post-Marxist critical stratification theory able to come to grips with the diversity and innovations of contemporary capitalist society without ignoring the Marxian achievement" (2). Reviews and critiques four recent types of Marxist theory relevant to class: theories seeking a substitute for the revolutionary role of the proletariat (Herbert Marcuse, for example), new working class theories (André Gorz), structuralist class analysis (Nicos Poulantzas and Erik Olin Wright), and the new intellectual class (Alvin Gouldner).

Colburn, Forrest D., ed., 1990. *Everyday Forms of Peasant Resistance*. White Plains, N.Y.: M. E. Sharpe. A collection of original essays based on peasant struggles.

Cullenberg, Stephen. 1991. "The Rhetoric of Marxian Microfoundations." *Review of Radical Political Economics* 23 (1 and 2):187–194. Critiques three approaches to the notion that holistic theories are functional and teleological and should be replaced by explanations in terms of the desires, motivations, and actions of individuals: the view that the behavior of the aggregate (state, firm, union, class) is "the summation of the individual actions comprising the totality" (Jon Elster being the foremost advocate of this view), the construction of a social totality based on a concept of equilibrium in Marxist Shraffian models and a preference for individual choice, and the autonomy of the individual (as in the work of Bowles and Gintis).

Dahl, Robert A. 1978. "Pluralism Revisited." *Comparative Politics* 10 (January): 191–203. Reworks his earlier view on pluralism to incorporate socialist as well as capitalist possibilities.

Dahrendorf, Ralf. 1959. *Class and Class Conflict in Industrial Society*. Stanford: Stanford University Press. A seminal sociological study.

Dean, Robert D. 1998. "Masculinity as Ideology: John F. Kennedy and the Domestic Politics of Foreign Policy." *Diplomatic History* 22 (Winter):29–62. Offers interesting insights into the ideology of powerful men and the impact of their masculinity on history.

Devine, James, and Gary Dymski. 1989. "Roemer's Theory of Capitalist Exploitation: The Contradictions of Walrasian Marxism." *Review of Radical Political Economics* 21 (Fall):13–17. A useful critical exposé.

Djilas, Milovan. 1957. *The New Class: An Analysis of the Communist System*. New York: Praeger. An indictment of communism in Yugoslavia.

Domhoff, G. William. 1976. "I Am Not an Instrumentalist: A Reply to 'Modes of Class Struggle and the Capitalist State' and Other *Kapitalistate* Critics." *Kapitalistate* 4–5 (Summer):221–224.

_____. 1978. *The Powers That Be: Process of Ruling Class Domination in America*. New York: Vintage Books. An empirical study of the ruling class in the United States based on network analysis.

Ehrenreich, Barbara. 1989. *Fear of Falling: The Inner Life of the Middle Class*. New York: Pantheon Books. A critical overview and history of the middle class since the late 1950s.

Ehrenreich, Barbara, and John Ehrenreich. 1977. "The Professional-Managerial Class." *Radical America* 11 (March-April):7–31. An important analysis of the middle class.

Elster, Jon. 1985. *Making Sense of Marx*. Cambridge, England: Cambridge University Press. A comprehensive and complex overview of weaknesses and inconsistencies in Marx, arguing that the basic problem is that much in Marx is teleological and cannot be demonstrated through quantitative and precise analysis. Judges Marx's contributions to be substantial and offers revisions to make his thought more useful and coherent.

_____. 1986. *An Introduction to Karl Marx*. Cambridge, England: Cambridge University Press. Offers a critique and reconstruction of Marxism based on mathematical models and an emphasis on the preferences of individuals. Employs rational actor game theory to show the inadequacy of Marx in relying on functional arguments. Argues that Marx failed to work out a detailed conceptualization of class and that class is determined by the relation of individuals or groups to the market.

Enloe, Cynthia. 1991. *Bananas, Beaches, and Bases: Making Feminist Sense of International Politics*. Berkeley: University of California Press. A scholarly effort at showing the significant role of women in the arena of international politics through examination of cases in tourism, the food industry, army bases, factories, and domestic work.

Esping-Andersen, Gosta, Roger Friedland, and Erik Olin Wright. 1976. "Modes of Class Struggle and the Capitalist State." *Kapitalistate* 4–5 (Summer):186–220.

Frankel, Boris. 1987. *The Postindustrial Utopians*. Madison: University of Wisconsin Press. Seeks to bridge the intellectual gap between the traditional left and proponents of alternative social movements. Systematically surveys and critiques various schools of postindustrial (utopian) thought that have emerged in recent decades. Concludes that the postindustrial theorists advocate a more tolerant, pluralistic, and democratic future but either ignore the incompatibility of new global forms of economic integration and desirable forms of decentralization and small institutions or fail to indicate how local movements will be linked with the outside world. Criticizes the utopian theorists for not comprehending how a postindustrial society might be feasible or how bureaucratic social wage programs can be transcended.

Frentzel-Zagórska, Janina, and Krzysztof Zagórski. 1989. "East European Intellectuals on the Road of Dissent: The Old Prophecy of a New Class Re-examined." *Politics and Society* 17 (March):89–113. Pessimism on a new intellectual class coming to power in state and socialist societies.

Fuentes, Marta, and André Gunder Frank. 1989. "Ten Theses on Social Movements." *World Development* 17 (February):179–191. A useful overview of the literature on social movements and its relevance to class theory and the prospects for changing traditional political and economic structures.

Gamble, Andrew. 1987. "Class Politics and Radical Democracy." *New Left Review* 164 (July-August):113–122. A thoughtful discussion of class and the search for participatory democracy.

Geras, Norman. 1987. "Post-Marxism?" *New Left Review* 163 (May-June):40–82. Criticism of Laclau and Mouffe (1985) for bringing "together all the key positions of a sector of the European left moving rightwards" (43). Examines their rejection of the position that "objective, or structural, class position is the primary historical determinant of social and political identities and alignments" (43).

_____. 1988. "Ex-Marxism Without Substance: Being a Real Reply to Laclau and Mouffe." *New Left Review* 169 (May-June):34–61. Continuation of the debate he initiated (1987).

Gerstein, Ira. 1989. "(Re)Structuring Structural Marxism." *Rethinking Marxism* 2 (Spring):104–133. Argues that the premature abandonment of structural Marxism necessitates its revision in order to deal with problems that blocked its theoretical development. Identifies two strengths of Althussserian structural Marxism: its attention to totalities and commitment to holistic social theory and its contribution to an understanding of historical materialism. Attempts to reconstruct the relationship between the mode of production and historical materialism through the concepts of hierarchy and mutual determination.

Giddens, Anthony. 1973. *The Class Structure of the Advanced Societies*. New York: Harper and Row. A review of approaches and theories of class in industrial societies.

Giele, Janet Z. 1988. "Gender and Sex Roles," pp. 291–323 in Neil J. Smelser, ed., *Handbook of Sociology*. Beverly Hills, Calif.: Sage Publications. A comprehensive overview of issues with regard to gender and sex, the new women's movements, and related topics.

Gorz, André. 1980. *Farewell to the Working Class*. London: Pluto Press. Turns from the working class to the new social movements and their potential impact.

Gramsci, Antonio. 1957. *The Modern Prince and Other Writings*. New York: New York University Press. The principal text in this collection, drawn from an analysis of Machiavelli, incorporates most of the important concepts of Gramscian thought.

Hall, Stuart. 1977. "Rethinking the 'Base-and-Superstructure' Metaphor," pp. 43–72 in Jon Bloomfield, ed., *The Communist University of London*. London: Lawrence and Wishart. A useful conceptual distinction.

Hartman, Heidi. 1981. "The Unhappy Marriage of Marxism and Feminism: Towards a More Progressive Crisis," in L. Sargent, ed., *Women and Revolution*. Boston: South End Press. Explores the problems and possibilities of combining Marxism and feminism.

Hindess, Barry. 1977. "The Concept of Class in Marxist Theory and Marxist Politics," pp. 95–107 in Jon Bloomfield, ed., *The Communist University of London*. London: Lawrence and Wishart. Looks closely at concepts of class and class struggle and takes issue with the views of Althusser and Poulantzas.

_____. 1987. *Politics and Class Analysis*. New York: Basil Blackwell. Critical assessment of traditions of class analysis, with attention to Marx and Weber.

Hobsbawm, Eric. 1989. "Farewell to the Classic Labour Movement?" *New Left Review* 173 (January-February):69–74. Pessimism for the labor movement in the face of bourgeois liberation.

Isaac, Jeffrey C. 1987. *Power and Marxist Theory: A Realist View*. Ithaca, N.Y.: Cornell University Press. An innovative theory of power.

Jameson, Fredric. 1989. "Marxism and Postmodernism." *New Left Review* 176 (July-August):31–46. Builds on his seminal article "Postmodernism, or the Cultural Logic of Late Capitalism," *New Left Review* 146 (1984):53–93. Clarifies his position as a Marxist critic of postmodernism and attempts to establish postmodernism as a historic moment in the culture of the third stage of capitalism as identified by Ernest Mandel in his *Late Capitalism*.

Johnson, Dale L., ed. 1982a. *Class and Social Development: A New Theory of the Middle Classes*. Beverly Hills, Calif.: Sage Publications.

_____. 1982b. *Middle Classes in Dependent Countries*. Beverly Hills, Calif.: Sage Publications. An anthology of original essays and case studies of the role of middle classes in dependent countries.

Kesselman, Mark. 1982. "The State and Class Struggle: Trends in Marxist Political Science," pp. 82–114 in Bertell Ollman and Edward Vernoff, eds., *Left Academy*. New York: McGraw-Hill. Focuses on Marxist trends in political science, with considerable attention to the role of state and class struggle but no reference to class theory.

Kirkpatrick, Graeme. 1994. "Philosophical Foundations of Analytical Marxism." *Science and Society* (Spring):34. This review essay emphasizes the link among these Marxists, first, in their criticism of the historical experience of capitalism; second, in their understanding of the strengths and weaknesses in Marxist theory and discourse; and, third, in their exploration of the problems and prospects for democracy under capitalism and socialism.

Laclau, Ernesto, and Chantal Mouffe. 1985. *Hegemony and Socialist Strategy: Towards a Radical Democratic Politics.* London: Verso. Adopts a post-Marxist position, favoring political parties and social movements rather than the working class, in the search for a politics of change.

———. 1987. "Post-Marxism Without Apologies." *New Left Review* 166 (November–December):79–106. A response to Geras (1987) arguing that the history of Marxism has been away from essentialism and toward the concept of hegemony. Views socialism and democracy as integrated and argues that the antagonism between workers and capitalists develops when workers seek to improve their situation by resisting the extraction of surplus value, a process that occurs through the extension of democracy.

Lafferty, George. 1996. "Class Politics and Social Theory: The Possibilities in Marxist Analysis." *Critical Sociology* 22 (1996):51–65. Examination of influential Marxist efforts to provide a conceptualization of class in contemporary capitalist society.

Lebowitz, Michael A. 1988. "Is 'Analytical Marxism' Marxism? *Science and Society* (Summer):191–214. Concludes that the methods and concepts of analytical Marxism are anti-Marxist, but it is useful for its challenge to teleological reasoning and functional explanations. Critiques methodological individualism of Elster and the analytical Marxism of Roemer in particular.

Levine, Andrew, Elliott Sober, and Erik Olin Wright. 1987. "Marxism and Methodological Individualism." *New Left Review* 162 (March–April):67–84. A review with criticism and self-criticism of the influences of Marxism on methodological individualism.

Lockwood, David. 1958. *The Blackcoated Worker: A Study in Class Consciousness.* London: George Allen and Unwin. An empirical study of consciousness in clerical and manual workers based on data relating to occupation and mobility, position in the division of labor, and status.

Luke, Timothy W. 1987. "Methodological Individualism: The Essential Ellipsis of Rational Choice Theory." *Philosophy of the Social Sciences* 17 (September):59–88. A useful critique and overview.

———. 1989. "Class Contradictions and Social Cleavages in Informationalizing Postindustrial Societies: On the Rise of New Social Movements." *New Political Science* 16–17 (Fall–Winter):125–153. Reviews the theoretical literature on the new social movements to derive a set of categories for understanding these movements.

Marable, Manning. 1983. *How Capitalism Underdeveloped Black America.* Boston: South End Press. A Marxist interpretation of the consequences of capitalism for black Americans, with attention to the ties of capitalism and race.

Masters, Marick F., and John D. Robertson. 1988. "Class Compromises in Industrial Democracies." *American Political Science Review* 82 (December): 1183–1201. A look at class conflict in politics and the economy. Assesses the role of the state.

Mayer, Thomas. 1989. "In Defense of Analytical Marxism." *Science and Society* 53 (Winter):416–441. Defines the Marxist project "as the effort to create a scientific theory of the practice of human emancipation from economic domination" (417). Looks at analytical Marxism as "the most interesting and hopeful development within contemporary Marxism" (417). Identifies the important analytical Marxists, describes what analytical Marxism is, and examines its arguments.

McCrate, Elaine. 1999. "The Growing Class Divide Among American Women." Paper presented to the Howard Sherman Festschrift Conference, University of California, Riverside, February 12. Focuses on the question of class and gender and, in particular, the class differences among working women. Examines women's position in ownership of firms, policymaking authority, and control of their own labor.

McNall, Scott G., Rhonda F. Levine, and Rick Fantasia, eds. 1991. *Bringing Class Back In: Contemporary and Historical Perspectives.* Boulder: Westview Press. An anthology of articles on class structure, class formation, class power, conflict, struggle, culture, ideology, and consciousness. Argues that "class has an objective and subjective component, is a process, is defined in opposition to other class processes, and is historically contingent" (4).

McQuarie, Donald, and Marc Spalding. 1989. "The Concept of Power in Marxist Theory: A Critique and Reformulation." *Critical Sociology* 16 (Spring):3–26. Critical overview of traditional understanding of power and class, especially in Marxism.

Meiksins, Peter. 1986. "Beyond the Boundary Question." *New Left Review* 157 (May-June):101–120. Advocates moving beyond static class analysis to focus on class conflict.

Mellor, Mary. 1992. "Eco-Feminism and Eco-Socialism: Dilemmas of Essentialism and Materialism." *Capitalism Nature Socialism* 3 (June), 43–62. Discusses ecofeminist philosophy and its prospects for understanding ecological problems.

Miliband, Ralph. 1969. *The State in Capitalist Society: An Analysis of the Western System of Power.* New York: Basic Books. An "instrumentalist" perspective on the capitalist state.

_____. 1973. "Poulantzas and the Capitalist State." *New Left Review* 82 (November-December):83–92. A rejoinder to Poulantzas (1973).

_____. 1985. "The New Revisionists in Britain." *New Left Review* 150 (March-April):5–26. Identifies four issues that exacerbate the crisis of Marxism: the rejection of "class politics," the underestimation of the power of the state and the dominant class, the emphasis on the decline of the working class, and the reduced attention to foreign policy.

Mills, C. Wright. 1951. *White Collar: The American Middle Classes.* New York: Oxford University Press. An early study of intermediate classes.

_____. 1956. *The Power Elite.* New York: Oxford University Press. A classic study of the power structure in the United States.

Mosca, Gaetano. 1939. *The Ruling Class: Elementi di scienza politica.* New York: McGraw-Hill. Edited and revised with an introduction by Arthur Livingston, translated by Hannah D. Kahn.

Navarro, Vicente. 1991. "Class and Race: Life and Death Situations." *Monthly Review* 43 (September):1–13. Argues that class as a category is obscured in statistical analysis by emphasis on race, gender, and region and the myth that most Americans are middle class. Suggests that this allows the dominant class in the United States, the most powerful in the world in a nation that has limited democracy, to divide the working class by pitting whites against blacks.

Offe, Claus. 1972. "Political Authority and Class Structures—An Analysis of Late Capitalist Societies." *International Journal of Sociology* 2 (Spring):73–108. Seeks to transcend Marxist and Weberian understanding of development in late capitalist societies.

Pareto, Vilfredo. 1966. *Sociological Writings*. New York: Frederick A. Praeger. Selected and introduced by S. E. Finer, translated by Derick Mirfin. Selections from his *Treatise on General Sociology*.

Parijs, Philippe Van. 1986–1987. "A Revolution in Class Theory." *Politics and Society* 15 (4):453–482. Aims "to rephrase and generalize the Roemer-Wright approach" to class analysis.

Parkin, Frank. 1979. *Marxism and Class Theory: A Bourgeois Critique*. London: Tavistock. A critique of the "professorial Marxism" that has emanated from the universities since the 1960s. Argues that although classical Marxism, including the applied and vulgar versions endorsed by the working class, posed a counterposition to bourgeois social theory, the intellectual variety is entrenched in bourgeois Western universities.

Poulantzas, Nicos. 1969. "The Problem with the Capitalist State." *New Left Review* 58 (November-December):67–78. Criticism of Ralph Miliband's theory of the state.

_____. 1973. *Political Power and Social Classes*. London: New Left Books and Sheed and Ward. A theoretical framework for study of class.

_____. 1976. *The Crisis of the Dictatorships: Portugal, Greece, Spain*. London: New Left Books. Comparative study of transitions from dictatorship to democratic rule.

_____. 1977. "The New Petty Bourgeoisie," pp. 113–124 in Alan Hunt, ed., *Class and Class Structure*. London: Lawrence and Wishart. Elaboration of a distinctive theory of the middle class.

_____. 1978. *State, Power, Socialism*. London: New Left Books. A clear statement of state and class with attention to class and social movements.

Reich, Robert B. 1991. *The Work of Nations: Preparing Ourselves for 21ˢᵗ-Century Capitalism*. New York: Alfred A. Knopf. Argues that national products, technologies, industries, and corporations are in decline as each nation turns to citizen skills and insights as its major assets in contending with the dominant global economy.

Resnick, Stephen, and Richard D. Wolff. 1982. "Classes in Marxian Theory." *Review of Radical Political Economics* 13 (Winter):1–18. An attempt to transcend the two-class approach evident in the Marxist tradition and the critiques of that approach by Poulantzas, Wright, and others.

_____. 1987. *Knowledge and Class: A Marxian Critique of Political Economy*. Chicago: University of Chicago Press. (See also their *Economics: Marxian Versus Neoclassical*. Baltimore: Johns Hopkins Press, 1987.)

_____. 1988. "Communism: Between Class and Classless." *Rethinking Marxism* 1 (Spring):14–42. Offers a definition of class "as the processes whereby some people in society produce more than they consume—the 'surplus'—so that others who produce no surplus can appropriate, distribute, and receive that surplus" (15). Argues that "Marxian class analysis suggests that there are different forms or types of communist class structure. These are the specifically collective ways of producing, appropriating and distributing surplus labor which distinguish communist class structures from the various forms of the capitalist, feudal, slave and other kinds of class structures" (17).

Rey, Pierre-Philippe. 1973. *Les alliances des classes*. Paris: Maspero. Sets forth a framework for analysis of modes of production.

Roemer, John. 1988. *Free to Lose*. Cambridge, Mass.: Harvard University Press. A digest of his previous work with attention to exploitation in property relations. Argues that wealth and domination but not exploitation contribute to class struggle

_____. 1989. "Visions of Capitalism and Socialism." *Socialist Review* 19 (July-August):93–100. Focuses on property rights rather than on the relations of domination at the point of production. Argues that through formal modeling one can "construct a microeconomic explanation of the formation of class and the existence of exploitation" (93). Endorses the postliberal thesis of Bowles and Gintis (1986) and expresses confidence in the flexibility of capitalism to eliminate coercion except that needed to maintain property relations: "I remain an unreconstructed Marxist in believing that democratic control of economic surplus, and not the workplace, is the real necessity for fundamental social transformation" (99). Insists that the required development of the productive forces will probably be more readily accomplished under a capitalist rather than socialist system.

Ross, Dorothy. 1991. *The Origins of American Social Science*. Cambridge, England: Cambridge University Press. Argues that American "exceptionalism" pervades social science thinking.

Ruccio, David. 1988. "The Merchant of Venice, or Marxism in the Mathematical Mode." *Rethinking Marxism* 1 (Winter):36–68. Shows that many Marxist economists are adapting mathematics to Marxist theory. Examines the analytical Marxists, especially Roemer, as an example of this approach. Opts for an alternative approach that assumes the impossibility of separating individuals from classes.

Scase, Richard. 1992. *Class*. Minneapolis: University of Minnesota Press. Argues that class is a vital concept for understanding contemporary capitalist society.

Ship, Susan Judith. 1994. "And What About Gender? Feminism and International Relations Theory's Third Debate," pp. 129–151 in Claire Turenne Sjolander and Wayne S. Cox, eds., *Beyond Positivism: Critical Reflections on International Relations*. Boulder: Lynne Rienner. Demonstrates and criticizes the dominance of male thinking in international relations.

Sitton, John F. 1990. "Citizens and Classes: Political Isolation and Class Formation." *Critical Sociology* 17 (Summer):3–33. Examines various theoretical positions of classical and current theorists with regard to whether the development of democracy under capitalism will help workers organize to pursue their own class objectives.

Smith, Tony. 1989. "Roemer on Marx's Theory of Exploitation: Shortcomings of a Non-Dialectical Approach." *Science and Society* 53 (Fall):327–340. A systematic rebuttal of four criticisms John Roemer makes of the Marxist concept of exploitation.

So, Alvin Y., and Suwarsono. 1990. "Class Theory or Class Analysis? A Reexamination of Marx's Unfinished Chapter on Class." *Critical Sociology* 17

(Summer):35–55. Shows the relevance of Marx's theory of class through an examination of his use of the term in two principal writings, *Manifesto of the Communist Party* and *The Eighteenth Brumaire of Louis Bonaparte*.

Sweezy, Paul. 1991. "Class Societies: The Soviet Union and the United States." *Monthly Review* 43 (December):1–17. Two interviews with the well-known American economist, who urges class analysis as a means of understanding rapidly changing conditions in the two countries.

Therborn, Göran. 1976. *Science, Class, and Society: On the Formation of Sociology and Historical Materialism*. London: New Left Books. Examines and critiques various lines of thinking in sociology in an effort "to develop a more systematic way of understanding the causal relations between the structural categories of Marxist theory and the level of appearances tapped in empirical investigation" (14). Draws concepts of overdetermination and structural causality from Althussser and other structuralist Marxists and elaborates six "modes of determination . . . within the global concept of structural causality": structural limitation, selection, reproduction/nonreproduction, limits of functional compatibility, transformation, and mediation. Diagrams the relationships among economic structures, state structures, state interventions, and class struggle.

_____. 1978. *What Does the Ruling Class Do When It Rules?* London: New Left Books. Sets forth a basic framework for analysis of the class character of state apparatuses. Defines the character of state power with a focus on the ruling class. Sees historical materialism as "an instrument of empirical investigation of men's social conditions and possibilities" (241) and argues that it must examine capitalism in relation to other modes of production, for example, in feudal and socialist states. Offers reflections on socialism and democracy.

Thompson, E. P. 1963. *The Making of the English Working Class*. New York: Vintage Books. Emphasis on class as an active process in the making of history.

Wacquant, Loic J. D. 1991. "Making Class: The Middle Class(es) in Social Theory and Social Structure," pp. 39–64 in Scott G. McNall, Rhonda F. Levine, and Rick Fantasia, eds., *Bringing Class Back In: Contemporary and Historical Perspectives*. Boulder: Westview Press. A very useful critical overview of approaches to the middle class in Marxist and non-Marxist analysis.

Weber, Max. 1958. *From Max Weber: Essays in Sociology*. New York: Oxford University Press. Translated with an introduction by H. H. Gerth and C. Wright Mills. Important essays, including his elaboration of class and status.

Wolff, Richard, and Stephen Resnick. 1986. "Power, Property, and Class." *Socialist Review* 16 (March-April):97–124. Attempts to define class in terms of Marx's original conception in an effort to avoid reductionism and determinism. Identifies different schools of class analysis, along lines of income, wealth, and property (C. Wright Mills and Paul Sweezy); power according to rule and dominance (Ralf Dahrendorf, Paul Baran, and Paul Sweezy); and ideology and consciousness (Nicos Poulantzas and E. P. Thompson).

Wood, Ellen Meiksins. 1982. "The Politics of Theory and the Concept of Class: E. P. Thompson and His Critics." *Studies in Political Economy* 9 (Fall):45–71. A critical assessment of Thompson's theory of class in his *The Making of the English Working Class* (1968). Shows that Thompson, in his effort to justify the concept of class in the face of bourgeois critics and to minimize the structural emphasis of

Marxism, insists that relations of production matter in different ways in different historical contexts: "Classes arise or 'happen' because people 'in determinative productive relations,' who consequently share a common experience, identify their common interests and come to think and value 'in class ways'" (51).

_____. 1986. *The Retreat from Class: A New "True" Socialism*. London: Verso. A systematic critique of Laclau and Mouffe (1985).

_____. 1989. "Rational Choice Marxism: Is the Game Worth the Candle?" *New Left Review* 177 (September-October):41–88. (With reply by Alan Carling, "In Defence of Rational Choice: A Reply to Ellen Meiksins Wood," pp. 97–109.) A systematic critique of rational choice Marxism.

Wright, Erik Olin. 1978. *Class, Crisis, and the State*. London: New Left Books. Includes thesis on contradictory locations of class.

_____. 1984. "A General Framework for the Analysis of Class Structure." *Politics and Society* 13 (4):383–423. Identifies various approaches to study of the middle class, then focuses on two theoretical alternatives, one based on exploitation and the other on the analysis of both capitalist and postcapitalist society.

_____. 1985. *Classes*. London: New Left Books. Influenced by author's association with analytical Marxists such as G. A. Cohen, John Roemer, Jon Elster, and Adam Przeworski, addresses criticism of his earlier formulation of contradictory relations within class relations (1978) and then presents a new formulation with emphasis on exploitation. Offers empirical data in support of this conceptualization. Burris (1988) critiques this work.

_____. 1987. "Towards a Post-Marxist Radical Social Theory." *Contemporary Sociology* 16 (September):748–753. A sympathetic review of Bowles and Gintis (1986). Criticizes its defense of a relatively weak thesis with which it is difficult to disagree and use of this as the basis for a stronger thesis without providing further arguments. Points out that authors argue against the primacy of economics but appear to emphasize class and economic analysis.

_____. 1988. "Exploitation, Identity, and Class Structure: A Reply to My Critics." *Critical Sociology* 15 (Spring):91–110. Restates his basic argument: "Classical Marxism contains a well developed concept of the fundamental classes of the capitalist mode of production—capitalists and workers—but does not provide a satisfactory way of conceptualizing what in common language is called the 'middle class.' . . . The 'middle classes' can then be understood as locations in the class structure which are exploited in terms of capitalist mechanisms of exploitation, but exploiters in terms of one or more of these secondary mechanisms of exploitation" (91–92).

_____. 1989. "What Is Analytical Marxism?" *Socialist Review* 19 (4):35–56. Justifies new directions in Marxism because of the defection of many intellectuals, lack of consensus over the core elements of Marxist theory, and the crisis of Marxism itself. Focuses on analytical Marxism as a "vibrant intellectual current in contemporary Marxism."

_____. 1991. "The Conceptual Status of Class Structure in Class Analysis," pp. 17–37 in Scott G. McNall, Rhonda F. Levine, and Rick Fantasia, eds., *Bringing Class Back In*. Boulder: Westview Press. Distinguishes between macro and micro approaches to class and justifies his micro approach as a basis for powerful analysis. Describes approaches through contradictory locations and multidimensional exploitation. Elaborates on the Marxian conception of class and compares it with the Weberian conception.

Wright, Erik Olin, et al. 1990. *The Debate on Classes.* London: Verso. Essays by progressive scholars with attention to Wright's concept of the new middle class.

Zeitlin, Maurice, W. Lawrence Neuman, and Richard Earl Ratcliff. 1976. "Class Segments: Agrarian Property and Political Leadership in the Capitalist Class of Chile." *American Sociological Review* 41 (December):1006–1029. Based on empirical investigation of the ruling class in Chile, shows "that the landed capitalists, who personified the coalescence of large agrarian property and corporate capital, played a disproportionate role in the political leadership of their class. This class segment formed the core of the class structurally and the center of its leadership historically" (1027).

4

THEORIES OF THE STATE

Theories of the state date to classical times and became especially prominent with the emergence of political economy in the eighteenth and nineteenth centuries. For political economists like Ricardo, Smith, Marx, Weber, and others, the state was one of the most important features, and their views weigh heavily on contemporary understandings of public life and how to shape it. Modern theories of the state have evolved from these early understandings and moved in two major directions, one liberal democratic and the other progressive (see Table 4.1). This chapter first delineates these two paths, with a focus on historical conceptions of the state while concentrating on theories that have evolved over the past two centuries, then offers a sketch of contemporary theoretical directions, and finally focuses on issues of state theory.

TWO CONCEPTIONS OF THE STATE

The Liberal State

The liberal democratic state evolved from classical thinking and in recent times has become part of the experience of industrial capitalism (see MacIver 1926, for example). Formal representative democracies date to the thirteenth-century parliamentary forms envisaged in the Magna Carta and represented by the English parliament and to the nobility's defense of its feudal rights against the absolute monarchs. Eventually, the state came to be seen as a guarantor of the common good in ensuring individual rights, placing constraints on the desire for material gain, and allowing the market to operate freely in civil society. The liberal state thus evolved from origins in antiquity through the classical political forms represented in Hobbes, Locke, Rousseau, and Montesquieu to the liberalism of Adam Smith, the utilitarianism of Bentham, and the liberal pluralism of Weber and Schumpeter.

TABLE 4.1   Liberal and Progressive Conceptions of the State

Liberal	Progressive
Antiquity: Plato and Aristotle	
Classical: Hobbes, Locke, and Rousseau	Classical: Hegel
Traditional: Smith	Traditional: Marx and Engels
Utilitarian: Bentham	Hegemonic bloc: Gramsci
Pluralism: Weber, Schumpeter, and Dahl	

In the eighth book of the *Republic,* Plato identified four types of government or state formations of classical times: timocracy, or timarchy, a "government of honor" or "government of the best" such as that of Crete or Sparta; oligarchy, a government resting on the value of property, in which the rich are powerful and the poor deprived; democracy; and tyranny. He described democracy as involving the rebellion of the poor against the rich or simply the withdrawal of the rich for fear of it. Under democracy, people are free and government is "full of variety and disorder."

In *Politics,* Aristotle conceptualized the state as a political community oriented to some good. Aristotle understood the state as having a "natural" history, with a basis in economics; the structure of the family; ethics; and the basic political forms of monarchy, aristocracy, and democratic polity, each with an inner history of its own and experiencing growth toward maturity and an impulse toward decay. These forms evolve through phases in which human action and will can be decisive. If maturity can be speeded up, decay can be avoided. The practice of politics is choice among these forms and their combinations.

Niccolò Machiavelli's sixteenth-century conception of the state was as a single structure the elements of which are responsive to a center of power. In his view, the state incorporates all the authority that exists in the territory it represents. Nothing is superior to the state. Thus, the powerful and well-organized state will enjoy the undisputed loyalty of all its citizens. It is a morally neutral and powerful entity used by those who control it for achieving whatever ends seem good to them. It is a complex of institutions that gives society its cohesion. The better constructed it is, the greater its stability and its strength. In the first chapter of *The Prince,* Machiavelli asserted that all states are either republics or monarchies and he concentrated on the monarchies.

This conception of the state is similar to Thomas Hobbes's idea of sovereignty and to the notion of the federal state shaped by its constitution and the deliberate division of power among various bodies whose mutual relations are defined by law. Hobbes argued that constitutions guide stable governments. Government is a form of collaboration and is thus always divided, because those who have power must follow rules in dealing with one another. Yet, Hobbes argued that the rules governing the use of power are more likely to be observed when authority is vested in a sovereign person or assembly rather than divided among several entities. Subjugation would thus be preferable to civil war, and the sovereign would respect his or her subjects to earn their support.

Aristotle's belief that government may produce equilibrium among the forces in the state influenced seventeenth-century thinkers such as John Locke, Jean-Jacques Rousseau, and Charles-Louis de Secondat, Baron de La Brède et de Montesquieu, who advanced theories of mixed government. Locke acknowledged that government may have arisen from paternal power, but he also argued that true political authority rests on consent. People submit to government, he believed, to preserve their property, liberties, and security, but they do not give up all their rights. They join together in society under a body of laws that govern power relations. They give up some rights to the state, however, as a means of avoiding conflict or war. No government should wield absolute power. It is for the people to decide if government is properly exercising power for the good of society. Thus, legislative power for Locke was paramount.

Rousseau understood the state as the arm of the wealthy in the guise of benefiting all, but he believed that a "social contract" in theory would guarantee freedom and equality. People place themselves and their power in common in "the general will" or state so that although receiving the right to civil freedom and ownership in what is possessed, individuals relinquish any right to everything else that tempts them or is desired. Rousseau saw the state as a potential intervenor to prevent inequality, and he felt that through education and goodwill that a balance could be attained between social and individual interest.

Montesquieu distinguished among three different types of government: republic, monarchy, and despotism. Unlike Hobbes, he believed that the power of every government is limited by its distribution among persons who exercise it and by the traditions on which authority rests. Constraints on power through laws allow for the possibility of individual freedom.

Skepticism about these theories of balance of power eventually led to the idea that it was the free market exchange of goods that would quell individuals' political ambitions and designs. Adam Smith argued that men were driven by material economic gain and that individual desires would collectively maximize the collective good. The individual drive to better oneself would not only carry society on to wealth and prosperity but also overcome the obstacles in human society. Thus, the undesirable trait of greed actually could result in good for the greatest number of people. Smith questioned the role of the state in regulating the market in the mercantilist capitalist economy of his day, arguing that the state should provide the legal framework to facilitate this market. In showing the relevance of Smith's formulation to contemporary North American thinking, Martin Carnoy suggests that

> the concept that each individual pursuing his or her own economic interests unwittingly provides the best possible formula for the collective good still holds a great deal of sway. The very assumption that individuals are the source of power, both in their pursuit of wealth and their control over their passions, and that social corruption, if it exists at all, is much more likely to emerge from the public than the private sector, underlie much of American political philosophy of this day. (1984: 29)

These ideas influenced Jeremy Bentham to advocate the free market at a time when the English bourgeois state was encountering the early stirrings of class conflict and labor agitation. The state was seen as protection for a system of capitalist enterprise and limitless private property. Bentham saw political power as linked to the electorate, but unlike Locke and Rousseau, who looked for equality and a new kind of man, he acknowledged that citizens were not all equal in their power and considered it essential for the voters to defend capitalism while ensuring that government not abuse the citizenry. Thus, the liberal bourgeois state was a representative and formal democracy controlled by a privileged segment of the citizenry, while the market distributed goods and services along with income and wealth. Under this utilitarian vision, notions of classless society and equality faded away.

The answer to this dilemma, according to Carnoy, was pluralism, an offshoot of the liberal doctrine. Several major influences shaped this revision. One of these was Max Weber's idea of a rational state capable of organizing and shaping the government and its bureaucratic agencies under a modernizing capitalism. Weber defined the state as "a human community" invested with the right to use physical force, even coercion, in situations in which the dominance of some over others is attained through competition among groups seeking power within an order of legitimate authority. Legitimacy implies routinization, harmony, efficiency, and order in the bureaucratic organization of the state. Weber was interested in the ideal and material interests of all members of the society. Another influence was Joseph Schumpeter's views about the prospects for democracy under the capitalist state. Schumpeter argued that individual opinions could not be translated into the will of the people—that citizens usually are uninterested or uninformed about political issues, will act in their individual rather than the common interest, and are easily misled by propaganda. Thus, his theory contrasts with classical liberalism: "Schumpeter reverses the roles; he makes the deciding of issues by the electorate secondary to the election of representatives who are to do the deciding" (Carnoy 1984: 34), and since "voters' decisions are based on a political version of neoclassical utility theory, the issue becomes one of the degree of consumer sovereignty in the market" (36). Third, Robert Dahl described the United States as a democratic order with power and authority dispersed among government officials, private individuals, and groups. Within this order, there were opportunities for freedom of thought, consensus, and participation in politics.

The Progressive State

Marx never formulated a definitive theory of the state, but several frameworks appear in his writings (see Shaw 1985 for an overview of issues in classical Marxist understanding of the state). The earliest conception is based on his critical assessment of Hegel. In his *Philosophy of Right and Law* (1821), Hegel worked out a detailed abstract conception of the state that differed from the utilitarian view of Bentham. He believed that the courts, the police, and the administrative departments were as much organs of civil society as of the state; they pertained to civil society, where their function was to promote personal or private interests, and to the state, where their function was to coalesce a community. Hegel distinguished three powers within the state—legislative, to determine the universal will; executive, to settle particular matters in conformity with the universal will; and sovereign, to make ultimate decisions and express the unity of the state. The sovereign power was related to the other two dialectically. An excerpt from his description sums up some of this understanding:

> The essence of the state is the universal, self-originated, and self-developed—the reasonable spirit of will; but, as self-knowing and self-actualizing, sheer subjectivity, and—as an actuality—one individual. . . . As a living mind, the state only is an organized whole, differentiated into particular agencies, which, proceeding from the one notion . . . of the reasonable will, continually produce it as their result. The constitution is this articulation or organization of state-power. It provides for the reasonable will . . . for that will being put in actuality, through the action of the government and its several branches. (Hegel 1974 [1821]: 285–286)

Marx characterized the Hegelian conception as idealist and a defense of the Prussian state of his times. Hegel recognized the state as separate from civil society, but he believed that the state moderates and resolves the conflicts that emerge in civil society. Thus, Hegel envisaged the state as the embodiment of the general interest of society and standing above particular interests and able to transcend any split between civil society and the state. Marx rejected this claim, arguing that in real life the state cannot represent the general interest but instead defends the interests of property.

After Hegel's death, his followers diverged in their understanding of the state. The Left or Young Hegelians criticized his idea of state. Among them, Marx argued that the state perpetuates a hierarchy of classes in the interests of the ruling class. Under capitalism, the state is the agency that maintains the property relations of the wealthy minority, and the consequence is the oppression of one class by another. The state does not stand above class but is always on the side of the rulers. Marx differentiated the legal and political superstructure of society, including the state, from its economic structural base of productive forces and social relations of production but viewed the two forms as entwined.

Marx worked out much of his early understanding through his critique of the Hegelian conception of state. Through an exhaustive paragraph-by-paragraph assessment in *Contribution to the Critique of Hegel's Philosophy of Law* (1843), he exposed the idealistic and abstract implications of the Hegelian view. For example, he showed how real and imaginary description can twist and confuse conceptualization:

> The idea is made the subject and the actual relation of family and civil society to the state is conceived as its internal imaginary activity. Family and civil society are the premises of the state; they are the genuinely active elements, but in speculative philosophy things are inverted. When the idea is made the subject, however, the real subjects, namely, civil society, family . . . become unreal objective elements of the idea with a changed significance. (1975 [1843]: 8)

Although Marx did not fully formulate a definitive theory of the state, at least four variants of the state are identifiable in his writings (Table 4.2). For Marx, the state was rooted in the material conditions of life rather than in Hegel's ideal notions. Although under capitalism the state is separate from the civil society, Marx asserted that individuals are also separate from each other because of the fragmentation of civil society by competing private interests. In Marx's view, the state legitimizes individuals' pursuit of particular interests through the possession of private property, and this leads to inequality, disunity, and a breakdown of community.

The view that the state is fundamentally an instrument of the ruling class appears in Marx and Engels's *Manifesto of the Communist Party* (1848). Under capitalism, a modern bourgeoisie consolidates its dominance not only of the economy but of the state. Its instrumental role was described accordingly: "The executive of the modern state is but a committee for managing the common affairs of the whole bourgeoisie" (Marx 1974 [1848]: 69).

TABLE 4.2   Variants of a Theory of the State in Marx

Position	Source
Early structuralist	*Contribution to the Critique of* Hegel's Philosophy of Law
Instrumentalist	*Manifesto*
Structural relative autonomy	*18th Brumaire*
Participatory democratic	*Critique of the Gotha Programme*

Another conception of the state appears in *The Eighteenth Brumaire of Louis Bonaparte* (1852), where Marx provides a class analysis of events in mid-nineteenth-century France. In the midst of the struggle, the bourgeoisie was unable to consolidate a dominant position, and it is clear that the state had considerable autonomy (see Gilbert 1981).

The participatory democratic position appears perhaps as early as in Marx and Engels's mention in *The German Ideology* (1846) of a contradiction between the interests of the individual and those of the community. Coercion has an impact on production and economic relations, and once coercion shifts from the economic base of society it tends to concentrate in the state or "the ideological superstructure." Once the state forms, it is divorced from the real interests of individual and community. Classes, based on the division of labor, shape struggles for domination: "All struggles within the State, the struggle between democracy, aristocracy, and monarchy, the struggle for the franchise, etc. etc. are merely the illusory forms in which the real struggles of the different classes are fought out among one another" (1970 [1846]: 54). The democratic view of the state is more explicitly expressed in *Critique of the Gotha Programme* (1966 [1891]: 17), where Marx shows that a class analysis is more complex than a simple dichotomy of working class and reactionary mass and that other classes are clearly identifiable in class struggle: "Freedom consists in converting the state from an organ standing above society into one completely subordinated to it." He goes on to ask what form the state takes under communism: "Between capitalist and communist society lies the period of the revolutionary transformation of the one into the other. There corresponds to this also a political transition period in which the state can be nothing but 'the revolutionary dictatorship of the proletariat'" (18). Marx was interested in the experience of the 1871 Paris Commune, which decreed an expansion of democracy by abolishing the army and subjecting elected officials to recall. Lenin refers frequently to this theme in Marx to suggest that although the state may be necessary only in class society and remnants of the capitalist state may be useful in the transition to socialism, the real changes must be initiated and implemented outside the state apparatuses.

In a historical overview entitled *Origin of the Family, Private Property, and the State* (1884), Engels examined coercion in stateless and state societies. In primitive stateless societies, for instance, coercion could be based on collective judgment and applied by the whole society. Once a society is divided into opposing social classes, its interests become fragmented and the power that makes coercion possible separates from the collectivity, thereby creating conditions for the emergence of the state:

> The state . . . is rather a product of society at a certain stage of development; it is the admission that this society has become entangled in an insoluble contradiction with itself, that it is cleft into irreconcilable antagonisms which it is powerless to dispel. In order that these antagonisms, these classes with conflicting economic interests, may not annihilate each other and society in sterile struggle, a power, apparently standing above society, became necessary for the purpose of moderating the conflict and keeping it within the bounds of "order"; and this power, arising out of society, but placing itself over it, and increasingly alienating itself from it, is the state. (n.d. [1884]: 140)

Engels explained that consumption and production were originally in common and collective before society experienced a division of labor, exchange between individuals, and commodity production. With the eventual exploitation of one class by another, the great majority became oppressed, and development was "a continuous contradiction." The only way to overcome this would be by finding a balance between the interests of society and individuals.

In *State and Revolution* (1932), Lenin succinctly outlined a theory of the state drawn from the thought of Marx and Engels while also arguing against what he called bourgeois distortions (Rothenberg 1995). In this political tract, Lenin argued that the state promotes rather than mitigates class struggle: "The state is the product and the manifestation of the irreconcilability of class antagonisms. The state arises when, where, and to the extent that the class antagonisms cannot be objectively reconciled. And, conversely, the existence of the state proves that the class antagonisms are irreconcilable" (Lenin 1932: 8). He saw the state as a force above society that could only be overturned by violent revolution and the destruction of the state apparatuses created by the ruling class. He advocated armed power among the working people as a force to contend with the state instruments of power, the standing army and the police. The workers or proletariat would seize power and transform the means of production from private to state property. Under the proletariat, a transition from capitalism to communism would evolve. Bourgeois democracy would become proletarian democracy as the majority suppressed the oppressive minority, and the functions of state power would devolve upon the people until there was no need for such power and the state disappeared altogether.

Lenin outlined several phases in this evolution. First, bourgeois society develops under capitalism. Second, a political transition occurs in which "the state can be no other than the revolutionary dictatorship of the proletariat" (1932: 71). Third, in an early phase of communism generally known as socialism, the means of production are no longer the private property of individuals but belong to the whole society, although the inequalities of capitalist society are not altogether eliminated. Fourth, in a higher phase of communism the bourgeois inequalities are eliminated, the state is replaced by the rule of all society, and the people work according to their abilities and receive according to their needs (78–81).

Antonio Gramsci, the Italian Marxist, who was a political prisoner under Mussolini's fascist government, wrote a series of political essays that have appeared as *Selections from the Prison Notebooks of Antonio Gramsci* (1971) and *Selections from Political Writings 1910–1920* (1977). His work is distinctive because of its emphasis on the state; its elaboration of the concept of hegemony; and its disdain for economism, in which causal explanation draws from significant developments in the economic base and political struggles are seen as determined by that base. The following synthesis of his understanding of hegemony and the state draws heavily on Carl Boggs (1984), Anne Showstack Sassoon (1980), and Roger Simon (1982).

With the concept of hegemony, Gramsci shifted emphasis from ruling-class power in the mode of production to state power in the superstructure. In particular, he addressed the issue of consensual power as it evolved in advanced European society. His definition of ideological hegemony related to special interests or even class interests:

> One's own corporate interests, in their present and future development, transcend the corporate limits of the purely economic class, and can and must become the interests of other subordinate groups too. This is the most purely political phase, and marks the decisive passage from the structure to the sphere of complete superstructures . . . thus creating the hegemony of a fundamental social group [class] over a series of subordinate groups. (quoted in Boggs 1984: 160)

For Gramsci, hegemony is the organization of consent through persuasion and coercion whereby a class and its representatives hold power over subordinate classes. The concept was originally used by Georgy Plekhanov and later Lenin to suggest how the working class might ally itself with the peasantry to overthrow the Russian tsar. In Gramsci's usage, hegemony became "a relation between classes and other social forces. A hegemonic class, or part of a class, is one which gains the consent of other classes and social forces through creating and maintaining a system of alliances by means of political and ideological struggle" (Simon 1982: 22–23). In other words, hegemony is impossible under the leadership of a single class and must take into account the democratic demands of the people. Gramsci referred to "the war of position" in building a broad bloc of forces. He wrote of "the passive revolution" as a strategy of the bourgeoisie when its hegemony is threatened, using the state to modify social and economic structure from above, and of the "anti-passive revolution" as the strategy of the working class in such a situation. Gramsci also distinguished the apparatuses of the state from the civil society where popular democratic and class struggles take place. Normally, the bourgeoisie holds decisive control over the productive process, but workers usually contest this, and control by capitalists is never absolute. Thus, Gramsci believed it was misleading to separate production from politics. Indeed, the social relations of civil society are linked to the relations of production, so that a hegemonic class must combine a bloc of social forces in civil society with its leadership in the sphere of production and in this manner build "a historic bloc." This process involves a "war of movement" but becomes a "war of position" as the working class seeks hegemony in the building of a new historic bloc. A transition to socialism is possible with the transfer of power from the bourgeoisie to the working class and the transformation of the capitalist state into a socialist state. (In addition to the above sources, see Bobbio 1978 and 1988 and Kesselman 1980 for elaboration on the importance of these concepts in a Gramscian theory of the state.)

Assessing the Dichotomy

Whereas the liberal conception of the state is as an institution above and outside society to which members relinquish individual rights, the progressive one is as an apparatus of power based on its class structure. It is the class nature of society that differentiates the progressive from the liberal perspective. Marx conceived of the state as a kind of superstructure of political institutions and ideological activity that reflected changes in the economic base and the intensification of contradictions and subsequent struggle among social classes. Weber was interested in the legitimation of the state through force and coercion and the achievement of stability and order in a modern productive society. He saw historical change as gradual and evolutionary progress as dependent on the fundamental conditions of each society. Critics have assessed these differences in interesting ways.

Frank Parkin (1979) criticized most contemporary mainstream or "bourgeois" theory for giving insufficient attention to the state. One problem he identified was its divorcing the state from the nation. Weber focused on power in a territorial context, a reflection of the nineteenth-century German concern with national unification. In Marx's writings on mid-nineteenth-century France, the state was an agency serving the collective purposes of the ruling class, although not necessarily as its direct representative: "Conceptions of the state that start off from the idea of a separate, independent source of state power are, after all, plentiful enough; but they stem from traditions completely alien to Marxism" (Parkin 1979: 126). Parkin suggested that Weber hinted at the idea of the state as a corporate interest group: "Although Weber speaks of bureaucracy as a corporate group within the state, it is only a small step to combine the two in the concept of a state bureaucracy, denoting a powerful stratum distinct from social classes" (127).

In large measure, inquiry about the state has been shaped by these contrasting perspectives. For example, in a study that evolved from his earlier attention to the welfare state, Claus Offe argued that the prevailing understanding of institutionalized or state political authority represented a position intermediate between Weber and Marx (1985: 4). Michael Mann (1986) moved beyond such orthodox frameworks as structuralism and structural-functionalism to examine overlapping and intersecting ideological, economic, military, and political power networks, employing a sociospatial and organizational model and a Weberian methodology of ideal types in an analysis of the development of Europe up to the eighteenth century. Richard Bellamy (1986) defended Hegel's claims for the state and then went to some length to reinstate the Hegelian conception of rationality as a way of examining contemporary political issues. Finally, in an effort to find a middle position in political science between those who focus the political system and those who place the state at the heart of the discipline, Seymour Mitchell argued that "we need to examine the detailed political processes through which the uncertain yet powerful distinction between state and society is produced" (1991:78). He suggested that the state should not be seen as a coherent entity separate from society but that the

> distinction between state and society should nevertheless be taken seriously, as the defining characteristic of the modern political order. . . . The state should be addressed as an effect of detailed processes of spatial organization, temporal arrangement, functional specification and supervision and surveillance, which create the appearance of a world fundamentally divided into state and society. (95)

Martin Carnoy (1984) and Bob Jessop (1982 and 1990) have concentrated on sorting out contemporary theories of the state, but always with reference to the early understandings. Table 4.3 provides a sketch of these theories and the differences and similarities elaborated by these authors.

TABLE 4.3   Themes in Classical Theories of the State

Carnoy	Jessop
Represents collective interests and classes (Hobbes, Locke, Rousseau, Smith, Weber, and Schumpeter)	Parasitic, lacking any key role in production or reproduction
An ideal form involving a just and ethical relationship of harmony among segments of society; society as an idealized collectivity (Hegel)	A surface reflection of property relations and class struggles
A materialist, historical context shaped by society and a dominant mode and relations of production (Marx and Engels, *German Ideology*)	Cohesive and a mitigating mediator of class conflict
Autonomous (Marx, *18th Brumaire*)	An instrument of the ruling class
An instrument of the ruling class (Marx and Engels, *Manifesto*)	A set of institutions and a public power emerging in the division of labor
An organ of class rule against which power must be exercised in the revolutionary struggle to achieve socialism and communism (Lenin, *State and Revolution*)	A system of political domination with impact on the class struggle
The complex of practical and theoretical activities through which the ruling class justifies and maintains its dominance but also seeks the active consent over whom it rules and achieves hegemony (Gramsci)	

Carnoy traces North American conceptions of the state to classical writings that contend with Marxist approaches and emphasizes the thought of Hegel, Adam Smith, Weber, and Schumpeter as a foundation for understanding mainstream approaches to the state. Most of his text, however, identifies the roots of state theory in the tradition of ideas, thinking, and theories in Marx and Engels and in Lenin. Jessop (1990: 26–29) lists six patterns of thought about the state in the traditional Marxist texts: (1) the rather traditional conception of the state as parasitic, exemplified by the case of nineteenth-century Prussia; (2) the notion of the state as a reflection of a system of property relations and class struggles, with revolution being engendered by the contradictions between forces and relations of production; (3) the idea (found in Engels) that the state mediates class conflict without undermining the ruling class and capitalist reproduction; (4) the emphasis on the state as an instrument of class rule; (5) a view of the state as a set of institutions and officials that dominate or repress in the name of a public power that emerges with a mode of production in which one class exploits another; and (6) the idea of the state as a system of political domination with emphasis on political representation and state intervention, ensuring a balance of forces favorable to a particular class or class fraction

TOWARD A THEORY OF THE STATE

Historically, the study of politics has incorporated an understanding of the state, and political science has dealt with the concept since its inception in the nineteenth century. John Gunnell has noted that "its adoption was most essentially a function of the Germanization and disciplinization of political science" (1991: 125). He traced the early work on the state to the German political scientist Johann Kaspar Bluntschli (1885 [1851]); Francis Lieber, a naturalized American and "the first to employ the concept of the state . . . and to make it an object of theoretical analysis"; and Theodore Woolsey, educated in Bonn and Paris and "the first of the major native American theorists of the state and political science." Gunnell argues that "the theory of the state, as advanced by Lieber, Bluntschli, and Woolsey, constituted a distinct and influential paradigm" and sees it as surviving in the work of Westal W. Willoughby (1896), the "last 'grand' theorist of the state in American political science" (125).

The social science interest in the state, of course, continued well into the twentieth century (see, e.g., Oppenheimer 1975 [1914]). Most of the writings implied a state formally conceived along traditional institutional lines, allowing for descriptive analysis, usually of national states.

By the 1950s, mainstream comparativists, led by Gabriel Almond and influenced by behavioralism, were interested in turning the study of politics into a science. They argued that there were already too many conceptions of the state. Indeed, as early as 1931, C. H. Titus had published an article identifying 145. They believed that the state would be better viewed as an aspect of the political system, along with political parties, interest groups, communication media, family, school, church, and so on. Instead of the formal study of the state and its executive, legislative, and judicial functions, examination of the political system would open the way for comparative analysis of the complex newly emerging countries of the Third World. In his introduction to *The Politics of Developing Areas* (1960), Almond argued that "state" was imbued with many meanings and could not be operationalized in current comparative investigation.

Outside the United States, however, social scientists divided into two camps during the 1960s. On the one hand, the behavioralists adopted a systems approach, following the sociologist Talcott Parsons and the political scientist David Easton. On the other, some traditional European political scientists continued with their descriptive analysis and attention to the formal institutions of the state, while progressive social scientists, influenced especially by the renewed interest in Marx, elaborated theory on the evolving capitalist state. Particularly significant was the debate over the instrumentalist conception of the state in the work of the British political scientist Ralph Miliband and the structural conception of the Greek political sociologist Nicos Poulantzas.

It was not until the mid-1980s that interest in the state revived in U.S. academic circles. A campaign to "bring the state back in" under the auspices of the Committee on States and Social Structures of the Social Science Research Council (SSRC) resulted in "a paradigmatic shift," and interest in the role of the state prevailed into the 1990s (Evans, Rueschemeyer, and Skocpol 1985). This effort met with criticism from several quarters. Almond continued to argue that any notion of the state should be assimilated into the framework of the political system (1988: 885). Parkin (1979) and Mitchell (1991) argued that there was nothing new in the committee's work. Jessop went so far as to expose its agenda and the preference for the capitalist state itself that appeared in analysis on

> the geopolitical position of different modern states within the international system of nation states and the implications for state action . . . the dynamic of military organization and warfare in the development of the modern state . . . the distinctive powers of the modern state . . . shaping the character of institutions and social forces beyond the state in the economy and civil society . . . the distinctive interests and capacities of "state managers" as opposed to other social forces. (1990: 279, 283–286)

Although elements of mainstream political science struggled to refocus attention on the state, a general decline in interest in a Marxist theory of the state was evident that Prabhat Patnaik (1995) characterized as a continuing general retreat. In general, this was attributable to the crisis of Western Marxism, including the depreciation of the substantial theoretical contributions of French philosopher Louis Althusser, who had sparked renewed interest in a Marxist theory of the state during the 1960s. The collapse of authoritarian regimes in Southern Europe during the 1970s and in Latin America in the 1980s coupled with the fall of the Berlin Wall and the breakup of the Soviet Union and much of Eastern

Europe also contributed to the shift away from Marxism. With these changes, attention was diverted from the state to democracy and the appearance of new social movements around such pressing issues as ecology and feminism.

In a general way, the state can be characterized as coalescing the political, economic, social, and cultural processes and relations of society. At a fundamental level, the state is

> a system of relationships which defines the territory and membership of a community, regulates its internal affairs, conducts relations with other states (by peaceful and by warlike means), and provides it with identity and cohesion. It consists of institutions and processes which are extremely various and complex, presiding over different spheres of the community, which distribute different social goods according to different principles. (Jordan 1985: 1)

From another vantage point, the state can be understood as overseeing the class struggle in the process of capital accumulation. This perspective attends to relations between political and economic life without reducing one to the other or understanding them as independent, it acknowledges historical and national differences, and it takes into account the influences of institutional and other nonclass forces (Jessop 1990: 25). Furthermore, the state may be envisaged as intervening in the uneven process of capitalist reproduction and as a provisional means for resolving crises: "The state activities always develop out of, and the social form of the state maintains itself through, class conflicts and the political struggles mediated through the basic social context of capitalist crises" (Hirsch 1978: 98). Thus, the state serves to regulate and mediate the interests of society. In the authoritarian or exceptional form of the state, rule tends to be autocratic, with formal competition absent and participation limited to the dominant classes and the privileged or favored groups. The state may also become relatively autonomous but dominant through its ideological and repressive apparatuses, with social classes being outside the state in the capitalist mode of production; the state may be relatively autonomous from these economic relations but perform its class role as the site where various competitive fractions (financial, industrial, commercial, agrarian, and mining) of the capitalist class are unified through hegemony.

The authoritarian or exceptional form of the state was evident during the Portuguese monarchy from its inception in the twelfth century until its demise in 1910 and during the dictatorship from 1926 until 1974. The parliamentary form of the state appeared during the two republican periods from 1910 to 1926 and from 1974 to the present. In the parliamentary form, formal competition enhances the possibility of state autonomy, under which political relations can develop independently of economic relations and the state implements policy formulated within recognized rules, procedures, and institutional bargaining the outcome of which may not be predetermined. Outside the state, in civil society, parliamentary and political party politics may extend hegemony to the inherently antagonistic working class. There may also be a possibility of meaningful informal and direct participation by groups and individuals who influence power and shape policy outside a parliamentary system. Through the state, especially in capitalist and industrial societies, social classes may be organized collectively so that individual class interests are undermined while the bourgeoisie and its allies are mobilized around national interests. Similarly, the state and its leaders may encourage the disunity of dominant classes so that individual capitalists or capitalist interests do not prevail. Coherent state policy is possible when the needs, interests, and conflicts of the dominant class fractions are mitigated. Furthermore, in times of economic crisis the state may mediate social pacts between labor and bourgeois elements, including parliament and political parties, to ensure economic and political stability and advance mutual interests.

The following discussion reviews and reformulates current thinking on the state. Detailed syntheses are available in Jessop (1982 and 1990) and in Carnoy (1984), as well as in my *Theories of Comparative Politics* ([1981] 1994). Among other useful attempts to classify various theories or interpretations of the state are Barrow (1993); Clark and Dear (1984); Deutsch (1986); Rosenau (1988); Gold, Lo, and Wright (1975); Esping-Andersen, Friedland, and Wright (1976); Wolfe (1974); and González Casanova (1988). See also Table 4.4.

CURRENT THINKING ON THE STATE

Mainstream Theories

Pluralist capitalist perspective.   The pluralist capitalist view of the state is as a political marketplace that filters the demands and interests of competing groups and individuals. One school of thought suggests that state agencies are neutral and capable of mediating conflict that arises from competition among political parties or various group interests. Another sees the agencies of the state in terms of differing bases of political power, with competition among the agencies for funding determined by their relationship to parties and interest groups. Both these views reflect the liberal tradition of U.S. social science, and both are consistent with the preferences of comparativists such as Gabriel Almond and Peter Evans, Dietrich Rueschemeyer, and Theda Skocpol. J. P. Nettl (1968) was the first to challenge the abandonment of study of the state in the 1960s, and he failed to persuade mainstream political scientists to change their course. The mainstream statist movement in the middle 1980s was an effort to re-

TABLE 4.4   Contemporary Theories of the State

Mainstream	*Alternative*
Pluralist capitalist	Pluralist socialist
Institutional	Marxist institutional
Corporatist	Instrumental
Bureaucratic authoritarian	Structural
Neoliberal	Regulationist
	Feminist

NOTE: This table draws heavily from but updates and expands the discussion in my *Theories of Comparative Politics* 1994 (1981).

but the theoretical and empirical pluralist and structural-functional literature, but Almond persisted in his view, asserting that "neostatism" was merely a "polemic internal to Marxism," an intellectual movement operating "from a social class reductionist set of assumptions" (1988: 868–869). He bitterly denounced the statists for leaving a generation of young scholars with "little more than a paradigmatic farewell" and the alternative of adopting "ambiguous phraseology in the place of a hard-won tradition of operational rigor" (872).

Robert Alford and Roger Friedland (1985: 16) began with a pluralist view of the state but distinguished three perspectives according to the level of analysis: pluralist—individual and based on interaction; managerial—organizational and rationalized; and class—societal and premised on class struggle. Central concerns from these perspectives are differentiation in a modernizing society (pluralist), rationalization in an industrializing society (managerial), and accumulation in a capitalist mode of production (class). Whereas the pluralist perspective emphasizes cultural values and the managerial wields political power, the class perspective is based on economic considerations. These different perspectives are linked to the democratic, the bureaucratic, and the capitalist state.

Institutional perspective.   The study of politics in the early twentieth century stressed the state conceived of as an institutional array of governmental agencies. A recent movement has returned attention to this conception. Asserting that the "range of options available to policymakers at any given point in time is a function of institutional capabilities that were put in place at some earlier period," Stephen Krasner has used an institutional perspective to understand the sovereign state (1988: 67). His position contrasts with utilitarian or functional approaches that see outcomes as the consequence of individual choice. Thus, the sovereign state has become the form of political organization acceptable to the modern world: "Path-dependent patterns of development have been important; once Europe was committed to a form of political organization based on sovereign states, other possibilities were foreclosed" (90). Arguing that such theories are normative, Elinor Ostrom (1990) suggests that a convergence is occurring in the acceptance of the proposition that individuals are rational but that rational choice behavior can be explained through a deep understanding of institutions.

This trend to institutionalism was also picked up by James Rosenau, who supported reinstating the concept of the state because of the "diminished effectiveness of whole systems" and "a deep disillusion with systems analysis" (1988: 22). He returned to the traditional literature to legitimize this institutional thrust, suggesting that "the state is deeply embedded in our terminology and is unlikely to yield to efforts to replace it" (27).

Corporatist perspective.   Corporatism was theoretically conceived as a basic ideological component of the fascist regimes in the Iberian peninsula and in the Southern Cone of Latin America during the 1930s and 1940s. The Romanian economist Mihail Manöilescu was especially influential with ideas about how economy and polity could be organized into formal corporations supervised by the state. Philippe Schmitter (1979) had picked up on the title of Manöilescu's essay *The Century of Corporatism* (1934) to describe what he called a new, social form of corporatism, a notion that stemmed from his fieldwork on interest groups in the authoritarian state of Brazil during the late 1960s. Schmitter defined the state as "an amorphous complex of agencies with ill-defined boundaries, performing a great variety of not very distinctive functions" (1985: 33).

The optimism over corporatism was based on the belief that the planning that was essential to modern capitalism called for an effective income policy and that policy depended on consensus among the affected groups. Thus, corporatist compromises, especially in Europe, between labor and capital sometimes evolved through the intervention of the state. M. Donald Hancock (1983) noted a paradigmatic shift from traditional mainstream concerns toward "societal" or "liberal" corporatism, as reflected in the work of Leo Panitch (1980). Schmitter (1989) argued that national negotiations are now of decreasing importance, because of policies aimed at improving productivity and international competitiveness and the shift of interest conflicts from class-based cleavages to social movements based on issues of gender, environment, consumer protection, and so on. He also noted that international competition had resulted in the displacement of workers from traditional industry to services and public employment. Consequently, he was "less and less concerned that corporatism . . . will survive, much less be as much an imperative for the future of capitalism" (72).

Jessop (1990) generally ignored mainstream theories of the state, but he did not raise questions about corporatism. First, he identified problems with the distinction between "societal" corporatism (characterized by autonomy of interest associations from the state) and "state" corporatism (the subordination of interest associations to the state in relation to crisis and authoritarian forces from above). For example, corporatism tends to envisage the state as rooted in the economy and civil society and as an instrument for endowing the bourgeoisie with the power to restructure society at will (1990: 112). R. E. Pahl and J. T. Winkler defined corporatism as "an economic system in which the state directs and controls predominantly privately owned business towards four goals: unity, order, nationalism, and success" (1976: 13). They believed that Britain was evolving toward fascism, in which authoritarianism would eventually replace the rule of law and inquisitorial justice would replace adversary justice. Jessop felt that this approach suffered from its narrow conception of capitalism and a neo-Ricardian subjective view of the state as autonomous and outside and above the economy (1990: 114). Jessop also looked at the work of Gerhard Lehmbruch, who favored liberal corporatism and the party system as a means of increasing the structural differentiation and functional specialization of the political system. He believed that even under liberal corporatism the parliamentary system would remain determinant (Lehmbruch, 1977: 91–127).

Jessop went on to argue that capital accumulation is dependent on finding ways to ensure the increasing creation and appropriation of surplus value. The laws of motion of capitalism, he argued, depend on a balance in the struggle between capital and labor. It follows that the growth of corporatism in advanced capitalist states may depend on a reestablishment of this balance and a restoration of the conditions favorable to accumulation.

Exploring the links between corporatism and social democracy, Jessop suggested that the latter was the appropriate social base for the former because "it secures the support of the largest and most powerful of the dominated classes in state monopoly capitalism" (1990: 131). He suggested that creeping authoritarianism would overtake parliamentarism in capitalist societies with the adoption of new technologies for political control and centralization. He envisaged a trend toward "a social democratic tripartism based on the articulation of corporatism and parliamentarism and unified through the location of a social democratic party at the apex of both the corporatist and parliamentary systems" as well as a secondary tendency toward the creation of a strong state based on a weakening of corporative bodies involved in representation and intervention (115).

Jessop suggested that corporatism was initially formulated as an ideological critique of liberal capitalism; later it became less ideological and more practical in form, as it did not so much oppose capitalism as struggle against the rise of labor and seek new forms of interest. This led to authoritarianism from above in the form of fascist regimes and later to forms of societal corporatism. Jessop believed that the crisis of industrialization had led to a crisis in corporatism but that corporatism has enduring value in contributing to a differentiated subsystem, revenue distribution, and private interest government (see Grant 1985 for a critical assessment of corporatism).

Bureaucratic authoritarian perspective.   Guillermo O'Donnell's (1988) effort to transcend the limitations of corporatism and account for authoritarianism under the state in Argentina during the 1960s and early 1970s is especially relevant to authoritarian situations elsewhere in Latin America. The emergence of transnational corporations after World War II led to the "new industrialization" of the Third World. The importation of new production processes and technology was accompanied by an increase in activism and mass political participation. O'Donnell argued that these changes were assimilated into an expansion of the state that in turn succumbed to a rash of military coups and their transformation into authoritarian corporatist regimes. In describing this evolution, Carnoy suggested that two models of the state appeared. One model, state capitalist, shows how state intervention foments a state bourgeoisie, a new class with control over resources rather than ownership over the means of production: "This bourgeoisie has interests in the State as the State itself rather than as a bureaucratic representative of class interests in civil society" (1984: 200). In the second model, bureaucratic authoritarianism, the state is "guarantor and organizer of the domination exercised through a class structure subordinated to the upper fractions of a highly oligopolized and transnationalized bourgeoisie" (O'Donnell 1979: 292). The state excludes the popular sectors, marginalizing them through a shift from social spending to infrastructure that assimilates foreign investment. In this process, the state functions like a public entrepreneur: "In bureaucratic authoritarianism, the public sector, the transnational corporation, and the modern capitalist sector of the national economy are joined" (Carnoy 1984: 201).

William Canak (1984) explored the expanding role of the state in the process of capital accumulation in Latin America. He suggested that a crisis appeared with the exhaustion of the import-substitution model of industrialization and the weakness of the national bourgeoisie. He suggested, however, that this characterization had become increasingly irrelevant because of the view that dependency and capitalist development were not necessarily incompatible: The increasing internationalization of production was undermining domestic industry; state expenditures and the extent of state intervention were increasing similarly in both core and peripheral nations; and delegitimization of the state was increasingly appearing everywhere.

Neoliberal perspective.   Like the classical form of liberalism, neoliberalism emphasizes freedom in terms of individual autonomy and pursuit of material gain in the marketplace. Neoliberals favor banishing government from the economic arena. They would privatize the economy, free markets of regulations, and open up the national economy to international trade and foreign investment and would cut government social spending and welfare programs. In effect, they would favor the market over the state. Outside the United States, neoliberalism became the preferred approach of the emerging representative democratic regimes that appeared during the 1980s, especially in Latin America, where military dictatorships had opened up domestic economies to the outside world while controlling power through the state. In the United States, such sentiments were manifested through the ultraconservative majority of the Republican party, but the ideology was labeled conservative in the face of traditional liberal sentiment. Curiously, under neoliberalism, despite the pretensions to do away with the state altogether and in spite of some privatization of public entities and deregulation, the capitalist state continued to be as dominant and intrusive as in the past. Although antistate rhetoric was manifested everywhere, the bottom line for most people was that at the root of politics the state was an institutional web of agencies and persons that shaped, guided, and regulated economic development, social security and welfare, and indeed most facets of political and social life (Fishlow 1990).

The recent experience of Latin America illustrates this assertion. The role of the state has changed over the past half century. Whereas the interventionist state of the 1950s and 1960s sometimes redistributed income to the lowest-income groups, the neoliberal state shifts income in favor of the highest-income groups at the expense of the poor. Yet, the state continues to promote civil society and plan the economy. Neoliberal rhetoric, however, and the appearance of changes in the state were a response to the need to deal with the substantial demands of a rapidly rising external debt, which in turn led to instability and the need to rely on central authority: "Anti-statist ideology served as a smoke screen to hide the unlimited exploitation of the state international and national economic powers" (Hinkelammert 1995: 13). Even today, the state cannot carry out its normal functions and often turns to authoritarianism to maintain stability, and its repressive apparatuses are decisively involved: "Where the state has not developed sufficiently, these apparatuses become the dominant power of the state" (15). The continuing strength of the state is also emphasized by Albert Fishlow (1990) in his assessment of the neoliberal push for a smaller role for the state, less government intervention, privatization of state enterprise, and a free market. He argued that the state continues to assume an active and positive role in the production of goods and services, management of revenues and expenditures, and regulation of private activity. Furthermore, it plans levels of capital accumulation and adjusts for a disproportionate concentration of private power to ensure some degree of social justice, provision of public services, and equality. It is hindered by such problems as fiscal shortfall, increase in government expenditure, and emphasis on industrialization rather than agriculture. An effective state is needed, and there is no assurance that privatization will increase efficiency. Democracy within the state was a starting point in a reformulation that would effectively require a new coalition of political support founded on both new and old realities.

In a twist on the neoliberal position and in line with the reality of continuing state involvement in the less developed economies, Luiz Carlos Bresser Pereira (1993) has argued that the growth of the state has led to its current weakness. Therefore, it must be reformed through a reorganization somewhat along lines of neoliberal thinking, but once it is reformed, contrary to neoliberal thinking it will be ready to grow and intervene on behalf of the economy and society. As a minister in the Brazilian neoliberal government during the late 1990s, Bresser Pereira attempted to implement his reforms with only modest success, but the effort to tie theory to practice was instructive. In another historical example, Eduardo Silva (1993) focused on domestic business owners and landowners and how they worked through coalitions and exercised influence on state policy during the repressive military dictatorship in Chile up to the late 1980s.

Alternative Theories

Pluralist socialist perspective.   Robert Dahl, a proponent of pluralism within the traditions of American democracy, eventually extended his thinking to suggest the possibility of pluralism in a decentralized socialist order. Early in the twentieth century, Gramsci explored various means of democratically gaining control over the state. Whereas Lenin saw hegemony as a strategy for revolution in which the working class and its representatives win the support of the majority, Gramsci extended the concept to the capitalist class and its possibilities for gaining state power. Hegemony could thus be understood as a relationship between classes and other social forces, evolving into a system of alliances to secure control over state and society.

The awakening of a radical social movement in 1968 was followed by the rediscovery of Gramsci, who had worked out a political analysis of advanced capitalism in a Marxist framework and whose thinking about links and alliances among parties, social movements, and classes suggested a pluralist socialist perspective. Whereas traditional Marxist studies emphasized capitalist control of material production, the new studies focused on state activity and class struggle (Kesselman 1982). Socialist pluralism was the rallying cry of many leftist Portuguese intellectuals after the fall of the fascist dictatorship in April 1974. The recent openings to representative and formal democracy in countries long dominated by authoritarian rule, either in fascist capitalist or state socialist regimes, were frequently associated with the view that pluralism could be compatible with socialism, with the state filtering the demands and interests of competing individuals, groups, and classes.

The pluralist socialist perspective has not been delineated in any definitive form, but several critical views may be helpful in working toward a theoretical understanding. A first emanates from a Hegelian interpretation of the state as being a mediator above particular interests and classes and ensuring orderly competition among individuals and groups while preserving the collective interests of society. Influenced by Hegel during his early years, Marx also saw the state as a political expression of class structure embedded in production. The philosopher Herbert Marcuse and others of the Frankfurt school were able to draw from these influences and promote a critical theory that exposed the mystification of the state and advocated the liberation of individuals and groups from the oppression of capitalism. A second view stressed the conflict between state and classes. Claus Offe (1985), for example, criticized interpretations that ignored the class character of the state, and James O'Connor (1973) pointed to the relationship of the class struggle to contradictions in the process of capitalist accumulation. A third position emphasized the social relations of state capitalism as a dominant form of the political economy. It distinguished between state capitalism (where government has primary control over capital resources and performs important industrial management functions) and military state capitalism (where the primary activity of government is military). For example, Seymour Melman (1991) argued that capitalism in both the Western business world and the former Soviet bureaucracy involved a pluralism through the separation of decisionmaking from production, a hierarchical organization of decisionmaking, and the propensity of managers to enlarge their powers. Thus, both U.S. and Soviet managers sought to broaden their power over production and production worker.

Marxist institutionalist perspective. With the revival of the state as a key concept in the middle 1980s, attention turned to the possibility of a progressive theory of institutional life. The linking of institutions to the state was an effort to move away from rigid premises and ideological assumptions about what to study in society. Progressive institutional theory derives from the work of Douglass C. North, who developed a framework for the study of central issues in economic history and a theory of institutional change that contends with both neoclassical and Marxist theory. In an effort to lay bare the assumptions and weaknesses of neoclassical theory, he proposed an institutional approach based on a theory of property rights related to individual and group incentives, a theory of the state as enforcer of property rights, and a theory of ideology. Generally overlooked in the economic history of secular change, the nature of the state "must provide an explanation both for the inherent tendencies of political-economic units to produce inefficient property rights and for the instability of the state in history" (1981: 17). North looked at two explanations of the state: contract theory, envisaging the state as an agency of a rule class or group, and exploitation, the extraction of the income of others in society on behalf of a dominant group or class.

This alternative view is at the heart of a comparison of institutionalism and Marxism by William M. Dugger and Howard J. Sherman (1994), who identified common ground in these differing perspectives. Their comparison was structured by questions about the fundamental relationships and the dynamics of social science activity: power relationships in society, class conflict, the relationship of technology to ideas, social explanations, and the role of the individual. They saw convergence in the emphasis on nonreductionist relational or holistic views of ideas, structures, and the individual and in a historical or evolutionary view of society as progress.

In an effort to move away from the Hegelian totality on which the methodological individualism of neoclassical economic theory and the economic determinism of classical Marxist theory are based, Stephen Cullenberg has sought a "new" Marxism based on institutionalism. He advocates concrete and historically specific analyses that avoid explaining causality in terms of individual agents or structures. In particular, he recommends a "decentered approach to social totality . . . as a framework for institutionalist thought" that attends to "social, political, and economic structures and the idea that individuals are embedded in, and constitutive of, these structures" (1999: 3–4). The new theory would also build on ideas such as Althusser's "overdetermination," which appears prominently in the thinking of Stephen Resnick and Richard Wolff. Overdetermination is a theory of causality in which everything determines everything else: "Nothing exists in and of itself, and therefore all aspects of a society exist only as the result of the constitution (mutual determination) of all of society's other aspects" (Cullenberg 1999: 18). Thus, it has to do with processes that are complex and contradictory and linked to other processes in the family, the church, enterprise, and the state.

Instrumental perspective.   The instrumental approach is generally attributable to Marx and Engels's *The German Ideology* and the *Manifesto*. The former advances the idea that members of the ruling class assert collective interests through the state and the latter the idea that the state is an executive or committee for managing the common affairs of the bourgeoisie of the modern state. Instrumentalism runs through the thought of those who followed Marx and Engels, such as Lenin, who once referred to the standing army and police as instruments of state power; Paul Sweezy, who viewed the state as an instrument in the hands of the ruling classes; and Ralph Miliband, who characterized the state as the instrument of the ruling class for domination of society. The instrumentalist perspective thus focuses on the class that rules and on the mechanisms that link ruling-class instruments and state policies.

Instrumentalism has frequently been criticized for economic reductionism and the assumption that the economic base determines political outcomes in the struggle for state power. Marxism-Leninism and Stalinism, which stressed an instrumentalist view of the state, especially came under criticism by the Marxist left during the 1960s. Various influences emerged from this criticism, including the capital logic school, with its Hegelian emphasis, in West Germany; Althusserian structuralism, which rejected individualism and class consciousness, in France; and the revision of Gramscian thought with attention to the relationship of state apparatuses and civil society elsewhere (Jessop 1990: 29–31). The criticism also led Nicos Poulantzas to identify state forms and distinguish normal states (where bourgeois hegemony is stable), exceptional states (where a crisis of hegemony exists), and authoritarian states (where the state controls socioeconomic life and there is a decline of representative democracy) (see Jessop 1990: 66).

Instrumentalism has stimulated contributions to class analysis. The analysis of Marx and Engels, for instance, not only revealed the complexities of power within the state but demonstrated the importance of struggle for control of the state agencies and their activities. The idea of the instrumentality of the state also facilitated analysis of economic policymaking by theorists influenced by David Ricardo. Finally, it was incorporated into the social democratic conception of the state, which in liberal parliamentary regimes is envisaged as a neutral instrument ready for capture through electoral victory and a step on the gradual and peaceful way to socialism (Jessop 1982: 14). This perception coincides with the assertion of Frank Parkin that the political character of the state varies: "The Marxist conception of the state as the servant and protector of a dominant class is far too narrow; the state can equally well serve the interests of a dominant racial group, a dominant religious community, or a dominant party" (1979: 138).

Structural perspective.   Writing on the state in *A Dictionary of Marxist Thought* (in Bottomore 1983), Ralph Miliband has compared instrumentalism and structuralism, noting that both approaches view the state as subordinated to and constrained by forces external to it. Yet, the question of autonomy remains relevant in the writing of Marx and Engels. Under Bonapartism, Marx observed, all classes appeared to have succumbed to the despotism of the dictator because the bourgeoisie had lost the struggle for power and the working class was incapable of ruling the country. Engels asserted that such moments were "exceptional" periods when the state emerged as an independent mediator between the warring classes.

Structuralism is relevant to understanding the distinction between the economic base or infrastructure and the superstructure, which incorporates the state and its apparatuses. Gramsci contributed to this in several ways (Hall 1977): by expanding the conception of what the superstructure can do for capital, by developing intermediary concepts (such as "hegemony" and "historical bloc") that allow for specificity in analysis of the superstructure, and by focusing on the capitalist state. Althusser and his followers, in particular Poulantzas, elaborated a Marxist theory of base and superstructure that showed that the economy could not be detached from political and ideological practices to exert its determination "in the last instance," thereby suggesting the possibility of eliminating the metaphor of base and superstructure altogether and arriving at a social formation in which overdetermination rather than determination is important. This makes the superstructure relatively autonomous.

The ideas of Gramsci especially influenced the thinking of Poulantzas on the question of hegemony and the state. Hegemony would ensure unity of dominant class fractions as well as the consensus of the dominated classes, with the state assuming the essential role as "an institutional ensemble which has a major function in organizing hegemony within the power bloc as well as in the mobilization of active consent vis-à-vis the dominated classes and thus society as a whole" (Jessop 1982: 155). Poulantzas conceptualized hegemony as part of capitalism and related it to the distinction between the state and civil society. He also differentiated between normal and exceptional states, the former corresponding to stable bourgeois hegemony and the latter to a crisis of hegemony in the capitalist state; the former might be characterized by the functioning of a plural party system not dependent on the central administration and the latter by the dominance of political apparatuses such as the fascist party, the army, and the secret police, which operate apart from the administration. Sometimes interpreted as an exceptional form of the state, Bonapartism is considered an intermediate case because it exists in a crisis of hegemony and representative politics remains subject to a centralized and unifying bureaucracy. Poulantzas also elaborated on a new form of the capitalist state called authoritarian statism, which was more normal than exceptional; its elements were a concentration of power in the executive, a fusion of the three branches of government and a disrespect for law, a decline in the influence of political parties, and the existence of power networks that are parallel and overlap the organization of the state.

Particularly important in Poulantzas's thinking on the state is the shift in his view about alliances and the role of intermediate classes, especially the ties of petty bourgeois fractions with the working class. Poulantzas noted the changing nature of the state under capitalism and denied the validity of the notion of a centralized popular power parallel and external to that of the state. He recognized the possibility of class struggle within the state apparatus and the polarizing of forces in the direction of a socialist transition. The idea that the state can serve as an instrument of the working class either through a frontal assault or through penetration from within was associated with the denial of the necessity for a single revolutionary or vanguard party as the catalyst for revolution. These views of Gramsci and Poulantzas were extended by Ernesto Laclau and Chantal Mouffe through what Jessop described as "discursive mechanisms through which hegemony can be achieved" or "discourses in the field of ideological struggle" (1982: 210).

Taking the position that there can be no general theory of the state, Poulantzas (1978) argued against traditional mechanistic economist and instrumentalist conceptions of the state. He identified apparatuses of the state such as the ideological apparatus as a means of identifying the form of the state and argued that the state "plays a constitutive role in the existence and reproduction of class powers, and more generally in the class struggle itself" (34). This position was drawn from the formulations of Althusser, who emphasized the "structured whole" within which there are various levels that are distinct and "relatively autonomous," and Etienne Balibar, who noted that in the capitalist mode of production, the "economic" instance is relatively separate from the "political" and "ideological" instances and is dominant and a determinant "last instance" (34).

In formulating the concept of the relative autonomy of the state, Poulantzas initially showed a relative separation of the economic and the political in the capitalist mode of production and sought an alternative to instrumental interpretations of a Marxist theory of the state. This changed as some writers began to assess the possibility of autonomy for states. Haldun Gulalp (1987) has argued that there are similarities between the Poulantzian formulation and the liberal conception of the state, that the shift from relative to potential autonomy is a consequence of separating the political and economic dimensions, and that analysis of the state should be grounded in the process of capital accumulation.

In his later work, Poulantzas integrated the class struggle into his conceptualization of the state without departing from the framework separating the political and the economic, and this meant identifying the class struggle with the political struggle. Arguing that this formulation resulted in a pluralist and therefore liberal conception that led critics such as Fred Block (1980), Theda Skocpol, and Miliband to conclude that relative autonomy was "class reductionist," Gulalp reviewed various conceptions of state autonomy in these and other writers and showed that they tended to separate the economic from the political and to envisage the state as an independent entity with power distinctive from the relations of class domination (1987: 305). He reformulated the role of the state in terms of the continuity of capital accumulation: "The role of the state in maintaining and reproducing the relations of domination should be seen in the light of its relation to capital accumulation rather than its direct or indirect links with the dominant class(es) or its fractions" (311).

James O'Connor's (1973) work is also relevant to a structural approach because he examined the state and internal class struggle in light of contradictions in the process of capital accumulation. In particular, he was interested in how class struggle constrains the ability of the state to rationalize capitalism and how the state structures serve as barriers to the challenge of the working class. In a follow-up work, he described the "accumulation crisis" in terms of the individualization of needs and the state response to supplying individual services and incomes: "The processes of production, distribution, exchange, consumption, and competition in the model of U.S. full capitalism were deeply inscribed by ideologies of individualism and their practices which, in turn, gave rise to different kinds of economic and social contradictions and crisis tendencies" (1984: 188).

Criticism of both structuralist and instrumentalist theory abounds. Structuralists minimize class activity and emphasize the political output of state activity that ensures capitalist domination. Instrumentalists stress the political input into the state and the unequal class distribution of power. "Neither approach can analytically distinguish the extent to which class action mediates between constraints and state structures, generates those constraints and structures, or at times is irrelevant to the relationship of economic constraints to the state" (Esping-Andersen, Friedland, and Wright 1976: 189–190). Focusing explicitly on industrial society, Offe (1972) steers away from traditional instrumentalist and structuralist approaches in his examination of the character of the capitalist state and its mechanisms that affect class. The political theorist David Easton (1981) offered a full assessment of Poulantzas and ultimately not only ignored his theory but concluded with a defense of a theory of the political system in place of the state. Other relevant writings include Adam Przeworski and Michael Wallerstein (1988) on the state and the market, Ben Fine and Lawrence Harris (1979) on state intervention on behalf of monopoly capital, and Richard Braungart and Margaret Braungart (1991) on the origins and structure of the modern state.

Regulation perspective.   Another alternative understanding of the state has embraced regulation theory as initially developed in Michel Aglietta's *Régulations et crises du capitalisme* (*A Theory of Regulation*, 1976; see annotated reference in Chapter 2) and Robert Boyer's *La théorie de la régulation: Une analyse critique* (1986; see annotated reference in Chapter 2). They argued that capitalism evolves through a succession of periods of crisis and periods in which a regularity of social relations and structure can be observed. A mode of regulation—that is, a set of coherent and predictable rules—corresponds to each period of stability and allows harmonious development of the system. In contrast, economic laws no longer function during the crisis because regulation is not always possible and the system is left to the whims of social struggle and political choices. Economic time is divided into periods of regularity, those of laws and regulation, and periods of crisis, those of chance (Fontvieille 1991).

In a retrospective analysis of regulation theory over the past twenty years, Aglietta takes issue with fashionable contemporary currents, especially neoclassical theory and its emphasis on equilibrium and the liberal notion of a free market. He argues that regulation theory was "concerned with heterogeneous economic processes in which necessity and contingency, the constraint of the past and the creation of the new, are intertwined" and, furthermore, involved "processes that emerge, are reproduced, then wither away under the effects of the unequal development inherent in capitalism" (1999: 44).

In a full-blown review and criticism of the regulation school, Jessop demonstrated its usefulness to a theory of the state. He dwelt on the regulationist use of key concepts such as "regime of accumulation" and "mode of regulation" and identified the diversity among the Parisian practitioners of this school. He also looked closely at related currents such as an Amsterdam school interested in international class formation and modes of regulation with emphasis on "the state's centrality in implementing a comprehensive concept of control at home"; a German school that tied state theory to regulation and focused "on the state's role in actively constituting a power bloc and, as a hegemonial structure, underwriting specific accumulation strategies and societalization forms"; and an American school (for example, Gordon 1991) the theory of which may be classified as social-structures-of-accumulation with attention to the democratic state "as a site of conflict between the logic of capital and the logic of citizenship." He showed that regulation theorists incorporate the state into a mode of regulation and concentrate on three theoretical aspects: "first, the specific object(s) of regulation which they examine; sec-ondly, the substantive theoretical framework in terms of which such ob-jects are studied; and, thirdly, for periodizing and/or conjunctural analy-sis" (1990: 312). He concluded, first, that although the state is never absent from the mode of regulation and regulation theorists incorporate it into their analysis, its role is "largely neglected" because of "the uneven development of the approach itself." Furthermore, the state ought to be seen as "an object as well as agent of regulation" and not as "a regulatory *deus ex machina* to be lowered on stage whenever the capital relation needs it" (315). Here, he alluded to the fact that the regulation literature stresses the fragmentation of the state as the source of the relative auton-omy of the political sphere.

Feminist perspective. Focusing on patriarchy and the domination of women by men, feminism looks at gender relations as an aspect of a power relationship and challenges traditional ways of studying political economy. In general, feminists have not elaborated a theory of the state, but it is essential to mention some efforts to relate gender to such a theory.

Men predominate not only in professional life and academia but also in politics in general. Women have long been neglected not only in political science and comparative politics but also in political economy. Their role in government is usually minimal. Bob Connell described it: "The state arms men and disarms women" (quoted in Jessop 1990: 13). In an attempt to move the feminist discourse in a critical direction, Kathy Ferguson (1983) argued that liberal feminists have become co-opted in the growing bureaucratization of political and economic institutions, including the state apparatuses, and that radical feminists should be wary of how the women's movements relate to this process. Heidi Hartmann (1979) voiced pessimism about a more radical outcome because of the inability of feminist theory to analyze the position of women within the dominant patriarchal society. Diana Coole revealed how through the state and its apparatus men sustain male power in both the public and private sectors: "Many feminists have found the impersonal and bureaucratic nature of the modern state problematic in relation to the personalized and partici-patory style of politics which they favour" (1990: 32). V. Spike Peterson pointed to "the gendered construction of the state" (1992), and Catharine A. MacKinnon (1983 and 1989) contended that there was no feminist the-ory of the state.

In exploring the question of feminism and Marxism as method in a search for an understanding of the state, MacKinnon emphasized the dif-ferences between them and noted that Marxists criticize feminism as bourgeois theory and practice and as serving the dominant class, and feminists view Marxism as male-dominated theory. Whereas Marxist method is dialectical materialism, feminist method is consciousness raising. In her view, feminism becomes Marxism's ultimate critique as Marxism serves to criticize classical political economy. Feminism turns Marxism on its head.

Feminist criticisms of Marxist state theories fall into three camps, according to Jessop: subsumption, in which all states are viewed as expressions of patriarchy and must be contested; derivation, in which the functions or forms of the state are understood as derived from the requirements of reproduction rather than production, changes in the form of patriarchal domination, and the nature of the domestic mode of production; and articulation, which links patriarchal and capitalist forms of domination (1990: 14).

ISSUES OF STATE THEORY

An interesting point raised by Jessop is that although critics acknowledge that Marx did not systematically develop a theoretical analysis of the state, they also recognized that other classical Marxist writings rarely focus on state power, capital accumulation, and the changing forms of the state (1990: 25). Table 4.5 not only incorporates these aspects but also serves to extend our discussion on contemporary lines of thinking by emphasizing major issues to consider.

Building on classical Marxist thought, Carnoy and Jessop have identified the principal contemporary currents of progressive thought on the state. First, they point to the emphasis in Ralph Miliband (1969) on an instrumentalist view of the state as a means of attacking liberal theories of pluralism and democracy, an approach that did not advance theory on the state because "he actually reproduces the liberal tendency to discuss politics in isolation from its complex articulation with economic forces" (Jessop 1990: 30). Carnoy also introduces the view of William Domhoff that the capitalist class dominates the state with its economic power and state personnel participate in the dominant class.

Second, there is opposition to instrumentalism as represented in the work of Nicos Poulantzas and an emphasis on the structurally determined role of the state and its complex of social relations in which class struggle occurs not only in civil society but also within the state. Carnoy and Jessop both argue that in this formulation it is not clear whether any class actually controls the state apparatus and, furthermore, that Poulantzas vacillates between a state that is completely independent and a state that is dependent on the economic base.

Third, theorists who follow in the Ricardian tradition emphasize how the state intervenes in the economy to influence distribution of income

TABLE 4.5   Contemporary Progressive Theories of the State

Carnoy	Jessop
State personnel are one and same as those located in higher branches of government who belong to the same class or classes that dominate civil society (Domhoff)	State power built on socialization into the ideology of the dominant class, with attention to instrumentalism in an exposé of the mystification of liberal pluralism (Miliband)
Capitalist class dominates state with its overall economic power, withholding capital, for instance	State viewed as a complex of social relations, cohesive and relatively autonomous (Poulantzas)
State is instrument of the ruling class (Miliband, in a qualified way)	State influence on the distribution of income between classes and state intervention to ensure corporate profits at the expense of wages (neo-Ricardians)
State as autonomous; no class has power to rule through the state in particular instances (exceptional state) (Poulantzas and Althusser)	State monopoly capitalism based on the laws of motion of capitalism; the class nature of the state depends on external factors
State theory derived from economic laws of capitalist development; state intervenes to offset declining rate of profit, extracts surplus from workers rather than mediates class struggle (Hirsch)	State as an ideal collective capitalist with the form of the capitalist state derived from the pure capitalist mode of production and its conditions of existence (Altvater)
State as dependent	State envisaged with historical specificity and class struggle (contemporary Frankfurt theorists)
State as democratic in the transition to socialism	Capitalist state and the popular-democratic struggle based on ideological hegemony (Gramsci and neo-Gramscians)

between classes and ensure corporate profit at the expense of wages; here, says Jessop, the approach ignores social relations of production and class struggle in its attention to struggles for income distribution, and the state is seen as a third force capable of intervention or subject to manipulation.

Fourth, theories of state monopoly capitalism incorporate laws of motion of capitalism, and the state either becomes the instrument of the dominant monopolies or fuses with monopoly capital to deny political power to medium-sized and small capital, which become potential allies alongside the petty bourgeoisie and the working class in an antimonopoly front. State theory may derive from economic laws of capitalist development so that the state intervenes to offset declining rates of profit or extracts surplus from workers rather than mediates class struggle.

Fifth, the state also is seen as the ideal collective capitalist in the form of a political institution corresponding to the common needs of capital, evident in the work of the capital logic school, which derives the general form of the capitalist state and its principal functions from the pure capitalist mode of production: "To the extent that it is not an actual capitalist but a distinct political institution corresponding to the common needs of capital, the state is an ideal collective capitalist" (Elmar Altvater, quoted in Jessop 1990: 35).

Sixth, the state is cast in a context of historical specificity and class struggle.

Seventh, the emergence of the capitalist state and the popular democratic struggle as advocated by the followers of Antonio Gramsci and the concept of ideological hegemony, which coalesces the capitalist state with the popular-democratic struggle.

In sum, the role of capital in the modern state can be understood in terms of instrumentalism, whereby the bourgeoisie or the capitalist class as a whole or fractions thereof manipulate the state as an instrument to promote their interests at the expense of other classes, or in terms of structuralism, whereby external constraints prevent the state from pursuing policies contrary to the interests of capital or the structure of the state system ensures that the interests of capital are favored in policy. The state is also envisioned strategically as a social relation where the state and its institutions are brought into play through representation and intervention.

Alluding to the problem of how Marxism draws on non-Marxist concepts and approaches in the search for solutions, Jessop suggests that Marxist analysis may dissolve into "a broadly pluralistic, eclectic account of the state" over such issues as "the alleged 'relative autonomy' of the state, the sources of the class unity of state power, the periodization of the state, its social bases, the precise nature of hegemony and its articulation with coercion, and the role of the nation-state in the changing world system" (1990: 196). At stake will be an assessment of law and legal domination within the capitalist state in its evolving forms (Santos 1980).

In its essence, the state has been described as comprising "a distinct ensemble of institutions and organizations whose socially accepted function is to define and enforce collectively binding decisions on the members of a society in the name of their common interest or general will" (Jessop 1990: 341). Jessop cautions that contradictions are evident in any conception of the state, so that the state is not the same as government, bureaucracy, a coercive apparatus, or any political institution. Although institutions make up the core of the state, their relationship with the state and society at large may be uncertain, depending on the social formation (for example, feudal or capitalist) and the historical experience. Furthermore, although the state employs coercion, all means of enforcement should be considered in assessing its intervention in society. Finally, the common interest and general will must be taken into account and privileged interests examined in light of interests that are marginalized.

Whatever preference may have dominated social science over the past century, the state is at the center of the study of politics. In progressive theory, the state is located in the superstructure where politics and ideology can shape outcomes and affect institutional and class activities. Analysis must also be directed to the productive base, where (class) relations of production can be understood as juxtaposed to forces of production in the prevailing mode of production (usually capitalism) and the social formation. Transcending capitalism has been perceived as possible for the state through either violent or peaceful means, but it has become evident in recent times that the transition to socialism or some system that provides for the basic needs of all people must involve movement in the direction of participatory democracy. The issue, therefore, is the nature of that democracy and of the role of authority and central control and planning in the transition process.

REFERENCES

Aglietta, Michel. 1999. "Capitalism at the Turn of the Century: Regulation Theory and the Challenge of Social Change." *New Left Review* 232 (November-December):41–90. A reassessment of the regulation approach.

Alford, Robert R., and Roger Friedland. 1985. *Powers of Theory: Capitalism, the State, and Democracy.* Cambridge, England: Cambridge University Press. Examines three theoretical approaches: pluralist (emphasis on political consensus and peaceful and evolutionary modernization); managerial or elite (stresses the dominance of an alliance of military, executive, and corporate bureaucracies over the democratic tradition of elections, parties, and legislatures); and neo-Marxist class (attention to capitalist accumulation as constraining state structure and policy): "For the pluralist perspective it is the individual; for the managerial, the organization; and for class, society. . . . An adequate theory of the state must incorporate all three levels of analysis" (6).

Almond, Gabriel A. 1988. "The Return to the State." *American Political Science Review* 82 (September):853–874. With responses, pp. 875–901, by Eric A. Nordlinger, Theodore J. Lowi, and Sergio Fabbrini. A review of the revival of interest in theories of the state. Concludes that the statist literature fails in its attack on pluralist reductionism. Criticizes "this intellectual episode" for not searching the literature of institutional and administrative history. Replies show weaknesses in his argument and supporting sources.

Andrews, William G. 1991. "Corporatist Representation in European International and Supranational Organizations." Paper presented at the 15th World Congress of the International Political Science Association, Buenos Aires, July 21–25. Advances the argument that corporatism is important in European international organizations and widely accepted in the institutions of the European Economic Community (EEC). Defines modern corporatism as "a system of official representation of interest communities and associations within the formal institutions of government and, by analogy, within international organizations" (1).

Barrow, Clyde W. 1993. *Critical Theories of the State: Marxist, Neo-Marxist, and Post-Marxist*. Madison: University of Wisconsin Press. A simplified approach to the classification of Marxist theory that nevertheless helps to sort out various lines of thinking.

Bellamy, Richard. 1986. "Hegel's Conception of the State and Political Philosophy in a Post-Hegelian World." *Political Science* 38 (December):99–112. Reviews liberal and Marxist criticism of the relationship between the state and authority and applies a Hegelian understanding of rationality to contemporary analysis.

Block, Fred. 1980. "Beyond Relative Autonomy," pp. 227–242 in Ralph Miliband and John Saville, eds., *Socialist Register 1980*. New York: Monthly Review Press.

_____. 1987. *Revising State Theory: Essays in Politics and Postindustrialism*. Philadelphia: Temple University Press. An effort to update and recast a theory of the state in terms of the "postindustrial" era.

Bluntschli, Johann Kaspar. 1885 (1851). *The Theory of the State*. Oxford, England: Clarendon Press. An influential work for early American political science, examining the conception of the state, its functions and forms, and its historical foundations (see Gunnell 1991 for a detailed review).

Bobbio, Norberto. 1978. "Is There a Marxist Theory of the State?" *Telos* 35:5–16.

_____. 1988. "Gramsci and the Concept of Civil Society," pp. 73–99 in John Keane, ed., *Civil Society and the State*. London and New York: Verso. Explores the conceptual roots of civil society in political thought up to Marx and then the thinking of Gramsci on the state and civil society.

Boggs, Carl. 1984. *The Two Revolutions: Gramsci and the Dilemmas of Western Marxism*. Boston: South End Press. An analysis of Gramscian thought and influence, with some attention to the question of the state and hegemony.

Braungart, Richard G., and Margaret M. Braungart, eds. 1991. *The Political Sociology of the State: Essays on the Origins, Structure, and Impact of the Modern State*. Chicago: JAI Press. Deals mainly with various aspects of American politics, policy, and regulation.

Bresser Pereira, Luiz Carlos. 1993. "Economic Reforms and Cycles of State Intervention." *World Development* 21:1337–1353. An advocate of continuing state involvement in the economy who believes that state activities must be trimmed and efficiently reorganized.

Canak, William L. 1984. "The Peripheral State Debate: State Capitalist and Bureaucratic-Authoritarian Regimes in Latin America." *Latin American Research Review* 19 (1):3–36. Analyzes two major conceptual frameworks useful for understanding the state in Latin America, the state capitalist and the bureaucratic-authoritarian. Points to similarities between the two theories (state structure

and policy are linked to crisis derived from exhaustion of the import-substitution model of industrialization, and the weakness of the state is linked to the
weakness of the national bourgeoisie).

Caporaso, James A., ed. 1989. *The Elusive State: International and Comparative
Perspectives*. Newbury Park, Calif.: Sage Publications. A collection of essays on
the state, including Bert Rockman and James Rosenau on conceptual variation,
Ted Robert Gurr on the coercive state, and Janice Thomson and Stephen
Krasner on sovereignty.

Carnoy, Martin. 1984. *The State and Political Theory*. Princeton: Princeton
University Press. A critical overview of theories and debates, with emphasis on
Marxist and progressive thinkers.

Clark, G. L., and M. Dear. 1984. *State Apparatus: Structures and Language of
Legitimacy*. Boston: Allen and Unwin. Review and critical assessment of eigh-
teen different theories of the state.

Coole, Diana. 1990. "Feminism and Politics," pp. 24–40 in Adrian Leftuich, ed.,
New Developments in Political Science. Hantis, England; and Brookfield, Vermont:
Edgar Elgar and Gower Publications. Argues that feminism allows for understanding of gender relations and the dominance of men, especially in the study
of politics.

Cullenberg, Stephen. 1999. "New Marxism, Old Institutionalism." Paper prepared
for the Howard Sherman Festschrift Conference, University of California,
Riverside, February 13. A response to criticisms of classical Marxism in which
the outline of a "new" Marxism is based on institutionalist thought derived
from Althusser, Hindess and Hirst, and Resnick and Wolff along with the contributions of Howard Sherman.

Deutsch, Karl W. 1986. "State Functions and the Futures of the State." *International
Political Science Review* 7:209–222. Includes an analysis of twelve types of states.

Dugger, William M., and Howard J. Sherman. 1994. "Comparison of Marxism and
Institutionalism." *Journal of Economic Issues* 27 (March):101–127. Identifies common ground in Marxism and institutionalism while acknowledging different
perspectives in each paradigm.

Easton, David. 1981. "The Political System Besieged by the State." *Political Theory*
9 (August):303–325. An appraisal of Poulantzas's conception of the state and a
defense of systems theory.

Engels, Frederick. n.d.(1884). *Origin of the Family, Private Property, and the State*.
New York: International Publishers. Departing from a critical assessment of the
anthropologist Lewis H. Morgan, elaborates an understanding of how society
has evolved from the family and become dependent on the state, especially under capitalism.

Esping-Andersen, Gosta, Roger Friedland, and Erik Olin Wright. 1976. "Modes of
Class Struggle and the Capitalist State." *Kapitalistate* 4–5 (Summer):186–220. A
critical examination of various theories of the state, with particular attention to
the role of classes and class struggle within the state.

Evans, Peter, Dietrich Rueschemeyer, and Theda Skocpol, eds. 1985. *Bringing the
State Back In*. Cambridge, England: Cambridge University Press. Gives renewed attention to the state in contemporary social science.

Ferguson, Kathy E. 1983. "Feminism and Bureaucratic Discourse." *New Political Science* 2 (Spring):53–71. Distinguishes between liberal and radical feminism in a criticism of the bureaucratization of society.

Fine, Ben, and Laurence Harris. 1979. *Re-Reading Capital: A Marxist Debate.* London: Macmillan. An analysis of state monopoly capitalism that transcends the limitations of the dominant Leninist work in this area and shows that state intervention can be a mediated process on behalf of monopoly capital and that monopoly capital as a stage can be distinguishable from state monopoly capitalism.

Fishlow, Albert. 1990. "The Latin American State." *Journal of Economic Perspectives* 4 (Summer):61–74. Argues that the state has played a significant role in development and will continue to exercise influence in the transformation of Latin America.

Fontvieille, Louis. 1991. "Long Cycle Theory: Dialectical and Historical Analysis." *Review* 14 (Spring):233–261. A useful although disjointed discussion of long-cycle theory and its application to an understanding of the failure of economists to give answers.

Gilbert, Alan. 1981. "Marx and the State," pp. 220–238 in his *Marx's Politics: Communists and Citizens.* New Brunswick, N.J.: Rutgers University Press. Discusses the development in Marx's writings of a new theory of the capitalist state as characterized by an independent bureaucracy "which soars above society as an alienated expression of its perverted common power" and "an instrument of violence which serves one class at the expense of others" (233).

Gold, David A., Clarence Y. H. Lo, and Erik Olin Wright. 1975. "Recent Developments in Marxist Theories of the Capitalist State." *Monthly Review* 27 (October): 29–43. An overview of approaches to understanding the capitalist state.

González Casanova, Pablo. 1988. "The Theory of the State and Today's World." *Socialism in the World* 11 (66):3–25. Examines various theories of the state: as power politics, as class struggle, as decolonization, as apparatus of the state, as instrument of free forces, as welfare state, as sovereignty of the people, and as hegemomic coalition. Turns briefly to contemporary liberalism, Marxism, and revolutionary nationalism to assess these theories.

Gordon, David M. 1991. "Inside and Outside the Long Swing: The Endogeneity/Exogeneity Debate and the Social Structures of Accumulation Approach." *Review* 14 (Spring):263–312. Examines the question of whether the long economic swings in capitalist economies are the consequence of self-generating economic dynamics. Argues for an alternative model based on social structures of accumulation.

Gramsci, Antonio. 1971. *Selections from the Prison Notebooks of Antonio Gramsci.* New York: International Publishers. Edited by Quintin Hoare and Geofrey Nowell Smith.

Grant, Wyn, ed. 1985. *The Political Economy of Corporatism.* New York: St. Martin's Press. Criticizes past and present thinking on corporatism.

Gulalp, Haldun. 1987. "Capital Accumulation, Classes and the Relative Autonomy of the State." *Science and Society* 51 (Fall):287–313. An excellent critical assessment of the question of relative state autonomy.

Gunnell, John G. 1991. "In Search of the State: Political Science as an Emerging Discipline," pp. 123–161 in P. Wagner, B. Whittrock, and R. Riley, eds., *Discourses on Society*. Dordrecht, The Netherlands, and Boston: Kluwer Academic Publishers. Examines theories of the origins of the state in theory and concept in nineteenth-century political science to throw light on current debates about the state.

Hall, Stuart. 1977. "Re-Thinking the 'Base-and-Superstructure' Metaphor," pp. 43–71 in Jon Bloomfield, ed., *Papers on Class, Hegemony and Party: The Communist University of London*. London: Lawrence and Wishart. A reexamination of the distinction between base and superstructure in the writings of Marx and Engels and those of Gramsci and Althusser.

Hancock, M. Donald. 1983. "Comparative Public Policy: An Assessment," pp. 283–307 in Ada W. Finifler, ed., *Political Science: The State of the Discipline*. Washington, D.C.: American Political Science Review. A comprehensive overview of the literature on comparative public policy studies, noting the diversity in scope, methods, and major research themes.

Hartmann, Heidi I. 1979. "The Unhappy Marriage of Marxism and Feminism: Towards a More Progressive Union." *Capitalism and Class* 8 (Summer):1–33. Argues for combining patriarchy and capitalism in an analysis of the role of women in society and suggests that feminism has been subordinated to Marxism.

Hegel, Georg. 1974 (1821). "Philosophy of Right and Law," partially reprinted, pp. 256–313, in Frederick G. Weiss, ed., *Hegel: The Essential Writings*. New York: Harper and Row. Useful for his understanding of the state, which provoked Marx in a criticism.

Hinkelammert, Franz J. 1995. "Our Project for the New Society in Latin America: The Regulating Role of the State and Problems of Self-Regulation in the Market," pp. 12–27 in Susanne Jonas and Edward J. McCaughan, eds., *Latin America Faces the Twenty-First Century: Reconstructing a Social Justice Agenda*. Boulder: Westview Press. Argues that the state has been restructured through demands to repay external debt and privatization of state enterprise internally.

Hirsch, Joachim. 1978. "The State Apparatus and Social Reproduction: Elements of a Theory of the Bourgeois State," pp. 57–107 in John Holloway and Sol Picciotto, eds., *State and Capital: A Marxist Debate*. London: Edward Arnold. Argues that no theory of the state in the phase of late capitalism and capitalist crisis has yet been fully developed.

Jessop, Bob. 1977. "Recent Theories of the Capitalist State." *Cambridge Journal of Economics* 1 (December):353–373. Identifies six conceptions of the state in the Marxist literature.

_____. 1982. *The Capitalist State*. Oxford, England: Martin Robertson. Builds on an essay (Jessup 1977) and reviews the literature on theories of the state, including attention to instrumentalism as well as debates between neo-Ricardians and fundamentalist theorists over state intervention; the Italian theorists; and American contributions.

_____. 1990. *State Theory: Putting Capitalist States in Their Place*. University Park: Pennsylvania State University Press. A collection of essays, some previously published, some revised, and some newly formulated, that constitutes an invaluable overview of theories of the capitalist state.

Jordan, Bill. 1985. *The State: Authority and Autonomy.* Oxford, England: Basil Blackwell. See especially Chapter 1, "Definitions, Methods, and Arguments."

Keane, John, ed. 1988. *Civil Society and the State: New European Perspectives.* London and New York: Verso. Explores the theoretical relationship of state and civil society.

Kesselman, Mark. 1982. "Socialist Pedagogy." *New Political Science* 9–10 (Summer-Fall):113–136. A critical examination of themes relevant to Marxism, with attention to the state, democracy, and socialism. Turns to Gramsci and others in an effort to resolve the lack of systematic political analysis in Marx's thought.

Krasner, Stephen D. 1988. "Sovereignty: An International Perspective." *Comparative Political Studies* 21 (April):66–94. Reprinted in Caporaso (1989: 69–96). Argues for an institutional as opposed to a utilitarian or functionalist perspective, asserting that the sovereign state was chosen long ago as the fundamental form of political organization.

Lehmbruch, Gerhard. 1977. "Liberal Corporatism and Party Governance." *Comparative Political Studies* 10:91–126. Ties corporatism to the role of political parties and their participation in government.

Lenin, V. I. 1932. *State and Revolution.* New York: International Publishers. A synthesis and polemic on the evolution of the state, with an attack on Kautsky.

MacIver, R. M. 1926. *The Modern State.* Oxford, England: Oxford University Press. Identifies and assesses seven conceptions of the state found in the traditional literature.

MacKinnon, Catharine A. 1983. "Feminism, Marxism, Method, and the State: An Agenda for Theory," pp. 227–256 in Elizabeth Abel and Emily K. Abel, eds., *The Signs Reader: Women, Gender and Scholarship.* Chicago: University of Chicago Press. A prelude to her 1989 work on the state and feminist theory.

_____. 1989. *Toward a Feminist Theory of the State.* Cambridge: Harvard University Press. Seeks an understanding of the state from a feminist perspective independent of Marxism.

Mann, Michael. 1986. *The Sources of Social Power: A History of Power from the Beginning to A.D. 1760.* Cambridge, England: Cambridge University Press. The first volume of a projected three-volume history of power relations in human societies. Argues that "societies are constituted of multiple overlapping and intersecting sociospatial networks of power" (1).

Marx, Karl. 1966 (1891). *Critique of the Gotha Programme.* New York: International Publishers. The subtitle, "Marginal Notes to the Programme of the German Workers' Party," reveals the intent to refine and contest concepts and phrases, identifying origins and contending with erroneous usages of the notions of the state and class struggle.

_____. 1974 (1848). *The Revolutions of 1848.* New York: Vintage Books.

_____. 1975 (1843). *Contribution to the Critique of Hegel's* Philosophy of Law *(Collected Works,* Vol. 3.). New York: International Publishers. A close critical assessment of the Hegelian conception of the state. Also under the title "Critique of Hegel's Doctrine of the State" in Karl Marx, *Early Writings*. Edited by Lucio Colletti. New York: Vintage Books.

Marx, Karl, and Frederick Engels. 1970 (1846). *The German Ideology*. New York: International Publishers. Edited by C. J. Arthur. An early text; includes a conceptualization of the state.

Melman, Seymour. 1991. "Military State Capitalism." *The Nation* 252 (May 20):664. Distinguishes between state capitalism and military state capitalism, offers a characterization of capitalism itself, and compares top managers in U.S. and Soviet industry in terms of decisionmaking power.

Miliband, Ralph. 1969. *The State in Capitalist Society: An Analysis of the Western System of Power*. New York: Basic Books. A somewhat traditional Marxist view of the state, arguing that the state is an instrumental force serving the interests of the ruling class.

Mitchell, Seymour. 1991. "The Limits of the State: Beyond Statist Approaches and Their Critics." *American Political Science Review* 85 (March):77–96. A useful review and critique of mainstream approaches to the state in American political science.

Nettl, J. P. 1968. "The State as Conceptual Variable." *World Politics* 20:559–592. A rebuttal to political scientists such as Almond and Easton who had abandoned the concept of state.

North, Douglass C. 1981. *Structure and Change in Economic History*. New York: W. W. Norton. Presents a framework for the study of central issues in economic history. Works toward a theory of institutional change and contends with neoclassical and Marxist theory.

O'Connor, James. 1973. *The Fiscal Crisis of the State*. New York: St. Martin's Press. Analyzes contradictions in the accumulation process and the internal structures of the state.

_____. 1984. *Accumulation Crisis*. Oxford, England: Basil Blackwell. Attributes the crisis of state in part to individualism and individual demands, needs, and ideologies in the U.S. capitalist system.

O'Donnell, Guillermo. 1979. "Tensions in the Bureaucratic Authoritarian State and the Question of Democracy," pp. 285–318 in David Collier, ed., *The New Authoritarianism in Latin America*. Princeton: Princeton University Press. Sets forth how his thesis on the bureaucratic state complements representative democracy.

_____. 1988. *Bureaucratic Authoritarianism: Argentina, 1966–1973, in Comparative Perspective*. Berkeley: University of California Press. The theory of this form of authoritarianism is understood through an analysis of military rule and the strong role of the state in Argentina from 1966 to 1973.

Offe, Claus. 1972. "Advanced Capitalism and the Welfare State." *Politics and Society* 2 (Summer):479–488. Examines the structural mechanisms that affect class relationships within the state.

_____. 1985. *Disorganized Capitalism: Contemporary Transformations of Work and Politics*. Cambridge, Mass.: MIT Press. Argues that the labor market is "the most significant feature of capitalist social structures" (2) and examines this proposition in the context of "institutionalized political authority" as an aspect of state theory.

Oppenheimer, Franz. 1975 (1914). *The State*. New York: Free Life Editions. An early effort to conceptualize the state.

Ostrom, Elinor. 1990. "Rational Choice Theory and Institutions." *American Political Science Review* 85:237–243. A review and sympathetic critique of the literature on rational choice and its compatibility with an institutional approach.

Pahl, R. E., and J. T. Winkler. 1976. "Corporatism in Britain," pp. 5–24 in *The Corporate State—Reality or Myth*? London: Centre for Studies in Social Policy.

Panitch, Leo. 1980. "Recent Theorization on Corporatism: Reflections on a Growth Industry." *British Journal of Sociology* 31:159–187. A review and critical synthesis of the literature on corporatism.

Parkin, Frank. 1979. "Social Cleavages and the Forms of State," pp. 119–142 in his *Marxism and Class Theory: A Bourgeois Critique*. London: Tavistock. Criticizes both Weber and Marx and shows the limitations of contemporary mainstream and alternative perspectives.

Patnaik, Prabhat. 1995. "A Note on the Political Economy of the 'Retreat of the State,'" pp. 194–210 in his *Whatever Happened to Imperialism and Other Essays*. New Delhi: Tulika. Critical examination of the impacts of neoliberal privatization of state-owned enterprise or production units.

Peterson, V. Spike, ed. 1992. *Gendered States: Feminist (Re)Visions of International Relations Theory*. Boulder: Lynne Rienner. A feminist perspective serves to criticize prevailing state theory.

Poulantzas, Nicos. 1978. *State, Power, Socialism*. London: New Left Books. Outlines a theory on the relative autonomy of the state.

Przeworski, Adam, and Michael Wallerstein. 1988. "Structural Dependence of the State on Capital." *American Political Science Review* 82 (March):11–29. Examines the social democratic criticism of the market and the role of the state. Argues that "the state is not structurally dependent on capital in the sense that virtually any distribution of consumption between wage earners and shareholders is compatible with continual private investment" (24).

Rosenau, James N. 1988. "The State in an Era of Cascading Politics: Wavering Concept, Widening Competence, Withering Colossus, or Weathering Change?" *Comparative Political Studies* 21 (April):13–44. Reprinted in Caporaso (1989: 17–48). Synthesis of diverse perspectives of the state with emphasis on "the norms governing relationships, the habits of voluntary and coerced compliance, and the practices of cooperation through which large numbers of people form and sustain a collectivity that possesses sovereign authority" (15).

Rothenberg, Mel. 1995. "Lenin on the State." *Science and Society* 59 (Fall 1995): 418–436. A useful analysis of Lenin's theory of state.

Santos, Boaventura de Sousa. 1980. "Law and Community: The Changing Nature of State Power in Late Capitalism." *International Journal of the Sociology of the Law* (8):379–397. Analysis of the theoretical model of legal domination in the capitalist state and assessment of the impact of reforms on the nature of state power.

Sassoon, Anne Showstack. 1980. *Gramsci's Politics*. Minneapolis: University of Minnesota Press.

Schmitter, Philippe C. 1979. "Still the Century of Corporatism?" pp. 7–75 in G. Lehmbruch and P. C. Schmitter, eds., *Trends Toward Corporatist Intermediation*.

London: Sage Publications. Reprinted from *Review of Politics* 36 (1976):85–131. An early exposition of the meaning of corporatism.

_____. 1985. "Neo-Corporatism and the State," pp. 32–62 in Wyn Grant, ed., *The Political Economy of Corporatism*. New York: St. Martin's. Elaboration on his thesis regarding corporatism and the modern state.

_____. 1989. "Corporatism Is Dead! Long Live Corporatism!" *Government and Opposition* 24 (Winter):54–73. A provocative retrospective on corporatism and its strengths and weaknesses as theory.

Shaw, Martin. 1985. "Marxism, the State and Politics," pp. 246–268 in his *Marxist Sociology Revisited: Critical Assessments*. New York: Macmillan. Examines central issues raised by classical Marxist analysis on the state and comments on the extent to which they have been resolved.

Silva, Eduardo. 1993. "Capitalist Coalitions, the State, and Neoliberal Economic Restructuring Chile, 1973–88." *World Politics* 45 (July):526–529. A useful case study that focuses on domestic capitalists (business owners and landowners) and their influence on state policy under the authoritarian Pinochet regime.

Simon, Roger. 1982. *Gramsci's Political Thought: An Introduction*. London: Lawrence and Wishart. A useful synthesis of the principal concepts in the thought of Antonio Gramsci.

Titus, C. H. 1931. "A Nomenclature in Political Science." *American Political Science Review* 25:45–60. A survey of definitions of the state.

Willoughby, W. W. 1896. *An Examination of the Nature of the State*. Norwood, N.J.: Norwood Press. Examines the state as a principal focus of study in political science.

Wolfe, Alan. 1974. "New Directions in the Marxist Theory of Politics." *Politics and Society* 4:131–160. A synthesis of state theories in Marxism.

5

THEORIES OF IMPERIALISM

"Imperialism" derives from the Latin word *imperium*, "command, supreme authority." Roman imperialism contrasted with modern imperialism in that it reinforced the traditional local ruling hierarchies instead of generating a new basis of power among subject populations (Miles 1990). In France during the 1830s, the term imperialism was associated with those who wished to restore the Napoleonic empire, and after 1848 it was used pejoratively to describe the pretensions of Napoleon Bonaparte. During the 1870s, it was employed as a characterization of the practices of expanding British colonialism, and by the end of the century it was commonplace in descriptions of the dominance of one nation over another (Cohen 1973: 10–11).

Joseph Schumpeter (1955 [1919]) examined the imperialist experiences of past centuries from ancient Egypt to the Arabs to Louis XIV and determined that imperialism was based on powerful drives and personal whims that capitalism fundamentally opposed. He believed that capitalism represented a potential new order of peace and compromise and that imperialism would ultimately be undermined by democracy and competition. In its broad meaning, imperialism is "the domination by one country or group of people over others, in ways that benefit the former usually at the expense of the latter" (Griffin and Gurley 1985: 1091).

The traditional conception of imperialism was tied to mercantile and early industrial capitalism. Harry Magdoff (1970) identified three periods in the history of traditional imperialism: from the late 1400s to the mid-1600s, characterized by European exploitation of the resources of peripheral areas, such as gold and silver in the Americas; 1650 to 1770, the era of slave labor and the search for commodities that would benefit England, Spain, and the other European powers; and the 1770s to the 1870s, when England sought new markets in Africa and Asia after losing most of its American colonies. This traditional conception was supplanted by that of a "new" imperialism characterized by intense rivalry

175

among the advanced European nations (see Koebner and Schmidt 1964 and also O'Connor 1970 for a useful definition). Aspects of this transition include the link between the industrial capitalism of the late eighteenth century in Britain and primitive accumulation, the division of labor between primary-producing underdeveloped states and industrialized states, U.S. and European expansion at the end of the nineteenth century, the European origin of export capital, the role of the large firm as an accumulator of capital, the relationship between neocolonialism and the old colonialism, and the similarity of Soviet imperialism to capitalist imperialism (Barratt Brown 1974).

Lenin, influenced by the English liberal John Atkinson Hobson and sharing with Rudolf Hilferding and Nicolai Bukharin what has been characterized as a classical Marxist understanding of imperialism, emphasized the merging of industrial and bank capital in finance capital, the expansion of capital exports, and the increase in military production and militarism. Others such as Bill Warren (1980) have stressed the penetration of capitalism into backward areas and the imposition of the capitalist mode of production on precapitalist or early capitalist systems. Magdoff (1969) saw imperialism as involving the penetration of the United States (the hegemony of which from 1946 to 1967 ensured its status as the dominant imperialist power) into Western Europe. Magdoff's colleague Paul Sweezy incorporated this conception into later (1989) analysis of U.S. imperialism, while together in their journal *Monthly Review* they interpreted the rapidly changing events of the early 1990s in terms of globalization at the center and the periphery of the world order.

Imperialism is sometimes thought of as formal or informal—that is, as involving direct control by a dominant country over a subordinate one, as in the case of colonialism, or control exercised less directly, as in situations in which countries have broken free of their imperial ties with European countries but remained under their economic domination, primarily through trade relations.

Hobson (1965 [1902]) distinguished "early imperialism" from "modern imperialism," the former motivated by the slave trade and lust for treasures, the latter by exploitation of "lower races": "The change is a twofold one: the legal status of slaves has given place to that of wage-labourer, and the most profitable use of the hired labour of inferior races is to employ them in developing the resources of their own lands under white control for white men's profit" (249).

An important historical explanation of the early experience of empire and mercantilism was based on the dominance of Spain, with its control of precious metals in South America, and, to a lesser extent, Portugal, through its commercial points of contact in Africa, Asia, and Latin America and its trade in spices, slaves, and ivory. Portuguese hegemony succumbed to that of Spain when the two monarchies were unified under Spanish control in the late sixteenth and early seventeenth centuries. As Spain and Portugal lost control over maritime traffic, the Dutch, then the English, and ultimately the French expanded their influence, moving slaves from Africa to the Americas, sugar from the Americas to Europe, and manufactured goods from Europe to Africa. During the eighteenth century, the influence of these nations extended to Asia, and in the nineteenth century they made territorial gains in Africa. About 1800, the mercantile period gave way to the emerging epoch of capital development (Brewer 1990 [1980]: 5); Britain became the dominant colonial power, with India as the crucial element in its empire and the industrial revolution serving as the underpinning of a new era promising mechanized production and the abolition of poverty.

In a revision of this interpretation, Giovanni Arrighi focused on two "genealogies of modern capitalism," the first involving a succession of world hegemonies and the second "a succession of systemic cycles of accumulation" (1994: 84). ("World hegemony" here refers to the power of a state over a system of sovereign states.)

The new imperialism was associated with the industrial revolution and, in particular, with the European push toward manufacturing, the demand for raw materials from the periphery, and the need to find markets for a surplus of production. Britain led the way in this era, given its dominance over world markets and its access to the raw materials of its vast empire, although the late nineteenth century saw a shift of influence to the United States in Latin America.

All these expansions produced a growing disparity between the advancing industrial and capitalist nations at the core of the international capitalist system and the undeveloped and backward nations at the periphery. Explanations of this disparity have absorbed the attention of many thinkers from Marx to the present day (see Rosen and Kurth 1974 and Rhodes 1970), and it is the purpose of this chapter to delineate the various lines of thought.

TRADITIONAL AND CLASSICAL IMPERIALISM

The thinking of the classical Marxists was largely inspired by the European experience. A rudimentary framework for a theory of imperialism is found in Marx's work. (See Table 5.1.)

Marx

Marx did not use the term imperialism, and later Marxist writers do not base their understandings of imperialism on his writings (Brewer 1990

TABLE 5.1   Theories of Imperialism

Theorist	Theory Emphasis	Strengths	Weaknesses
Hobson	Domestic underconsumption	Focused on financiers	Descriptive, lacking analysis
Hilferding	Finance capital	Thorough analysis of joint stock companies; major Marxist contribution to a theory of imperialism	Dated analysis, perhaps exaggerated emphasis on role of banks
Luxemburg	Capital accumulation and penetration in primitive societies	Anticipated negative impact of capitalism on noncapitalist nations	Undue attention to underconsumption rather than profit; Bukharin labeled it "voluntarist"
Bukharin	Monopolies of banks and corporations in advanced stages of capitalism	Combined anaylsis of internationalization of capitalist relations of production with formations of blocs of finance capital	Stressed the contradictions of capitalist modernization process rather than its imperfect and uneven development
Lenin	Imperialism as monopoly and highest stage of capitalism	Clearly articulated	Eclectic, polemical, and political
Kautsky	Peaceful resolution by capitalist class	Advocated theory of ultra imperialism	Optimism on progressive nature of capitalism
Schumpeter	Withering away of imperialism	Provided a historical context for showing that imperialism is based on interests of ruling classes	Misguided emphasis on political imperialism as well as its demise

[1980]: 25). Marx and Engels in the *Manifesto of the Communist Party,* however, came close to a conception of imperialism in their reference to the need of the bourgeoisie for a constantly expanding international market: "It must nestle everywhere, settle everywhere, establish connections everywhere. . . . In place of the old local and national seclusion and self-sufficiency, we have intercourse in every direction, universal inter-dependence of nations" (Marx and Engels 1958 [1848]: 37).

Noting that Marxism has become a "weapon" with which the underdeveloped Third World attacks the European vision of the developed and industrialized capitalist world, Shlomo Avineri suggests that Marx's own thinking on the non-European world has been largely misunderstood and that an early conception of imperialism can be discerned in his thinking. Avineri suggests that Marx saw capitalism as a necessary step toward development and that his views on European capitalist expansionism must therefore be examined carefully. In particular, Marx's attention to the Asiatic mode of production extends the analysis on primitive accumulation in the first volume of *Capital,* where he traced the path of Western European capitalism out of feudalism.

Avineri suggests that Marx worked out a sophisticated understanding of the Asiatic mode of production based on the absence of private property in India and the combination of agriculture and home manufacture in China and India: "Both Indian and Chinese villages are based on a peculiar union of agriculture and manufacture, which makes each village into a self-sufficient and self-contained microcosm, autonomous, autarchic, inward-working, cut off from the outside world and hence capable of serving as the basis of conservatism, immobility and stagnation" (1976: 240). Marx seemed to be suggesting here that Asian society possessed no internal mechanisms of change as had evolved in European society—that the Asiatic mode of production did not create conditions for its overthrow and therefore an outside force in the form of English colonialism and imperialism was necessary to destroy the Asiatic mode and establish the foundation for Western capitalism. Avineri notes that the process of European expansion and the integration of China and India into the world market leads to a two-way process in which not only does Asia become dependent on Europe, but Europe becomes dependent on Asia. The control of Indian markets by British capital, for instance, was achieved at the high cost of protective duties and the necessity of providing India with an irrigation and communications system and a network of railways. Furthermore, the necessary flow of capital from the metropolis to the colonies created a negative balance of payments.

Avineri argues that this shows "Marx's sophisticated understanding of the dialectics of historical development" and points to "the ultimate contradiction in colonial trade . . . the dialectical analysis of realizing the in-

ternal structural tensions of capitalist society" (246–247). "When Marx
later discusses the overall economic benefits Britain is reaping from
India, he comes out with a far more complex theory than such a simplistic view of 'exploitation.'" For example, although British penetration may
have exploited Indian labor and allowed a small segment of the British
working class to benefit, when one distinguishes "between the benefits
derived from India by the British economy and society as a whole, and
the specific benefits derived from India by individuals and groups in
England . . . Marx argues that as far as the British public is concerned, the
cost of administering India exceeds the income derived from it" (247). In
other words, incomes from India were less than the cost of the administration that collected them, so that "it was Britain, and not only India,
that was being exploited for the benefit of the English ruling classes
through British rule in India" (248). Avineri concludes that it is unfortu-
nate that Marx was unable to incorporate these understandings of non-
European society into his universal framework and that Marxist interpretations of Asian history have been misguided, for example, by the belief
that revolution requires the mobilization of the underdeveloped world
against the industrialized nations. Michael Howard and J. E. King suggest that Marx and Engels were unable to focus on the link between economic crisis, the concentration of capital, and the drive toward imperialism (1989, 1: 91).

Kenzo Mohri (1979) reminds us that for Marx in the 1840s and 1850s
British capital would have a revolutionary role in the destruction of the
old society, but after 1860 he "became well aware that the destruction of
the old society would not necessarily give rise to the material conditions
for a new society" (40). He believed that Ireland's poverty was due to
English exploitation. Every effort to industrialize the country ended in a
return to agriculture, because Ireland was unable to withstand English
competition. The solution, then, was tariffs and protection against British
imports, and he envisioned a national rather than a socialist revolution in
Ireland. Jie-hyun Lim (1992) has elaborated on this perception of the Irish
question and argued that a rudimentary understanding of imperialism allowed Marx to transcend an earlier Eurocentric and historical-materialist
conception of the nation.

Marx understood that whereas merchant capital exploits without transforming, industrial capital undermines vestiges of precapitalism while
transforming. This process was especially evident in feudal Europe.
Indian society, in contrast, was based on the Asiatic mode of production,
characterized by communal village agriculture, handicrafts, a hereditary
division of labor, and an absence of private property in land. In India, the
surplus was absorbed not by the landlords but by the state through taxation. Anthony Brewer has shown that Marx's emphasis on the Asiatic

mode has been questioned by Marxists who tend to ascribe social ills to foreign oppressors and see the nation as progressive (1990 [1980]: 56). Thus, different modes of production helped to produce the different patterns of development in Europe and Asia.

We are reminded that after Marx's death in 1883 Engels studied the imperialism of his times and concluded that although domestic capitalist crises could be temporarily resolved, "they would only make the final collapse of capitalism more certain in the long run—for they accelerated the processes of capitalist development, including the concentration of capital" (Griffin and Gurley 1985: 1095).

Hobson

John Atkinson Hobson gave an economic interpretation to imperialism, and his work is believed to have influenced those who followed, including Lenin. The outlines of his writing on the subject took shape in the middle 1880s, and his major book, *Imperialism*, was published in 1902. The book begins with a definition of imperialism that contrasts it with nationalism. It is divided into two parts, the first on the economics and the second on the politics of imperialism.

Political union on the basis of nationality was a major force in the nineteenth century, followed by a trend toward federations of states and later by the drive to divide up territory into colonies and establish empires. Nationalism began as a territorial and dynastic phenomenon and evolved with "racial, linguistic, and economic solidarity" (1965 [1902]: 5). Internationalism consisted of union among "powerful self-respecting nationalities" (10). Colonialism involved an "overflow of nationality" and the transplanting of "civilization" (7). In the scramble for Africa and Asia, for example, imperialism "became a constant agent of menace and of perturbation to the peace and progress of mankind" (12) and undermined any movement toward internationalism, because hostility and national self-consciousness emanated from competition among empires.

Hobson traced British imperialism to the period 1870–1885 with the partition of African lands. He briefly examined German, U.S., French, Italian, Portuguese, Spanish, Belgian, and Russian imperial designs. He characterized the new imperialism as distinct from the colonization of sparsely peopled lands in temperate zones where whites carried with them the civilization of the mother country. He examined the "commercial value of imperialism" and argued for the expansion of the home market, believing that the loss of foreign markets would be less than expected. He held that imperial expansion brought no value in trade with the colonies: "The distinctive feature of modern Imperialism, from the commercial standpoint, is that it adds to our empire tropical and subtropical regions with which our trade is small, precarious and unprogressive. . . . As for the territories acquired under the new imperialism . . . no serious attempt to regard them as satisfactory business assets is possible" (38). He noted that other industrialized nations had not become involved in developing the tropical or subtropical countries.

Hobson argued that imperialism was the consequence of the drive for private gain of a small group of capitalists and their special interests: "It has been good business for certain classes and certain trades within the nation" (46). Imperialism was reflected in the "growing cosmopolitanism of capital" (51), its influence being particularly pervasive among financiers and finance capital: "The final determination rests with the financial power. The direct influence exercised by great financial houses in 'high politics' is supported by the control which they exercise over the body of public opinion" (59–60).

Hobson showed that other industrialized nations were eager to become involved in imperialism and therefore Britain should not weaken itself politically or financially through further expansion. Such competition made it "more and more difficult to dispose of the full surplus of our manufactures at a profit" (72). In particular, U.S. manufactures were saturated with capital and could absorb no more. One after another, they sought refuge from the waste of competition in "combines" that secured a measure of profitable peace. They faced two alternatives: One was employing full production and using the savings to increase business capital while regulating output and prices for the home market and at the same time dumping surplus goods in the foreign markets; the other was employing savings in investments outside the country, first repaying their debt to Britain and other nations for the establishment of infrastructure. But it was the direct control over politics by its business owners that led the United States to the new imperialism:

> American imperialism was the natural product of the economic pressure of a sudden advance of capitalism which could not find occupation at home and needed foreign markets for goods and for investments. . . . Everywhere appear excessive powers of production, excessive capital in search of investment. . . . It is this economic condition of affairs that forms the tap root of Imperialism. (78–79)

Financial imperialism involved the manipulation of government by private interests to secure for them economic gains outside their country: "The capitalist-imperialist forces, the pivot of financial policy . . . must be regarded as the true determinant in the interpretation of actual policy" (96). "The economic root of imperialism is the desire of strong organized industrial and financial interests to secure and develop at the public expense and by the public force private markets for their surplus goods and their surplus capital. War, militarism, and a 'spirited foreign policy' are the necessary means to this end" (106). Hobson went on to discuss public debts as a means of escaping taxation on income and property. He argued that Britain and the United States would both "succumb more and more to the money lending classes dressed as imperialists and patriots" (109).

Hobson contrasted the democratic tendencies in English politics with the political nature of imperialism abroad: "We have taken upon ourselves in these little islands the responsibility of governing huge aggregations of lower races in all parts of the world by methods which are antithetical to the methods of government which we most value for ourselves" (117). The new imperialism had spread to tropical and subtropical areas that the English were unable to colonize, an extension of British "despotism, far outbalancing the progress in population and in practical freedom attained by our few democratic colonies" (124). He contrasted this new imperialism with the older colonialism, which seemed to him to have worked well:

> Modern British colonialism has been no drain upon our material and moral resources, because it has made for the creation of free white democracies, a policy of informal federation, of decentralisation, involving no appreciable strain upon the governmental faculties of Great Britain. Such federation, whether it remains informal with the slight attachment of imperial sovereignty which now exists or voluntarily takes some more formal shape, political or financial, may well be regarded as a source of strength, political and military. (125)

He made clear the contradiction: "Imperialism is the very antithesis of this free, wholesome colonial connection, making, as it ever does, for greater complications of foreign policy, greater centralization of power, and a congestion of business which ever threatens to absorb and overtax the capacity of parliamentary government" (125). Competing cliques of business owners usurp the "authority and voice of the people, use the public resources to push their private interests, and spend the blood and money of the people in this vast and disastrous military game, feigning national antagonisms which have no basis in reality" (127). "Imperialism . . . implies militarism now and ruinous wars in the future" (130).

Hobson showed how military expenditure conflicted with the need for social reform and how imperialism as public policy undermined responses to other problems at home. Indeed, war distracted attention from those problems: "It has become a commonplace of history how governments use national animosities, foreign wars and the glamour of empire-making, in order to bemuse the popular mind and divert rising resentment against domestic abuses" (142). He went on to discuss imperialism and popular government and the contradiction between them: "Imperialism poisons the springs of democracy in the mind and character of the people. . . . The spirit, the policy, and the methods of imperialism are hostile to the institutions of popular self-government, favouring forms of political tyranny and social authority which are the deadly enemies of effective liberty and equality" (150, 152).

He examined moral and sentimental factors, for example, condemning the influence of imperialism on education:

> To capture the childhood of the country, to mechanize its free play into the routine of military drill, to cultivate the savage survivals of combativeness, to poison its early understanding of history by false ideals and pseudo-heroes, and by a consequent disparagement and neglect of the really vital and elevating lessons of the past, to establish a "geocentric" view of the moral universe in which the interests of humanity are subordinated to that of a country . . . is as foul an abuse of education as it is possible to conceive. (217)

Imperialism pervades not only the school but the party, the press, and the church and molds public policy with false idealization "of those primitive lusts of struggle, domination and acquisitiveness" and "weaves thin convenient theories of a race struggle for the subjugation of the inferior peoples, in order that we, the Anglo-Saxon, may take their lands and live upon their labours" (221–222).

Since imperialism evolved in the form of rents, monopoly profits, and unearned or excessive income having no relation to production, Hobson advocated a more equal distribution of income so as to eliminate what he called excessive saving and ensure full employment for capital and labor at home: "The only safety of nations lies in removing the unearned increments of income from the possessing classes, and adding them to the wage-income of the working classes or to the public income, in order that they may be spent in raising the standard of consumption" (89). He saw trade unionism and socialism as the only enemies of imperialism. He argued that a serious attempt should be made to revive agriculture and return people to the soil through land reform and also through taxes on imported grain, cattle, and agricultural products. Finally, he looked to some sort of an international council to bring harmony and goodwill to the world.

Prior to Hobson, two "neutral" connotations of imperialism had prevailed, one advocated by those who wanted to keep British settlements under control rather than allow them independence and the other associated with expansionism and control of uncivilized parts of the world (Fieldhouse 1961: 187–188). Hobson's theory of underconsumption or oversaving had appeared earlier in a book by A. F. Mummery, *The Physiology of Industry* (1889), that examined the economic and political sides of imperialism but emphasized the central role of financiers. With the publication of *Imperialism* at the turn of the century, these two elements were elaborated in an economic theory that high levels of foreign investment, spurred on by monopoly or trusts, resulted in excessive savings that would not be necessary if income were redistributed and a political theory that tied foreign investment to imperialist policies.

In developing his thesis of underconsumption or oversaving, Hobson sought to discredit contemporary arguments for the pursuit of imperialist policies. Using aggregate economic and demographic statistics, he demonstrated through a cost-benefit analysis that imperialism was economically inefficient. He also showed that those who advocated imperial expansion as "an outlet" for British emigration were mistaken in that the vast majority of emigrants did not move into regions under direct British imperial control. Another myth that Hobson felt obliged to dismantle was the notion that territory acquired through imperial conquest must be diligently protected lest some other imperialist nation should usurp the benefits of its exploitation. He saw that the amount of trade between the imperialist nations massively outweighed the trade between any single imperialist country and its imperial holdings and therefore argued that there was no economic justification for the high costs associated with sealing off a conquered region from other imperialist interventions.

Hobson's theory of imperialism has been characterized positively for having provided a "material explanation . . . rather than a vulgar, jingoistic or militaristic one" (Kenneth Tarbuck in Bukharin and Luxemburg 1972 [1921 and 1924]: 34) and negatively for its "dogmatic interpretation" (Fieldhouse 1967: 188). One concern is that it "describes what would happen if monopoly grew, or, more generally, if inequality increased, *while other factors remained constant*, which they did not" (Brewer 1990 [1980]: 81). The central problem, however, is its "making capital investment abroad dependent on underconsumption at home" (Lichtheim 1971: 39).

The model will have its predicted effects of recession due to savings only if there is no essential change in methods of production in the economy, interest rates have no effect on the level of savings, and the labor force is limited. It is possible to argue that an excess of savings could depress interest rates, if other things are held constant. This in turn would stimulate investment, which may be viewed as consumption of capital goods. But would a market exist for the consumer goods that are the product of these capital goods? Hobson did not think so and ignored the effects of an injection of funds into the economy brought on by an increase in investment, implicitly assuming that future consumption and investment possibilities were fixed. An increase in the rate of savings may increase output and consumption unless growth is curtailed by limitations on labor and natural resources. Thus, it seems that Hobson was assuming an economy operating at full productive capacity.

But all these complications are unnecessary, for an excess of savings is not required to explain the capitalist compulsion for export markets and investment opportunities. If interest rates fall because of an increase in savings to a level below rates of return on investment abroad, capital will be directed abroad. But capitalist investment is a function not just of savings but also of the expected rate of return, and the effect of the latter may well outweigh that of the former.

Hobson identified financiers and investors as the main beneficiaries of imperialism. He failed to identify their specific interests and vaguely asserted that these lay in turbulence; this rendered his theory capable of explaining any event, however bizarre or irrational, without examining its specifics. Although some critics have dismissed this reference to financial interests as irrelevant, Brewer asserts that "it is precisely the conspiracy of financiers that gives Hobson's theory what explanatory force it has" (1990 [1980]: 84). Brewer, however, is uncertain whether Hobson saw any conflict between financiers and industrialists, although it is clear he envisaged conflict between financiers and the people.

Hilferding

Rudolf Hilferding believed that monopolies would form on a national basis and would require protection through tariffs to achieve a dominant position. This analysis was prevalent during his times; his contribution was "to build it into a Marxist analysis of the rise of finance capital" (Brewer 1990 [1980]: 97). Hilferding concentrated on the centers of finance capital in the advanced industrial countries, but he also commented on their impact on less developed areas of the world. He understood that capitalist expansion was accompanied by force: "Violent methods are of the essence of colonial policy, without which it would lose its capitalist rationale" (Hilferding 1981 [1910]: 319). The export of capital was responsible for this force; as capital spread into precapitalist societies, it destroyed the old social relations and involved all countries in the international capitalist system: "The export of capital, especially since it has assumed the form of industrial and finance capital, has enormously accelerated the overthrow of all the old social relations, and the involvement of all the world in capitalism" (322). Hilferding believed that the penetration of capital into the less developed nations could be beneficial, especially in the early stage of building infrastructure, but because this capital was directed to the extraction of raw materials for export to the industrialized world there could be a drain of profit abroad, resulting in economic and political dependence (330): "Hilferding thus anticipated themes developed by later writers" (Brewer 1990 [1980]: 104).

Industrial and financial capital were unified by finance capital. Representatives of banks served on boards of industrial firms and representatives of the firms sat on bank boards, so that economic, social, and family ties were all evident in the ruling class. The characterization of the new ruling class is reminiscent of the thinking of Hobson: "unified in political affairs under the leadership of the 'magnates of finance capital,' corresponding to a relatively unified and hierarchical economic structure ... [and] a change in its relation to the state, a relation which became much more close and direct" (Brewer 1990 [1980]: 105–106).

Hilferding refrained from using the term imperialism and instead spoke of "protectionist policy" or "colonial policy" or "external policy of finance capital." Imperialism usually meant militarism and expansionism in association with capitalism.

His was, however, the first serious Marxist theory of imperialism, and his major work *Finance Capital* "has proved to be the most influential text in the entire history of Marxist political economy, only excepting *Capital* itself" (Howard and King 1989: 100). Brewer calls Hilferding "the real founder of the classical Marxist theory of imperialism" (1990 [1980]: 108). Without doubt, *Finance Capital* can be viewed as an extension of Marx's project. Its fundamental thesis is that the concentration of capital changes the competitive structure of capitalism and facilitates the emergence of cartel price-fixing schemes. Hilferding examined the concentration of financial capital and the reduction of the number of firms involved in production and development. His theory stressed the collusion of industrial and financial capital in a new form of capital, which he called finance capital, that was mobilized through banks and extended to large enterprises in exchange for shares of stock. He identified three stages in the history of capitalism: usurer capital; industrial capital; and finance capital, the latter characterized by monopoly capital and a shift from competitive to cartel industries. The pursuit of imperialism was inevitable, he argued, as finance capital sought to establish the largest possible territory, to provide protective tariffs to undermine foreign competition, and to exploit outlying areas: "Finance capital, in its maturity, is the highest stage of the concentration of economic and political power in the hands of the capitalist oligarchy. It is the climax of the dictatorship of the magnates of capital" (quoted in Howard and King 1989: 99).

Brewer systematically examines Hilferding's treatment of the theory of money; the rise of the joint stock company, a coalition of capitalists who share the profits and control the firm ("really the first thorough Marxist discussion of this important topic" [1990 (1980): 90]); and monopoly viewed as control through banks (Brewer states that his position was based on the German experience and raises some questions about it). "Hilferding took Marx's separation of capital (finance, industrial, commercial) and showed that finance and industrial capital merged. Finance capital evolves from the fusion of industrial and financial capital" (93).

Paul Sweezy (1942: 269) considered the notion of finance capital as the foundation of imperialism to have been made obsolete by the emergence of the monopoly corporation that was capable of financing its own ventures around the world by drawing on its own surplus rather than on bank capital. Critics such as Michael Barratt Brown (1970) argue not only that bank capital has become less important to imperialism but that Hilferding's emphasis on protectionism to ensure profits for monopoly capital in the world markets has proved misplaced.

Luxemburg

Rosa Luxemburg, a Polish Marxist whose later years were devoted to German socialism as a leader of the left wing of the Social Democratic party, developed a theory of imperialism to explain continuous capital accumulation. A central concern was capital penetration in primitive economies. She identified three phases of capital accumulation: first, the struggle of capital with natural economy in areas where there are primitive peasant communities and common ownership of land or a feudal system or an economic organization oriented to internal demand where there is little surplus production or demand for foreign goods; second, capitalist struggles with a commodity economy; and, third, imperialism: "For capital, the standstill of accumulation means that the development of the productive forces is arrested, and the collapse of capitalism follows inevitably, as an objective historical necessity. This is the reason for the contradictory behavior of capitalism in the final stage of its historical career: imperialism" (Luxemburg 1951 [1913]: 417). Luxemburg understood imperialism as the conversion of surplus into capital and its spread throughout the world economy. In its final phase, capitalism "has adopted such an unbridled character that it puts the whole civilization of mankind in question" (Bukharin and Luxemburg 1972 [1921 and 1924]: 143).

In *The Accumulation of Capital* (1951 [1913]), Luxemburg returned to Marx for an analysis of imperialism and capital accumulation. Her argument centered on what she saw as a flaw in Marx's logic on capitalist commodity production and the system's ability to reach equilibrium. Production is in a sense meaningless unless the surplus value is realized, so that the accumulation cycle can continue and increase the profits of capitalists. For Luxemburg, this raised the question whether the expenditures of capitalists and workers could be sufficient to permit continuous realization of the surplus value generated by expanding commodity production. Capitalism had been growing for more than a century, and Luxemburg looked to historical case studies to bolster her case. Her analysis incorporated a concern with underconsumption, but like Lenin she stressed the export of finance capital via the international loan system, citing the British-American case. "It was no more income (used by Americans to purchase British goods) but rather English capital which was used to push on consumption. The English themselves bought and paid for their own goods which they sent to America and thereby went the pleasure of using these goods" (Luxemburg 1951 [1913]: 423–424). Here, Luxemburg saw the limits of the capitalist market as being set by the income of workers and capitalists, which would limit domestic consumption. Furthermore, she saw international loans as having three functions: converting money or lower-middle-class savings of noncapitalist groups into capital, with money thus becoming a commodity equivalent and a fund for the capitalist class; transforming money capital into productive capital by means of state enterprise such as railroad building and supplying the military; and diverting accumulated capital in the form of bonds from the old capitalist countries to new ones (Luxemburg 1951 [1913]: 420). Her description implies emphasis on dependency.

Here, Luxemburg has been heavily criticized for her supposed failure to discuss how people in noncapitalist nations become consumers without foreign capital. She dealt with this point in her discussion of the transformation of the noncapitalist economy from a natural to a commodity economy. Her case-study-based discussion of the breakdown of the existing social structures and the appropriation of land is penetrating and rings true for those familiar with the contemporary development literature. Somewhat dubious is her faith in peasants' being able to sell all their produce for capital and have any capital left over for purchasing foreign manufactured goods. This is a point seemingly ignored by her critics, who are content with sweeping away her work in favor of Lenin and Hilferding.

Luxemburg's work provides us with a rich discussion of the relation between the state and capital and between militarism and racism, providing a deeper analysis than that of Hobson. Her discussion of militarism and its virtual creation of a new market is relevant to what Seymour Melman (1971) has called the "permanent war economy" of today. Most important, in pointing to the way in which capitalism is thrust on noncapitalist nations it anticipated by decades the need for students of development to look at imperial relations. *The Accumulation of Capital* was, however, severely criticized, and in 1915 she wrote a reply that was eventually published in 1921 as *Anti-Critique* (Bukharin and Luxemburg 1972 [1921 and 1924]). Howard and King (1989) argue that her principal theme, similar to that of Kautsky, was that the evolution of capitalism depended

on the search for noncapitalist markets and this brought about the contradictory transformation of backward economies as advanced industrial
nations competed for territory. Here, "Luxemburg criticizes Marx, and
does so as openly and energetically as any revisionist" (107). She argued
that in volume 2 of *Capital*, Marx essentially employed a stable equilibrium model within a closed system, and she proposed an economic
model in which one department reflected the means of production and
the other the means of consumption, revealing "a deep and fundamental
antagonism between the capacity to consume and the capacity to produce
in a capitalist society, a conflict resulting from the very accumulation of
capital which periodically bursts out in crises and spurs capital on to a
continual extension of the market" (Luxemburg 1951 [1913]: 347). It was
recognition of the contradiction that made a theory of imperialism possible, because Marx's analysis implied that capital accumulation was limitless. "Luxemburg's conception of imperialism is a distinctive one. It does
not depend upon formal colonization, and has little in common with
Hilferding's emphasis on the growth of monopoly or the increasing dominance of the banks" (Howard and King 1989: 111). She argued, first, that
the imperialist phase of capitalist accumulation involved industrialization and capitalist development of the hinterland where capital once realized surplus value and, second, that imperialism was the political expression of capital accumulation involving the competitive struggle for
control of the noncapitalist world and leading to conflicts, the advocacy
of protectionism and abandonment of free trade, and militarism and
expansionism.

The Bolshevik theoretician Nicolai Bukharin argued that Luxemburg's
theory of imperialism implied the harmonious development of capitalism
and that it was "voluntarist" and reminiscent of Hobson's. Howard and
King argue that

> she herself is mistaken in imputing to the capitalist system as a whole the
> goal of expanding human consumption. . . . At the level of the individual
> capitalist she is equally wrong. The capitalist is motivated by profit, not by
> concern for the growth of consumption. . . . Her vigorous attack on dispro-
> portionality theories of economic crises . . . is similarly flawed. . . . It is diffi-
> cult to reconcile Luxemburg's treatment of military expenditure with her dis-
> missal of Malthusian "third persons." [Her] discussion of imperialism
> concerns the effect of exports to pre-capitalist markets, which, if they are off-
> set by an equivalent amount of imports, have no direct impact on the level of
> demand. (1989: 112–113)

They go on to cite Bukharin as pointing out that "Luxemburg's belief in
the imminence of capitalist collapse is inconsistent with the logic of her
position, for the overwhelming majority of the world's population still

belongs to the category of 'third persons'" (114). Bukharin relies on Arnold Bauer's work on accumulation in rejecting Luxemburg's (118).

Brewer, in his summary of Luxemburg's thinking on imperialism, suggests that her work revolves around two central arguments: that Marx's analysis of expanded reproduction is in error and capitalism can exist only in the presence of noncapitalist forms and that capitalist firms and states tend to trade with precapitalist economic formations and eventually to destroy them. Brewer feels that the first of these arguments is incorrect (1990 [1980]: 59). The idea that there must be consumers outside capitalist relations of production, following the line of underconsumption, is a misconception, because in contrast to individual capitalists, organizations, and so on, capitalism as a system is decentralized and without purpose. He also takes issue with her view that the exchange of surplus product among capitalists results in continuous increase in production. Furthermore, he discounts her view that capitalists need to accumulate capital, because, rather than hoarding, they tend to put it to use as profit-making capital and turn surplus value into money: "She insisted that the problem of realization must be examined on the level of the aggregate social capital, but she treated the aggregate capital as though it were individual capital which has to sell to others, and buy from others. She seems to have been unwilling to recognize the difference between a system and a component element within a system" (63). Furthermore, "the conceptual framework of her analysis was, however, rather crude. She dealt . . . in a single and undifferentiated concept of 'capital,' without any clear specification of the stages of development which capitalism goes through, of the possible divergent interests of particular sectors, or of the political mechanisms by which the interests of 'capital' are translated into the policies of particular national states" (67–68).

Although discounting the argument that capitalism requires a noncapitalist setting, Brewer agrees with Luxemburg's position that capitalism was able to grow in such a setting. Thus, European capitalism emerged out of feudalism and outside Europe. Furthermore, capitalism can expand more easily in the colonies than at home. Here, he recalls Marx's argument that worldwide expansionism is associated with capitalism: "Luxemburg brought this aspect of Marx's thinking back into the limelight. She was surely right to argue that, in the real history of capitalism, the expansion of capitalist relations of production is one of the most important, perhaps the most important process at work" (1990 [1980]: 70).

The importance of her work lies in her distinction between capitalist and noncapitalist modes of production. Rather than focus on advanced industrial societies, she turned to the less developed societies and how they were or were not being incorporated into the capitalist mode of production:

Imperialism brings catastrophe as a mode of existence back from the periphery of capitalist development to its point of departure. The expansion of capital, which for four centuries had given the existence and civilization of all noncapitalist peoples in Asia, Africa, America and Australia over to ceaseless convulsions and general and complete decline, is now plunging the civilized peoples of Europe itself into a series of catastrophes whose final result can only be the decline of civilization or the transition to the socialist mode of production. (Luxemburg in Bukharin and Luxemburg 1972 [1921 and 1924]: 147–148)

Brewer supports this emphasis in Luxemburg's thinking, asserting that "her real contribution was to insist that the mechanisms of primitive accumulation, using force, fraud and state power, were not simply a regrettable aspect of capitalism's past, but persist throughout the history of capitalism at the margin where capitalist and pre-capitalist economic systems meet" (1990 [1980]: 72).

Griffin and Gurley (1985: 1097) summarize the flaws mentioned by critics of Luxemburg:

She assumed constant consumption demand by workers and, based on this, the folly, within a closed capitalist system, of continued capital accumulation by capitalists out of their profits (more properly, surplus value). Hence, her conclusion: use the profits to produce goods that are sold outside of the system. But, if wages and consumption grow in a developing system, further capital accumulation could grow, too, with purpose and profit. Nikolai Bukharin pointed this out in 1924, Sweezy in 1942, as did many others in between and since.

Norman Geras rebuts another criticism, emphasized by Arnold Bauer, that Luxemburg offers a conception of capitalist collapse and that her formulations are economist, fatalist, and spontaneist but acknowledges that her "revolutionary catastrophism did have its negative effects. Although it opposed her to the liberal and reformist illusion that everything must automatically continue to get better, it led also to an underestimation of bourgeois democracy's resilience and capacity for integrating the masses" (1983 [1976]: 198).

Bukharin

Nicolai Bukharin envisaged imperialism as an advanced stage of capitalism in the world economy. He argued that the world economy consisted of a system of production and exchange relations on a world scale. Exchange relations were a primitive form, whereas trusts and cartels represented the highest form of capitalist organization at the international level. Uneven development reflected differences in the productive forces of various countries, but rapid development of the productive forces of world capitalism was responsible for the expansion of the world economy since the end of the nineteenth century. This expansion was accompanied by the emergence of new economic formations, particularly capitalist monopoly organizations such as trusts and cartels and the banks that financed them. Banking capital would be transformed into industrial capital to become finance capital, and capitalist monopolies would transcend national boundaries, resulting in a consolidation of developed powers at the center and undeveloped countries in the periphery: "A few consolidated, organised economic bodies ('the civilized powers') on the one hand, and periphery of underdeveloped countries with semi-agrarian or agrarian system on the other" (Bukharin 1973 [1917]: 74). National capitalism, Bukharin believed, sought expansion into three spheres of the world economy: markets for the sale of commodities, markets for raw materials, and capital investment. The result was capitalist expansion and imperialism: "The faster the tempo of capitalist development . . . [and] the stronger . . . the competition between industrially developed countries for the possession of backward countries, the more unavoidable becomes an open conflict between them" (95).

Bukharin criticized interpretations of imperialism relating to race and conquest and defined imperialism as a policy of finance capital: "It upholds the structure of finance capital; it subjugates the world to the domination of finance capital; in place of the old pre-capitalist, or the old capitalist, production relations, it puts the production relations of finance capital. . . . Imperialism is a policy of conquest. But not every policy of conquest is imperialism. Finance capital cannot pursue any other policy" (1973 [1917]: 114). As a policy of finance capital, imperialism was not necessarily pursued by a single nation but emerges with the rivalry among many nations; it was the reproduction of capitalist competition on a world scale.

In his essay in *Imperialism and the Accumulation of Capital,* Bukharin presented a forceful critique of every aspect of Luxemburg's *The Accumulation of Capital* (Bukharin and Luxemburg 1972 [1921 and 1924]). He attacked it from two angles, one that accepted accumulation as a problem—and another that dismissed it. The crucial difference between the two works lay in their views of the motivations for imperialism: For Luxemburg it was the realization of surplus value and for Bukharin it was profit.

Whereas Luxemburg overlooked the "money phase" of capitalism (she saw the important issue as surplus, not money), Bukharin saw it as essential and linked it with the gradual realization of surplus value. Through Bukharin's analysis, we see that Luxemburg's underconsumptionist stance was somewhat extreme, perhaps exaggerating the incapacity of the

workers to absorb the surplus value and failing to explain how this defi-
ciency would be remedied. Again, Bukharin did not see expansion as the
only solution for accumulation; the growth of credit could increase at the
same speed as that of commodities. Bukharin went on to criticize
Luxemburg for separating production from consumption and specifically
for failing to see the dependency of consumption on the social production
of capitalism. The underlying problem here, he said, was that Luxemburg
treated the capitalist system as an individual capitalist, failing to see the
compromises that producers made to continue making a profit and to
preserve the system as a whole.

Bukharin's analysis of crisis differed from those of Luxemburg and
Hilferding (who thought that crisis was caused by disequilibrium between the different branches of production) in focusing on disproportions
in social production. Many of his criticisms were convincing, but in the
end he did not succeed in completely demolishing Luxemburg, perhaps
because at the heart of the disagreement were motivations, which are
difficult to demonstrate or disprove. Ultimately, Bukharin accused
Luxemburg of being an apologist for capitalism. Interestingly, Luxemburg's view that production expands for its own sake, with its suggestion
of the absurdity of this, does not fit Bukharin's portrayal of her as moderate and reformist.

Bukharin drew on Hilferding's *Finance Capital*, as did Lenin, and in
1915 wrote the bulk of his *Imperialism and World Economy*, for which Lenin
wrote a preface apparently a few months before his own treatise on the
subject. Bukharin's writing on the subject was not particularly original,
but it was a coherent presentation that combined theory with evidence.
He closely followed the argument of Hilferding, in particular elaborating
on the organization of capital on a national level, where overcoming competition was simpler than on a world scale. Brewer (1990 [1980]: 112–113)
considers this theme important today, when the role of the nation-state is
often obscured by that of the internationalization of capital. "Whereas
Hilferding had concentrated upon the structure of advanced national
economies, Bukharin followed Rosa Luxemburg—although not her underconsumptionist economics—in locating all national economies as
units of a world market, to whose laws they were subject. These laws
were those of capitalist commodity production as analyzed in Marx's
Capital" (Howard and King 1989: 245).

According to Howard and King, Bukharin stressed the central contradiction of modern capitalism, operating simultaneously both to national-
ize and to internationalize capital. His intellectual debt to Hilferding is
obvious in *Imperialism*, and it is through the reorganization of Hilferding's
ideas that Bukharin made one of his three principal contributions.

A second contribution was Bukharin's claim that

the national centralization of capital has moved beyond finance capital to form a set of "new Leviathans," or quasi-totalitarian state capitalisms. ... Each national bourgeoisie therefore represented a qualitative new unity. Parliaments had become anachronistic because there was no longer a pressing need for a forum in which the sectional interests of different bourgeois groups could be reconciled. (Howard and King 1989: 246)

A third contribution was the recognition that "the specific nature of the system determines the form of its overthrow." Breaking completely with Hilferding, Bukharin argued that there could be "no question of simply taking over the existing state machine in order to use it as an instrument of proletarian power" (Howard and King 1989: 248).

In sum, Bukharin argued that the contradictions of contemporary capitalism were a consequence of the modernization process, not of its imperfect and uneven development.

Lenin

According to Lenin, Hobson, "whose point of view is that of bourgeois social-reformism and pacifism, which, in essence, is identical with the present point of view of the ex-Marxist, Karl Kautsky, gives a very good and comprehensive description of the principal specific economic and political features of imperialism" (1967: 684). Lenin also drew on the idea in Hilferding that imperialism in the form of finance capital was a late and highly developed form of capitalism: "In spite of a certain inclination on his part to reconcile Marxism with opportunism, this work gives a very valuable theoretical analysis of 'the latest phase of capitalist development'" (684). Lenin defined capitalism as "commodity production at its highest stage of development, when labour-power itself becomes a commodity" (723). Under the new capitalism, the export of capital by monopolies became a major characteristic of imperialism, and it was associated with uneven development and the accumulation of a surplus of capital in the advanced nations under the control of a financial oligarchy of bankers who increasingly invested their money in industry and became industrial capitalists (710–711). Thus, finance capital and the financial oligarchy reigned supreme over all other forms of capital (721).

For Lenin, imperialism was monopoly capitalism, identifiable in four manifestations: the formation of the capitalist associations, cartels, syndicates, and trusts as monopoly arises out of the concentration of production; the monopoly control of the most important raw materials; the emergence of banks as the monopolies of finance capital; and the division of the colonial world into spheres of influence, a reflection of the struggle of finance capital for raw materials and of the export of capital. Brewer argues that Lenin essentially popularized the theory of Hilferding and Bukharin and at the same time drew heavily from the thought of Hobson.

Lenin's pamphlet *Imperialism: The Highest Stage of Capitalism* (1937 [1917]) was largely derived from the work of others, especially Hilferding and Bukharin, but it has nevertheless been central to subsequent thinking on imperialism. Although it is theoretically unoriginal for the most part and analytically disconnected at times, to dismiss it would be unfair because Lenin's purpose was political rather than scholarly; the work was designed to provide a basis, even a call, for political action.

Lenin noted the increasing monopolization or "cartelization" of the economy that simultaneously yields a higher rate of profit and a slower growth in output, the result being the contradictory conditions of expansion of the economy and the increasing appropriation of surplus value. These tendencies appear in the banking industry as large banks align themselves with industry and holding companies form conglomerates to control the market and ensure large profits. With the accumulation of large surpluses, the capitalist class invests abroad because of stagnation in the home market (the consequence of monopolization), and this leads to the need for the political division of the world under military control. Imperialism is seen as the highest stage of capitalism.

Lenin identified five characteristics of monopoly capital: the concentration of production and capital, the creation of finance capital and a financial oligarchy through the merging of bank capital and industrial capital, the export of capital rather than commodities, the formation of international monopoly capitals that controlled the world order, and the division of the world among the capitalist powers (1967: 745–746). He was vague, however, about the mechanisms that led to the export of capital overseas. He did, however, suggest one strong motive for imperialist expansion: to seize control of the raw materials inputs of an industrial economy.

The effect of this export of capital, in Lenin's view, was to slow development in capital-exporting countries and accentuate it in capital-importing countries, but he failed to clarify whether the capitalist economy was the nation-state or the entire capitalist world. He suggested that it was national groups of finance capitalists that had divided the world into economic spheres, but it is unclear why these groups should form on a national basis, capitalists, like workers, being after all stateless.

One interesting idea in Lenin's work is that of "the labor aristocracy." Although the theory of imperialism suggested how antagonisms between the ruling classes of different countries could lead to nationalism, it did not explain how the proletariat came to be infected with such nationalism. According to Lenin, small sections of the working class did benefit from monopoly capital, and this divided the proletarian front. He repeatedly used the term "bribe," suggesting a conscious policy of division on the part of capital, but conceded that nationalistic feelings within the working class might well have a material basis.

Lenin's position was similar to but more complex than that of Bukharin. They agreed that war was rooted in modern capitalism, that capitalism in achieving its highest stage generated a revolutionary situation that would culminate in socialism, and that the opportunism of the Second International was no accident but stemmed from the very nature of imperialism. Lenin probably saw Bukharin's view of capitalism as exaggerated. Not until 1916 did he accept the proposition that the idea of state capitalism was appropriate for characterizing the metropoles (Howard and King 1989: 249).

Howard and King have argued that Lenin's *Imperialism* claimed no originality and was but a sketch of what he conceptualized as the highest stage of capitalism, and John Willoughby (1995) believes it is reductionist, but Terrence McDonough (1995) considers Lenin's concept of a stage of capitalism significant in resolving a major crisis of Marxism. In an essay on Lenin's treatise on imperialism, Prabhat Patnaik asserts that "while providing an explanation of the origin and nature of the first world war ... it simultaneously provided the theoretical basis for a correct definition of the Marxist attitude to the developing struggles of the colonial peoples" (1995: 80). He makes the point that for Lenin imperialism was monopoly capital, essentially a twentieth-century phenomenon. In the line of Bukharin, Lenin advanced several assumptions: that the development of state monopoly capitalism comes into play, that the bourgeois democratic revolution needs to be transcended, and that the dictatorship of the proletariat eventually takes hold. Howard and King criticize Lenin's work as "loosely connected theoretically," offering only a superficial economic analysis of monopoly capitalism, failing to distinguish various features of imperialism, and lacking the capacity to explain the connections between the centralized economic control exercised under monopoly capitalism and the decentralized conception of the proletarian state (1989: 259–260).

Lenin's pamphlet on imperialism was a political statement, identifying a series of trends in the development of capitalism and its spread throughout the world, and a response to the polemics of Kautsky and other "ex-Marxists," in particular to Kautsky's theory of ultraimperialism—the notion that the capitalist nations would eventually rationally and peacefully divide up the underdeveloped world.

Although Lenin provided an influential description of a world divided among rival empires, his analysis had several shortcomings. He separately described tendencies without analyzing their relationships. He often engaged in polemical attacks, on Kautsky in particular. Brewer feels that because Lenin believed that capitalism was in a stage of decay and

dissolution, ensuing Marxists were unable to explain not only the resilience of capitalism but its advances. He also believes that Lenin failed
to clarify the role of the nation-state in the world economy and the link-
ages among monopoly, capital export, and the division of the world (1990
[1980]: 122–123). After the formation of the Communist International,
Lenin argued for temporary alliances between communist and bourgeois
democratic movements and considered the possibility that backward areas might advance to socialism without passing through a capitalist
stage. After his death, the Comintern revised its traditional position that
capitalism and imperialism would promote development and proclaimed
that instead the colonies and backward areas would suffer from imperialism. Al Szymanski (1981) and, in particular, Bill Warren (1980) blamed
Lenin for this shift in view and for its influence on later dependency
thinking. Brewer does not give much credence to this position, arguing
that Lenin emphasized that the export of capital expanded and deepened
capitalism everywhere: "Bukharin and Hilferding came closer to the dependency theorists than Lenin did" (1990 [1980]: 134).

Kautsky

Karl Kautsky was a leading advocate of the theories of Marx and Engels.
Born of Czech parents, he lived most of his life in Germany and participated in the German Social Democrat party. Lenin associated himself
with many of Kautsky's views until disagreements and debates divided
them after 1914. Key issues of imperialism revolved around the contradiction in the German experience of political expansionism, military power,
and the evolution of capitalism.

Kautsky suggested as early as 1884 that the colonies were necessary for
capitalist expansion. In his *Class Struggle* (1910 [1892]), he argued that the
evolution of markets was tied to territorial expansion and that European
colonial policy would lead either to war or to a union of European states
(a notion he later called "ultraimperialism"). He envisioned capital as being transformed into a single world entity, a universal world trust.
Bukharin and others considered this idea theoretically possible but irrelevant to the practical world of national states. In his early writing, Kautsky
did not question the need for overseas expansion as a rational practice of
the capitalist class, but in his article "Colonial Policy Old and New," published in 1897–1898, he "distinguished 'labour colonies' based on
European settlement from 'exploitation colonies' where plunder of the
large native populations was the rule" (Howard and King 1989: 93).
Kautsky initially viewed merchant capital as monopolistic and militaristic and industrial capital as tending toward peace and order and opposing colonialism. By the turn of the century, however, he anticipated both

Hilferding and Lenin by focusing on the struggle for markets as European nations overproduced and by noting a trend toward the formation of cartels, tariff protectionism, and military expansion.

Although Kautsky drew from Hobson the idea of imperialism as a manifestation of protectionism and militarism, he envisioned an imperialism in which there would be collective exploitation of the world by international finance. At the same time, he considered the interests of the capitalist class as a whole to be in conflict with those of a minority of powerful capitalists who depended on military means to support their expansionist efforts. An internationally united finance capital might bring about a peaceful resolution of conflict generated by the rivalry of national finance capitals. This was the reasoning behind the idea that the major powers would reach consensus on their collective exploitation of the world rather than struggle to divide it. The argument was similar, as Lenin mentioned, to the notion of "interimperialism" in the work of Hobson. Lenin questioned the idea of ultraimperialism on the ground that struggle among the leading powers would inevitably lead to a collapse of capitalism. Although Kautsky's hopes for a peaceful alliance of international capital were undermined by war and violence throughout the twentieth century, his position continues to carry weight, for example, in the view of S. M. Miller, Roy Bennett, and Cyril Alapatt (1970) that the majority of capitalists will eventually oppose and prevent military imperialist expansion.

Although the published writings of Edward Bernstein on imperialism were sparse and contradictory and it is not clear that they influenced Kautsky, some of the two men's thinking was similar. Bernstein believed that free trade and international harmony would ensue in a world demarcated by a new expansionism. The "liberal optimism" of Bernstein was manifested in his view that the "most industrially developed countries are simultaneously competitors and customers of one another; likewise, their trade relations expand simultaneously with their mutual competition. . . . We have entered a new epoch, an epoch in which international law will prevail" (quoted in Howard and King 1989: 92).

Kautsky believed that Lenin and the Bolsheviks had undermined the democratic base of Marxism and had established a dictatorship not of the proletariat but of the party. He felt that a democratic revolution could not take place without evidence of conditions of advanced capitalism, including industrialization and a working class that favored socialism. He argued that the class conflicts within capitalism along with capitalism itself would eventually diminish through peaceful processes:

> The so-called method of the class struggle, which is confined to non-militant methods, parliamentarism, strikes, demonstrations, the press, and similar

means of pressure, will retain its importance in every country according to the effectiveness of the democratic institutions which prevail there, the degree of political and economic enlightenment, and the self-mastery of the people. (Kautsky 1964: 37–38)

Schumpeter

Joseph Schumpeter was born in 1883 into a well-established family; briefly became finance minister of the new Austria after World War I; served as head of a small Viennese banking house; taught at the University of Bonn; and finally emigrated to the United States, where he became a professor of economics at Harvard University. In 1908, he published his first important work, *The Nature and Essence of Theoretical Economics*. His most renowned work was the 1911 *Theory of Economic Development*. During his European period, he was a defender of aristocratic elitism and conservative bourgeois democracy (Swedberg 1991: 12), but he served on the German Socialization Commission, chaired by Karl Kautsky, having been invited by Rudolf Hilferding. During his American period, he published *Business Cycles* (1939), *Capitalism, Socialism and Democracy* (1942), and the posthumously published *History of Economic Analysis* (1954). Early on, he was critical of the social sciences but respectful of the "scientific talent" of Marx. He was also an admirer of Max Weber, whom he thought of first as a sociologist and second as an economist. A major biographer comments, "During the early period, Schumpeter was the *enfant terrible* of European economics; and during his late period he was a mature and respected economist in the United States" (Swedberg 1991: 33).

Written after Bukharin, Hilferding, Hobson, Kautsky, and Luxemburg had advanced their imperialist theories, Schumpeter's *Imperialism and Social Classes* (1955 [1919]) attempted an alternative explanation. Schumpeter was highly critical of what he considered to be the economic determinism of the Marxist school and claimed that it viewed imperialism "simply as the reflex of the interests of the capitalist upper stratum, at a given stage of capitalist development" (7). Schumpeter believed that imperialism was best conceived of not as a policy always and everywhere serving some concrete interests but as "the objectless disposition on the part of the state to unlimited forcible expansion" (50).

His essay on imperialism was first published in 1918–1919 in *Archiv für Socialwissenschaft und Sozialpolitik*, and in 1951 it first appeared in English translation. Schumpeter thought the essay important, and the political scientist Karl Deutsch called it a minor classic. The essay breaks into two parts: the first comprises a definition alternative to the Marxist and a series of historical examples from antiquity to the absolute state in the seventeenth and eighteenth centuries, and the second examines the relationship of capitalism to imperialism, suggesting that there would be no imperialism in a purely capitalist world because of the ubiquity of free trade and markets and that competitive capitalism would lead to peace rather than war. He acknowledged that modern imperialism was the consequence of nations' erecting tariff barriers and encouraging monopolies and nationalist rivalries.

Schumpeter insisted on a common sociological explanation for imperialism, both ancient and modern. This led him to assert that the impact of the productive forces on imperialism represented the persisting effects of past productive forces maintained through some political organization. He substantiated this argument with reference to historical examples: England in the nineteenth century; the Egyptian, Abyssinian, and Persian empires as "a form of popular imperialism" (171); Alexander the Great; Rome; and the modern absolute monarchy in Europe.

The connection of capitalism to the imperialism referred to by Marxist theoreticians was, for Schumpeter, inherently flawed. The relation was to be understood not as logically necessary but as the result of specific historical circumstances: "Protectionism is not an essential characteristic of the capitalist economy. . . . it is apparent that any economic interest in forcible expansion on the part of a people or a class is not necessarily a product of capitalism" (76). In fact, capitalism, he believed, was associated with opposition to imperialism arising from five conditions: opposition to war associated with the expansion of capitalism, the rise of strong peace parties once capitalism becomes evident, the vigorous dissent from imperialism of industrial workers and peasants, the establishment of mechanisms and institutions to counter imperialist tendencies, and the withering away of precapitalist elements in advancing capitalist centers (213).

The distinction that Schumpeter drew between real interests served by imperialist expansion under capitalist relations of production and the logical mechanics of capitalism as a system of production can be accepted as useful—indeed, as a strong position from which to undertake social-scientific inquiry that might have proved helpful to recent interpretations of the world system of capitalist production. The question, however, is whether his critique of economic determinism is buttressed by an adequate explanation that relies on the exercise of a state's military power in the interest of its economic ruling class. According to Swedberg, "Schumpeter's attempt to introduce elements of economic theory into his theory of imperialism is not very successful. The transition from the economic argument about free trade to the thesis that capitalism is by nature peaceful is not convincing" (1991: 51). Eliminating his notion of the inherently peaceful nature of imperialism would leave only a sociological theory of imperialism, a point that Karl Deutsch stressed in a political context: "Whenever new social changes create a set of military habits, politically influential groups or classes, and important social institutions, all dependent for their continued functioning on sustained politics of warfare or at least war preparations, there the pattern of seemingly irrational imperialistic behavior . . . may come to be acted out all over again" (quoted in Swedberg 1991: 51).

At the outset, Schumpeter dissociated himself from the Marxist view of imperialism as "the reflex of the interests of the capitalist upper structure, at a given stage of capitalist development" (1955 [1919]: 7). He recognized that historically imperialism had been irrational, a reflection of the needs of people who wanted to survive and a response to the social and economic interests of ruling classes and individuals. Imperialism thus stemmed from past conditions. It was precapitalist and therefore would disappear in a rational and progressive capitalist era: "If our theory is correct, cases of imperialism should decline in intensity the later they occur in the history of a people and of a culture" (65). He argued that a concrete interest need not be economic in nature and continued:

> No one calls it imperialism when a state, no matter how brutally and vigorously, pursues concrete interests of its own; and when it can be expected to abandon its aggressive attitude as soon as it has attained what it was after. The word "imperialism" has been abused as a slogan to the point where it threatens to lose all meaning, but up to this point our definition is quite in keeping with common usage, even in the press. For whenever the word "imperialism" is used, there is always the implication—whether sincere or not—of an aggressiveness, the true reasons for which do not lie in the aims which are temporarily being pursued, of an aggressiveness that is only kindled anew in each success, of an aggressiveness for its own sake, as reflected in such terms as "hegemony," "world dominion," and so forth. (5)

Schumpeter defined imperialism generally as the "objectless" and "unlimited forcible expansion" of the state, but his understanding influenced other meanings of the term. For example, he referred to a social imperialism as evident where entrepreneurs co-opt workers by means of social welfare concessions that appear to depend on monopolistic control over exports. Curiously, the term "social imperialism" was later incorporated by Szymanski (1981) in a Maoist criticism of Soviet socialism and other perspectives during the 1970s. Social imperialism has also been associated with European fascism. Schumpeter may also have inspired the rational choice approach that came to be influential during the 1980s and 1990s: "In *An Economic Theory of Democracy* Anthony Downs refers explicitly to *Capitalism, Socialism and Democracy* and states that Schumpeter's analysis of democracy 'forms the inspiration and foundation for our whole thesis'" (Swedberg 1991: 61). A relevant effort to demonstrate the importance of the rational choice approach is that of Robert Bates (1988).

CONTEMPORARY ANALYSES OF IMPERIALISM

The positions of the United States and Europe at the June 1992 Rio de Janeiro conference on the environment prompted the Malaysian Prime Minister Mahathir Mohammed to exclaim that the North must clean up its industry and pollution and stop blaming the South as the scapegoat for ecological devastation: "The eco-imperialism of the North ought to be put to rest once and for all" (*Los Angeles Times*, June 2, 1992). A conference of officials from nineteen countries in Ottawa, Canada, early in 1998 agreed to form a protective international cultural alliance in reaction to fears that the world was being engulfed in a rising tide of U.S. dominance in cultural production of films, television, and other entertainment. The United States was even charged with manipulating human rights in its own interests as part of a policy characterized as "human rights imperialism" (Heuer and Schirmer 1998). These views reflect the ongoing concern about the imperialism of the advanced industrial nations.

After World War II, as the old empires began to break up and many new nations, especially in Africa and Asia, were about to become independent, new modes of thinking appeared. Two principal directions are identifiable. One built on the classical theory of imperialism, adapting it to new conditions, in particular the rise of multinational corporations with capital that transcended the boundaries of many nations around the world. The other was a reaction, on the one hand, to neoclassical and mainstream developmental economists who argued that the problems of the Third World would be solved by the diffusion of capital and technology from the advanced nations to the backward nations and, on the other, to theorists of imperialism who emphasized external factors as the explanation for the backwardness of the nations of the periphery that were seeking means of autonomous development (for useful overviews, see Girvan, 1961; Griffin and Gurley 1985; and Morgan 1982).

Adapting Classical Imperialism to New Conditions

Historians have not neglected imperialism as, is evidenced by Eric J. Hobsbawm's *The Age of Empire, 1875–1914* (1987), William Appleman Williams's *Empire as a Way of Life* (1980), and Gore Vidal's historical novel *Empire* (1987). Combining an economic history of uneven economic expansion with an analysis of the resulting wealth and poverty of nations around the world, David Landes (1998) carries historical debate into the

1990s. In his exploration of how capitalism came to dominate the world economy, the consequences of imperialism, the nature of uneven development, and the Marxist understanding of these questions, Brewer critically assesses the influence of both classical and contemporary thinkers on imperialism, focusing on "the logical coherence of the economic theory that underlies a particular political position" (1990 [1980]: 3).

The economist Paul Baran said of the understanding of imperialism in the work of Marx and others, "The powerful tendencies towards stagnation, imperialist conflagrations and severe political crises discerned by Marx . . . and analyzed by Hobson, Lenin, Hilferding, Rosa Luxemburg, and others, expressed themselves so manifestly as to give cause for alarm to all but the most complacent" (1960 [1957]: 6). He went on to examine "the economic strangulation of the colonial and dependent countries by the imperialist powers that stymied the development of indigenous industrial capitalism, thus preventing the overthrow of the feudal-mercantile order and assuring the rule of the comprador administrations" (196). Baran sought to correct the shortcomings of previous treatments of the development of capitalist relations on a world scale, with particular attention to the less industrialized areas. He identified various kinds of surplus (actual, potential, and planned) in an effort to explain backwardness in many parts of the world. He believed that Marx's assumption that capitalism would play a progressive role in development was founded on assumptions relating especially to the European experience: "That in reality things have not developed in this way . . . was actually determined by the nature of Western European development itself" (144). Thus, imperialism can be understood as the failure to reinvest the surplus material benefits as development was diverted from its normal path to suit the purposes of the imperialists. In the tradition of Lenin, who had written about underdevelopment and backwardness in Russia (1956 [1899]), Baran seriously examined the process of underdevelopment in the Third World and distinguished between the capitalism of the less developed nations and that of the advanced industrial countries. This pioneering work was supplemented and elaborated by another creative analysis on underdevelopment by the Indian economist Amiya Kumar Bagchi (1982). In an essay endorsing the advances of Baran and Bagchi, Patnaik (1995) has argued that the underdeveloped countries must establish institutions relevant to a different mode from that generating capitalist growth.

Pointing to Hilferding, Luxemburg, and Lenin as major contributors to a Marxist theory of imperialism, Paul Baran and Paul Sweezy (1966) set forth a theory that explains international relations in the capitalist world, clarifies the development of social and economic conditions in capitalist countries, and analyzes the unequal relations between advanced and underdeveloped nations. Their particular contribution to a theory of imperialism emphasized what happens to economic surplus, defined as the difference between what a society produces and the costs of producing it. They also turned to monopoly capital in an effort to update and advance the thinking on imperialism of Lenin and his followers, based on the prevalence of monopoly in the advanced capitalist nations, and they insisted that contemporary analysis abandon the competitive model that absorbed the attention of Marx for one of monopoly and oligopoly.

Baran and Sweezy neglected the role of the working class, and their definitions of surplus and monopoly capitalism were criticized as imprecise and ambiguous. They were also labeled "underconsumptionists" for suggesting that it was the limited purchasing power of workers that accounted for lack of demand in capitalist economies (Brewer 1990 [1980]: 137). Their attention to monopoly capital influenced other writers, however, such as Harry Magdoff, who examined the impact of U.S. foreign policy on the international expansion of U.S. business. Magdoff described a new imperialism characterized by the rise of such industrial powers as the United States, Germany, France, and Japan to challenge England and, by shifts of power to large integrated industrial and financial firms, the multinationals that came to predominate after World War II. Magdoff pointed to "the shift of the main emphasis from rivalry in carving up the world to the struggle against the contraction of the imperialist system; the new role of the United States as organizer and leader of the world imperialist system; and the rise of a technology which is international in character" (1969: 40). He marshaled data on to the foundations of the expanding U.S. empire that linked the military and political presence of the United States abroad, the dominance of U.S. capital in the multinationals, and the importance of international banking. He identified three stages of U.S. expansion: supplier of food and raw materials to the rest of the world, competitor with other industrialized nations and exporter of manufactured goods and capital, and dominant capitalist economy and the world's banker. This analysis led him to conclude that "economic theory and analysis which omit imperialism and militarism from their underlying paradigm are far removed from the reality of today's world" (1970: 12). Challenging Magdoff, Miller, Bennett, and Alapatt (1970) have argued that capitalism can exist without imperialism, but Magdoff has countered that capitalism thrives in the advanced industrial countries where competition requires imperialism and the exploitation of the less developed countries.

Richard Barnet and Ronald Muller (1974) argued that global corporations had become the supreme imperial power, opportunistically manipulating "its resources from industry to industry and country to country and by keeping its overriding goal simple—worldwide profit maximization" (363). Likewise, Norman Girvan (1961) emphasized the contemporary importance of imperialism and later identified a system of international capital that understands power in terms of owners and managers of capital who seek to enhance their accumulation of capital and whose activities are institutionalized as transnational corporations. These corporations adopt a "decentralization-centralization" pattern to coordinate different production, marketing, and research and development strategies that "when reproduced on a world scale and transposed onto the center-periphery pattern of the international capitalist economy, gives rise to the phenomenon that we have called corporate imperialism" (1976: 25).

Although these examples focus on corporate capital, Marxist scholars have been divided over the question of whether corporate or bank capital is more important in the world today. Whereas Baran and Sweezy (following Bukharin and Lenin) believed that large corporations had broken the hold of the bank owners and stockholders, others have stressed the significance of bank control and industry. James O'Connor (1968), for example, delineated these opposing theoretical positions and argued for the development of a more systematic theory of corporate capital.

Barnet and Muller critically examined how multinationals wield imperial power in the world economy. They looked at the "world managers" and their vision of peace and abundance in a world corporate society and assessed the challenge of the Third World for the multinationals. In this analysis, they dismissed the concept of finance capital (1974: 135), instead focusing on distribution of goods, resources, and technology and attributing the problems of the Third World to institutional weaknesses, including a weak labor movement.

Giovanni Arrighi addressed the conceptual ambiguities of imperialism, beginning with Lenin and Hobson:

> The real meaning of the postulate of an identity between "imperialism" and "monopoly stage of capitalism" may be an attempt to unify three diverse ideological representations: that of the oppressed nations of the world (to whom the expression "imperialism" relates); that of the working class (to whom the expression "capitalism" relates); and that of the peasant or artisan petty bourgeoisie (to whom the expression "monopoly" and/or "finance" relates). (1978: 21)

Arrighi identified four primary elements of the "geometry" of a theory of imperialism: colonialism, formal empire, informal empire, and imperialism, "themselves ideal types of 'expansionism' or 'imperialism' in the broad sense" (28). Having offered a reconstruction of Hobson's theory as his starting point, he concluded with a critique of it as "unstable and transitory."

Moving in a different direction, Arghiri Emmanuel (1972) offered a theory of unequal exchange with attention to "the imperialism of trade." Brewer considers it an original contribution because it deviates from the main traditions of Marxist thought on imperialism and differs substantially from non-Marxist theories. Emmanuel showed that free trade between capitalist countries can be unequal. Brewer offers a synopsis of his thinking: "Emmanuel's arguments mainly come down to asserting that high wages are the key to development, and that unequal exchange is important in permitting wage disparities to exist without corresponding inverse differences in profit rates. High wages, we are told, promote development, first, by creating a larger local market, and, second, by encouraging mechanization" (1990 [1980]: 218).

Arguing against the "reductionism" of the Leninist view of imperialism and suggesting that imperialism is a structural relationship between collectivities, Johan Galtung provided a structural theory: "Imperialism is a system that splits up collectivities and relates some of the parts to each other in relations of *harmony of interest,* and other parts in relations of *disharmony of interests,* or *conflict of interest*" (1971: 81). He classified imperialism in terms of a number of relationships between the center and the periphery: economic, in which the means of production develop in the center, not in the periphery; political, where position is strengthened in the center and the periphery; military, represented by the development of the means of destruction in the center, with no such production in the periphery; communication, which is developed in the center and underdeveloped in the periphery; and cultural, which results in a sense of self-reliance and autonomy in the center and dependency in the periphery. The principal problem with this conceptualization is that it tends to deprive the term of theoretical significance.

Imperialism may not be the monopoly stage of capitalism as Lenin said but instead a permanent feature of the capitalist world system. Christopher Chase-Dunn, for instance, argues that it is this larger world system, not national societies, that determines the nature of imperialism, and he develops the view that even the socialist states have been incorporated into the capitalist world economy: "The history and developmental trajectory of the socialist states is explained as socialist movements in the semiperiphery which have attempted to transform the basic logic of capitalism but which have ended up using socialist ideology to mobilize industrialization in order to catch up with core capitalism" (1990: 68). "The recent moves toward further opening and marketization are simply the latest developments in a process that has long been underway. The big political changes are largely a matter of the superstructure catching up with the economic base" (74).

In a view critical of Schumpeter but nevertheless resting on progressive capitalism, Henry Pachter envisaged imperialism as "a deliberate, well-profiled policy, executed with powerful means and accompanied by an ideology that justifies the striving for empire and domination" (1970: 461). He argued that the underdevelopment of nations was a consequence not of imperialism but of the population explosion and that these nations had to "telescope the three industrial revolutions through which the West has passed into the lifetime of one generation" (485). Reforms that would enhance this process, he believed, included the establishment of common markets that would allow the less developed nations to protect their markets, agreements to stabilize prices and allocate the production of raw materials and foodstuffs, national control over national resources, and a shift from foreign to state ownership of industry. He saw imperialism not as a consequence of economic activity but as the reflection of polemics, "exaggerated, perverted, unleashed functions of the legitimate security interests of the national states" (487).

Further views that assess classical imperialism in terms of later times include David Fieldhouse's critical review of theories of imperialism in the work of Hobson, Hilferding, Luxemburg, and Bukharin. He explained the continuing interest in a capitalist theory of imperialism in terms of "its sheer probability, coupled with its neatness and universality" (1967: 192). Additionally, he emphasized that the Marxist insistence that capitalism would stagnate at some historical moment continued to influence thinking on imperialism.

Likewise, George Lichtheim depicted a nondogmatic interpretation of imperialism as "the relationship of a hegemonial state to peoples or nations under its control" (1971: 5). Domination and subjection were the elements of imperialism, and the loss of sovereignty or autonomy implied that a nation was under imperial domination. Lichtheim traced theories of imperialism from Roman times to the present to shed light on the changing nature of imperialism and the need for clarity in its conceptualization. He argued against a determinist and economistic explanation of imperialism by suggesting that a political and ideological explanation helps in understanding the persistence of the concept. He believed that most theories of imperialism were fragile: The liberal view had been proved theoretically inadequate, the fusion of social imperialism with social Darwinism in the theory and practice of European fascism had been discredited, and Marxist-Leninist analysis of capitalist imperialism had become suspect. He looked to the possibility of implementing the ultra-imperialism of Kautsky.

Examining imperialism in the light of dependency theory, Ronaldo Munck pointed out that the Communist party of Mexico, although recognizing dependency theory's positive role in breaking with old dogmas of the Communist International, considered it an obstacle to the advance of Marxism. Among its negative aspects were its rejection of capitalism as a system of social relations of production, its failure to recognize the bourgeoisie as a class enemy, and its characterization of imperialism as the principal enemy of the revolution without placing the anti-imperialist struggle in the context of the development of the forces of production (1981: 162–163). Munck recalled Florestán Fernandes's argument that there was no dependency theory, only a theory of imperialism relating to the impact of imperialist domination on the peripheral nations of the Third World. Thus, according to Munck, this approach "locates imperialism at the center of the theory and focuses on relations of dependency as seen in the light of the dynamics of expansion of large corporations, the modern capitalist state, and the model for control of the periphery" (166).

In a more traditional understanding, Bill Warren (1973 and 1980) begins with Marx's assumptions about the historically progressive nature of capitalism, reminding us that initially Lenin also advocated these views but later "initiated the ideological process through which the view that capitalism could be an instrument of social advance in precapitalist societies was erased from Marxism" (1980: 8).

The Chinese revolutionary Mao Tse-tung envisaged socialism as inevitably displacing capitalism and believed that U.S. imperialism had taken the place of fascism after the defeat of Germany, Italy, and Japan. The United States, like all reactionary countries, was a paper tiger not to be feared: "From the long-term point of view, the really powerful strength lies not with the reactionaries, but with the people" (1958: 18).

The Albanian communist and Stalinist Enver Hoxha focused on imperialism in two contexts. One was the U.S. imperialism that after World War II "mobilized all the reactionary forces of the capitalist world to rescue the old capitalist order and crush any revolutionary and national liberation movement which endangered it, to destroy the socialist camp and restore capitalism in the Soviet Union and the countries of people's democracy, and to establish its hegemony everywhere in the world" (1979: 14). The other was Soviet (after Stalin) and Chinese (after the Cultural Revolution) social imperialism in opposition to Marxism-Leninism. Soviet imperialism was characterized by domination over satellite states, struggle for new markets and spheres of influence, and the extension of neocolonialism to the Third World, all under the pretext of following a Leninist and internationalist policy as an ally and defender of the new national states and the less developed countries. China also pursued social imperialism, in the view of Hoxha, by undermining the socialist character associated with its liberation struggle and allowing the old and new capitalist bourgeoisie to dominate the Chinese people.

RESPONSES TO IMPERIALISM: UNDERSTANDING DEVELOPMENT AND UNDERDEVELOPMENT

Partly in reaction to the failure of classical and contemporary interpretations of imperialism to address the internal conditions of countries in the Third World, scholarship and polemic have turned to a number of ideas that arise from thinking about ways to overcome imperialism. These ideas have to do with the legacy of imperialism in developmental theory, the dimensions of development under capitalism and socialism, and various policy approaches to development.

The Legacy of Imperialism in Developmental Theory

The idea of a sequence of stages in the process of development is inherent in evolutionary theory of the nineteenth century. Lenin's concept of stages of capitalism was a response to the first major crisis in Marxist theory, initiated by Edward Bernstein's revisionist interpretation of the capitalist recovery from the great depression of the late nineteenth century, and it was a seminal influence on subsequent Marxist discussion of capitalist history. For instance, Lenin's concept of monopoly as the highest imperialist stage of capitalist history directly inspired the Baran-Sweezy monopoly capital school, the North American social-structures-of-accumulation framework, and Ernest Mandel's idea of a stage of late capitalism. The Japanese Uno school's theory of mercantilism, liberalism, and imperialism as stages of capitalism (see Itoch 1988) is also traceable directly to Lenin's *Imperialism* (McDonough 1995: 340). Baran and Sweezy (1966), Brewer (1990 [1980]), and Fieldhouse (1967) focused on the impact of advanced capitalism, especially in its monopoly form, on colonial and less developed areas, whereas Gabriel Palma (1978) examined Lenin's thought for the roots of a theory of underdevelopment. Whereas these writers stressed the negative consequences of the imperialist advance, some on the left, for example, Bill Warren (1980), have attempted to demonstrate that imperialism tends to destroy precapitalist social formations and pave the way for capitalist development everywhere.

Dependent capitalism, according to Ruy Mauro Marini (1978), is incapable of reproducing itself through the process of accumulation. Where an authoritarian military takes charge, however, the economy can be sometimes reorganized with the working class and the opposition oppressed to create favorable conditions for a project of subimperialism. The regime facilitates foreign investment and technology and increases domestic industrial capacity but must seek new markets by expansion into neighboring countries. The dependent country thus becomes an intermediary between imperialist countries and other less developed countries that are vulnerable to exploitation. Subimperialism has two elements, "a medium organic composition on the world scale of national productive apparatus, and . . . the exercise of a relatively autonomous expansionist policy" (34–35). It contributes to the concentration of industrial capital and U.S. hegemony over a world system of production. Criticism of this perspective focuses on its economic determinism and its implication that the exploitation involved can be overcome only by revolution.

Christian Palloix's (1975 and 1977) theory of the internationalization of capital addressed the movement of capital and class struggle on an international level, particularly investment and capital accumulation in the developing countries by capitalist enterprises of the center and the rapid growth in the internationalization of other forms of capital such as private and public export credits, bank loans, and commodity exports. Palloix drew on volumes 2 and 3 of *Capital* to produce an analysis of capital and labor, the mode of accumulation, and the social relations of production as the basis for a Marxist appraisal of the world economy. His concentration on the shift of circuits of capital from the national to the international level allowed analysis of the recent historical experience of multinationals in "underdeveloped" nations. He argued that the international mode of accumulation linked more countries to a worldwide division of labor and reduced the opportunities for autonomous development, thus leading to an intensification of the contradictions in capitalism and an increase in class struggle. The internationalization of capital can be understood as an alternative to development strategies of import substitution and export-led industrialization (Yaghamaian 1990). With the appearance of new forms of internationalization of capital—for example, the rise of oil prices in 1973 and the ensuing economic crisis in Europe and most of the world—capital could be directed from the center to the periphery in pursuit of new investments and markets, permitting national capital accumulation in some countries while others continued to suffer from blocked development or dependency. Under such conditions, autonomous development might occur in the periphery, resulting in new forms of production and reproduction, including manufacturing, rather than the traditional reliance on raw materials and increasing technology and exports.

A further example of the influence of classical imperialism is evident in the notion of a postimperialism. David Becker and Richard Sklar argued that global institutions tend to promote the integration of diverse national interests on a new international basis by providing access to capital resources and technologies. This postimperialism is reflected in "the mutuality of interest between politically autonomous countries at different stages of economic development. . . . Their interests are not fundamen-

tally antagonistic and do not entail automatically the intensified domination of the less developed countries by the more developed" (1987: 6).
Becker and Sklar suggest the formation of a transnational class based on
the "coalescence of dominant class elements across national boundaries"
(9). This class necessitates the location of both foreign labor and management in the dependent country as well as local participation in the ownership of the corporation. In such a situation, two segments of a new social
class appear: privileged nationals or a managerial bourgeoisie and the
foreign nationals who manage the businesses and transnational organizations. This coalescence of dominant class elements across national boundaries suggests the rise of an international oligarchy. A theory of postimperialism serves as an alternative to a determinist Leninist understanding
of imperialism and to dependency orthodoxy, according to Becker.
International capital has dominated Third World situations, however, and
there is little evidence that a managerial national bourgeoisie will emerge
as hegemonic and other classes will decline. Stuart Corbridge (1990) argues that postimperialist analysis moves away from the theoretical impasse stressed by David Booth (1985) and allows for the combining of
Marxism with a nonessentialist approach.

Dimensions of Development in Capitalism and Socialism

The economic, social, and political dimensions of development vary with
the system, whether capitalist or socialist (Table 5.2). Development may
be defined as meeting the basic needs of all people (Dube 1988), and
Hanna Park (1984) has identified these needs as survival, belongingness,
leisure, and control. It is obviously problematic whether capitalist societies can meet such needs as health, food, shelter, and employment, although the politically representative character of many of them is usually
viewed as a step in this direction. Yet, in capitalist societies large numbers
of people often absent themselves from the electoral process, political
participation is minimal, and grassroots political involvement may be
dwarfed by electoral campaigns influenced by moneyed interests.
Although socialist societies have generally been able to deal with basic
human needs through the socialization of most means of production and
the planned distribution of resources, they generally have not established
either effective representative or participatory democracies. Thus, societal
development must account for these needs in all classes, groups, and individuals, as Denis Goulet (1989) and Gerald Kruijer (1987) advocate.
Otherwise, human development is undermined by international trade
policies, capital movements, flows of labor, and international governance
(Griffin and Khan 1991).

Capitalist and socialist systems relate to this proposition about development in different ways. Primitive accumulation is a starting point in

TABLE 5.2   Dimensions of Development Under Capitalism and Socialism

Dimensions	Capitalism	Socialism
Economic	Monopoly capital and state through capitalist market	State planning and state bureaucrats through socialist market
Social needs	Basic services through welfare reforms in advanced industrial societies	Basic human needs and egalitarianism
Political	Bourgeois representative formal and indirect democracy	Participatory informal and direct democracy

capitalism, where the producers or laborers are separated from the means of production. Accumulation under capitalism underlies the economic base, generating a deep-rooted division of labor, social class distinctions, and income gaps between rich and poor. Accumulation may occur under both competitive and monopoly capitalism, with attention to the market for the production of commodities. Accumulation also takes place in socialism, where the state and state workers usually coordinate the economy through central planning. Experience shows that socialist systems have generally provided well for the basic needs of their people, and that some social democratic regimes in industrialized European countries have done so for a large portion of their populations. What remains is to combine these forms of economic and social development with the opening of space for citizens to participate in political and economic matters affecting their lives (Goulet 1989). Bureaucracies need not be hierarchical, and central planning can be controlled by institutionalized democratic structures.

Policy Approaches to Development

Approaches to development today are borrowed from the past experiences of nations everywhere. Prominent policy options include diffusionist, self-reliant and autonomous, state and export-oriented, and sustainable development (Table 5.3).

Diffusionist development.   Capital and technology may be transferred from the advanced capitalist centers to the periphery to promote development there. Such development is implicit in the "invisible hand" notion of Adam Smith and other neoclassical economists who believe that eventually all the world will rise under capitalism. It also is associated with

TABLE 5.3   Development Approaches and Policies

Approach	Theoretical Basis
Diffusionist development	
	Neoclassical economic theory
	Neoliberal theory
	Modernization theory
	Postmodernization theory
Autonomous or self-reliant development	
	Inward-directed development
	Export-oriented development
	Underdevelopment theory
	Dependency theory
	Associated dependent development
	Sustainable development

the neoliberal notions of prosperity for all under a presumably laissez-faire economy and a diminished state and government. Diffusionism has also been associated with modernization in various forms, for example, the political aspects of democracy, particularly formal representative democracy, in advanced capitalist nations as espoused by North American political science in writings such as James Bryce's *Modern Democracies* (1921), Carl J. Friedrich's *Constitutional Government and Democracy* (1937), and Seymour Martin Lipset's *Political Man* (1960).

During the 1950s and 1960s, modernization was also linked to nationalism, a European idea that originated with attention to such cultural traditions as symbols of national experience, institutional solidarity, sovereignty of the state, and a creed of loyalty and common feeling or will associated with the consciousness of the nation in the minds of the people. The concept of modernization appears to have evolved from nineteenth-century theories of evolution and the belief that the Western world would civilize other less developed areas by spreading Western values, capital, and technology. The U.S. economic historian Walt W. Rostow, in his *Stages of Economic Growth* (1960), and the political scientist A. F. K. Organski, in his *Stages of Political Development* (1965), outlined stages through which modernization evolved. The political scientists David Apter and Samuel Huntington elaborated on the concept of modernization, the former distinguishing development and modernization in *The Politics of Modernization* (1965) and the latter placing emphasis on the need to maintain stability in the face of rapid social and economic changes that accompany modernization in *Political Order in Changing Societies* (1968). These mainstream trends were critically reviewed by Joel Migdal (1983), who argued that Huntington was especially influential because of his in-depth attention to institutions.

During the late 1950s, some conservative and liberal mainstream writers suggested the possibility of transcending the turmoil and exploitation wrought by capitalism. Daniel Bell, in *The End of Ideology* (1960), affirmed that the old ideologies such as liberalism and socialism were fading in the face of advancing society, and later in *The Coming of Post-Industrial Society* (1973) he projected moving beyond capitalism. This theme was picked up in the 1980s by Alvin Toffler in his *Third Wave* (1980), which envisaged the future in terms of individual and small-group activities in the age of computers, with an improvement in living standards; a closing of the gaps between classes through mass education, mass production, and mass consumption; and a diminishing of ethnic, linguistic, regional, and religious loyalties and a marginalization of total ideologies.

Expressing variants of this thought, Amitai Etzioni has spoken of "the post-modern era," George Lichtheim of "the post-bourgeois society," Herman Kahn of "post-economic society," Murray Bookchin of "the post-scarcity society," and Kenneth Boulding of the "post-civilized society" (see Frankel 1987 for a critical analysis of these and other "post" forms). Radical criticisms of these views have not deterred some left theorists from incorporating a postmodernism and even a post-Marxism into their efforts. These "utopians," as Boris Frankel characterized them, have shifted their attention from the national industrial society to a more globally linked society, introducing the ideas of mixed-economy societies, the combination of socialist state planning and decentralized production, and self-sufficiency. Their discussion of alternative decentralized and cooperative economies and welfare services, guaranteed-income schemes, disarmament, and other ideas has contributed to the search for a new politics—a politics of transition in an era of capitalist national and international reorganization, the introduction of new technology and change in labor processes, the erosion of planning, and an increase in alienation and dissent. They have advocated limits on state political and administrative institutions that are distinguishable from civil society and rejected Marxist class theory in favor of new social movements or a bureaucratized technostructure in which no one holds power.

Postmodernism obscures progressive thinking concerned with criticism of the bourgeois order, the dilemmas of capitalism and socialism, and class struggle. It has, in the view of John Bellamy Foster, "an anti-totalizing, anti-generalizing bias with respect to society, rejecting . . . the Marxist critique of capitalism, or even the more chaotic approach to society, which is viewed as inherently fragmented" (quoted in Wood and Foster 1997: 185). The new thinking excises not only classes from a socialist perspective but dissent from the traditional Marxist view that the working class is essential for its revolutionary potential because of its structural position as the class that produces capital. Postmodernists generally avoid analysis of the exploitative relations between capital and labor. Furthermore, their emphasis on politics and ideology as autonomous from economics undermines the attention to political economy that has been of interest to classical and contemporary Marxists. Debate on the nature of the capitalist mode of production no longer appears important, and classes and class struggle are displaced by an emphasis on political pluralism, political organizations, and interest groups.

Ellen Meiksins Wood decries the postmodernist rejection of the possibility of an emancipatory politics based on broad knowledge or vision. Postmodernism, she insists, "is a product of consciousness formed in the so-called golden age of capitalism" (quoted in Wood and Foster 1997: 3). Analysis of the state, for instance, may stress differences between the power bloc and the people while overlooking the opposition between capital and labor. There may also be a tendency to focus on a single or a few political institutions; the segmenting of political forces may limit prospects for a societal overview. Political movements attempting to penetrate the mainstream may be isolated; populist strategies designed to challenge the establishment may be diffused and weakened by the separation of particular interests.

Autonomous and self-reliant development.   Advocated by the Argentine economist Raúl Prebisch and the Economic Commission for Latin America (ECLA), autonomous, self-reliant, or domestic capitalist development called for the imposition of tariff barriers, the building of an infrastructure for the local economy, and import substitution to stimulate production. Essentially, this approach sought ways in which the less developed nations could adjust to international conditions through government intervention, but its reformist solutions to underdevelopment were usually insufficient to overcome the dominance of international capital.

The argument that capitalism creates underdevelopment as capital and technology diffuse from the advanced capitalist to the backward nations runs through an important literature emanating especially from Paul Baran's *The Political Economy of Growth* (1960 [1957]) and was influential and popular among Third World scholars and students, particularly in Latin America. Baran despaired that "the colonial and dependent countries today have no recourse to such sources of primary accumulation of capital as were available to the now advanced capitalist countries" and that "development in the age of monopoly capitalism and imperialism faces obstacles that have little in common with those encountered two or three hundred years ago" (16). Among the major regional studies that analyzed this theme were André Gunder Frank's *Capitalism and Under-*

development in Latin America (1967), Walter Rodney's *How Europe Underdeveloped Africa* (1974), Malcolm Caldwell's *The Wealth of Some Nations* (1977), and Manning Marable's *How Capitalism Underdeveloped Black America* (1983). Frank (1966) believed that national capitalism and the national bourgeoisie, historically unlike their counterparts in England and the United States, could not promote development in Latin America. He argued that the contradictions of capitalism had led to the expropriation of economic surplus that generated development in the metropolitan centers and underdevelopment in the peripheral satellites. Bruce Cumings (1984) elaborated on the significance of this problem for the Asian political economy. Criticism of these views relates to emphasis on commercial patterns of international trade rather than on processes and relations of production (see Bernstein 1979; Booth 1985; Brenner 1976; Cammack 1988; Chew and Denemark 1996; Cooper et al. 1996; Corbridge 1990; Kay 1989; Laclau 1971; and Mouzelis 1988).

Three forms of dependency appear in history: colonial dependency, evident in trade monopolies over land, mines, labor; financial-industrial dependency, accompanied by imperialism and the expansion of big capital at the end of the nineteenth century; and the new dependency, characterized by the capital of multinational corporations in industry oriented to the internal markets of underdeveloped nations after World War II. Theotônio dos Santos (1970) described this new form as conditioned by the relationship of the dominant to the dependent country with the expansion of the dominant country having either a positive or negative impact on the development of the dependent one. Enrique Dussel (1990) and Kenzo Mohri (1979) criticized the dependency theorists for failure to root their conceptualization in the method of Marx (for other criticisms, see Brewer 1990 [1980] and Munck 1981). Robert Packenham (1992) indicted them for their Marxism but, curiously, overlooked most of the Latin American Marxists who assimilated dependency into their thinking, such as Sergio Bagú, dos Santos, Silvio Frondizi, Pablo González Casanova, and Marini, along with many others who rejected dependency altogether.

Associated dependent capitalist development is a situation in the periphery in which the domestic bourgeoisie associates itself with international capital and through the mediation of the state stimulates capitalist accumulation. According to Fernando Henrique Cardoso (1973a, 1973b), who used Brazil as an example, the accumulation and expansion of local capital thus depended on the dynamic of international capital. Socialist critics argue that this view promotes capitalist exploitation. Cardoso referred to "situations" rather than to a theory of dependency and argued that dependency approaches had to consider forces of change and relate them to a global perspective. Cardoso emphasized a relationship between dependency and imperialism but considered the thinking of Lenin was in need of revision to accommodate the new phase of imperialism, capital expansion, and accumulation since World War II. Criticism of these ideas included the observations that the association of dependency with capitalist accumulation was simply a manifestation of bourgeois nationalism and that there was disproportionate emphasis on dominant rather than exploited classes and the notion that the national bourgeoisie might produce a developmental solution.

Extraction and exports of raw materials by foreign enterprise historically characterized the exploitation of many countries in the Third World. Especially in Latin America, the extraction of a single commodity such as bananas in Central America, coffee in Brazil, or oil in Venezuela was associated with "enclave" economies. Since about the 1960s, many countries have adapted to world markets as a means of improving the material existence of people in general and of promoting industry for export, premised on low-cost labor. Particularly conspicuous in this process initially were the capitalist experiences of the "tigers" of East Asia, including Hong Kong, Singapore, South Korea, and Taiwan, although other nations, such as China, adapted their socialist experiences and reforms under a communist party to the opening of markets to the international capitalist world. Alice Amsden (1990) has characterized the export model as a form of late industrialization and exceptionalism facilitated through the state and the mechanism of the market. This form of development has usually occurred under dictatorships or highly centralized bureaucratic authoritarian regimes in which popular forms of participation are limited or absent.

The concern in sustainable development is with a capitalist or socialist economy that enhances the quality of life of contemporary peoples without impairing the welfare of future generations. Development must be designed to ensure basic needs are met while protecting the environment on a global scale. At the same time, there must be recognition that capitalist development usually leads to an increase in the numbers of poor and vulnerable people while degrading the environment. Thus, individual countries must assert their particular preferences within a globalized and interdependent world. Economic development must not lead to depletion of natural resources and environmental degradation. Both for industrial and for less developed countries, the struggle to overcome poverty and inequality must be combined with protection of the earth. Keith Griffin and Azizur Rahman Khan (1991) show the discrepancy between economic growth and human development, attributable principally to high concentration in the ownership of productive assets, inequality in income distribution, and entrenched power structures. In a detailed review of the sustainable development literature, Sharachchandra Lele (1991) criticizes mainstream perspectives as suffering from a weak theoretical framework, including an incomplete perception of poverty and environmental degradation and a misunderstanding of the role of economic growth and participation. Lele identifies five concerns: abandoning the focus on economic growth as the means for eliminating poverty and sustaining the environment; moving away from neoclassical economic arguments about the environment; acknowledging structural, technological, and cultural causes of poverty; understanding the multiple dimensions of the sustainable; and assessing the compatibility of resource demand with ecological sustainability (618). (For elaboration of the idea of sustainable development, see World Commission on Environment and Development 1987.)

INNOVATIVE THEORIES OF CAPITALIST AND SOCIALIST DEVELOPMENT

Advocacy of reformist capitalism was initially associated with a strong state through policies oriented to building infrastructure in each backward nation and implementing protectionist policies and import substitution. Subsequent thinking envisaged the state as combining reforms with foreign and domestic capital that would overcome backwardness and promote capitalism in its belated forms. Socialist aspirations were often linked to theoretical positions on backwardness, underdevelopment, and dependency, with policy and action oriented toward confronting imperialist capital through either peaceful or revolutionary means. The discussion and Table 5.4 delineate these distinctions and characterizes the principal lines of thinking (see also Chilcote 1984, 1991, 1992) and their strengths and weaknesses.

Reformist, Nationalist, and Capitalist Theories

Concern about imperialism, especially in the Third World, provoked a nationalistic turn inward. Although the new thinking retained the diffusionist belief in the possibility of positive capitalist development, it also recognized limitations and Western biases toward modernization based on past European and North American experiences. Thus, nationalism was combined with opposition to imperialism in the idea that backward countries might be able to transform themselves through an expanding capitalism that developed autonomously. Ensuring *autonomous development* was the concern of Raúl Prebisch and the development economists of the Economic Commission on Latin America (ECLA) such as the Brazilian Celso Furtado and the Chilean Osvaldo Sunkel. They favored a strong state that could create barriers to unwanted foreign capital and trade in the form of subsidies, tariff protection, or import substitution. Rather than

TABLE 5.4   Innovative Theories of Capitalist and Socialist Development

Reformist, Nationalist, and Capitalist	Revolutionary and Socialist
Inward development (Prebisch, Sunkel, Furtado)	Early dependency (Frondizi, Bagú)
Poles of development (Perroux)	Backwardness and surplus (Baran)
Internal colonialism (González Casanova)	Capitalist development of under-development (Frank)
Associated dependent capitalist development (Cardoso)	New dependency (dos Santos)
World systems (Wallerstein)	Unequal development (Amin) Unequal exchange (Emmanuel)
Regulation theory (Aglietta)	Late capitalism (Mandel) Combined and uneven develop-ment (Trotsky) Modes-of-production (Rey)

socialize the means of production, their state would coordinate private and public enterprise in overcoming obstacles generated from outside.

The French economist François Perroux and followers such as the Brazilian geographer Manuel Correia de Andrade pursued this direction with a focus on *poles of development*. Their idea was that the economic activities of new autonomous development poles in outlying areas should be integrated into and linked with the regional or national economy. Thus, primary processing of raw materials would be linked with enterprise oriented toward domestic producers and consumers. Several development poles could be combined in a development area. Inequity between centers and peripheries could be mitigated through central planning. The idea was to link these centers or poles in an integrated national scheme of development, to establish national control, and to ensure a balance with regard to international investment and involvement.

The concept of *internal colonialism* signifies a relationship similar to the colonial ties between nations but involving dominant and marginal groups within a single society. For example, according to the Mexican political sociologist Pablo González Casanova (1969), internal colonialism was represented by the monopoly of the ruling metropolis in Mexico City over the marginal Indian communities. The underdevelopment and deformation of the marginal society is the consequence of its exploitation by and dependence on the developing metropolis. During the early 1970s, this view was applied by social scientists in the United States to minority groupings and poor ghettos of African Americans and barrios of Latinos and was extended to an analysis of internal colonialism in the Soviet Union (Gouldner 1977–1978). Joseph Love (1989) shows how the concept has been used by various schools of thought and refers to the Italian Antonio Gramsci in the Marxist tradition and the Romanian economist Mihail Manöilescu in a conservative tradition. He suggests that Manöilescu's ideas have much in common with those of Prebisch, especially on the deterioration of terms of trade between industrial and agricultural countries. This in turn influenced economists such as Furtado to examine the Brazilian Northeast in terms of its backwardness as a region, its potential for development, and the impact of foreign trade. This approach was abandoned, however, in the face of criticism that it served only to influence liberal interpretations of minority groups and did not incorporate an analysis reflecting class struggle. Roxanne Dunbar Ortiz (1992) suggests, for example, that backwardness is the consequence of Spanish conquest and five centuries of "brutal colonialism" and imperialism that devastated indigenous populations in the Americas.

During his 1994 presidential campaign, the renowned social scientist and later president of Brazil Fernando Henrique Cardoso proclaimed that all his past thinking was irrelevant to what he would do during his term in office, but in fact his theory of *associated dependent capitalist development* served as a guide for his policies. First, Brazil was a dependent nation long oriented to serving the needs of both international and domestic capital. Second, industrialization and capital accumulation could be promoted through state mediation of international and domestic capital while placing limits on state intervention and privatizing much state enterprise. Third, unlike those who viewed capitalism as leading to stagnation and underdevelopment in the periphery, Cardoso argued that the penetration of the periphery by industrial-financial capital accelerated the production of surplus value and intensified the productive forces. He identified new patterns of capitalist accumulation; suggested the compatibility, in certain situations, of capitalist development and monopoly penetration as advanced sectors were linked to the international market; and foresaw ties between national bourgeoisies and advanced nations.

World systems theory derives from the methodology of the French historian, Fernand Braudel, his journal *Annales,* and his renowned work on European capitalism, which deals with the history of the world from the fifteenth to the nineteenth centuries. Immanuel Wallerstein (1974, 1979, 1980, 1989) drew from Braudel and set forth the essential concepts for the study of the world capitalist system. He distinguished between two types of world systems: world empires that were great civilizations such as those of China, Egypt, and Rome; and world economies dominated by nation-states and their colonial networks, exemplified by Britain and France. Supportive of thinkers such as Frank and Sweezy, Wallerstein (1974) turned to the experience of Europe, where he identified three essential elements of the world system: a core area in northwestern Europe, where there was highly skilled labor in agricultural production; a periphery in Eastern Europe and the Western Hemisphere, where agricultural exports, slavery, and coerced cash-crop labor were predominant; and a semiperiphery in Mediterranean Europe. Within these three categories, he examined a single market, state structures that distort the capitalist market, and the appropriation of surplus labor—all aspects that lead to class struggle within nations and across national boundaries. This perspective was criticized by Robert Brenner (1976), who insisted that it was flawed by an emphasis on trade rather than class analysis. Wallerstein and Frank, Brenner argued, repeated the mistake of Ricardo and Smith by not recognizing the effect of capitalism on innovation in the productive process as well as increases in relative surplus value. Wallerstein tended to emphasize the capitalist mode of production in understanding underdevelopment rather than examining the internal structure of countries, which might or might not be influenced by international capital. That is, the dominant class in the Third World might function similarly to feudal lords in blocking development on behalf of particular interests, with the result that underdevelopment becomes the consequence of noncapitalist privileges that impede the free development of capitalism. Robert Denemark found Wallerstein's approach "better suited to explaining social and political phenomena than Brenner's state-level analysis" (1988: 49) but saw flaws in Wallerstein's argument as well (see also Gerstein 1977 for an appraisal).

As set forth by the French regulation school, *regulation thinking* has evolved since about 1970 as an analysis of the contemporary capitalist system and its problems and transformations. Critical of the ahistorical and static analysis of neoclassical and orthodox economics, the regulationists seek to interpret the history of capitalism as a succession of phases and to understand how networks of institutions affect capitalist accumulation. Originally conceived by Michel Aglietta in *A Theory of Regulation: The U.S. Experience* (1976), this theory is apparent in the work of Robert Boyer, Alain Lipietz, and Benjamin Corriat. The regulationists emphasize structural forms such as mode of regulation, regime of accumulation, and mode of development as well as political and class struggles (see Bernis 1990). Although one serious review of these ideas (Brenner and Glick 1991) recognizes the similarity but sees as unclear the relationship of regulation theory to Marxism, another review (Mavroudeas 1999) sees it as failing to meet its aims. David Ruccio (1989), however, understands it as contributing explicitly to a Marxist class analysis of contemporary capitalism. This view is reinforced by Corbridge (1990), who argues that the regulation school and postimperialist analysis move Marxist thought away from teleology and emphasize the diversity of relations and regimes of accumulation.

Despite their obvious differences, all these various theories take the position that Third World countries may be able to transform through an expanding and autonomous capitalism. Capitalism and autonomous development constituted the vision of Prebisch, whereas Furtado and Sunkel looked to nationalist planning under the capitalist state. Perroux and Andrade searched for capitalist autonomy and multinational investment, whereas González Casanova and Cardoso recognized limitations of capitalist development influenced by imperialism but viewed capitalism as progressive, and later Cardoso pushed for the integration of Brazilian capitalist development into the global economy. Prebisch early insisted on dividing the world into center and periphery, a structural approach generally adopted in developmental perspectives (Sunkel 1992). Most of the approaches assumed a central role for the state in national planning. Most were concerned with backwardness and lack of development. Most focused on markets and trade. Implicit in some of these approaches was that their advocacy of capitalism was necessary en route to socialism, although this ideal of socialism was obscured by changes in the late 1980s and the influence of neoliberalism in the 1990s.

Revolutionary and Socialist Theories

In contrast to the reformist traditions, a parallel mode of thought sought to establish a scholarly basis for a revolutionary response to backwardness, exploitation, and underdevelopment. For the most part, these ideas were generated by prominent left writers, many of them in Latin America, who criticized imperialism and combined their concern about external influences with analysis of internal structural conditions in their countries. They tended to identify the national bourgeoisie or domestic capitalist class with imperialism and to be pessimistic about the prospects for a bourgeois democratic revolution. Implicitly, their analysis suggested that significant change could be realized only through revolution in the direction of socialism.

The earliest of these socialist thinkers included two Argentine scholars. As early as 1944 to 1946, the historian Sergio Bagú set forth ideas on the relationship between the advanced capitalist countries and the backward colonial areas. He argued that capitalism made its impression on Latin America very early in the colonial period. In discussing the relationship of the city to the countryside, he reaffirmed that "colonial capitalism" and not feudalism was responsible for backwardness. In 1947, Silvio Frondizi, a Marxist law professor, expressed concern with questions of dependency and underdevelopment. The roots of his thinking appeared in an essay on capitalism and world integration in which he elaborated a thesis of two imperialisms, British commercial and U.S. industrial. He exposed the weaknesses of the Argentine bourgeoisie in the face of both these imperialisms. He believed that neither a strong state nor a national bourgeoisie could overcome imperialism through a bourgeois democratic revolution. Thus, an underdeveloped country would tend to be more dependent on the capitalist centers of the world. He was one of the first to suggest the notion of dependency that was to become popular fifteen years later.

In his explanation of backwardness, Paul Baran argued that "the backward world has always represented the indispensable hinterland of the highly developed capitalist West" (1960 [1957]: viii). In showing that the underdeveloped countries were also dependent, Baran equated colonialism with dependency and argued that the dependent countries could not achieve accumulation as the advanced countries had. He condemned the devastating impacts of capitalism on the Third World, and toward the end of his life he visited Cuba and recognized its revolutionary example as a principal form of resistance to the world capitalist system and struggle for socialism. He understood that Cuban agriculture had become at an early stage an appendage of monopoly capital but had not evolved into a feudal system; peasants had fought both for ownership of the soil they tilled and for steady employment and adequate wages along with more humane working conditions.

Elaborating on the provocative analysis of Baran, André Gunder Frank set forth his thesis on the *capitalist development of underdevelopment*, beginning with the proposition that "the now developed countries were never *under*developed, though they may have been *un*developed" (1966: 17–18). He posited that the metropoles at the center tended to develop and the satellites at the periphery to underdevelop. Satellites developed only when their ties to the metropoles were weakest, for example, during a depression or a world war. Furthermore, areas that appeared to be feudal and backward were once in fact not isolated and precapitalist but capable of providing primary products and capital to the world metropolis until they were abandoned and fell into decline. Initially, Frank's work was broadly influential, but it fell victim to criticism that its historical analysis lacked depth and failed to emphasize a class analysis. (See Frank 1991, 1992 for a retrospective.)

Whereas Frank emphasized underdevelopment, the Brazilian political economist Theotônio dos Santos refined the idea of *dependency*: "By dependence we mean a situation in which the economy of certain countries is conditioned by the development and expansion of another economy to which the former is subjected" (1970: 231). Dos Santos focused on dependency in countries that suffered from the expansion of dominant countries. His theory incorporated the expansion of imperialist centers and their domination over the world economy, but it also looked at the laws of internal development in countries impacted by that expansion. Bill Warren criticized dependency theory for a number of reasons, including it failed to attend to the possibility that dependency might be declining, its center-periphery paradigm is largely unexamined, and its view of imperialism as a monolithic structure is incorrect (1980: 163–170).

Conceptualization of *unequal development* tends to divide the world into developed and underdeveloped societies, some capitalist and others socialist, all integrated into a commercial and financial capitalist network on a world scale. Samir Amin (1976) analyzed unequal development in terms of disarticulation of different sectors of an economy, domination from the outside, and dependence caused by large foreign industrial business. His analysis moved toward a reformulation of a theory of imperialism (1977) as he focused on the social formations of peripheral capitalism and precapitalist modes of production. He also examined the capitalist mode of production, autocentric accumulation, and international trade patterns and monetary flows and concluded that dependency was related to the need of central capitalism for cheap labor in the periphery. Unevenness of development was, he believed, the consequence of unequal exchange on a world scale, evident in the impoverishment of the masses and the integration of a wealthy minority into the world system. Criticism of Amin's formulation included a recognition of his effort to update and reconstruct Lenin's theory of imperialism and Luxemburg's theory of capitalist accumulation but also concern over his lack of attention to the state and the process of state formation and imprecision in dealing with relations of production. J. Medley (1989) identified inconsistencies in Amin's analysis of unequal development.

Elaborated by Arghiri Emmanuel (1972) and based on David Ricardo's thesis on comparative costs and natural advantages of countries participating in commercial exchange, the theory of *unequal exchange* portrays capitalist production relations as penetrating a world economy the units of which are distinguished by differences in specialization in the international division of labor and by unequal wage levels. Emmanuel based his theory on a close reading of *Capital* and the application of what he called "the imperialism of trade" to the exploitation of poor nations and peoples. He was able to explain why wealthy nations become wealthier and poor nations poorer. Criticism included the observation that his emphasis on exchange rather than forces and relations of production obscured the exploitation of working peoples.

Late capitalism was the construct of Ernest Mandel (1975) in his overview of capitalism since World War II. He identified it as a consequence of the integrated international system that necessitates the transfer of surplus from underdeveloped regions to industrialized regions and thereby delays the development of the former. Some less developed countries have tried to minimize this tendency by nationalizing international capital (Mexican petroleum in 1938 and Chilean copper during the early 1970s). The notion of late capitalism is similar to the new dependency perspective, which also attributed a lack of development to the rise of multinational corporations and new forms of capitalism after 1945.

The theory of *combined and uneven development* was that the most backward and the most modern forms of economic activity and exploitation are found in variable forms in different countries and may be linked or combined, especially under the impact of imperialism. For example, in the period of transition from a precapitalist to a full capitalist economy, elements of feudalism and capitalism may coexist (see Löwy 1981). Richard McIntyre (1993) has noted that the notion of uneven development is not explicitly found in Marx but instead originates with Trotsky, who considered it an essential law of historical process. Trotsky concentrated on three forms of unevenness: between Russia as a backward country and other advanced European countries, between advanced capitalist sectors and primitive sectors of the Russian economy, and between new forms of economic relations and traditional forms of cultural and political relations. The conditions for socialism were dependent, he believed, on the combined and uneven interactions of the advanced and backward sectors; the dominance of the center and exploitation of the periphery would create the conditions for the overthrow of capitalism (McIntyre 1993: 78). Trotsky extended his analysis to imperialism and saw capitalism as a global system linked by national units so that no isolated socialist revolution could succeed. Thus, a revolution in one country could triumph only if extended to other parts of the world economy so that international capital was progressively weakened.

Lenin also utilized the notion of uneven development in his analysis (1956 [1899]) of the slow development of late-nineteenth-century Russia in relation to other capitalist nations, which he attributed to the resiliency of traditional institutions, competition from Western Europe, and a weak bourgeoisie. Nevertheless, he held that capitalist development was under way in Russia and that different modes of production coexisted.

In a later version of the idea, Bill Warren (1980) argued that capitalism developed unevenly in two ways: First, it could evolve in an environment of noncapitalist social relations; and, second, it could occur in association with technical change that allows some sectors to expand. Neil Smith (1986) examined uneven development in the context of geographical change and in the tendency toward dynamic equilibrium as capital developed certain geographical spaces at the expense of others. The idea of

combined and uneven development is similar to Frank's thesis of capitalist development of underdevelopment in that the evolution of capitalism
and a world market both confronted and penetrated all forms of precapitalist formations. The essential difference between the two theories is the
latter's association of capitalism with the conquest of the Americas and
the former's assumption that the capitalist mode of production did not
fully establish itself even in Europe until the nineteenth century. In a
search for conceptual clarity and influenced by Trotsky's original usage of
combined and uneven development, McIntyre employed conceptions of
overdetermination and contradiction and argued for "a concept of existence that implies unevenness and change both across and within each
social site, with no necessary direction to history except that which is produced in each conjunctural moment" (1993: 83).

Other treatments of uneven development include the view of Samir
Amin (1976) that a definite logic of underdevelopment in the periphery
guaranteed the development of the center. McIntyre cited the criticisms
of Medley (1989) and noted a teleological theory of development in the
thought of Amin in that this "development-underdevelopment-revolu-
tion is based on a simple, Hegelian contradiction. Each region is governed
by a driving essence and their combination necessarily produces socialist
revolution" (81). McIntyre also referred to the work of Barry Bluestone
and B. Harrison, who argued that competitive markets failed to remain
competitive, resulting in booms and busts and disequilibrium. Obstacles
to the expression of free and individual self-interest resulted in uneven
development of the economy; McIntyre criticized these writers for thinking in terms of dynamic equilibrium and failing to address "either the interaction of the economic and the noneconomic or the capitalist and the
noncapitalist" (84). Donald Harris (1985) also argues that capitalism develops unevenly in two ways: First, it can evolve in an environment of
noncapitalist social relations; and, second, it occurs in association with
technical change that allows some sectors to expand and others to retard.
McIntyre suggests that this conception of uneven development "results
from his understanding of the nonapplicability of the neoclassical model
to actually existing capitalism rather than as a consequence . . . of basic
Marxian categories of social existence and change" (1993: 86).

The *modes-of-production* approach departs from the premise that development is largely determined by the level of forces of production—the
capital and technology, labor skill, and efficiency attained by society.
Capital accumulation and reproduction are essential for the maintenance
and expansion of the capitalist mode of production (Rey 1973). Crucial in
promoting the forces of production, especially in the Third World, is
whether capitalism itself must be strengthened en route to socialism or
the capitalist stage can be skipped altogether. Amin identified precapital-

ist modes, including the communal, the tribute paying, the feudal, and the slave owning, which combined in social formations, "concrete, organized structures that are marked by a dominant mode of production and the articulation around this of a complex group of modes of production that are subordinate to it" (1976: 16). As prerequisites for the development of capitalism, he identified proletarianization and an initial accumulation of capital. Lawrence Simon and David Ruccio (1986) suggested that conceptualization could be profitably organized in terms of three approaches—articulation of modes of production, colonial mode of production, and internationalization of capital—and pointed to the need to overcome the tendency toward economic determinism and to combine economic and noneconomic as well as class and nonclass aspects of social reality in theories of development. This approach sought to circumvent the common criticisms of a focus on modes of production for the determinism of its reliance on successive stages of development and its reliance on predetermined modes that may not appear in some societies in particular historical periods (see Foster-Carter 1978; Gerstein 1977; Simon and Ruccio 1986; and Taylor 1979). Despite this criticism, however, modes-of-production analysis may be more fruitful than the influential world systems theory described above.

Hundreds of important criticisms constitute an overview and critical appraisal of these ideas on the prospects for revolutionary and socialist development. Griffin and Gurley (1985) establish a link between imperialism and developmental theories, Chilcote (1974) and Munck (1981) review the debates on dependency and underdevelopment, and Chilcote (1992) synthesizes theoretical currents with regard to development. Both Grosfoguel (1996, 1997) and Moore (1995) offer useful retrospectives that identify the historical influences and contributions, especially since 1945. Ozay Mehmet (1995) shows the limitations of Eurocentric ideas on development theory.

In a provocative overview, David Booth (1985) has lamented the lack of Marxist theory on development and offered a critique of dependency theory, especially emphasizing the flaws in the work of Frank, the imperialist theory of Warren, and the modes-of-production debate. Alejandro Portes and A. Douglas Kincaid (1989) have joined Booth in this concern, and Cristóbal Kay (1993) has called for a revival of developmental theory. All of them see an impasse in theory, but Booth asserts that the dependency literature has not died and continues to influence contemporary social science. He suggests a shift in emphasis: "Curiosity about why the world is the way it is, and how it may be changed, must be freed not from Marxism but from Marxism's ulterior interest in proving that within given limits the world has to be the way it is" (1985: 777).

Seeking a way out of the impasse, Enrique Dussel has argued for a return to the methodology and theory of Marx and its link to the contemporary period: "The concept of dependency is the only one that can provide a theoretical framework for a political understanding of the situation of domination" (1990: 95). This link between past and present perspectives will help in attaining a sufficient understanding of the weakened capitalism of peripheral countries. There must be liberation from dependency and liberation of the oppressed people of these nations.

In another serious effort to return to the classical writings, Gabriel Palma examined theories of imperialism, especially in the thought of Lenin, in an attempt to relate the early thought to contemporary writings on dependency. He believed that comprehension of capitalism could be anchored in specific historical conditions corresponding to a Marxist theory of capitalism and the phases of imperialism: the economic and the class structure of advanced capitalist societies and the relations between them, the economic and political relations between advanced and backward nations within the world system, and the economic and class structure of the more backward nations. Palma saw Lenin's theory of imperialism as an advance that helped in filling gaps in Marx's depiction of the capitalist mode of production. Assessing dependency approaches, he found the perspective of Cardoso most useful because its systematic critique exposed fundamental errors in dependency theory and contended with its underlying propositions that capitalist development in Latin America was impossible, that dependent capitalism was premised on the exploitation of labor, that local bourgeoisies were unimportant, that penetration by multinational firms resulted in expansionist policies and subimperialism, and that the only political alternatives were fascism or socialism. Palma concluded that these theories of dependency "are mistaken not only because they do not fit the facts, but also because their mechanical nature renders them both static and ahistorical" (1978: 911).

STRATEGIES AND ISSUES OF CAPITALIST AND SOCIALIST DEVELOPMENT

A capitalist path to development is likely to emphasize growth over providing for the needs of people, although the welfare schemes of advanced societies have dealt to some extent with issues such as housing, food security, education, and health care (see Table 5.5). In contrast, most socialist societies have attempted to deal with those and other concerns directly. Issues such as private or public ownership impact both capitalism and socialism, although capitalist societies tend to reinforce the notion of private ownership, and the ownership role of the state becomes a crucial

TABLE 5.5   Strategies and Issues of Capitalist and Socialist Development

Strategies	Issues
Capitalism versus socialism	Growth or human needs
	Private or public ownership of means of production
	Market or planned economy
	Capitalist path or noncapitalist path
	One path or multilinear paths
	· Physical investment (plant and equipment) or human capital investment
	Evolution versus revolution
	Growth or distribution of resources
	Reforms or radical restructuring
Endogenous versus exogenous orientation	Self-reliance or interdependence
Market or planning	Industrial or agricultural
	Industrial or environmental protection
	Development or nondevelopment
Aid versus trade	Import substitution or export promotion

issue in both capitalism and socialism. Socialist societies usually have planned economies, but these may be centralized or decentralized, and recently there has been interest in encouraging a socialist market economy. Successful capitalist societies employ central planning at the state level in conjunction with domestic and foreign capital. No socialist society has skipped capitalism altogether, but socialist objectives do not usually include the development of the capitalist forces of production en route. Development orientations may be endogenous or exogenous. In the choice of a marketing or planning strategy, emphasis on industrial or agricultural activity depends on the availability of resources, the drive toward industrialization in the face of the degradation of natural resources and the environment, and the desired pace of growth. Whether development relies on aid or trade depends on the extent to which domestic production can be protected against outside penetration and exports can be promoted to generate foreign exchange earnings needed for investment in capital goods and other essentials. Imperialist aid programs are conducted by such international agencies as the World Bank, the International Monetary Fund, and the U.S. Agency for International Development (Hayter 1971).

The theoretical literature conspicuously skirts empirical reference to real situations, but there are many case studies that reflect different developmental strategies. For instance, Amsden has observed that although dependency theories have been unable to explain the rapid growth of East Asia, it is important to examine late industrialization as "a new paradigm, in terms of the operation of the market mechanism and the role of the state" (1990: 31). Tying theory to experience, Girvan (1976) examined the nature of corporate imperialism in mineral export economies with attention to three examples (Chile, Caribbean, and Guyana) of dependent underdevelopment. Denemark (1988) assessed the Brenner-Wallerstein debate through a case study of Poland during the fifteenth and sixteenth centuries. In a look at Third World problems and solutions, Gerald Kruijer (1987) has examined a variety of strategies designed to free people to participate in the struggle against poverty and oppression. Describing the development paradigm in terms of the established system of economic, social, and cultural inequalities; the measurement of all commodities in terms of money; and the exploitation and oppression of people through old and new forms, Bharat Patankar has suggested an alternative paradigm of liberation from exploitation and the negative consequences of prosperity in relation to forest, land, water, industry, and human resources: "We want to think about alternative models of development from the perspective of obtaining a sustainable, growing and healthy prosperity and liberation through the increased democratic participation of toiling men and women" (1995: 29). In a twist on his Brazilian government's neoliberal orientation, Luiz Carlos Bresser Pereira (1993) has favored the reduction of state functions and privatization in response to excessive and distorted state growth. He advocates a reorganized state capable of intervention and growth rather than the minimal state envisaged by neoliberals. Berch Berberoglu (1992) has emphasized the developmental role of the state in his study of economic development in several countries including Turkey, Tanzania, Peru, and India, whereas Peter Evans (1989) has stressed a comparative approach to the question of development in the Third World, asserting that the state must have a decisive role in solving the developmental problems of poor nations. Denis Goulet (1989) has reviewed paths toward a popular and participatory developmental process by offering a simple typology of participation illustrated with the experiences of Sri Lanka and Brazil. Thomas Schoonover has reviewed the imperial experience of the United States in Central America with emphasis on social imperialism, defined as "a link between metropole and periphery in which the preservation of well-being and security in the metropole rested on its ability to ameliorate domestic social woes through its ties to the periphery" (1992: 3). Finally, Tony Smith, in an examination of the historical experience of Britain and the United States in the Latin world, has questioned "dependency's myth of imperialism" as well as "its myth of the logic of change on the periphery." Whereas it may be possible

> to accept dependency interpretations of history where they seem appropriate . . . that is not good enough for the advocates of dependency; like proponents of any holistic ideology, they are intensely suspicious of eclecticism. For the unity of the movement to be irredeemably shattered intellectually, it is not necessary, in short, to maintain that dependency is always and everywhere mistaken, but only that it is no better than a partial truth. (1981: 557)

WHITHER IMPERIALISM AND DEVELOPMENT THEORY?

The answer to the question whether the contemporary Third World has a theory of development in the face of imperialism and international capital may be affirmative or negative depending on the particular situation and one's own perspective. For example, Arturo Escobar (1995) has pointed to the ethnocentrism, ideology, and bias that permeate theories of development and concluded that no particular model of development applies to the diverse cultures of the Third World. Similarly, Catherine Scott (1996) has insisted that masculine conceptions permeate development theory, including dependency. Statements like these do not help in sorting out the confusion of theoretical directions in the development literature.

Much of this confusion can be attributed to the ideological preference for formal democracy and capitalism characteristic of the early North American literature on political development and modernization. Paul Cammack (1997) points to the theory of liberal democracy in the work of Joseph Schumpeter and Robert Dahl, argues that Gabriel Almond's attention to functionalism and political culture was insignificant for developmental theory, and exposes the limitations of the orthodox interpretations of Samuel P. Huntington. Cammack analyzes in particular the criticism of Charles Tilly and others of the effort to weave theory into comparative history. Turning to the literature of the 1980s on transitions to democracy in Europe and Latin America, he shows that a "new orthodoxy" was based on the legacy of the earlier period: "It took up precisely where the literature of the 1960s left off. It was devoid of theoretical ambition, highly elitist, and overwhelmingly concerned with pragmatic policy advice to aspiring political leaders" (223). Cammack argues that the developmental literature has been largely ideological and that it has mystified the relationship between liberal democracy and capitalism. He goes on to suggest that a Marxist analysis is helpful for understanding the absence of a satisfactory theory of development.

During the 1970s and into the 1980s, theories of dependency and underdevelopment were the center of debate in the field of development and constituted an alternative to mainstream liberal developmental theory. Significantly, progressive intellectuals looking for ideas to interpret and lead their societies into the modern world of capitalism and socialism debated, identified theoretical weaknesses and strengths, and moved on to alternative understandings as dependency and underdevelopment theory gained popularity and influence in mainstream social science. As these ideas began to fade in the 1990s, some mainstream scholars began to ask what had happened to the old ideas. Robert Packenham's belated response (1992) reflected his preoccupation with the penetration of much of this thinking by Marxism—a curious characterization given that by that time most Marxists had abandoned it and that they had rarely attributed it to Marx and the classical Marxist thinkers. The changes in the world of socialism and the end of the cold war had further obscured some of the old questions. In the face of the "new international order," was it assumed that Third World theories of underdevelopment and dependency were no longer relevant?

The new international order appeared to consist of three economically powerful blocs of nations in the North (Europe in collaboration with Eastern Europe and Russia; the United States, working under the North American Free Trade Agreement and/or through some Pacific Rim bloc in an effort to reassert its own hegemony; and an Asian bloc, including Japan and in the new millennium quite likely China). Given the rivalry between these blocs and the U.S. preoccupation with its own problems, some response might well emerge from the marginalized less developed nations of the South in the form of resistance, violence, and revolution. Other than these significant political and economic realignments, it might be argued that little had changed. A return to Marx's *Capital* (see Foley 1986) remained a good starting point for understanding the contemporary evolution of capitalism.

As development specialists searched in vain for new ideas, concepts, and theories, it became clear in the middle 1980s that they confronted an impasse (see Booth 1985). Some of them began to recycle or reformulate the discredited modernization theory of a half century earlier. For instance, in overviews of developmental approaches S. C. Dube (1988) reassessed the idea of modernization and Alvin So (1990) offered a sympathetic reappraisal of modernization ideas. Many others, both mainstream and progressive, continued to refer to dependency-oriented research, somewhat nostalgically offering retrospective assessments of the earlier work (Brohman 1996; Brewer 1990 [1980]; Cypher and Dietz 1997; Frank 1992; Hettne 1990; Kay 1989; Larraín 1989; Lehmann 1990; Preston 1997; and Rapley 1996). Peter Evans and John Stephens (1988) saw a para-

digmatic shift in comparative political economy away from Marxist theories and toward comparative and historical comparisons, and they emphasized recent research on states and markets, development and democracy, and accumulation and distribution.

A persistent theme in this survey has been the ties of contemporary
thinking to the past. For instance, the dependency idea can be understood
as a reflection of competitive capitalism and its idealistic projection of an
outcome based on utopian socialism, seen as a recycling of nineteenth-
century ideas such as those of the Russian Narodniks (Johnson 1981).
Again, the concerns with dependency and underdevelopment after
World War II were somewhat similar to those on imperialism at the turn
of the century, the difference being between the progressive European
disenchantment with imperialism in the earlier period and the progressive Third World resistance to imperialism in the later period and the effort to turn inward to an understanding of why development was not taking place. The focus of attention in both situations was the imperialist
advanced capitalist core. Efforts to understand the capitalist system in its
advanced monopolistic form provided a certain unity to theoretical and
empirical work on imperialism.

When attention turned to underdevelopment and the failure of capitalism or late capitalism in the peripheral areas, unity in theory was evident
in moments of outside aggression or economic penetration in the periphery. The introduction of formal democracy usually implied more subtle
forms of cooperation with the imperialist powers, concessions and compromises, and confusion over theory and policy. Most of the literature
tended to focus on conditions of backwardness, inequality, exploitation,
and underdevelopment in early studies and to challenge traditional interpretations on the question of feudalism and dual society (Stern 1988; see
annotated reference in Chapter 2).

Theory benefited from innovative questioning of late capitalism and
explanations for underdevelopment such as those of Baran on surplus
and backwardness, Frank on capitalist underdevelopment, dos Santos on
the new dependency, Cardoso on dependent development, and Marini on
subimperialism. Critical attention to capital accumulation, international
capital, and the hegemony of the international capitalist system opened
up possible different paths to capitalism and socialism and led to empirical studies based on a theory of capitalism in the periphery. Rather than
any single unified theory, however, a variety of theoretical trends became
discernible. On the development side, there were theories of inward-
oriented development, associated dependent capitalist development,
export-oriented development, sustainable development, and late capitalism. On the underdevelopment side, there were development of underdevelopment, new dependency, internal colonialism, subimperialism,

combined and uneven development, unequal development, unequal exchange, and so on. This thinking often involved revolutionary assumptions and the jump to the socialist stage (Baran, Frank, and Marini). Finally, the developmental literature has neglected traditional relevant Marxist theory, for example, on Ireland and India (Mohri 1979), on Marxist method (Dussel 1990), on Lenin and Russia (Palma 1978), and on the significance of Trotsky's theory of combined and uneven development. The lack of direct attention to classical Marxist theory may explain the emphasis on conditions of exploitation, poverty, and inequality in relation to exchange, circulation, and trade rather than to production and relations of production. Furthermore, inattention to much of the classical imperialist theory may account for neglect of issues around the role of the state and class and capitalist accumulation. Overlooking the planned economy or specific market mechanisms may explain the paucity of analysis of a socialist transition, whether real or anticipated.

Some of these problems are due to setting aside old conceptualizations, for example, imperialism, without regard for their potential utility. In their determination to find a concrete analysis of internal structural conditions that reflected external circumstances, many theorists of the Third World moved away from the polemic on imperialism. Brewer (1990 [1980]), however, turned this discourse on its head and looked at theories of underdevelopment and dependency in terms of imperialism. Recently, several Brazilian intellectuals (Ianni et al. 1996) have debated the usefulness of imperialism rather than globalization in conceptualizing the changing capitalist world. Ira Gerstein (1977) criticized development theory in terms of the idea of imperialism, including an appraisal of Wallerstein's world system as ahistorical, emphasizing circulation rather than production and class struggle; Amin's world complex of market relationships, which ignores class struggle and emphasizes national autonomous development; Palloix's model of social formations at an international level, which is incapable of analyzing the dissolution of nation-states undermined by multinational domination; and Nicos Poulantzas's idea of an imperialist chain, which abstractly distinguishes modes of production from social formations and emphasizes class struggle. Gerstein compared and contrasted these respective theoretical positions with respect to the capitalist mode of production, class struggle, periodization, division of labor, and contemporary political struggle.

This review has shown that theoretical lines have become blurred and conceptualization imprecise, even as theory is frequently abandoned altogether. Is it that Amin's recognition long ago that all the world was essentially capitalist, even in those areas where socialism had taken hold, became even more pronounced after 1989? Are present-day allusions to a new international order, global markets, and globalization simply distortions of imperialism and failure of capitalist development in the periphery? Inherent in much of the revisionist literature of the 1990s is the notion that the advanced capitalist world may not be totally responsible for the wretchedness and exploitation of the Third World. Once a part of the left intelligentsia, the Peruvian novelist Mario Vargas Llosa, an unsuccessful presidential candidate and now an advocate of neoliberalism, has placed the blame on the poor countries:

> Today poverty is produced, as is wealth, and both are options available to any country. Many underdeveloped countries, due to the infinite corruption of their ruling classes, the demential dilapidation of their resources, and the unreasonable economic policies of their governments, have become very effective machines that produce the atrocious conditions in which their people live. (quoted in Grosfoguel 1996: 131)

And the renowned Fernando Henrique Cardoso, now president of Brazil, has revised his thinking:

> Currently the majority of sociologists and political leaders, especially those from developing countries, identify the integration to, and the participation in, the international system with the solution to their problems rather than with the cause of their difficulties. . . . The new concept is not based on winners and losers, but on the equilibrium of interests based on peaceful negotiations between states. (quoted in Grosfoguel 1996: 132)

Further evidence of a conceptual shift by intellectuals once on the left to a moderate position is the case of the Brazilian economist Luiz Carlos Bresser Pereira, who in 1997 as finance minister called for fiscal discipline, trade liberalization, and privatization, and in the 1990s as minister of administration advocated reduction of state enterprise and other activities so as to better prepare the state to intervene on behalf of the capitalist economy (1993).

All these responses from intellectuals-turned-politicians reflect pragmatic positions on their involvement in mainstream politics. The broad pattern of accommodation to a politics centered on global reorganization (see Tonelson 1997) is not, however, without its dissenters, as in the case of Portes and Kincaid (1989), who urged a return to "national development"; Evans (1989), who turned to the state; and Alec Nove (1983), who has sought a feasible socialism combining state and markets within the capitalist world.

REFERENCES

Amin, Samir. 1976. *Unequal Development: An Essay on the Social Formations of Peripheral Capitalism.* New York: Monthly Review Press. A clear exposition of five modes of production: primitive communal, tribute paying, slave owning, simple petty commodity, and capitalist.

———. 1977. *Imperialism and Unequal Development*. New York: Monthly Review Press. A reworking of the analysis of unequal development with a focus on imperialism.

Amsden, Alice H. 1990. "Third World Industrialization: 'Global Fordism' or a New Model?" *New Left Review* 182 (July-August):5–31. Argues that although dependency theories have been unable to explain the rapid growth of East Asia, economic development must be understood not from the perspective of advanced countries but as "a new paradigm, in terms of the operation of the market mechanism and the role of the state" (31).

Arrighi, Giovanni. 1978. *The Geometry of Imperialism*. London: Verso. Offers a conceptualization comprising four elements, including imperialism, colonialism, and formal and informal empires.

———. 1994. *The Long Twentieth Century: Money, Power, and the Origins of Our Times*. London: Verso. An interpretive analysis of the rise and decline of powerful city-states and nations in Europe. Attributes decline to financial capital.

Avineri, Shlomo. 1969. *Karl Marx on Colonialism and Modernisation*. New York: Anchor Books. Especially "Introduction," pp. 1–31. Reprinted under the same title as the book in Part 5 "Imperialism," pp. 235–256 in M. C. Howard and J. E. King, eds., *The Economics of Marx: Selected Readings of Exposition and Criticism*. Harmondsworth, England: Penguin Books. Draws out ideas that show Marx was concerned with a theory of underdevelopment.

Bagchi, Amiya Kumar. 1982. *The Political Economy of Underdevelopment*. Cambridge, England: Cambridge University Press. Focuses on the concept of retardation. Patnaik (1995: 58–79) sees it as a logical successor to the work of Paul Baran (1960 [1957]).

Baran, Paul. 1960 (1957). *The Political Economy of Growth*. New York: Prometheus. A major work on the causes of backwardness, examining a variety of forms of surplus to show that capitalist development in the less advanced areas was diverted and distorted as a consequence of Western imperialism.

Barnet, Richard J., and Ronald E. Muller. 1974. *Global Reach: The Power of the Multinational Corporations*. New York: Simon and Schuster. Critical examination of how multinationals wield imperial power in the world economy. Discusses the "world managers" and their vision of peace and abundance in a world corporate society, the challenge of the Third World for the multinationals, and the impact on the United States of global corporate expansion. Dismisses the Bukharin-Hilferding-Lenin concept of finance capital (135), instead focusing on distribution of goods, resources, and technology.

Barratt Brown, Michael. 1974. *The Economics of Imperialism*. Harmondsworth, England: Penguin. An interpretive essay with a focus on a number of important historical problems. See also his *After Imperialism*, 2d ed., London: Merlin Press, 1970; and *Essays on Imperialism*, Nottingham, England: Bertrand Russell Peace Foundation, 1972.

Bates, Robert H., ed. 1988. *Toward a Political Economy of Development: A Rational Choice Perspective*. Berkeley: University of California Press. A collection of original essays on the political essence of economic development. Argues that political elites behave in irrational ways but politically are rational. Rational choice approaches by Robert Gilpin, Douglass North, and Mancur Olson are evaluated by Ronald Rogowski in an essay on structure, growth, and power.

Becker, David G., and Richard L. Sklar. 1987. "Why Imperialism?" pp. 1–18 in David G. Becker, Jeff Frieden, Sayre P. Schatz, and Richard L. Sklar, *Post-imperialism, International Capitalism, and Development in the Late Twentieth Century*. Boulder: Lynne Rienner. Argues that the national distinctions so crucial to the maintenance of intraimperialist power struggles have been broken down by the multinationals and a postimperialism has emerged in the world order.

Berberoglu, Berch. 1992. *The Political Economy of Development: Development Theory and the Prospects for Change in the Third World*. Albany: State University of New York Press. Examines the role of the state in the economic development of several countries, including Turkey, Tanzania, Peru, and India.

Bernis, Gerard Destanne de. 1990. "On a Marxist Theory of Regulation." *Monthly Review* 40 (January):28–37. Elaboration of regulation theory by one of its leading proponents, based on ideas developed by the Research Group on the Regulation of the Capitalist Economy at the University of Grenoble.

Bernstein, Harry. 1979. "Sociology of Underdevelopment vs. Sociology of Development," pp. 77–106 in David Lehmann, ed., *Development Theory: Four Critical Essays*. London: Frank Cass. A critical assessment of underdevelopment and development theory.

Booth, David. 1985. "Marxism and Development Sociology: Interpreting the Impasse." *World Development* 13:761–787. A provocative assessment of dependency theory and the lack of a Marxist theory of development.

Brenner, Robert. 1976. "The Origins of Capitalist Development: A Critique of Neo-Smithian Marxism." *New Left Review* 104 (July-August):25–92. Argues that Wallerstein and Frank are "Smithian" in their emphasis on the quantitative effect of a division of labor and the primitive accumulation that accompanies absolute surplus extraction.

Brenner, Robert, and Mark Glick. 1991. "The Regulation Approach: Theory and History." *New Left Review* 188 (July-August):45–119. A systematic review of the French regulation school and its analysis of capitalist crisis through historical phases.

Bresser Pereira, Luiz Carlos. 1993. "Economic Reforms and Cycles of State Intervention." *World Development* 21:1337–1353. Argues that the downsizing of state functions and privatization are but a reflection of excessive and distorted state growth. Rather than the minimal state envisaged by neoliberals, he believes that a reorganized state, capable of intervention and growth, will emerge.

Brewer, Anthony. 1990 (1980). *Marxist Theories of Imperialism: A Critical Survey*. Revised edition. London: Routledge and Kegan Paul. A very important survey of classical and contemporary theories of imperialism, with attention to major thinkers such as Marx, Luxemburg, Hilferding, Bukharin, and Lenin. Among the contemporary writers included in this useful account are Baran, Frank, Wallerstein, Rey, Arrighi, Emmanuel, and Amin.

Brohman, John. 1996. *Popular Development: Rethinking the Theory and Practice of Development*. Oxford, England: Blackwell. Critical evaluation of development approaches, mainstream and alternative, and their impact on Africa and Latin America.

Bukharin, Nicolai. 1973 (1917). *Imperialism and World Economy.* New York: Monthly Review Press. Original copyright, International Publishers, 1929. Introduction by V. I. Lenin dated December 1915. A preface by Bukharin, dated November 25, 1917, states that his manuscript was written and published in 1915. Includes chapters on the internationalization of the world economy, the process of nationalization of capital and the world economy, imperialism and capitalist competition, and the future of imperialism and the world economy.

Bukharin, Nicolai, and Rosa Luxemburg. 1972 (1921 and 1924). *Imperialism and the Accumulation of Capital: An Anti-Critique.* New York: Monthly Review Press. Edited and with a preface by Kenneth J. Tarbuck. Bukharin's systematic critique, written in 1924, of Luxemburg's 1951 (1913) analysis of the reproduction of capital together with a reply to critics written by her during imprisonment and published originally in 1921.

Cammack, Paul. 1988. "Dependency and the Politics of Development," pp. 89–125 in P. F. Leeson and M. M. Monogue, eds., *Perspectives on Development: Cross-Disciplinary Themes in Development Studies.* Manchester, England: Manchester University Press. A critical overview of dependency and the political implications of development theory.

_____. 1997. *Capitalism and Democracy in the Third World: The Doctrine for Political Development.* London: Leicester University Press. Departing from a Marxist stance and a defense of historical materialism, analyzes and critiques efforts to elaborate political development theory. Points to the failed attempt to build a universal theory around the process of capitalist modernization.

Cardoso, Fernando Henrique. 1973a. "Associated-Dependent Development: Theoretical and Practical Implications," pp. 142-176 in Alfred Stepan, ed., *Authoritarian Brazil.* New Haven: Yale University Press. Outlines the thesis that within a dependent situation capitalist development is possible.

_____. 1973b. "Imperialism and Dependency in Latin America," pp. 7–33 in Frank Bonilla and Robert Girling, eds., *Structures of Dependence.* Stanford, Calif. Reviews and criticizes Lenin's theory of imperialism in relation to contemporary thought on dependency.

Chase-Dunn, Christopher. 1990. "Socialism and Capitalism on a World Scale," pp. 67–86 in William K. Tabb, ed., *The Future of Socialism: Perspectives from the Left.* New York: Monthly Review Press. Suggests that imperialism is not the monopoly stage of imperialism in the present period as Lenin had asserted but a necessary and permanent feature of the capitalist world system.

Chew, Sing C., and Robert A. Denemark, eds. 1996. *The Underdevelopment of Development: Essays in Honor of André Gunder Frank.* Thousand Oaks, Calif.: Sage Publications. A collection of essays on the early underdevelopment and later world systems ideas and writings of Frank.

Chilcote, Ronald H. 1974. "Dependency: A Critical Synthesis of the Literature." *Latin American Perspectives* 1 (Spring):4–29. A critical appraisal of the dependency literature.

_____. 1984. *Theories of Development and Underdevelopment.* Boulder: Westview Press. Suggests a dichotomy of views between perspectives that advocate reformism and capitalist development and those that emphasize revolution and socialism.

_____. 1991. "Capitalism and Socialist Perspectives in the Search for a Class Theory of the State and Democracy," pp. 75–97 in Dankwart Rustow and Kenneth Erickson, eds., *Comparative Political Dynamics: Global Research Perspectives.* New York: HarperCollins. Criticizes the notion of "post" forms of development and distinguishes between capitalism and socialism as perspectives affecting approaches to development. Shows the usefulness of class analysis.

_____. 1992. "Development," pp. 616–637 in Mary Hawkesworth and Maurice Kogan, eds., *Encyclopedia of Government and Politics,* Vol. 1. London: Routledge. A conceptualization of developmental theory and policy, identification of the major approaches and schools of thought, and bibliography of principal sources.

Cohen, Benjamin J. 1973. *The Question of Imperialism: The Political Economy of Dominance and Dependency.* New York: Basic Books. Defines imperialism as a form of dominance or dependence of one over another given the necessary force to maintain such dominance. Reviews nineteenth-century theories of imperialism and argues that political imperialism predates contemporary capitalist relations. Concludes that imperialism can best be defined as "anarchic" competition between sovereign nation-states.

Cooper, Frederick, et al. 1996. *Confronting Historical Paradigms: Peasants, Labor, and the Capitalist World System in Africa and Latin America.* Madison: University of Wisconsin Press. Critically examines historical analysis of development and underdevelopment in Africa and Latin America. Focuses on ethnocentrism and the distortions of outside models for understanding developmental patterns in these regions.

Corbridge, Stuart. 1990. "Post-Marxism and Development Studies: Beyond the Impasse." *World Development* 18 (May):623–639. Departs from the critique by Booth (1985) to offer a defense of dependency theory and elaborates on the merits of the regulation school.

Cumings, Bruce. 1984. "The Origins of Development of the Northeast Asian Political Economy: Industrial Sectors, Product Cycles, and Political Consequences." *International Organization* 40:195–238. Examines the positive and negative consequences of capitalist development in northeast Asia.

Cypher, James M., and James L. Dietz. 1997. *The Process of Economic Development.* New York: Routledge. Focuses on theories of development and underdevelopment; structural transformation; and problems and issues including environment, debt, export-led industrialization, and import substitution.

Denemark, Robert A. 1988. "The Brenner-Wallerstein Debate." *International Studies Quarterly* 32 (March):47–65. Starting from the argument in Brenner (1976) that the world systems theory of Immanuel Wallerstein is flawed by an emphasis on trade rather than class analysis, explores the elements of the debate and assesses the merits of the arguments on both sides.

dos Santos, Theotônio. 1970. "The Structure of Dependence." *American Economic Review* 60:231–236. An early and widely accepted conception of the new dependency.

Dube, S. C. 1988. *Modernization and Development: The Search for Alternative Paradigms.* London: Zed Press and Tokyo: United Nations University. A useful critique of old and new theories oriented to overcoming problems of underdevelopment.

Dussel, Enrique. 1990. "Marx's Economic Manuscripts of 1861–63 and the 'Concept' of Dependency." *Latin American Perspectives* 17 (Spring):62–101. Examines the concept of dependency and its weaknesses as reflected in the writings of major thinkers in an effort to demonstrate the need to return to Marx's methodology and theory.

Emmanuel, Arghiri. 1972. *Unequal Exchange: A Study of the Imperialism of Trade.* New York: Monthly Review Press. Drawn from Marx's *Capital*, elaborates a theory of unequal exchange.

Escobar, Arturo. 1995. *Encountering Development: The Making and Unmaking of the Third World.* Princeton: Princeton University Press. Argues that there is no model of development that applies to the diverse cultures of the Third World and that ethnocentrism, ideology, and bias permeate development theory.

Evans, Peter. 1989. "Predatory, Developmental, and Other Apparatuses: A Comparative Political Economy Perspective on the Third World State." *Sociological Forum* 4 (December):561–587. Argues for emphasis on the state as a means for solving developmental problems in poor countries.

Evans, Peter B., and John D. Stephens. 1988. "Development and the World Economy," pp. 739–773 in Neil J. Smelser, ed., *Handbook of Sociology.* Newbury Park, Calif.: Sage Publications. A critical overview of debates on modernization, dependency, and world systems approaches and suggestions for a new way of understanding development.

Fieldhouse, David K. 1967. *The Theory of Capitalist Imperialism.* London: Longman, Green. Argues that the capitalist theory of imperialism is an inductive theory derived from a body of economic concepts dating to the eighteenth century and encompassing both liberal and Marxist theories. Finds fault with the theory but calls for work on imperialism at the core rather than the periphery.

Foley, Duncan K. 1986. *Understanding* Capital. Cambridge, Mass.: Harvard University Press. Accompanies the three volumes of Marx's *Capital* to clarify its content and reveal how people can understand and transform their lives.

Foster-Carter, Aiden. 1978. "The Modes of Production Controversy." *New Left Review* 107:47–77. A review of the origins and debates of modes-of-production theory.

Frank, André Gunder. 1966. "The Development of Underdevelopment." *Monthly Review* 18 (September):17–31. Seminal essay and thesis that capitalism promotes underdevelopment, especially in the Third World. Suggests a model of satellites and metropolises whose relationships reflect the world order.

_____. 1967. *Capitalism and Underdevelopment in Latin America.* New York: Monthly Review Press. Argues that capitalism promotes backwardness.

_____. 1991. *Underdevelopment of Development.* Stockholm: Bethany Books and Scandinavian Journal of Development Studies. A retrospective.

_____. 1992. "Latin American Development Theories Revisited: A Participant Review Essay." *Latin American Perspectives* 19 (Spring):125–139. A critical review of five recent books on development theory: Hettne (1990), Hunt (1989), Kay (1989), Larraín (1989), and Lehmann (1990).

Frankel, Boris. 1987. *The Post-Industrial Utopians*. Madison: University of Wisconsin Press. A critical appraisal of various "post" forms of society with a focus on postindustrialism.

Galtung, John. 1971. "A Structural Theory of Imperialism." *Journal of Peace Research* 7 (2):81–117. A theory of imperialism based on relations of harmony and disharmony of interest.

Geras, Norman. 1983 (1976). *The Legacy of Rosa Luxemburg*. London: Verso. See also "Rosa Luxemburg after 1905," *New Left Review* 89 (January-February 1975):3–46. A detailed analysis of the thought of Luxemburg, comparing and contrasting it with emphases in Lenin, Stalin, and Trotsky.

Gerstein, Ira. 1977. "Theories of the World Economy and Imperialism." *Insurgent Sociologist* 7 (Spring):9–22. A critique of bourgeois conceptions of world economy, along with a critical appraisal and comparison of the approaches of Wallerstein, Amin, Palloix, and Poulantzas.

Girvan, Norman. 1961. "Imperialism: An Historiographical Revision." *Economic History Review,* 2d series, 14 (2):187–209. A cogent assessment of the literature on imperialism.

_____. 1976. *Corporate Imperialism: Conflict and Expropriation. Transitional Corporations and Economic Nationalism in the Third World*. White Plains, N.Y.: M. E. Sharpe. Examination of the nature of corporate imperialism in mineral export economies with attention to three examples (Chile, Caribbean, and Guyana) of dependent underdevelopment. Attempts to bridge the gap between classical theories of imperialism and concrete analyses of dependency.

González Casanova, Pablo. 1969. "Internal Colonialism and National Development," pp. 118–139 in Irving Louis Horowitz, Josué de Castro, and John Gerassi, eds., *Latin American Radicalism*. New York: Vintage Books. Drawn from his *Sociología de la explotación* (2d edition, Mexico City: Siglo Veintiuno, 1970).

Gouldner, Alvin W. 1977–1978. "Stalinism: A Study of Internal Colonialism." *Telos* 34 (Winter):5–48. Reviews the historical significance and impact of Stalinism in terms of internal colonialism, viewed as "the use of the state power by one section of society . . . to impose unfavorable rates of exchange on another part of the same society" (13).

Goulet, Denis. 1989. "Participation in Development: New Avenues." *World Development* 17 (February):165–178. A review of paths toward popular and participatory forms in the developmental process. Offers a simple typology of participation and illustrates with the experience of Sri Lanka and Brazil.

Griffin, Keith, and John Gurley. 1985. "Radical Analyses of Imperialism, the Third World, and the Transition to Socialism: A Survey Article." *Journal of Economic Literature* 23 (September):1089–1143. A major review of the literature, the first two-thirds of it dealing with imperialism. Examines definitions and theoretical trends and provides an assessment of this vast literature.

Griffin, Keith, and Azizur Rahman Khan. 1991. "Human Development: The International Dimension." Manuscript. Riverside, Calif. Examines international trade, flows of capital, inequality, regional economic blocs, and global governance.

Grosfoguel, Ramón. 1996. "From *Cepalismo* to Neoliberalism: A World Systems Approach to Conceptual Shifts in Latin America." *Review* 19 (Spring):131–154. A useful overview and synthesis that not only links the early ideas of the Economic Commission on Latin America with those of contemporary neoliberalism but also connects developmental thinking since World War II with ideas dating to the nineteenth century.

———. 1997. "A Time-Space Perspective on Development: Recasting Latin American Debates." *Latin American Research Review* 20 (Summer-Fall):465–540. An overview of "developmental ideology" since the colonial period in Latin America, with emphasis on the 1945 to 1990 period. Shows how earlier debates are replicated in the recent period.

Harris, Donald. 1985. "The Theory of Economic Growth: From Steady States to Uneven Development," pp. 378–394 in G. Feiwel, ed., *Issues in Contemporary Microeconomics and Distribution*. London: Macmillan. Identifies the nuances of uneven development.

Hayter, Teresa. 1971. *Aid as Imperialism*. Harmondsworth, England: Penguin Books. Exposes the myth that aid is "a form of disinterested international munificence" and shows how the aid policies of international agencies serve the purposes of imperialism in the struggle against nationalism and socialism.

Hettne, Bjorn. 1990. *Development Theory and the Three Worlds*. London: Longman; and New York: John Wiley. An overview of development theory.

Heuer, Use-Jens, and Gregor Schirmer. 1998. "Human Rights Imperialism," *Monthly Review* 49 (March):5–16. Shows how nations like the United States and Germany manipulate human rights policy in their own interests and tend to ignore human rights in their own territories. Identifies an "ideological pattern" that shows how human rights are separated from the state and politics and from the governing principles of international law.

Hilferding, Rudolf. 1981 (1910). *Finance Capital: A Study of the Latest Phase of Capitalist Development*. London: Routledge and Kegan Paul. A major study of finance capital written in Vienna about 1905 and usually considered an advance in Marxism.

Hobson, J. A. 1965 (1902). *Imperialism: A Study*. Ann Arbor: University of Michigan Press. Seeking a solution to British imperialism, Hobson sets forth a theory of underconsumptionism to explain domestic chaos.

Howard, Michael, and J. E. King. 1989. *A History of Marxist Economics*. Vol. 1, *1883–1929*. Princeton: Princeton University Press. A critical survey of Marxist economic thought since the death of Marx. Includes useful biographies of the major Marxists of the period and an incisive summary of their works and ideas.

Hoxha, Enver. 1979. "The Strategy of Imperialism and Modern Revisionism," pp. 9–68 in his *Imperialism and the Revolution*. Chicago: World View Publications. Attacks the social imperialism of the Soviet Union and China.

Hunt, Diana. 1989. *Economic Theories of Development: An Analysis of Competing Paradigms*. Hemel Hemstead, England: Harvester Wheatsheaf; and Savage, Md.: Barnes and Noble Books. An overview of economic theories, which begins with a general discussion of theoretical paradigms, including classical and Keynesian theories, then moves on to ECLA structuralism and contemporary theories.

Ianni, Octávio, et al. 1996. "Debate: Imperialism e globalização." *Crítica Marxista* 1 (3):130–152. Debate among Brazilian Marxists over imperialism and globalization. Reflects differences among Third World intellectuals, with Ianni seeing imperialism as subsumed under globalization but the two terms as representing different totalities.

Itoch, Makoto. 1988. *The Basic Theory of Capitalism: The Forms and Substance of the Capitalist Economy*. Savage, Md.: Barnes and Noble Books. Sets forth Marx's economic method in line with the Japanese school of Marxism and the work of Kozo Uno. In his review of this work, John Bellamy Foster (*Monthly Review* 40 [January 1990]:51–55) suggests that Itoch overcomes problems with Uno's emphasis on the stage theory of Hilferding's *Finance Capital* and Lenin's *Imperialism*, especially the need to link theory and history.

Johnson, Carlos. 1981. "Dependency Theory and Processes of Capitalism and Socialism." *Latin American Perspectives* 8 (Summer and Fall):55–81. An attack on dependency theory.

Kautsky, Karl. 1964. *The Dictatorship of the Proletariat*. Ann Arbor: University of Michigan Press. Views democratic revolution as dependent on advanced capitalism, through which imperialism and class conflicts will diminish in time.

Kay, Cristóbal. 1989. *Latin American Theories of Development and Underdevelopment*. London and New York: Routledge. A major synthesis of Latin American theories—their origins and influence, strengths and weaknesses.

_____. 1993. "For a Renewal of Development Studies: Latin American Theories and Neoliberalism in the Era of Structural Adjustment." *Third World Quarterly* 14 (4):691–702. Reviews advances in developmental theory since World War II in the light of the countertrend in neoclassical and neoliberal thinking. Focuses on structural adjustment, the new world order, state and markets, and development strategies.

Koebner, Richard, and Helmut Dan Schmidt. 1964. *Imperialism: The Story and Significance of a Political Word, 1840–1960*. New York: Cambridge University Press. Explores the history of the term "imperialism."

Kruijer, Gerald J. 1987. *Development Through Liberation: Third World Problems and Solutions*. Atlantic Highlands, N.J.: Humanities Press International. Suggests a variety of strategies for freeing people to participate in the struggle to overcome poverty and oppression.

Laclau, Ernesto. 1971. "Feudalism and Capitalism in Latin America." *New Left Review* 67 (May-June):19–38. Criticizes André Gunder Frank for emphasis on circulation rather than production.

Landes, David S. 1998. *The Wealth and Poverty of Nations: Why Some Are So Rich and Some So Poor*. New York: W. W. Norton. An economic history of the enormous and uneven global economic expansion and the consequent income gap between poor and wealthy nations. Emphasizes how the West took advantage of its unique characteristics. In a review (*Los Angeles Times Book Review*, March 15, 1998), the historian Eric Hobsbawm called this book "a polemical tract for the times" and "an intervention into the ideological and policy debates of the 1990s."

Larraín, Jorge. 1989. *Theories of Development: Capitalism, Colonialism, and Dependency*. London: Polity Press. An incisive theoretical essay that examines the origins and evolution of development theory and reveals its strengths and weaknesses.

Lehmann, David. 1990. *Democracy and Development in Latin America: Economics, Politics, and Religion in the Postwar Period*. London: Polity Press. An imaginative and interesting review of development theory, with emphasis on the period of transitions from dictatorship to democracy and especially the influence of the theology of liberation and the new social movements.

Lele, Sharachchandra M. 1991. "Sustainable Development: A Critical Review." *World Development* 19 (6):607–621. A detailed review of the literature on sustainable development with criticism of the mainstream.

Lenin, V. I. 1937 (1917). *Imperialism: The Highest Stage of Capitalism*. New York: International Publishers. A political tract, emphasizing ideas from Hobson and Hilferding.

_____. 1956 (1899). *The Development of Capitalism in Russia: The Process of the Formation of a Home Market for Large-Scale Industry*. Moscow: Foreign Languages Publishing House. Examines capitalism and feudalism in Russia, with emphasis on the unevenness and exploitation of capitalist development.

_____. 1967. *Selected Works in Three Volumes*. Moscow: Progress Books.

Lichtheim, George. 1971. *Imperialism*. New York: Praeger. A systematic review of theories of imperialism dating from Roman times to the present. Examines the various meanings of imperialism. Shows the persuasiveness of imperialism, as legitimation for rulers of all kinds. See also "Imperialism," *Commentary* 49 (April 1970):42–75 and 49 (May 1970):33–58.

Lim, Jie-hyun. 1992. "Marx's Theory of Imperialism and the Irish National Question." *Science and Society* 56 (Summer):163–178. Suggests that in their concern with the Irish question Marx and Engels escaped from their earlier Eurocentrist views, using a rudimentary understanding of imperialism to broaden their historical-materialist conception of the nation.

Love, Joseph. 1989. "Modeling Internal Colonialism: History and Prospect." *World Development* 17:905–922. A very useful historiography on the concept of internal colonialism, defined as a "process of unequal exchange, occurring within a given state, characteristic of industrial or industrializing economies" (905).

Löwy, Michael. 1981. *The Politics of Combined and Uneven Development: The Theory of Permanent Revolution*. London: Verso. Draws on the thinking of Trotsky.

Luxemburg, Rosa. 1951 (1913). *The Accumulation of Capital*. London: Routledge and Kegan Paul. Examines the relation between the state and capital and between militarism and racism, together with finance capital and the impact of capitalism on noncapitalist nations. (See Bukharin and Luxemburg (1972 [1921 and 1924]) for a debate on this work.)

Magdoff, Harry. 1969. *The Age of Imperialism: The Economics of U.S. Foreign Policy*. New York: Monthly Review Press. A Marxist appraisal of U.S. foreign policy as significant in the new imperialism.

_____. 1970. "Militarism and Imperialism." *Monthly Review* 21(February):1–14. Ties U.S. militarism to imperialism in an effort to demonstrate that economic processes must be considered together with the political force that plays a major role.

Mandel, Ernest. 1975. *Late Capitalism*. London: New Left Books. Analysis of why capitalism arrived belatedly in the Third World.

Mao Tse-tung. 1958. *Comrade Mao Tse-tung on "Imperialism and All Reactionaries Are Paper Tigers."* Beijing: Foreign Languages Press. A compilation of quotations and statements on imperialism.

Marable, Manning. 1983. *How Capitalism Underdeveloped Black America*. Boston: South End Press. Draws on a Third World thesis to suggest the cause of backwardness in the United States.

Marini, Ruy Mauro. 1978. "World Capitalist Accumulation and Sub-imperialism." *Two Thirds* 1 (Fall):29–39. Focuses on the international capitalist system after World War II and argues that U.S. imperialism moved in two directions: toward establishment of an international market and international financial institutions that permitted disposal of an enormous commercial surplus and toward the extension of the sphere of capital accumulation, which led to a system of subimperialism in the Third World.

Marx, Karl, and Frederick Engels. 1958 (1848). "Manifesto of the Communist Party," pp. 33–65 in their *Selected Works in Two Volumes*, Vol. 1. Moscow: Foreign Languages Publishing House.

Mavroudeas, Stravos. 1999. "Regulation Theory: The Road from Creative Marxism to Postmodern Disintegration." *Science and Society* 53 (Fall):310–337. Argues that regulation theory fails to fulfill its purpose of explaining capitalist development on a historicist and institutional basis.

McDonough, Terrence. 1995. "Lenin, Imperialism, and the Stages of Capitalist Development." *Science and Society* 59 (Fall):339–367. Analysis of how Leninist theory filled a vacuum caused by a crisis in Marxist theory.

McIntyre, Richard. 1993. "Theories of Uneven Development and Social Change." *Rethinking Marxism* 5 (Fall):75–105. Argues that Marxist theories of uneven development have not been carefully set forth, partly because Marx at times emphasized the linear progression of history and so did some of those who followed him. Favors Trotsky's original usage.

Medley, J. 1989. "Concepts of Capital Accumulation and Development: Samir Amin's Contradictions." *Rethinking Marxism* 2 (Spring):83–103. Shows the inconsistencies in the work of Samir Amin (1976) on unequal development.

Mehmet, Ozay. 1995. *Westernizing the Third World: The Eurocentricity of Economic Development Theories*. New York: Routledge. Critique of Eurocentric development theories and prescriptions, with attention to mainstream classical and neoclassical approaches.

Migdal, Joel S. 1983. "Studying the Politics of Development and Change: The State of the Art," pp. 309–338 in Ada W. Finifler, ed., *Political Science: The State of the Discipline*. Washington, D.C.: American Political Science Association. An interpretive overview of mostly mainstream political science endeavors in development theory. Also looks at corporatism and bureaucratic authoritarianism, with attention to interest representation and the state.

Miles, Gary B. 1990. "Roman and Modern Imperialism: A Reassessment." *Comparative Studies in Society and History* 32 (October):629–659. Questions "why movements of national independence have occurred in modern times, but not in

Roman antiquity" (629) and examines the difference in the historical experiences associated with imperialism during the Roman empire and in modern times.

Miller, S. M., Roy Bennett, and Cyril Alapatt. 1970. "Does the U.S. Economy Require Imperialism?" *Social Policy* 1 (September-October):13–19. Draws on Kautsky's thesis that an internationally unified finance capital might effect a peaceful resolution of conflict between rival national finance capitals. Argues that capitalism will eventually overcome world conflict and imperialism. Criticizes Magdoff's (1969) thesis of a new imperialism, with reply by Magdoff, pp. 19–29.

Mohri, Kenzo. 1979. "Marx and Underdevelopment." *Monthly Review* 30 (April):32–42. Argues that scholars should return to Marx to discover the double mission of capitalism—on the one hand, penetrating and destroying the precapitalist social formations to allow the development of the capitalist forces of production and, on the other hand, imposing protective tariffs and other measures that open the way for autonomous development.

Moore, David B. 1995. "Development Discourse as Hegemony: Towards an Ideological History—1945–1995," pp. 1–53 in David B. Moore and Gerald J. Schmitz, eds., *Debating Development Discourse: Institutional and Popular Perspectives*. New York and London: St. Martin's Press/Macmillan. Examines the developmental discourse in the context of ideological history and hegemony. Develops two themes: two phases of development in the postwar era—international Keynesianism and state-mediated capitalism and the neoliberal deregulated capitalism that emerged in the 1970s—and ideological concepts about development (equity, democracy, and sustainability) during the past half century.

Morgan, I. 1982. "Theories of Imperialism: A Bibliographical Sketch." *Journal of Area Studies* 6 (Autumn):18–22. A comprehensive bibliographical review of the literature on imperialism, looking first at empires in history (empires based on slave labor, mercantile empires based on exploitation of commerce, and fully developed capitalist empires) and at classical theorists (Gibbon, Spencer, Weber, Hobson, Lenin, Bukharin, Kautsky, Hilferding, Luxemburg, and Schumpeter) and then at postclassical views: imperialism as a manifestation of power disequilibrium; politico-strategic considerations; center-periphery division; settler colonialism; servitor or social imperialism; and state-collectivist societies.

Mouzelis, Nicos. 1988. "Sociology of Development: Reflections on the Present Crisis." *Sociology* 22 (February):23–44. Analyzes the impasse in left perspectives on development.

Munck, Ronaldo. 1981. "Imperialism and Dependency: Recent Debates and Old Deadends." *Latin American Perspectives* 9 (Summer and Fall):162–179. Updates Chilcote (1974).

Nove, Alec. (1983). *The Economics of Feasible Socialism.* London: George Allen & Unwin. Examines a theory of state and market in the search for a viable socialism.

O'Connor, James. 1968. "Finance Capital or Corporate Capital?" *Monthly Review* 20 (December):30–35. Distinguishes two Marxist approaches to understanding the dominant form of capital.

_____. 1970. "The Meaning of Economic Imperialism," pp. 101–150 in Robert I. Rhodes, ed., *Imperialism and Underdevelopment: A Reader*. New York: Monthly Review Press. A comprehensive synthesis and conceptualization of the literature on imperialism.

Ortiz, Roxanne Dunbar. 1992. "Aboriginal People and Imperialism in the Western Hemisphere." *Monthly Review* 44 (September):1–12. A theoretical analysis.

Pachter, Henry. 1970. "The Problem of Imperialism." *Dissent* 17 (September-October):461–488. A non-Marxist explanation of imperialism critical of Lenin.

Packenham, Robert A. 1992. *The Dependency Movement: Scholarship and Politics in Development Studies*. Cambridge, Mass.: Harvard University Press. A detailed look at the movement, with particular attention to Cardoso and the Marxist underpinnings of dependency theory.

Palloix, Christian. 1975. *L'Internationalisation du capital*. Paris: François Maspero. Sets forth the thesis of internationalization of capital.

_____. 1977. "The Self-Expansion of Capital on a World Scale." *Review of Radical Political Economy* 9 (Summer):1–28. A Marxist analysis of the multinational corporation and its emergence in an international system of capital, a new international mode of accumulation, and an increase in worldwide class struggle.

Palma, Gabriel. 1978. "Dependency: A Formal Theory of Underdevelopment or a Methodology for the Analysis of Concrete Situations of Underdevelopment?" *World Development* 6:881–924. Examination of theories of imperialism, especially in the thought of Lenin, in an effort to relate the early thought to contemporary writings on dependency.

Park, Hanna S. 1984. *Human Needs and Political Development: A Dissent to Utopian Solutions*. Cambridge, Mass.: Schenkman. Development defined as meeting and sustaining human needs.

Patankar, Bharat. 1995. "The Alternative Development Paradigm." *New Political Science* 32 (Summer):28–42. An interesting effort to identify the established development paradigm of inequality and exploitation and suggest an alternative liberating approach.

Patnaik, Prabhat. 1995. *Whatever Happened to Imperialism and Other Essays*. New Delhi: Tolika. Includes his essay "On the Political Economy of Underdevelopment" (12–79), in which he departs from a Marxist framework, with emphasis on mode of production and three related elements—accumulation, concentration, and centralization—and elaborates on the beginnings of underdevelopment, the record of capitalist development, and the role of the state.

Portes, Alejandro, and A. Douglas Kincaid. 1989. "Sociology and Development in the 1990s: Critical Challenges and Empirical Trends." *Sociological Forum* 4 (December):479–503. Overview of the impasse in developmental theory.

Preston, P. W. 1997. *Development Theory: An Introduction to the Analysis of Complex Change*. Oxford, England: Blackwell. Reviews the major directions in theories of Third World development since World War II.

Rapley, John. 1996. *Understanding Development: Theory and Practice in the Third World*. Boulder: Lynne Rienner. Focuses on the shift from state-based to market-based development theory. Uses case studies to show the success and failure of various theories since the 1970s.

Rey, Pierre-Philippe. 1973. *Les alliances de classes*. Paris: Maspero. See also "The Lineage Mode of Production." *Critique of Anthropology* 3 (Spring 1975):27–70. Sets forth his theory of modes-of-production.

Rhodes, Robert I., ed. 1970. *Imperialism and Underdevelopment: A Reader*. New York: Monthly Review Press. A collection of essays, with two major pieces by James O'Connor and André Gunder Frank on imperialism and others dealing mainly with aspects of underdevelopment in the Third World.

Rosen, Steven J., and James R. Kurth, eds. 1974. *Testing Theories of Economic Imperialism*. Toronto and London: Lexington. Includes essay by Karl Deutsch that identifies various types of imperialism (folk, conservative, liberal, Marxist, sociological and psychological, and dependency theories); essay by Andrew Mack that examines and compares theories of economic imperialism; and essay by Thomas Weisskopf that looks at imperialism in terms of national interests.

Ruccio, David F. 1989. "Fordism on a World Scale: International Dimensions of Regulation." *Review of Radical Political Economics* 21 (Winter):33–53. A review of the French regulation school, especially the work of Lipietz. Examines global Fordism and peripheral Fordism in the Marxist agenda for theorizing capitalist development. Shows how the regulation school focused initially on a North-South model and the ways of regulating the advanced capitalist economies. Sees this school as a recent effort to complete Marx's project on international trade and world market.

Schoonover, Thomas D. 1992. *The United States in Central America, 1860–1911: Episodes of Social Imperialism and Imperial Rivalry in the World System*. Durham, N.C.: Duke University Press. On the basis of doctoral research on imperialism in Central America during the 1823 to 1929 period, introduces a political economy theoretical framework as a basis for archival research, narrative, and historical method.

Schumpeter, Joseph. 1955 (1919). *Imperialism and Social Classes*. New York: World Publishing, Meridian Books. English edition first published in 1951. Argues that imperialism will be insignificant in an era of advanced capitalism.

Scott, Catherine V. 1996. *Gender and Development: Rethinking Modernization and Dependency Theory*. Boulder: Lynne Rienner. Argues that masculine concepts permeate modernization and dependency theory alongside Marxism.

Simon, Lawrence H., and David F. Ruccio. 1986. "Methodological Aspects of a Marxist Approach to Development: An Analysis of the Modes of Production School." *World Development* 14 (February):211–222. Critical look at the modes-of-production school with focus on theoretical sources in Marxist theory, three approaches, and criticism.

Smith, Neil. 1986. "Uneven Development and the Geography of Modernity." *Social Concept* 3 (2):67–90. Builds on his 1984 work, *Uneven Development: Nature, Capital, and the Production of Space*. London: Basil Blackwell.

Smith, Tony. 1981. *The Pattern of Imperialism: The United States, Great Britain, and the Latin-Industrializing World Since 1815*. New York: Cambridge University Press. Argues that one must explode "dependency's myth of imperialism at the same time as its myth of the logic of change on the periphery" (557).

So, Alvin Y. 1990. *Social Change and Development: Modernization, Dependency, and World-System Theories*. Newbury Park, Calif.: Sage Publications. A critical overview and synthesis of three major schools of developmental thinking.

Sunkel, Osvaldo, ed. 1992. *Development from Within: Toward a Neostructuralist Approach for Latin America*. Boulder: Lynne Rienner. A collection of essays on the structuralist approach to development, influenced by ECLA.

Swedberg, Richard, ed. 1991. *Joseph A. Schumpeter: The Economics and Sociology of Capitalism*. Princeton: Princeton University Press. A biography and analysis of the thought of Schumpeter.

Sweezy, Paul M. 1942. "Imperialism," in his *The Theory of Capitalist Development*. New York: Monthly Review Press. Follows Lenin's definition, with emphasis on monopoly capital, in discussing imperialism in terms of nationalism, militarism, and racism and relating it to classes, the state, and wars of redivision.

_____. 1989. "U.S. Imperialism in the 1990s." *Monthly Review* 41 (October):1–17. Reviews the impact of U.S. dominance in the world capitalist system since the 1960s, identifies the symptoms of decline since the defeat in Vietnam, analyzes the failure of the Reagan administration to reverse the trend, and suggests that in the 1990s the U.S. empire will disintegrate and be replaced by a system of competing trade and currency blocs.

Szymanski, Al. 1981. *The Logic of Imperialism*. New York: Praeger. A systematic and critical overview of theories of imperialism, including the Marxist mainstream, Marxist dependency theory, the historical development of imperialism, the development of imperialism and the transformation of the periphery, and the decline of U.S. hegemony and interimperialist rivalry.

Taylor, John G. 1979. *From Modernization to Modes of Production: A Critique of the Sociologies of Development and Underdevelopment*. London: Macmillan. Through criticism of past and present theory, works out a distinctive approach to the modes of production.

Tonelson, Alan. 1997. "Globalization: The Great American Non-Debate." *Current History* 96 (November):353–359. A useful mainstream overview of the debates and contrasting perspectives around issues of globalization. Considers globalization a reality to which U.S. policy fails to adjust because many Americans equate it with trade and refrain from critical thinking about its implications.

Wallerstein, Immanuel. 1974, 1980, 1989. *The Modern World System*. 3 vols. New York: Academic Press. Influenced by Fernand Braudel, elaborates a theory of the world system with a reinterpretation of European history since the fifteenth century.

Warren, Bill. 1973. "Imperialism and Capitalist Industrialization." *New Left Review* 81 (September-October):3–44. A defense of imperialism as a means for promoting capitalist industrialization. Argues that imperialist rivalries in the form of trade and foreign investment allow Third World nations to grow and give them a bargaining position in the extraction and manufacturing sectors. Calls on the left to reexamine the anti-imperialist struggle and to consider national independence and full capitalist development means for achieving socialism.

_____. 1980. *Imperialism: Pioneer of Capitalism*. London: New Left Books. Returns to the Marxist assumption that capitalism is progressive and therefore imperialism will serve to push the less developed areas toward progressive social change.

Willoughby, John. 1995. "Evaluating the Leninist Theory of Imperialism." *Science and Society* 59 (Fall):320–338. Asserting that the Leninist theory of imperialism effectively focuses on the evolving forms of capital accumulation, argues that its attempt to reduce political domination to economic tendencies is misleading and that it must take into account evolving state structures and personnel in the state apparatus.

Wood, Ellen Meiksins, and John Bellamy Foster, eds. 1997. *In Defense of History: Marxism and the Postmodern Agenda*. New York: Monthly Review Press. A series of essays identifying and criticizing postmodernism.

World Commission on Environment and Development. 1987. *Our Common Future*. New York: Oxford University Press. The detailed report of the United Nations commission concerned with sustainable development, the management of resources, and the protection of the environment in the rapidly changing international order.

Yaghamaian, Behzad. 1990. "Development Theories and Development Strategies: An Alternative Theoretical Framework." *Review of Radical Political Economics* 22 (Summer and Fall):174–188. Uses a theory of the internationalization of capital to argue that import-substitution industrialization and export-led industrialization are "two stages of the internationalization of production" (174).

6

THEORIES OF DEMOCRACY

All the great revolutions of recent centuries have focused on one or another aspect of democracy. The French and English experiences reflected class distinctions and social inequalities and involved struggle for individual freedoms and rights in the society at large. The American upheaval was not only to gain independence but to ensure a political system of fair representation through the formal institutions of government and the state. The Russian, Chinese, and Cuban revolutions involved struggles between social classes; the overturning of injustices; and the goal of economic, social, and political equality. Revolution, however, does not necessarily ensure the attainment of these objectives, and all these cases have suffered from aberrations along the revolutionary path. Historically, democracy seems to have signified the struggle to eliminate class discrepancies, but in recent years, especially since World War II in the United States and conspicuously through the work of Arthur Bentley, David Truman, and Robert Dahl, democracy has come to mean a politics of bargaining and consensus.

Webster's Third New International Dictionary reminds us of the Greek roots of "democracy": *demos*, "people," and *kratia*, "authority," suggesting government in which supreme power is held by the people and exercised either directly or through a system of representation. This distinction is relevant to our assessment of capitalist or socialist experiences in which different forms of democracy have appeared, and it is at the root of essential questions we may raise in comparative inquiry. We may ask, for instance, whether formal or representative democracy is a precondition for participatory and ultimately pure democracy en route to some higher form of society, be it postcapitalist, socialist, capitalist, or something else, or whether these two forms are merely variants on the way to higher forms. Is formal democracy a necessary condition for the transition to socialism? Is a change in regime or in the apparatuses of the state also a condition for such a transition? If the state has some relation to democracy, then what about civil society? These questions hint at the complexity of realizing any vision of democracy in the contemporary world and indicate why the theory of democracy is so varied and imprecise.

Initially, the search for a definition of democracy might take us to the ancient texts on Athenian democracy. For example, the view that Athenian democracy involved direct participation has been articulated by Sheldon Wolin (1993), and in an acknowledgment of the Athenian legacy Sidney Verba (1993) has suggested that citizen initiatives should be taken into account alongside electoral and representative forms of democracy. Our impressions of this ancient democracy have been shaped by the critiques of Aristotle, Plato, and Thucydides and by the interpretations of later advocates of democracy such as James Madison and Alexander Hamilton, who in *The Federalist* characterized it as nothing but mob rule (Hamilton, Madison, and Jay, 1961). A revision of these understandings emerges, however, in the reassessments of Mogens Hansen in *The Athenian Democracy in the Age of Demosthenes* (1991), Donald Kagan in *Pericles of Athens and the Birth of Democracy* (1991), and R. K. Sinclair in *Democracy and Participation in Athens* (1988). In these and other recent works, Athenian democracy is revealed as a complex system of checks and balances:

> Looking to this scholarship we do not see either direct mass rule or concealed elite dominance; rather, it is a complex system but once we recognize the institutional richness of the Athenian system, we ought to be suspicious of overly romanticized notions of Athenian democracy that render it indistinguishable from modern notions of pure participatory democracy. (Grofman 1993: 471)

Sheldon Wolin, comparing the Periclean Athens of the fifth century B.C. with the New England township of the Jacksonian era, noted that Tocqueville slighted ancient Athens with his claim that American democracy was "more perfect than antiquity had dared dream of" (quoted in Grofmann 1993: 475). For Wolin, Tocqueville's comparison has left modern liberals and even radical democrats with the impression that Athenian democracy was impractical or extremist: "It is no exaggeration to say that one of the, if not the, main projects of ancient constitutional theorists, such as Plato (*The Laws*), Aristotle, Polybious, and Cicero, as well as of modern constitutionalists, such as the authors of *The Federalist* and Tocqueville, was to dampen, frustrate, sublimate, and defeat the demotic passions" (Wolin quoted in Grofman 1993: 476). J. Peter Euben admonishes us to "be alert to the conservative if not anti-democratic impulses of liberal constitutionalism and the inadequacies of relying on rights," pointing out that in a society professing formal rights social inequalities may prevail and rights may not be effective when most needed (in Grofman 1993: 479). For the Athenians, he reminds us, "Democratic excess was to be contained by the political education in civic virtue that came from living a public life" (479).

Focusing on the thought of Protagoras, who advanced "the only systematic argument for democracy to have survived from antiquity," Ellen Meiksins Wood (1995: 192–194) has described how Plato, in a refutation of these ideas, set forth the agenda for his later philosophical writing and, in particular, emphasized a division of labor between those who rule and those who are ruled. In contrast to Plato, other classical writings reveal an Athenian culture in which peasants and artisans enjoyed full rights of citizenship. Jean Elshtain, for instance, contrasted Plato's arguments against democracy with the idealization and uniqueness of Greek democracy portrayed by Pericles (1995: 92–104). In his defense of democracy, Protagoras argued that everyone who lives in a civilized community is exposed to learning processes that inculcate civic virtue through experiences in the family, the school, and political life. Thus, "nowhere . . . was the typical pattern of division between rulers and producers broken as completely as it was in the Athenian democracy" (Wood 1995: 190–191). Although differences and tensions between rulers and ruled persisted, civic identity and political status were dissociated from socioeconomic status and class inequality: "Democratic citizenship in Athens meant that small producers were to a great extent free of the extra-economic exactions to which direct producers in pre-capitalist societies have always been subject" (202). Citizenship meant that political equality could coexist with and even transform socioeconomic inequality, so that "democracy was more substantive than 'formal'" (202). This ancient Greek relationship was precluded in feudalism, where political rights were not redistributed, and in capitalism, where "democracy could be confined to a formally separate 'political' sphere while the 'economy' followed rules of its own" (203).

For a better understanding of democracy, one starting point might be the work of Giovanni Sartori, who in *Theory of Democracy Revisited* (1987) defends the mainstream theory of democracy and, in particular, the notion that restraint of arbitrary state power through the rule of law is the essence of modern civilization. This work distinguishes between elitist and participatory forms of democracy and expresses enthusiasm for the former. Norberto Bobbio (1987) follows this line of thinking with a minimal definition of democracy as "a set of rules" that determine who can make collective decisions through representative forms of government and competitive political parties.

Dankwart Rustow (1970) identified three conceptions of democracy: one associated with economic and social criteria such as per capita income, literacy, and urban residence as identified by Seymour Martin

Lipset in *Political Man* (1960 and 1994); another linked to political culture and certain beliefs or attitudes among citizens in civil society, as in *The Civic Culture* (1963), by Gabriel Almond and Sidney Verba; and a third tied to conflict and reconciliation, as in *The New Belief in the Common Man* (1942), by Carl Friedrich, and *Class and Class Conflict in Industrial Society* (1959), by Ralf Dahrendorf. Rustow's scheme serves as a point of departure for Terry Karl's middle-range definition of democracy "as a set of institutions that permits the entire adult population to act as citizens by choosing their leading decision makers in competitive, fair, and regularly scheduled elections which are held in the context of the rule of law, guarantees for political freedom, and limited military prerogatives" (1990: 2). In a related essay, Karl and Philippe Schmitter observe that "for better or worse, we are 'stuck' with democracy as the catchword of contemporary political discourse. It is a word that resonates in people's minds and springs from their lips as they struggle for freedom and a better way of life; it is the word whose meaning we must discern if it is to be of any use in guiding political analysis and practice" (Schmitter and Karl 1991: 75). They define political democracy today as "a system of governance in which rulers are held accountable for their actions in the public realm by citizens, acting indirectly through the competition and cooperation of their elected representatives" (76). They recast this definition as follows: "Modern democracy, in other words, offers a variety of competitive processes and channels for the expression of interests and values—associational as well as partisan, functional as well as territorial, collective as well as individual. All are integral to its practice" (78). They further identify concepts and ideas that relate to the discourse on democracy but are outside their "generic" definition of democracy: consensus, participation, access, responsiveness, majority rule, parliamentary sovereignty, party government, pluralism, federalism, presidentialism, and checks and balances (83–85).

Robert Dahl 1982: 11) has outlined a set of minimum conditions for modern political democracy: control constitutionally vested in elected officials over government decisions about policy, fair and frequent elections of public officials, adult suffrage and access to running for office, freedom of citizens to express political preferences, availability of alternative sources of information, and freedom to form independent parties and interest groups. These conditions approximate the essential components of democracy identified by Richard Sklar (1987): electoral practices, constitutional norms, and economic and social pluralism. A principal problem, Sklar argues, is the prevalent belief that mass political participation is detrimental to capital accumulation. What is needed is attention to accountability, which he believes underlies developmental democracy and fosters pluralism in political and economic life: "The norm of accountability appears to be the most widely practiced of democratic principles; it is by far more prevalent in the world than freedom of association to compete for governmental office, or popular participation in authoritative decision making" (Sklar 1987: 714).

This link of political and economic considerations and the relationship of capitalist accumulation to democracy is of concern to both Evelyne Huber Stephens (1989) and John Stephens (1993). Historically associating democratic tendencies with industrialization or with situations involving elite contestation, such as agricultural export expansion, Evelyne Stephens concludes that democracy emerged when pressure from the subordinated classes was perceived as a threat by economic elites and export pressures mobilized class alliances through political parties. This analysis suggests an evolution reminiscent of Daniel Levine's (1988: 383) notion of democratization, first in the sense that democracy is created in stages and second in the emphasis on the evolution of egalitarian social relations.

These mainstream understandings, with emphasis on the American variant of democracy, are widely accepted in academia today but they are not without criticism. Wood's allusion to the participatory inclinations of Athenian democracy serves as backdrop for her indictment of American representative democracy. She traces it to the tradition of "popular sovereignty," in which the *demos* was not the people but the privileged aristocracy of landlords. In her view, this resulted in a "check on monarchy and state centralization," but "the 'political nation' which grew out of the community of feudal lords retained its exclusiveness and the political subordination of producing classes" (1995: 205). In England, this exclusive political nation was represented in Parliament, whereas the American experience was shaped by the Federalists, whose "task was to produce an ideology, and specifically a redefinition of democracy, which would disguise the ambiguities in their oligarchic project" (214). Wood goes on to show how this conception of democracy evolved into its liberal form, "based on pre-modern, pre-capitalist forms of power" and dependent on "the emergence of capitalist social property relations" that allowed for "an economic sphere with its own power relations not dependent on juridical or political privilege" (234). In other words, under liberal or formal democracy the sphere of domination under capitalism and private property was relatively untouched by political power, the consequence of a flawed liberalism that was "not equipped to cope with the realities of power in a capitalist society, and even less to encompass a more inclusive kind of democracy than now exists" (237).

David Held has described five different conceptions and models of democracy, from the Greeks to Marx: competitive elitism, pluralism, neopluralism, neo-Marxism, and corporatism. The central tenet of competitive elitism was that political life in modern industrial society had little room for either democratic participation or individual or collective development. This theory was important to both Max Weber and Joseph Schumpeter, who wanted their democratic theories to be grounded in reality, transforming "apparent historical necessities into positive theoretical virtues" (Held 1987: 158). They believed that the apathy of most citizens was necessary for the smooth operation of a democratic system. In their restrictive vision of democracy, the role of the mass electorate was limited to choosing decisionmakers and curbing their excesses. They believed that most people were emotional and not qualified to participate directly in political life and policy decisions. Weber even referred to the primary function of the masses as democratically selecting "an elected dictatorship." Democracy was seen as a mechanism that allowed for registration of the broad desires of ordinary people while leaving actual public policy to the qualified few. Schumpeter attacked the idea of a "popular will" as lacking any rational basis because of the impact of propaganda, advertising, and promotion on individual choices and desires. Held argues that democratic theory has here come almost full circle from the broad participation under the Athenian system to an apparent abandonment of decisionmaking power to the elites. He considers this theory too quick to accept that those traditionally in power will remain there and that a "vicious circle of limited or non-participation" will prevail (175).

Pluralism, a conception of democracy that prevailed during the 1950s and 1960s, revolved around Madisonian democratic theory and the writings of Robert Dahl. It focused on the dynamics of group politics and explored the relationship between electoral competition and the activities of organized interests. In contrast with the Schumpeter/Weber model, it argued that concentration of power in the hands of competing elites was not inevitable. The purpose of government was seen as protecting the freedom of factions to further their political interests while preventing any one of them from undermining the freedom of others. A tyrannous majority was considered improbable because elections reflect preferences of various competitive groups rather than a firm majority. The democratic system thus functioned as a "polyarchy" of interest groups competing openly for the electoral support of a large population. Held takes issue with this approach, arguing that pluralism too narrowly defined democracy in terms of the existing features of Western politics and ignored questions such as citizen participation that have been part of democratic theory since the Greeks. He also calls attention to the fact that in the face of pluralism government does not necessarily listen to all groups equally or communicate beyond the leaders of power centers.

Neopluralism recognizes the problems of classical pluralism and acknowledges disparities in the distribution of power. It suggests that interest groups should not be treated as equal and that the state cannot be thought of as a neutral arbiter among them. Access to government and decisionmaking is limited. Furthermore, business corporations may wield disproportionate influence over the state, and state managers may develop their own aims and objectives.

Neo-Marxism takes a different tack, arguing that a dominant or ruling class owns and controls the means of production, has ties with powerful institutions, and is disproportionately represented at all levels of the state apparatus. This was Ralph Miliband's position, and Nicos Poulantzas criticized it, emphasizing the fracturing of structural elements in the face of competitive pressures and viewing the state as an arena in which class forces struggled for power and relative state autonomy might prevail.

Finally, a democratic theory is inherent in the literature on corporatism and the notion that traditional representative political institutions have been progressively displaced by tripartite decisionmaking between business, labor, and the state. Held questions these assumptions, suggesting that tripartite relations began to erode during the 1970s, when severe economic difficulties exposed the limited common ground between labor and capital and dominant capitalist groups were able to prevail and marginalize certain groups.

Many of the books on democracy are concerned with its political implications and representative forms of government. Particularly useful are James Bryce's *Modern Democracies* (1921), Robert A. Dahl's *A Preface to Democratic Theory* (1956), Harry Eckstein's *A Theory of Stable Democracy* (1961), and Carl J. Friedrich's *Constitutional Government and Democracy* (1937). A fundamental classical work on democracy, based on the early experience of establishing formal representative government and the implications for a society evolving within capitalism, is Alexis de Tocqueville's *Democracy in America* (1873), which considered social equality despite different economic conditions essential for democracy. Barrington Moore Jr., in his *Social Origins of Dictatorship and Democracy* (1966; see annotated reference in Chapter 1), examined the modern history of a number of societies, including the United States. The *Journal of Democracy*, which first appeared in 1990, was established by the National Endowment for Democracy under the editorship of Marc F. Plattner and Larry Diamond and seeks a blend of scholarly analysis and reports from democratic activists. Recent comparative studies include Arend Lijphart's (1984) application of a model of majoritarian and consensus democracy to the experience of twenty-two regimes and Lawrence Jacobs's (1994) study of liberal democracy.

DEMOCRACY AND CAPITALISM

Democracy has been associated both in theory and in practice with capitalism and socialism. The political scientist Samuel Huntington (1991) believes that the world is now engaged in its third wave of democratization. The first wave, in the hundred years from the 1820s to 1920s, brought democracy to some thirty nations; the second, after the defeat of fascism in World War II, raised the number to thirty-six; the third began with the Portuguese coup of April 1974 and increased the number to more than sixty. Each wave has confronted a backlash. Huntington's notion of democracy is close to that of Dahl, including political and civil rights, fair elections, the right to form political associations, sources of news that are not monopolized by the government or powerful interests, and a national electorate open to all. Representative, formal democracy thus forms the essence of these emerging experiences, and these political criteria are associated with capitalist development everywhere in the contemporary world.

Gabriel Almond, focusing on Schumpeter's *Capitalism, Socialism, and Democracy* (1942), argued that "the relation between capitalism and democracy dominates the political theory of the last two centuries. ... Capitalism is positively linked with democracy, shares its values and culture, and facilitates its development. This case has been made in historical, logical, and statistical terms" (1991: 468). As we shall see, however, the contradictions of capitalist development may interfere with the implantation of formal democracy. In his *Capitalism and Democracy in the Third World* (1997; see annotated reference in Chapter 5), Paul Cammack has argued that an ideological preference for formal democracy and capitalism underlies the abortive efforts of North American social scientists to elaborate a theory of development. The development literature tends to mystify the relationship between liberal democracy and capitalism. Irene Gendzier (1985) explains this mystification in terms of the cold war debates of the 1950s and 1960s. For the emerging democracies of the 1980s, capitalism, according to the Brazilian political scientist Francisco Weffort, often led to an insurmountable "profound and prolonged economic crisis that resulted in social exclusion and massive poverty." Indeed, many of these countries were "building democracy on top of a minefield of social apartheid" (1992: 20).

A collection of essays organized by Marc Plattner and Larry Diamond (1992) exposes the weaknesses of democratic capitalism and advocates democratic socialist alternatives. For example, Adam Przeworski (in Plattner and Diamond 1992: 55) shows how development linked to national, economic, and political independence has shifted to modernization through a process of internationalization that relinquishes national sovereignty. He demonstrates that neoliberal reforms, implemented without political participation, have painful social costs. Elsewhere, however (1991), Przeworski is pessimistic about the prospects for socialism.

The extent to which the capitalist state can be democratic is at issue today (Berger 1992). Russell Hansen (1989) has shown how the notion of democracy has changed in the course of the twentieth century. Originally, it was generally conceived of in terms of class, with the people constituting a mass of political consumers (the productive class) opposed to the aristocrats (the wealthy unproductive class). About the time of the New Deal this conception evolved into a compromise between classes so that democracy and plutocracy might live in harmony; the class divisions and conflicts of society became less conspicuous. A recent study on inequality and participation in the United States reaffirms the importance of class. In *Voice and Equality: Civic Voluntarism and American Politics,* Sidney Verba, Kay Lehman Schlozman, and Henry Brady (1995) note that participants in voting and politics tend to be well educated and have higher incomes. Despite the relative inattention to class in the mainstream literature, which they attribute to emphasis on multiculturalism, changing occupational structure, and the declining appeal of Marxist analysis, "when it comes to political participation, class matters profoundly for American politics" (1997: 80).

Advocates of the capitalist state consider the modern state uniquely responsive to popular demands and interests and therefore democratic. For them, there is no power struggle between the capitalist ruling class and the working class. Indeed, the interests of the two may overlap or merge, and various lines of political involvement and interests may prevail along with a pluralistic politics based on consensus and checks and balances in a complex and highly differentiated society. Almond and others believe that constitutions, the rule of law, and elections are forms of representation that reflect the will and participation of the people. For example, Robert Dahl, in *Pluralist Democracy in the United States* (1967), described the democratic order in terms of a wide dispersion of power and authority among government officials and private individuals and groups alike. The structure of power is segmented, not organized in a clear hierarchical pattern. Characteristic of this democratic order are opportunities for freedom of thought, consensus and dissent, and participation in politics; the peaceful management of conflict and constraints on violence; and widespread confidence in and loyalty to a constitutional and democratic polity. In reality, however, formal democracy is limited by structural constraints, the nature of the political party system and its agenda, and the indirect control of capital over the state. These constraints date to classical conceptions of government, as Noam Chomsky (1991), pointing to David Hume's paradox of government, reminds us: The few govern the many, and most are resigned to the situation.

This notion of the democratic state has been taken up in recent literature on institutionalization and the prospects for civil society (Hirst and
Khilnani 1996). Ruth Berins Collier (1999) sifts through 17 historical cases
and 10 contemporary cases to assess the role and influence of the working
class in the process of democratization. She finds labor in a weak and
marginalized position in the face of emerging democratic regimes. Theda
Skocpol (1997) has found that although most of the large voluntary associations of the nineteenth century survive today, better-educated
Americans are withdrawing from broad community groups. She argues
that Americans need a new emphasis on working together and helping
the poor.

Alan Wolfe (1997), more optimistic, sees civil society as having under-
gone a revival during the 1980s, when it was argued that families, voluntary organizations, and spontaneous political movements were more important. He shows how left, right, and center became enamored of the
idea and how his own *Whose Keeper? Social Science and Moral Obligation*
(1989) helped legitimize the concept in academia. He contends, however,
that today we are less likely to find civil society in neighborhoods, families, and churches and more likely to see it in the workplace, in cyber-
space, and in less organized forms of political participation outside the
political parties. "Civil society, is not obsolete; it can never be. Without a
realm of associational and communal life independent of the market and
the state, we cannot experience the richness of citizenship and the rewards of personal and group responsibility" (12).

In reality, capitalism, in the name of a formal freedom and equality in
the marketplace as well as a plurality of political power, mobilizes a politics of hegemony to ensure stability in the formal practice of democratic
government. Bob Jessop captures the essence of this: "Hegemony involves political, intellectual and moral leadership rather than the forcible
imposition of the interests of the dominant class on dominated classes."
This leadership becomes hegemonic through a national popular project
that expresses national interests through a set of policies or goals and "requires systematic consideration of the demands and interests of various
individuals and social groups, compromise on secondary issues to maintain support and alliances, and the continuing mobilization of support
behind the national-popular project" (1990: 181).

Amartya Sen (1999) seeks a way out of this dilemma by focusing on the
capabilities or freedoms of people to acquire sufficient food, avoid dis-
ease, access education, obtain employment, and participate in community. He argues that people of different cultures share many values and
are capable of agreeing on common commitments. Many socialists assume that a pluralist politics is not possible in a capitalist society. Jessop,
in contrast, argues that pluralism has its "roots in capitalist social rela-

tions and provides the basis of the distinctive forms of capitalist politics" but socialists "are committed to developing a counter-hegemonic project which will progressively polarize the majority of these pluralist forces around support for socialist democracy and progressively neutralize support for capitalist hegemonic projects" (1990: 184). Indeed, Robert Dahl (1979) had long ago suggested that pluralism and socialism were compatible and referred to several European cases as examples. Jessop also contends with the liberal assumption that the modern capitalist state serves the public interest and is not necessarily an instrument of class rule at home and abroad. According to this view, the state mediates competing interests and represents the public and national interests rather than any particular segment of society. The state does not directly act in the interests of capital. Jessop makes clear that the long-term interests of capital, however, cannot be understood as harmonious and without contradictions, especially in the face of crises and various paths of capitalist accumulation.

It is often suggested that gradual reforms will serve to mitigate the problems and limits of the modern state. The inadequacies and problems of the system may be manifested through democratic accountability or pressures from unrealistic popular expectations, say, among trade unions or business associations. Excesses can be dealt with by limiting the scope of government and educating the public. Jessop extends this point by arguing that the struggle for democracy is not the same as the struggle against capitalism and that socialists, in order to win hegemony, must fight enemies of democracy on the left and the right as well as "draw attention to the increasing atrophy of parliamentary institutions and civil liberties in the advanced capitalist states themselves together with a growing ideological antipathy to democracy" (1990: 187). He advocates working within the system to expose its limitations while winning short-term concessions, developing an alternative hegemonic project that links these short-term interests to democracy, and transforming the separation between economic and political life "through the introduction of a coordinated system of industrial self-government and democratic economic planning and . . . reorganiz[ing] the state itself through the extension of democratic accountability" (189).

The question of liberal democracy's relationship to capitalism and its prospects of evolving from authoritarian regimes and dictatorship received considerable attention in the 1970s and 1980s. The basic premises of liberal democracy were frequently extended to the Third World, but these attempts were rejected by social scientists in the area such as the Egyptian Samir Amin. The idea, for example, that the market represents economic rationality could be countered by the proposition that social relations determine the market and that there is no rationality in capitalism.

Also questioned was the notion that without capitalism there can be no democracy. The idea that a wide-open door to the world system or free trade ensures development is countered by the scarcity of evidence that peripheral areas have been able to overcome many of the problems of underdevelopment and the fact that the masses of people have received minimal benefits. These questions can be explored through a plethora of interesting studies comparing transitions in Southern Europe and in South America, including Baloyra (1987); Bresser Pereira, Maravall, and Przeworski (1993); Chilcote et al. (1990); Di Palma (1990); Diamond, Linz, and Lipset (1988–1989); O'Donnell, Schmitter, and Whitehead (1986); and Poulantzas (1976; see annotated reference in Chapter 1). Lowenthal (1991); Mainwaring, O'Donnell, and Valenzuela (1992); Malloy and Seligson (1987); and Rueschemeyer, Stephens, and Stephens (1992) focus on transition and democracy in Latin America. Useful criticisms of some of this work appear in Levine (1988) and MacEwan (1988), although the discussions do not necessarily yield any particular model of democracy. John Markoff has reassessed the many forms of democracy and concluded that there is no unified definition of the term; instead, we should adapt our understanding to changing conditions in social conflict: "We need to understand not some ideal and the history of our failed approximations, but the history of really existing democracies, including the ideals nourished in struggles around and within them" (1997: 68).

Many beliefs about democracy emanate from perceptions and understandings about the American system of capitalist democracy. Joshua Cohen and Joel Rogers have argued that the relationship between capitalism and democracy is not a harmonious union but a temporary alliance in an "unstable structure of inner antagonisms, each striving to forsake the other" (1987: 49). Workers have formal and procedural but not substantive political rights and are therefore not in a position to influence national policy. Capitalist democracy directs the exercise of political rights toward the satisfaction of certain interests (51) and is "capable of satisfying the standards of rational calculation encouraged by its structure" (52). Capitalist democracies create the conditions of rationality within the system and tolerate only the short-term struggles that they can absorb. "The achievement of short-term material satisfaction often makes it irrational to engage in more radical struggle, since that struggle is by definition directed against those institutions which provide one's current gain" (57).

Herbert Marcuse, in *One-Dimensional Man* (1964), asserted that mass culture was an integral part of the consumer society, a new configuration of capitalist modernity in which culture and aesthetics blended with production and advertising to create a way of life focused on consumption of goods, services, mass images, and spectacles. Marcuse saw the culture industries as functioning mainly to shape the needs, attitudes, and behavior of individuals so as to integrate them in the consumer society. He anticipated current debates over needs, commodities, and consumer policies and was among the first to see the importance of these issues for critical social theory and public policy.

Criticisms of American society may be limited by constraints of American politics on left intellectuals in their struggle whether or not to enhance democracy under capitalism (Kopkind et al. 1992). This paradox appears with the futilities of some minorities. In a provocative opinion piece, Lani Guinier has called attention to the need to focus on the problems affecting marginalized groups in the United States—in particular, to reform the legislative decisionmaking process by providing "mechanisms to ensure that disadvantaged and stigmatized minority groups also have a fair chance to have their policy preferences satisfied" (1993). She characterizes liberal or capitalist representative democracy as the tyranny of the majority (1994). She argued that majoritarian systems with mostly single-representative districts such as in the United States tend to produce winning candidates who are unwilling to share power. Such systems favor incumbents, discourage voter participation, limit competition and choice, and marginalize third parties. Guinier proposes various forms of proportional voting to overcome these limitations, among them cumulative voting (which promotes minority rights, encourages competition and choice, and promotes cross-racial alliances) and preference voting (which encourages coalitions and alliances). The latter method was used in some U.S. cities between 1920 and 1950 but was dropped when communists (in New York City) and persons of color (in Cincinnati) were elected to office. Guinier suggests shifting to a representative democracy in which participation is meaningful and every vote counts (Guinier 1994).

Examining British politics, Ralph Miliband described how a plurality of competing political parties interacts with the state. In this form of democracy, a tension persists between the democratic idea of equal citizenship rights and the structure of inequality in the capitalist economy. Furthermore, the structures of capitalist democracy constrain popular pressures or influences from below. Miliband identified two alternatives to capitalist democracy: capitalist authoritarianism, in which pressures from below are arrested by a monopolistic state party, as in fascism or by military rule under military dictatorships, and socialist democracy, characterized by the direct and unmediated participation of the people in the administration of all public affairs, as was attempted under the Paris Commune of 1871 or during the early months of the October 1917 revolution in Russia. Miliband, of course, favored socialist democracy but without the distortions of past socialist movements (Schwartzmantel 1995).

Wood (1995) argues that although the Greeks did not invent slavery, they did invent free labor, which "has never been accorded the historical importance typically attributed to slavery in the ancient world" (182). She acknowledges the existence of slavery in ancient Greece, perhaps involving 20 to 30 percent of the population, but asserts that "while various forms of unfree labour have been a common feature in most places at most times, the status enjoyed by free labour in democratic Athens was without known precedent and in many respects has remained unequaled since" (185). She points out that under modern capitalist democracy socioeconomic inequality and exploitation exist alongside civic freedom and equality. Capitalism can coexist with formal democracy, but civic equality does not affect socioeconomic position and class inequality. Under capitalism, workers must exchange their labor power for wages as a means of subsistence. In contrast, under ancient democracy, workers were generally free to enter the labor market and ensure their subsistence: "Democratic citizenship in Athens meant that small producers were to a great extent free of the extra-economic exactions to which direct producers in pre-capitalist societies have always been subject" (202). Wood emphasized that the ruling classes in Europe and America were reluctant to extend political rights to workers and that formal democracy in the political sphere could be separated from economics. In England, parliamentary supremacy reigned against the threat of popular power; propertied elite dominated over the laboring mass. The American experience with democracy also was decisive, as the modern conception of democracy essentially evolved as antidemocratic in the hands of the founding fathers:

> The Federalist ideal may have been to create an aristocracy combining wealth with republican virtue . . . but their practical task was to sustain a propertied oligarchy with the electoral support of a popular multitude [and] to produce an ideology, and specifically a redefinition of democracy, which would disguise the ambiguities in their oligarchic project. (214–215)

A movement to transcend this liberalism is under way in the form of "a new pluralism," as Wood characterizes it, and comprises diverse interests in the search for a democratic community that acknowledges all kinds of difference—of gender, culture, sexuality—and that "encourages and celebrates these differences, but without allowing them to become relations of domination and oppression." Ideally, this community unites diverse human beings, all free and equal, while "suppressing differences or denying their special needs." The new social movements that contribute to this new pluralism emphasize a "politics of identity," but, Wood argues, they are also limited, both theoretically and politically, when "we try to situate class differences within its democratic vision" (258). "By all means let us have diversity, difference, and pluralism; but not an undifferentiated and unstructured pluralism. What is needed is a pluralism that does indeed

acknowledge diversity and difference, not merely plurality or multiplic-
ity" (263).

The contradictory relationship between capitalism as a mode of production and democracy as a political regime has been explored in industrial societies by Göran Therborn (1977) but became particularly clear for
Latin America, according to Atilio Borón, when in the mid-1960s military
dictatorships proved necessary to ensure the deepening of capitalist development, thereby exposing the myth that through capitalist development the region's chronic authoritarianism could be eradicated and bourgeois democracy secured. Borón describes how the earlier revolutionary
and liberating substance of democratic ideas has given way to a convergence of democracy and capitalism with varying results: "When bourgeois hegemony succeeded in introducing into the consciousness of the
subordinated classes the ideological justification of its class domination,
the democratic state could coexist" without force, yet when "bourgeois
hegemony was not achieved, the faulty constitution of democratic capitalism rapidly gave way to fascism or dictatorship" (1995: 8).

DEMOCRACY AND SOCIALISM

Democracy is usually associated with Western forms of government, especially parliamentary activity and political parties, but it was also a
concern in the classical Marxist literature and it is relevant to socialism
everywhere. Frank Cunningham's *Democratic Theory and Socialism* (1987)
includes a wide-ranging discussion of issues of interest to democratic socialists, among them the limits of democracy in socialist societies dominated by bureaucratic and authoritarian rule. Paul Buhl's (1987 [1991],
1990) studies of Marxism in the Unites States delve into the search for a
democratic path. The excesses of socialist regimes in the former Soviet
Union and Eastern Europe serve as a backdrop for Howard Sherman's
conception of a socialist democracy and a critical Marxism free of deter-
ministic tendencies. Sherman dismisses the old official Marxism and describes a new Marxism that is "unofficial, independent, profoundly democratic, critical of all existing societies, and critical of all old, rigid ideas"
(1995: 3). Whereas most Marxist research has focused on the conflict between capitalism and democracy, with the demise of the Soviet Union it
should be easier to define socialism in terms of both political and economic democracy: "Economic democracy must entail the main socialist
goals: ending exploitation, enough democratic planning to guarantee
full employment, and a widespread system of free goods and services"
(337).

Early in his writings, especially in "On the Jewish Question" (1843),
Marx suggested that the differences between representative and partici-

patory democracy may not be substantial, since the state has the power to shape and determine what rights citizens have and how they may exercise them. Antonio Gramsci and, more recently, Nicos Poulantzas have emphasized that law and violence are inherent in the modern capitalist state. Both looked to authoritarian and fascist forms of the capitalist state. In *Selections from the Prison Notebooks of Antonio Gramsci,* Gramsci envisioned the state as seeking to form "a certain type of civilization and of citizen . . . and to eliminate certain customs and attitudes and to disseminate others. . . . The law will be its instrument for this purpose" (1971: 246). In his *State, Power, Socialism,* Poulantzas incorporated these elements: "By issuing rules and passing laws the state establishes an initial field of injunctions, prohibitions, and censorship, and thus institutes the practical terrain and object of violence" (1978: 72–73). In effect, the state permeates all social life. An assault on the state might resolve the dilemma, but changes might also be effected through the institutions and values of representative democracy alongside direct popular democracy in the transition to socialism.

In *The Civil War in France* (1871) Marx discussed socialist democracy in connection with the Paris Commune (1871). Carl Boggs reminds us that Marx was interested in the popular character of its governmental system: The armed populace replaced the standing army, the political power of the police was reduced, and all public servants were elected and subject to recall. Marx's reflections on the commune raised the issue of the role of democracy in the transition to socialism, for he believed that ultimately the inherent contradictions of capitalism would lead to a higher form. In the 1880s and toward the end of his life, Marx, in an era of parliaments, political parties, and universal suffrage in Europe, envisaged participation in the capitalist state as one instrument of class struggle, but he did not elaborate any theory of socialist democracy. Later, Engels wrote on German social democracy, envisioning electoral politics as a useful means of educating, organizing, and mobilizing workers for change through meaningful reforms. Boggs asserts that for Marx and Engels,

> the ideal of socialism meant public ownership of the means of production, abolition of inequality and exploitation, breakdown of the old social divisions—and democracy. It is hard to doubt the democratic sensibilities and intentions of classical Marxism: if capitalism signified oligarchy and domination by its very logic, then socialism was inherently democratic. (1995: 31–32)

Stanley Aronowitz goes a step farther to suggest that the critique of bourgeois democracy by Marx and Engels did not neglect the use that the working class could make of the liberal state and its civil liberties "for the purpose of organizing to overturn and replace it." Indeed, a socialist conception of democracy derived from Marx "consists in a 'free association' of individuals each of whom is expected to participate fully in the decisions affecting the collective" (1990 [1981]: 256–257).

But the classical Marxist literature describes no clear strategies for the democratic socialist transformation. "The absence of a political theory of the transitional process was one of the most striking features of early Marxism, with profound consequences for twentieth-century socialist politics" (Boggs 1995: 33). After Marx, the search for a political strategy was accompanied by debates and factional schisms around four tendencies (36–37): the orthodox or centrist Marxism of Karl Kautsky and Austro-Marxist thinkers; the reformist-evolutionary line of Edward Bernstein; the vanguardist-insurrectionary tendency of Lenin; and the radical left thrust of Rosa Luxemburg. Kautsky advocated a (bourgeois) parliamentary road to socialism through which the capitalist economy would gradually be overturned. Bernstein believed in a relatively smooth evolutionary transition to socialism through the parliamentary institutions of liberal democracy. Lenin proposed a revolutionary assault on the capitalist state that would lead to direct democracy, but he also spoke of a vanguard party and hegemony under firm political and economic discipline. Luxemburg felt that the imminent crisis of capitalism blocked any parliamentary transformation within the bourgeois state and that authoritarianism under the vanguard party would undermine democracy in the long run. Unlike Kautsky, Bernstein, and Lenin, according to Boggs, "Luxemburg was the first important Marxist theorist to pose the question of socialist democracy" (1995: 50). Eventually she and others worked out an institutional alternative to a party-centered socialism in the form of a federal system of local councils in which popular control could emanate from the workplace and the community.

The rise and recent fall of authoritarian, bureaucratic, or state socialist regimes in Eastern Europe and the Soviet Union has produced some new thinking, reassessment, and criticism of the prospects of democracy under socialism. Michael Löwy (1991) has argued that Western characterizations of communist states and Eastern descriptions of "really existing socialism" were false and misleading. Little private capital existed in these societies, and thus they could claim not to be capitalist, but they lacked democracy and excluded the majority from political power. Löwy asserts that what is dying is not communism but a moribund bureaucracy, the radical movements advocating socialist and democratic alternatives having been defeated. Although there is not much reason for optimism in the short run, socialist democracy remains a possibility. Even though the left is in a state of profound ideological confusion and disarray, Marxism serves to remove obstacles to the free development of the productive forces and functions through praxis and the dialectical materialist method as a means of criticizing all ideas and practices.

Other prominent political thinkers have dealt with the aftermath of the collapse of socialist regimes in Eastern Europe. Whereas the German political scientist Claus Offe (1991) has explored the prospects for reforms and assessed the relationship of representative democracy and emerging capitalism in the early democratic regimes, the Swedish sociologist Göran Therborn (1992) has examined these problems through a retrospective assessment of socialism, and John Keane (1988) has looked at the role of the state and civil society in exploring the problems of democracy and socialism in Europe.

The structural changes and new direction appear to comprise two fundamental struggles: one against the bureaucratic-authoritarian socialist state, the other against the neocapitalist and neocolonial state and capitalist monopolies. At the state level, the bourgeoisie was made up of state officials, the middle classes, and a petty bourgeoisie, but it was divided among supporters of authoritarian socialism, democratic socialism, and capitalism. The split was caused, on the one hand, by corrupt bureaucrats with power and special privileges who defended the restoration of the market economy to benefit themselves and, on the other hand, by democratic socialists aligned with honest officials.

In response to these changes in the socialist world, Keith Graham (1986) suggests reconsidering a "strictly defined" or orthodox Marxism—questioning the traditional stress on the abolition of private ownership of the means of production and its replacement by social or common ownership. According to Pat Devine, a reassessment of the relationship between legal ownership, actual control, and exploitation; between planning and the market; and between individual freedom, planning, and the market yields the possibility of a regulated socialist market in which the market mechanism is used as a tool of planning, economic production units respond to the use of economic regulators through fiscal and monetary policy, and the market environment reflects collectively determined as well as individual priorities (Devine, comment in Taub 1990).

Also questioning traditional assumptions about socialism, Jürgen Habermas (1990) outlines three interpretive models that are representative of recent critical thinking. First, in response to the postmodern critique of reason and its characterization of nonviolent upheavals as "a revolution to end the epoch of revolutions," the revolutionary collapse of bureaucratic socialism is taken as a sign that modernity and the spirit of the West are penetrating the East not only as a technological civilizing influence but also as a democratic tradition. Second, from the anticommunist point of view the revolution has turned against its origins through an international civil war conceived by intellectual elites and carried to a global level. Third, the liberal perspective sees the end of state socialism as signifying the beginning of the eventual disappearance of totalitarian-ism from Europe, to be replaced by constitutional democracy, market economy, and social pluralism. Habermas goes on to fault Western Marxism for continuing to root its critique in the characteristics of early industrialization and an analysis based on labor, class division, and conflict among social classes. He criticizes social democratic reformism for underestimating the resistance inherent in state power and for advocating a welfare state that proved an illusion. He argues that academia is now in a position to benefit from theoretical revisions and cross-fertilization of Marxist with, especially, Weberian thought. The challenges of the moment call for a radical democratic universalization of interests through institutions for the formation of public opinion and political will.

This argument suggests that orthodox interpretations of Marx are of limited value because the relationship of capital to society has fundamentally changed since Marx's time. Global capitalism has rendered Marx's conception of the early industrial character of nineteenth-century societies largely irrelevant. Given the complexity of modern society, the alternative is to pursue the democratic ideals through discourse.

The sort of approach suggested by Habermas might be applied to the experience of the Sandinistas in Nicaragua throughout the 1980s. Although some interpretations may have characterized this experience as emulating traditional authoritarian models, the practices and objectives of the ruling party were actually inclined toward encouraging broad participation and democracy. For instance, prevailing sentiment opposed permitting the vanguard party to devolve into authoritarian and repressive institutions. The party undertook a pluralist project of national unity in an effort to assimilate three major factions and their constituencies. Economically, it sought not to expropriate the means of production but to bring the financial apparatus and foreign marketing under state control. Important to the success of these policies was a model in which the leadership sought to become hegemonic rather than dictatorial. An essential challenge to the revolutionary party was how to hasten the formation of the mass social movements that were perceived as crucial to maintaining popular support once revolutionary activity had been initiated. Honest elections initially provided legitimacy to the revolution, but eventually the process of building a mass base was insufficient to sustain a counterrevolutionary opposition bolstered financially and materially by the United States. Although the Sandinistas eventually succumbed to this opposition, the lessons of the Nicaraguan revolution give credence to the possibility of radical political democracy. The party was able to activate the mass struggle not through some preconceived master plan but through direct experimentation and building on the revolutionary experience.

This experience mirrors the thinking of Marta Harnecker, a Marxist theorist and activist who observed participatory experimentation in

Chile under Salvador Allende (1970–1973) and later in Cuba and Nicaragua. She questions the failure of the orthodox Marxist-Leninist left and the more open new left to recognize democracy as an immediate goal of the majority of people struggling for changes in the Third World. She defines democracy in a socialist context in terms of three fundamental elements: political democracy in the form of representation and citizen rights (government of the people), substantial or social democracy (government for the people), and participatory democracy (government by the people). Any left project, she argues, must assimilate these three types of democracy:

> Socialism as a project, then, cannot be separated from democracy; it can only be a highest expression and an enormous expansion of democracy in relation to limited bourgeois democracy. Democracy is a cause championed by revolutionaries, and not by the bourgeoisie who appropriated it, taking advantage of the deficiencies of the socialist countries. (1992: 62–63)

Harnecker identifies a shift in left thinking from a dogmatic Marxism and Leninism to a preference for Marxism because of Leninism's association with Stalinism, from a view of social movements as party appendages to a recognition of their autonomy, from a single-party-and-vanguard to a multiparty-and-shared-vanguard practice, and from armed struggle to peaceful coalitions that unmask the intentions of repressive military forces. She advocates a broad democratic project

> based on respect for political and ideological pluralism; abandonment of hegemonism and sectarianism; a search for each country's own road based on respect for national traditions; the search for a language that permits communication with the people, reaching its deepest sentiments; and finally, a style of leadership that is not top-down and that allows people to appropriate the project, make it their own, and feel encouraged to enrich the project with their initiatives and to correct errors and deviations with their criticisms. (73)

ALTERNATIVE DIRECTIONS:
TOWARD PARTICIPATORY DEMOCRACY

The forms of democracy associated with capitalism tend to be representative, but participatory forms have also appeared under both capitalism and socialism. Pauline Rosenau and Robert Paehlke (1990) have identified the perspectives of conservatives, liberals, new right conservatives, Western Marxists, and Marxist-Leninists on the question of participation. They show that both liberals and Western Marxists are optimistic about the participation of the disadvantaged whereas conservatives and Marxist-Leninists may be pessimistic; they conclude that there are similarities between left and right on the role of political participation of the poor. Since the late 1980s, for example, a series of meetings by left intellectuals and practitioners in Latin America has revealed their willingness to abandon revolution and armed struggle for liberal or bourgeois political forms, participate in electoral strategies, encourage pluralism, and seek reforms in the direction of radical change (Robinson 1992). Some of this congruence is due to shifting allegiances in a rapidly changing world dominated by expansive and dominant international capitalism, but some of it may simply reflect the exhaustion of revolutionary impetus in the face of international support for counterrevolutionary causes.

This is not to suggest that ideological tensions and class conflict have disappeared. Indeed, direct democratic participation may well increase as capitalist interests favor the rich and ignore the poor. Anticipating this possibility, Matthias Stiefel and Marshall Wolfe have suggested various dimensions of participation: encounters between the excluded and the elements of society that enforce the exclusion; efforts among the poor and marginalized to work through movements and organizations; participation through programs or projects proposed by government agencies, voluntary organizations, or international bodies; participation as a component of national policy; and participation through resistance to antiparticipatory structures and ideologies of modernization (1994: 6–11). They also explore various means for achieving participation through such mechanisms as pluralist democracy, self-reliance among the poor, revolutionary and postrevolutionary mobilization, conscientization and self-liberation, collective action, worker management, and defense of the natural order (22–34).

Mobilization Around Moral and Human Issues

A sketch of participatory politics since World War II suggests at least three levels of activity (Boyte 1990). Initially, the U.S. civil rights movement and its leadership were successful in mobilizing moral protest against the inhumanity of segregation. The movement evolved organizationally and attracted wide support but eventually splintered. A second level involved local organizations moving beyond the efforts of civil rights movements and working around basic issues with an approach that included political education alongside action programs, for example, Saul Alinsky's Industrial Areas Foundation (IAF). A third level of organizing was that of the citizen initiatives of recent years, with a shift from particular to broader concepts that have the potential for democratic politics. In California, for instance, many successful initiatives on protection of the environment, campaign reform, and other topics illustrate the possibilities of direct citizen decisionmaking on issues of great importance. A fourth level involved popular protest in college towns such as Berkeley, California; and Madison, Wisconsin, in the 1950s and 1960s, with the emergence of the new left and its politics of change through radical and democratic means. This movement received the intellectual support of important academics, among them the sociologist C. Wright Mills and the historian William Appleman Williams. Much of the theoretical thought of the times appeared in the quarterly *Studies on the Left* and its successor, *Radical America*.

The Students for a Democratic Society, for example, expressed their passion for direct action, community, and self-action in the "Port Huron Statement." Years later, Tom Hayden and his then-wife, Jane Fonda, carried some of these ideas in a grassroots effort to mobilize progressive movements around essential issues and to influence the political process at the local level. Eventually, Hayden became involved in electoral politics as a California state senator. Participatory democracy was also part of Md Anisur Rahman's reflections (1992) on development through collective local initiatives and Stan Burkey's methodology (1992) for achieving local development through self-reliance, participation, cooperation, and consciousness raising.

New Social Movements and Identity Politics

The new social movements—unique in that they were not always working class led or based—represent an alternative to traditional participation in politics. The tumultuous student protests and worker strikes of 1968 were driven by some of these social movements. Whatever their importance historically, they were temporary and did not assume a position of prominence in a reformulated political economy. Because of the widespread disillusionment over the ineffectiveness and decline of the labor movement, however, they attracted considerable attention. The social movements of recent decades have tended to involve identity politics.

Stanley Aronowitz (1994) has described two ideological factions on the left: the "redistributive" left, including trade unions; the civil rights movement; single-issue groups in housing, education, welfare, and social security; liberal democrats; and socialist parties, and the new social movements of feminism, black nationalism, and ecological concerns. He identifies radical democracy as a unifying concept for the disparate social movements, drawing its inspiration from the French Revolution of 1789 and the Paris Commune of 1871 and characterized by an insistence on (1) direct popular participation in crucial decisions affecting economic, political, and social life and institutions; (2) democratic management in state-owned enterprises and changes in work time and size of enterprises and social institutions; (3) plural universalism, whereby the power to make decisions rests on those affected by them. Aronowitz saw radical democracy as "a universal . . . that is hostile to the tendency of modern states to centralize authority . . . [that] entails limiting the power of representatives by genuine self-management of leading institutions . . . [and that] refuses the imperative of hierarchy and privilege based upon economic power" (1994: 64–65). He sums up the radical strategy as addressing "the politics of family, school, and neighborhood from the perspective of individual and collective freedom—not from the viewpoint of control and reproduction of processes of individual and generational development" (70).

Another advocate of participatory democracy, Carole Pateman (1991), has exposed the past practices of the male-dominated discipline of political science that have opposed equality on racial and gender terms. Theorists associated with the revival of interest in participatory democracy, she argued, have also tended to neglect the feminist literature. This criticism is backed by Anne Phillips (1991), who argues that theoretical writings about democracy in general have neglected the feminist perspective. Finally, in a critical examination of left differences on socialism and ecology, Ted Benton (1989) has shown how influential traditions of the left have created tensions in these two movements and elaborated a socialist critique of ecological politics. He argues for a "green historical materialism" that incorporates Marx's incisive understanding of capitalist accumulation.

Market Socialism

Progressive intellectuals dissatisfied with the rigid formulas of communist theoreticians and practitioners after World War II have searched for alternatives within Marxism. One perspective that caught their attention during the 1980s was market socialism. In *The Economics of Feasible Socialism* (1983; see annotated reference in Chapter 2), Alec Nove, perhaps its major proponent, suggested how socialism could be responsive to the market, solve the problems of inefficient distribution and rigid pricing, and involve the population in the economy.

Market socialism undoubtedly appealed to the nondogmatic left, especially in Europe, but Nove's ideas appear to have served also as an option for a left that has encountered difficulty in rejecting statism in the face of the ideological hegemony of the new right and neoliberalism nearly everywhere. Devine, for example, has suggested that in the absence of any serious alternative many on the left have "fallen for the market" (in Taub 1990: 195). Nove's model is vague and not based on any particular experience, although it clearly reflects familiarity with the European scene. Experimentation with the market by formerly socialist economies in Eastern Europe appeared to be leading those countries along the path of Latin Americanization, implying not only integration with world markets and capitalism but an increasing inability to cope with problems associated with foreign capital, such as debt; a lack of autonomy and planning; and an inability to provide the basic services structured under the previous socialist governments (see Nove, 1990). Furthermore, market socialism may have been utopian in the face of the fundamental conflict between private capital and state enterprise and policy. Questionable too was the logic that nondiscriminatory regulation treats all enterprises the same when, in fact, in local situations the market is coercive, nontransformable, and alienating.

Self-Management

Throughout history, there have been occasional moments of spontaneity in which workers organized and worked out schemes of self-management. In Portugal during 1974 and 1975, for example, some owners fled their factories and their workers occupied the premises and became involved in issues of age, gender, status, and unemployment. The factory committees became the new management and although international capital was uncooperative with regard to sales, credits, and raw materials the enterprises continued to function for a brief period.

This sort of moment was conceptually elaborated by Cornelius Castoriadis, who anticipated the new left critique of bureaucracy by advocating a system of direct democracy through councils of workers. He recognized the potential role of social forces outside the sphere of production such as youth, minorities, and women but did not incorporate them in his framework. In his conception of socialism, the working class achieves power for itself:

> The only total form of democracy is therefore direct democracy. . . . To achieve the widest, the most meaningful direct democracy will require that all the economic, political, and other structures of society be based on local groups that are concrete collectivities, organic social units. Direct democracy certainly requires the physical presence of citizens in a given place, when decisions have to be made. But this is not enough. It also requires that these citizens form an organic community, that they live if possible in the same milieu, that they be familiar through their daily experience with the subject to be discussed and with the problem to be tackled. (1988–1993, 2: 98–99)

The approach has been criticized as impractical, misdirected, and incoherent: "Rather than engaging the state system with the aim of democratically transforming it, he largely ignored it. . . . This strategy is hopelessly inadequate in confronting the pervasive nature of state power in modern society" (Boggs 1995: 190).

Postliberalism

Disillusioned with the prospects for democracy under either liberalism or socialism, some intellectuals have searched for a middle path. For example, in a defense of the theoretical effort by C. B. Macpherson to retrieve liberal democracy for socialism, Frank Cunningham (1990) has offered a somewhat parallel line of thinking with his notion that a liberal democrat will favor socialism because of its economic egalitarianism. Likewise, Chantal Mouffe (1991 and 1992) has envisioned an articulation between liberalism and socialism, following Paul Hirst and Norberto Bobbio, who believed that socialism's objective should be the deepening of liberal democratic values (see Anderson 1988 for discussion of Bobbio's thought). Mouffe's principal concern is how to defend the greatest possible pluralism without destroying the framework of the democratic political community.

On the economic side, a search for democratic practices underlies the emphasis of David Gordon, Samuel Bowles, and Thomas Weisskopf (1990) on equality and income distribution. A theoretical conceptualization of economic democracy, including democratic control of investment and production, is elaborated by Bowles and Herbert Gintis in *Democracy and Capitalism* (1986; see also 1989). They point to the heterogeneity of power and suggest that democratic societies in Europe and North America are driven not by class struggle or economic tensions but by contradictions between different structures of power. They focus on the conflict between personal and property rights at the heart of discourse on democratic capitalism and suggest that four "institutional accommodations" have taken place in history: the Lockean, which extended political participation to property owners; the Jeffersonian, which distributed property widely among the citizenry; the Madisonian, which divided citizens so as to prevent a unified movement of the nonpropertied; and the Keynesian, which fostered the sharing of interests by the dispossessed and wealthy through the redistribution of income. They argue that personal rights will eventually triumph over property rights, reaching into all aspects of social life to produce a really radical or postliberal democracy, and that the left should use this language of liberalism rather than socialist rhetoric in the popular struggles in which it is involved.

Bowles and Gintis offer a series of propositions about the relationships of domination that characterize capitalist society: that class domination or exploitation need not be any more important than race, gender, or other forms of oppression; that the class relationship between capital and labor is largely political; that class conflicts do exist in the workplace; that liberal democratic capitalism is a system of contradictory rules; that liberalism provides the language for progressive movements in advanced capi-

talist countries; and that the role of revolution as a means of resolving societal inequities has been exaggerated.

In an incisive critique of their project of extending democratic rights
from the state to civil society, Michael Burawoy (1989) acknowledges the
validity of criticizing life in the United States and the usefulness of an
agenda for its transformation but argues that Bowles and Gintis fail to explain how the struggle for postliberal democracy will take place. He
agrees with them that the sphere of production has a political and ideological dimension as well as an economic one but suggests that they do
not take their analysis far enough. He particularly attacks their Gramscian view of state politics as compromised by a view of state production
politics: "Once we allow a Gramscian view of production, . . . we see that
the distinctiveness of production regimes in advanced capitalism lies in
their hegemonic character" (72–73).

Jeff Goodwin is concerned that radical socialists have abandoned much
of the old socialism for democracy. He identifies a loose theoretical unity
among them in their neglect of nonclass and noneconomic forms of domination, their belief that it is broad popular alliances rather than class
struggle alone that will bring about human liberation, their conviction
that socialism represents only one moment on the way to a free society,
and the premise that those seeking human liberation should abandon socialism and look for a different and more comprehensive democratic ideology or discourse (1990: 132). In particular, Goodwin criticizes the
postliberal democracy of Bowles and Gintis, suggesting that their account
of struggle between personal and property rights is problematic and not
clearly differentiated from the class analysis they wish to avoid. He faults
them for an attack on Marxism that is illiberal and antidemocratic in its
assumption that democracy and freedom are exclusively associated with
liberalism. Goodwin shows that instead the extension of democratic
rights to the economy is precisely what socialism is all about and, furthermore, that Marxism can be used to exploit the ambiguities and contradictions of the liberal discourse.

Moments of Participatory Democracy

Throughout the twentieth century, experiments with participatory
democracy have often appeared in revolutionary and liberating settings.
Usually, they have been localized and not influential elsewhere, but they
are instructive with regard to the possibilities of participation on a mass
scale.

The Portuguese coup of April 25, 1974, represented not only the fall of
the half-century-old dictatorship but the beginning of a new struggle
throughout Southern Europe against authoritarian rule. Similar regimes

also fell in Greece and Spain. All the world turned its attention to Portugal, surprised by the uprising and the prospects for a revolutionary outcome at a time when Europe appeared economically and politically stable. The possibilities for democracy in Portugal ranged from a formal representative politics in concert with the drive to open up the country to international capital to participation in European markets and technological expansion to a more informal and direct participatory system associated with revolutionary ideals. Ultimately, formal, parliamentary democracy emerged victorious in this ideological struggle. Although the revolutionaries and idealists of the radical left faded, reformist social democratic and socialist parties emerged to wield power throughout the ensuing decades. In the period from 1974 to 1976, however, there were all sorts of participatory experiences, including leftist revolutionary political parties and social movements oriented around gender and feminism, peace, ecology, and other issues in search of involvement outside parliamentary and formal representative institutions; grassroots neighborhood and civic organizations that operated outside established channels; and renegade peasant and labor groups that typically ignored nationally organized labor unions.

The failure of a revolutionary outcome in most of these situations signified a shift in the ideological parameters of democratic struggle, away from the twentieth-century political tendencies associated with socialist revolutionary experiences in Russia and China and toward a mainstream representative and formal democracy based on parliaments and political parties. The brutal military intervention in the Chilean Unidad Popular experiment during the 1970s had brought an end to an evolving attempt to provide for needs of people and promote socialist development through a legitimate and democratically elected government under Salvador Allende. During the 1980s, the military regimes in Argentina, Brazil, Chile, and Uruguay succumbed to democratic forces organized around labor movements and popular social movements, but inevitably they too evolved toward formal political systems. Toward the end of the decade, the bureaucratic and stagnant socialist regimes of Eastern Europe and the Soviet Union also crumbled, with a mix of forces attempting to fill the political vacuum and shift economic preferences from socialist to capitalist outcomes.

A purer revolutionary thrust remained in some parts of the world. The Cuban Revolution of 1959 experimented with both orthodox and alternative approaches to socialism and concentrated on developing the economy and providing people with ways to meet their basic needs. The Sandinista Revolution of 1979 dealt with basic needs and, in the face of a devastated economy, sought to build a pluralistic political system that ultimately brought about its defeat through electoral means. Armed struggles elsewhere, conspicuously in El Salvador but also in Guatemala, ended in negotiated outcomes generally consistent with formal and representative democratic experiences in the form of parliaments, political parties, and electoral practices. The emergence of an indigenous movement in Chiapas, Mexico, also challenged the dominant ruling party, raising the possibility of autonomy in that region and elsewhere in the country.

In one form or another, each of these efforts at liberation ultimately failed. Carollee Bengelsdorf (1994) has discussed the failed experiences of the former Soviet Union and Eastern Europe as a backdrop to a critical assessment of Cuba in the decades since 1959, focusing on its failure to achieve democracy, especially on the political level. Although she is pessimistic about the prospects for a real socialist democracy, it is important to recognize the complexity of each situation and to look for moments of promise based on the past experience. In all these situations, the task of an isolated country or movement was complicated by both external political and economic forces, and autonomy was becoming increasingly difficult to achieve in the face of international capitalism and policies aimed at integrating the world under the United States and other dominant nations. Each situation provided a lesson in how broadly based democracy might function effectively. Each offered hope that a synthesis of the various moments of opening to alternative experiences might yield a reformulation of democracy that would truly involve popular participation in decisions of economy and political life and ensure provision of basic human needs for all.

Toward a Model of Empowerment and Transformation

In his studies of Sweden and Turkey, Dankwart Rustow (1970) outlined a model in which, given national unity as a background condition, democratization begins with a preparatory phase of prolonged and inconclusive political struggle associated with intense economic development and the rise of new social classes—in short, a phase of *polarization*. In the ensuing phase, the top political leadership of a country makes a conscious *decision* to shift from oligarchy or some authoritarian form to democracy. This decision is likely to involve compromise, universal suffrage, and recognition of change. Finally, the *habituation* phase represents the implementation of policies to fulfill the promises of the decision phase. Conciliation and accommodation appear in the political process, which also addresses economic and social issues. Politicians and citizens learn from the resolution of some issues to put their confidence in the new rules, competitive recruitment and democratic practices become commonplace, and political parties link politicians with the mass electorate. In sum, the model suggests a sequence from national unity through struggle, compromise, and habituation to democracy. Yet, there are few experiences—none of any substantial duration—that have succeeded in involving masses of people in meaningful ways.

Michael Albert and Robin Hahnel (1991a and 1991b) abandon traditional approaches for a participatory scheme aimed at a modified socialism. Their model, as described in the introduction to a debate over its merits, "uses new production, consumption, and allocation institutions to promote solidarity, variety, and participatory self-management" (Alperovitz et al. 1991: 62). Their vision is based on three elements: the elimination of hierarchy in work relationships so that "conceptual" workers do not dominate "manual" workers; the attainment of "material equity" through promotion of consumption in relation to need and effort; and "proportionate participation" of all workers and consumers in "an informed negotiation" in which all of them collectively determine "what is produced, with what methods, and how it is distributed, all in light of one another's circumstances and with a say proportionate to their involvement in each decision's implications."

In Albert and Hahnel's model each unit, however large, has to make its decisions while maintaining material and social equality throughout the economy. This allows consumers to exercise power over their own consumption as well as over workers as they are affected by the products and the side effects of production, whereas workers exercise power not only over their own labor but also over consumption, producing what others consume: "We therefore self-consciously advocate separate but interactive consumer and producer economic institutions because that is the nature of economic activity where there is any significant division of labor" (1991a: 83–84). This approach envisages a new culture oriented to the community at large. In its rejection of current beliefs about the rationality of markets, the productive efficiency of central planning, and the rationalization of consumption through economies of world scale, it is far removed from systems of contemporary capitalism and socialism.

In a sympathetic but critical review of this approach, Robert Heilbroner (1993: 153) argues that Albert and Hahnel's (1991a) popular vision is not viable and calls attention to the more formal and technical analysis in *The Political Economy of Participatory Economics* (1991b), in which they envision a society that maximizes participation rather than competition and antagonism. In Heilbroner's summary,

> Its internal coherence would be achieved by a system of "voting" that would establish the overall shape of productive flows. The "socialist" aspect of the economic plan would reside more in the social constraints affecting voters' choices than in the planning process itself. A solidaristic ethos would be en-

couraged by obliging all members to undertake some work outside their principal tasks, on a regular basis. (153)

A third model of self-governing socialism has been suggested by Devine. Economic democracy requires social control over the use of the means of production at the level of society as a whole. At the level of the production unit, those who work in it are directly affected, but so are others, such as people concerned with environmental effects: All should be involved in the decisionmaking process, as distinguished with self-government determined by representatives of all social groups with a significant interest in its activities. All those involved in a particular branch of production come together to negotiate over decisions that affect the future of production units:

> The model assumes a democratic society, in which people participate through a variety of self-governing and representative bodies, with decision making decentralized as much as possible, both functionally and vertically. At each level, representative assemblies, democratically elected in a context of political party pluralism, are vested with ultimate political power. Civil society is populated with autonomous, self-governing interest groups. (Devine, quoted in Taub 1990: 199)

There would be negotiation among coordinated bodies, crosscutting representation, and openness of information.

Stanley Aronowitz has argued for a democracy "constituted only by understanding citizenship as self-management in economic, social, and cultural aspects." He suggests that a new historic bloc of forces could emerge from "a micropolitics of autonomous oppositional movements": "There would be no question of the hegemony of the working class, as traditionally constituted, over the historic bloc, nor of the claim of Marxism to represent more than its own historic perspective" (1990 [1981]: 167). Indeed, the new historic bloc would be counterhegemonic in its drive toward socialist transformation. Marxism would remain significant in its insistence on emancipation but not dogmatic. These ideas are drawn from Gramsci's theory of ideological hegemony: "Gramsci inverted the Hegelian concept of civil society, and Marx's appropriation of it as the economic infrastructure, by positing the so-called superstructures—particularly ideology and its apparatuses—as the major condition for bourgeois hegemony" (168).

Having all but abandoned the socialist project of moving industrial society toward the Marxian vision of an egalitarian, democratic order, abolition of classes, workers' self-management, and socialization of public life, Carl Boggs has argued that "the only transformative agenda that stands a reasonable chance of success, particularly in the industrialized countries,

is designed around a radical-democratic extension of collective and cooperative forms in all spheres of life" (1995: 180). The struggle for a radical
transformation of society, he argues, must seek new practices, meanings,
and identities. Ultimately, it must undermine the legitimacy of the structures of domination and search for a fuller understanding of mass consciousness and collective will. Although the old agenda of historical materialism and hierarchical party-centered models must be abandoned,
according to Boggs, the thought of Rosa Luxemburg, Georg Lukács,
Antonio Gramsci, Herbert Marcuse, Erich Fromm, and Jean-Paul Sartre
remains relevant. He identifies particularly with Cornelius Castoriadis as
an intellectual who experienced many influences, including Marxism and
Trotskyism, and came to see bureaucracy as a phenomenon that dominated all aspects of life and undermined the possibility of a critical mass
consciousness. Rejecting both Soviet communism and Western capitalism, Castoriadis believed that revolution would come from below
through autonomous struggles and direct democracy. The practical roots
of an alternative can be found in experiences such as the 1956 Hungarian
revolution or the May 1968 upheavals in France against the old forms of
capitalist, bureaucratic, and cultural domination. Its thrust suffered from
"fascination with direct democracy and social solidarity that, it was
thought, could be achieved without confronting the power structure itself. . . . It was hardly surprising that the American new left . . . never really attempted to forge a social theory appropriate to its own experience"
(Boggs 1995: 200–201).

Boggs urges "an entirely new approach to development consonant
with human needs, self-management, and ecological balance, tied to a
system of socialized ownership, planning, and investment." His approach incorporates a process of collective empowerment and recovery of
citizenship that "stands at odds with the main organized currents of the
socialist tradition" (220).

This review of various theories, frameworks, and ideas about democracy is relevant to the span of ideas covered in this book's attention to
comparative political economy. I hope that the reader is now motivated to
delve deeply not only into the diversity of theory but also into case studies in order to evaluate the successes and failures of past and present experience and formulate an approach that might be useful in analyzing the
complexity of the modern world.

REFERENCES

Albert, Michael, and Robin Hahnel. 1991a. *Looking Forward: Participatory Economics for the Twenty-First Century*. Boston: South End Press. A challenge to the
assumption that a successful economy is impossible without a hierarchical di-

vision of labor. Sets forth an alternative model for a truly participatory and efficient economy.

_____. 1991b. *Political Economy of Participatory Economics*. Princeton: Princeton University Press. Similar to 1991a but more detailed and scholarly.

Almond, Gabriel A. 1991. "Capitalism and Democracy." *PS* 24 (September): 467–473. A defense of the "civilizing" impact of capitalism. Identifies various lines of thinking in the literature on democracy: Capitalism supports democracy, capitalism subverts democracy, democracy supports capitalism, and democracy fosters capitalism.

Alperovitz, Gar, et al. 1991. "Looking Forward: A Roundtable on Participatory Economics." *Z Magazine* (July-August):61–91. Critical assessment of works on the participatory economics by Michael Albert and Robin Hahnel, with their rejoinder.

Anderson, Perry. 1988. "The Affinities of Norberto Bobbio." *New Left Review* 170 (July-August):3–36. Briefly mentions efforts to synthesize liberal and socialist traditions (C. B. Macpherson, John Rawls, Robert Dahl, David Held, John Dunn, Joshua Cohen and Joel Rogers, Samuel Bowles and Herbert Gintis are mentioned as examples) but concentrates on the work of Bobbio on democracy and socialism.

Aronowitz, Stanley. 1990 (1981). "Marxism and Democracy," pp. 256–304 in his *The Crisis of Historical Materialism: Class, Politics and Culture in Marxist Theory.* Minneapolis: University of Minnesota Press. Concluding chapter of a book critical of traditional theory, especially Marxism, which sets forth an approach for adapting Marxism to the ideal of democracy. Argues that democracy must "be constituted only by understanding citizenship as self-management in economic, social and cultural aspects" (257) and that this principle is inherent in Marx and his thought.

_____. 1994. "The Situation of the Left in the United States." *Socialist Review* 23 (3):5–79. A very useful review of the U.S. left, past and present, that advocates a radical participatory democracy as opposed to socialist currents of identity representation, including Marxist and social movements (feminist, ecological, and so on). Followed by a series of critical commentaries by prominent writers on the left.

Baloyra, Enrique, ed. 1987. *Comparing New Democracies: Transition and Consolidation in Mediterranean Europe and the Southern Cone.* Boulder: Westview Press. Examines various cases of shifts from authoritarian to representative democratic regimes.

Bengelsdorf, Carollee. 1994. *The Problem of Democracy in Cuba: Between Vision and Reality.* New York and Oxford, England: Oxford University Press. Contrasts bourgeois and Marxist formulations of democracy and focuses on the debates since 1959, problems in political and economic institutionalization, and the failure to resolve the issue of political democracy.

Benton, Ted. 1989. "Marxism and Natural Limits: An Ecological Critique and Reconstruction." *New Left Review* 178 (December):51–86. Exposes differences within left currents of socialism and ecology in an effort to demonstrate that the tensions and oppositions between them are rooted in influential traditions of the left and to suggest ways that a Red and Green dialogue can be facilitated.

Berger, Peter. 1992. "The Uncertain Triumph of Democratic Capitalism." *Journal of Democracy* 3 (3):7–17. A conservative analysis emphasizing the association of emerging democracy with the hegemony of capitalism.

Bobbio, Norberto. 1987. *The Future of Democracy: A Defense of the Rules of the Game.* Minneapolis: University of Minnesota Press. Combines a historical understanding of the meaning of democracy with political and social theory.

Boggs, Carl. 1995. *The Socialist Tradition: From Crisis to Decline.* New York: Routledge. Examines Marx's own conception of democracy, traces the rise and decline of Eurocommunism and Eurosocialism, and suggests an approach to the "radical challenge."

Borón, Atilio. 1995. *State, Capitalism, and Democracy in Latin America.* Boulder: Lynne Rienner. A solid analysis of the role of the state and the constraint of capitalism in the democratic openings since the 1980s.

Bowles, Samuel, and Herbert Gintis. 1986. *Democracy and Capitalism: Property, Community, and the Contradictions of Modern Social Thought.* New York: Basic Books. A search for a postliberal form of democracy with capitalism in an effort to find middle ground between liberal and Marxist ideas.

_____. 1989. "Democratic Demands and Radical Rights." *Socialist Review* 18 (4):67–72. Considers the prospects for employing the language and practices of democratic liberalism in progressive movements in advanced capitalist countries.

Boyte, Harry C. 1990. "The Growth of Citizen Politics." *Dissent* 37 (Fall):513–518. Focuses on an alternative understanding of popular participation in the form of the citizen-based politics that evolves out of grassroots networks formed in response to local issues.

Bresser Pereira, Luiz Carlos, José María Maravall, and Adam Przeworski. 1993. *Economic Reforms in New Democracies: A Social-Democratic Approach.* New York: Cambridge University Press. Examines experiences of transition in Southern Europe, Latin America, and Eastern Europe in an attempt to identify conditions allowing for change. Argues that the most successful reforms are those worked out through a process of negotiation and democratic institutions.

Buhl, Paul. 1987 (1991). *Marxism in the United States.* London: Verso. A history of the Marxist left and its influences in the United States.

_____, (ed). 1990. *History and the New Left.* Philadelphia: Temple University Press. A collection of twenty-eight memoirs of radicals who participated in the new left in Madison, Wisconsin, and founded the journal *Studies on the Left.* Important for understanding progressive thought on democracy and transformation.

Burawoy, Michael. 1989. "Should We Give Up on Socialism?" *Socialist Review* 18 (1):59–74. Critique of Bowles and Gintis (1986).

Burkey, Stan. 1992. *People First: A Guide to Self-Reliant Participatory Rural Development.* London: Zed Press. Sets forth methodology around grassroots, popularly controlled, and environmentally friendly development activity. Combines theoretical understanding with field experience to emphasize self-reliant participatory rural development. Based on work in Latin America and South Asia.

Castoriadis, Cornelius. 1988–1993. *Political and Social Writings.* 3 vols. Minneapolis: University of Minnesota Press. Translated and edited by David Ames

Curtis. Criticizes the left and right in a search for an alternative model incorporating democracy.

Chilcote, Ronald H., Stylianos Hadjiyannis, Fred A López III, Daniel Nataf, and Elizabeth Sammis. 1990. *Transitions from Dictatorship to Democracy: Comparative Studies of Spain, Portugal, and Greece.* New York: Taylor and Francis. Retrospective assessments of the transitions from dictatorship to representative democracy and the prospects for participatory democracy and socialism through three case studies originally examined by Nicos Poulantzas in *Crisis of the Dictatorships* (1976; see annotated reference in Chapter 1).

Chomsky, Noam. 1991. "Force and Opinion. " *Z Magazine* (July-August):10–24. A critique of governmental force and the rule of the few.

Cohen, Joshua, and Joel Rogers. 1987. *On Democracy: Toward a Transformation of American Society.* New York: Penguin Books. An assessment of American capitalist democracy in search of a strategy of direct opposition to the oppression of that system.

Collier, Ruth Berins. 1999. *Paths Toward Democracy: The Working Class and Elites in Western Europe and South America.* Cambridge, England: Cambridge University Press. Focuses on the working class in the process of democratization.

Cunningham, Frank. 1987. *Democratic Theory and Socialism.* New York: Cambridge University Press. A critical assessment of socialism and its prospects for democracy in the face of bureaucratic and authoritarian rule.

_____. 1990. "The Socialist Retrieval of Liberal Democracy." *International Political Science Review* 11 (1):99–110. Defense of C. B. Macpherson's attempt to retrieve liberal democracy for socialism.

Dahl, Robert. 1982. *Dilemmas of Pluralist Democracy.* New Haven: Yale University Press. An update on earlier writings on pluralism with attention to procedures.

Diamond, Larry, Juan Linz, and Seymour Lipset, eds. 1988–1989. *Democracy in Developing Nations.* 4 vols. Boulder: Lynne Rienner. Covers theoretical and overall trends and then examines case studies in Africa, Asia, and Latin America.

Di Palma, Giuseppe. 1990. *To Craft Democracies: An Essay on Democratic Transitions.* Berkeley: University of California Press. Theoretical overview of transitions from authoritarian to democratic rule.

Elshtain, Jean Bethke. 1995. *Democracy on Trial.* New York: Basic Books. An interpretive inquiry into the problems of American democracy.

Gendzier, Irene. 1985. *Managing Political Change: Social Scientists and the Third World.* Boulder: Westview Press. An in-depth account of the cold war milieu out of which evolved the development debates of the 1950s and 1960s and the relationship among theories of political development, mass society, and liberal democracy.

Goodwin, Jeff. 1990. "The Limits of 'Radical Democracy.'" *Socialist Review* 19 (4):131–144. Criticizes radical socialists who have abandoned traditional principles of socialism in favor of liberal democracy.

Gordon, David, Samuel Bowles, and Thomas Weisskopf. 1990. "An Equality-Efficiency Trade-Off?" *Dissent* 37 (Fall):510–512. Demonstrates that greater equality in income is associated with better economic performance in both advanced and developing countries.

Graham, Keith. 1986. *Battle of Democracy: Conflict, Consensus, and the Individual*. Totowa, N.J.: Barnes and Noble. Focusing on recent British and North American debate, concludes that the most coherent expression of democracy can be found in a reconsideration of "strictly defined Marxism."

Gramsci, Antonio. 1971. *Selections from the Prison Notebooks of Antonio Gramsci*. New York: International Publishers. Most of the major writings, written when he was a political prisoner during the 1920s.

Grofman, Bernard. 1993. "Lessons of Athenian Democracy." *PS* 26 (September): 471–494. Introduction to five essays—by Michael T. Clark, J. Peter Euben, Josiah Ober, Arlene W. Saxonhouse, and Sheldon Wolin—on democracy after the reforms of the Greek Cleisthenes. Compares a romanticized vision of Greek democracy with contemporary notions of democracy.

Guinier, Lani. 1993. "Minority Goal Must Be Equality in Fact." *Los Angeles Times*, May 27. Argues that "substantive equality should be measured by equality in fact; the process must be equal but the results must also reflect the effort to remedy the effects of a century of official discrimination."

_____. 1994. *The Tyranny of the Majority: Fundamental Fairness in Representative Democracy*. New York: Free Press. Reviewed favorably and in some detail in George Pillsbury, "Understanding Lani Guinier: Her Ideas for Election Democracy in the United States," *Socialist Review* 24 (1994):185–196.

Habermas, Jürgen. 1990. "What Does Socialism Mean Today? The Rectifying Revolution and the Need for New Thinking on the Left." *New Left Review* 183 (September-October):3–21. Argues that the reforms in the Soviet Union and Eastern Europe were largely introduced from above as a "rectifying revolution" intended to return to constitutional democracy but were characterized by a "total lack of ideas that are either innovative or oriented towards the future" (5) and rejected for the most part by the population.

Hamilton, Alexander, James Madison, and John Jay. 1961. *The Federalist Papers*. New York: Mentor Books. Introduction by Clinton Rossiter.

Hanson, Russell L. 1989. "Democracy," pp. 68–89 in Terence Ball, James Farr, and Russell L. Hanson, eds., *Political Innovation and Conceptual Change*. New York: Cambridge University Press. Attempts to deal with problems posed by the contemporary popularization of democracy. Shows how the concept of democracy has shifted from a conception in which people were juxtaposed with the wealthy productive class to one in which the class conception has evolved to a notion of compromise between classes, and class divisions thus become less conspicuous.

Harnecker, Marta. 1992. "Democracy and Revolutionary Movement." *Social Justice* 19 (4):60–73. Redefines democracy from a left perspective.

Heilbroner, Robert. 1993. *21st Century Capitalism*. New York: W. W. Norton. Follows up on his earlier affirmation of the victory of capitalism over socialism. Outlines the dynamics of and the obstacles to socialism. Sees the possibility of socialism but is pessimistic about participatory economic democracy.

Held, David. 1987. *Models of Democracy*. Stanford: Stanford University Press. Provides an overview of political thought on democracy from the Greeks to Marx and then assesses the desirability and possibility of liberal social democracy.

Hirst, Paul, and Sunil Khilnani, eds. 1996. *Reinventing Democracy*. Cambridge, England: Blackwell. Examines democracy in Europe in general and England in particular. Especially interesting are contributions by John Stewart on local government, Paul Hirst on civil society, Andrew Gamble on the limits of democracy, and Benjamin Barber on reinventing democracy.

Huntington, Samuel. 1991. *The Third Wave: Democratization in the Late Twentieth Century*. Norman: University of Oklahoma Press. Retrospective on democratic trends through history.

Jacobs, Lawrence R. 1994. "Studying Substantive Democracy." *PS* 27 (March): 9–17. Emphasizes mainstream political science perspectives and representative democracy. Provides an extensive bibliography.

Jessop, Bob. 1990. "The Democratic State and the National Interest," pp. 170–189 in his *State Theory: Putting Capitalist States in their Place*. University Park: Pennsylvania State University Press. Critical examination of four arguments about the democratic nature of the capitalist states.

Karl, Terry Lynn. 1990. "Dilemmas of Democratization in Latin America." *Comparative Politics* 23 (October):1–22. Points to contradictions that emerge as Latin American countries move from dictatorships to democracies. Advocates an interactive approach to their study that relates structural constraints to the shaping of choice and examines the different types of democracy that emerge from the transitional cases.

Keane, John. 1988. *Democracy and Civil Society: On the Predicaments of European Socialism, the Prospects for Democracy, and the Problem of Controlling Social and Political Power*. London and New York: Verso. Explores the dilemmas and contradictions of European socialism and the possibilities for democracy

Kopkind, Andrew, et al. 1992. "The Democratic Moment: Toward a New Politics." *The Nation* 255 (July 20–27):81–105. Articles by Kopkind and Alexander Cockburn, Katha Pollitt, Gloria Steinem, Ralph Nader, Sandy Pope, and Joel Rogers on the eve of the Democratic party convention, offering views on how democracy can be enhanced and the left's role.

Levine, Daniel H. 1988. "Paradigm Lost: Dependence to Democracy." *World Politics* 40 (April):377–393. A review of O'Donnell, Schmitter, and Whitehead (1986), with attention to the close relation between an analysis of transitions and attention to democracy. Argues that there is a fit between dependency theory and current conceptions of democracy and that liberal democracy has been undervalued; the popular support for pacts and accommodations has been ignored; ties between elites and popular groups, especially those worked out through political parties, are not examined; and democracy itself has been inadequately analyzed.

Lijphart, Arend. 1984. *Democracies: Patterns of Majoritarian and Consensus Government in Twenty-One Countries*. New Haven: Yale University Press. A comparison of the majoritarian and consensus models of democracy. Despite the subtitle, describes the experience of twenty-two democratic regimes.

Lipset, Seymour Martin. 1994. "The Social Requisites of Democracy Revisited." *American Sociological Review* 59 (February):1–22. A useful retrospective overview of democracy and its elements. Sets forth concepts and incorporates a synthesis of the mainstream literature.

Lowenthal, Abraham F. 1991. *Exporting Democracy: The United States and Latin America*. Baltimore: Johns Hopkins University Press. Focuses on historical themes and case studies of democratic attempts and possibilities in Latin America.

Löwy, Michael. 1991. "Twelve Theses on the Crisis of 'Really Existing Socialism.'" *Monthly Review* 43 (May):33–40. Discusses changes in former economic and political systems of Eastern Europe and the Soviet Union.

MacEwan, Arthur. 1988. "Transitions from Authoritarian Rule." *Latin American Perspectives* 15 (Summer):115–130. A critical assessment of O'Donnell, Schmitter, and Whitehead (1986). Argues that "real democracy . . . cannot exist while the military remains intact as an institution. Neither can real democracy be attained within the existing structure of power and privilege" (130).

Mainwaring, Scott, Guillermo O'Donnell, and J. Samuel Valenzuela, eds. 1992. *Issues in Democratic Consolidation: The New South American Democracies in Comparative Perspective*. South Bend, Ind.: University of Notre Dame Press. Focuses on the problem of implementing democracy in the face of enormous difficulties. Examines transitions from authoritative rule to civilian government and the process of institutionalizing democracy.

Malloy, James M., and Mitchell Seligson, eds. 1987. *Regime Transition in Latin America*. Pittsburgh: University of Pittsburgh Press. Case studies of transition from authoritarian to democratic regimes.

Markoff, John. 1997. "Really Existing Democracy: Learning from Latin America in the Late 1990s." *New Left Review* 223 (May-June):48–68. A review of various forms of democracy since the eighteenth century, with attention to current debates and conceptualizations.

Mouffe, Chantal. 1991. "Liberal Socialism: Which Perspective?" Paper prepared for the 15th World Congress of the International Political Science Association, Buenos Aires, July 21–25. A look at the prospects for a liberal socialism, given the "collapse of actually existing socialism."

_____, (ed). 1992. *Dimensions of Radical Democracy: Pluralism, Citizenship, Community*. London: Verso. A collection of original essays by Quentin Skinner, Sheldon Wolin, and others on how citizen and community fit a radical and plural form of democracy.

Nove, Alec. 1990. "'Market Socialism' and 'Free Economy.'" *Dissent* 37 (Fall): 443–446. A response to East European economists disillusioned with socialism and Nove's ideas for market socialism.

O'Donnell, Guillermo, Philippe C. Schmitter, and Laurence Whitehead, eds. 1986. *Transitions from Authoritarian Rule*. Baltimore: Johns Hopkins University Press. Published in cloth as a single volume and in paperback as a series of volumes with different subtitles: *Prospects for Democracy; Southern Europe; Latin America; Comparative Perspectives*; and *Tentative Conclusions About Uncertain Democracies*. Papers originally commissioned for a conference sponsored by the Woodrow Wilson International Center for Scholars between 1979 and 1981.

Offe, Claus. 1991. "Capitalism by Democratic Design? Democratic Theory Facing the Triple Transition in East Central Europe." Paper prepared for the 15th World Congress of the International Political Science Association, Buenos Aires, July 21–25. Explores the prospects for transition to democracy under current reforms and examines the relationship of capitalism and representative democracy.

Pateman, Carole. 1991. "A New Democratic Theory? Political Science, the Public, and the Private." Paper presented to the plenary session "Democratic Theory Today" at the 15th World Congress of the International Political Science Association, Buenos Aires, July 21–25. Examines the question of democracy with a focus on exposing the failure of political science as a discipline to recognize the role of women. Pateman also authored *Participation and Democratic Theory*, New York: Cambridge University Press, 1988.

Phillips, Anne. 1991. *Engendering Democracy.* Berkeley: University of California Press. Critically examines contemporary theories of liberal, participatory, and republican democracy from a feminist perspective.

Plattner, Marc F., and Larry Diamond. 1992. "Capitalism, Socialism, and Democracy." *Journal of Democracy* 3 (July):3–137. Essays in remembrance of Joseph Schumpeter and his book with the same title published a half century earlier. Particularly useful are essays by Peter L. Berger on doubts over democratic capitalism, Adam Przeworski on the neoliberal fallacy, and Robert Dahl on mixed economies in contrast to free market or centralized planned economies.

Poulantzas, Nicos. 1978. *State, Power, Socialism.* London: New Left Books. A clear statement of state and class with attention to class and social movements.

Przeworski, Adam. 1991. "Could We Feed Everyone? The Irrationality of Capitalism and the Infeasibility of Socialism." *Politics and Society* 19 (March):1–38. With critical comments by Joshua Cohen, pp. 39–58, and Zhiyuan Cui, pp. 59–69. Argues that "the socialist critique of the irrationality of capitalism is valid, but the socialist alternative is infeasible" (24) and that whether we could feed everyone depends as much on politics as on economics.

Rahman, Md Anisur. 1992. *People's Self-Development: Perspectives on Participatory Action Research.* London: Zed Press. Influential ideas based on fieldwork and participatory initiatives in Africa and Asia. Questions both liberal and socialist development and sets forth an alternative approach.

Robinson, William I. 1992. "The São Paulo Forum: Is There a New Latin American Left?" *Monthly Review* 44 (December):1–11. Reports on shifting trends among left intellectuals in Latin America. Sets forth a number of propositions that move the discourse toward pluralism and politics.

Rosenau, Pauline M., and Robert Paehlke. 1990. "The Exhaustion of Left and Right: Perspectives on the Political Participation of the Disadvantaged." *International Political Science Review* 11 (1):123–152. Suggests congruencies between efforts of left and right in seeking the political participation of the disadvantaged.

Rueschemeyer, Dietrich, Evelyne Huber Stephens, and John D. Stephens. 1992. *Capitalist Development and Democracy.* Chicago: University of Chicago Press. Using case examples from the industrial world along with Latin America and the Caribbean, argues that capitalism transforms class structure by enlarging the working and middle classes while weakening the landed bourgeoisie. Focuses on the balance of power among social classes, power relations between the state and society, and transnational structures of economic and political power.

Rustow, Dankwart A. 1970. "Transitions to Democracy." *Comparative Politics* 2 (April):337–363. Sketches a model of democratization based on the experiences of Sweden and Turkey.

Sartori, Giovanni. 1987. *The Theory of Democracy Revisited.* 2 vols. Chatham, N.J.: Chatham House. Deals with contemporary debate and distinctions between normative and empirical theory, then examines traditional or classical themes of democracy beginning with those in ancient Greece.

Schmitter, Philippe C., and Terry Lynn Karl. 1991. "What Democracy Is . . . and Is Not." *Journal of Democracy* 2 (Summer):75–88. Identifies concepts that make democracy unique as a system for organizing relations between rulers and the ruled, looks at procedures or rules needed for democracy to persist, and identifies two operative principles that make democracy function.

Schwartzmantel, John. 1995. "Capitalist Democracy Revisited," pp. 207–224 in Leo Panitch, ed., *Socialist Register 1995.* New York: Monthly Review Press; and London: Merlin Press. Critical examination of the concept of capitalist democracy in the thought and writing of Ralph Miliband.

Sherman, Howard. 1995. *Reinventing Marxism.* Baltimore: Johns Hopkins University Press. Seeks a critical and useful Marxism.

Sklar, Richard L. 1987. "Developmental Democracy." *Comparative Studies in Society and History* 29 (October):686–714. Identifies important components of democracy and points out that "development theory faces the challenge of democracy" (708).

Skocpol, Theda. 1997. "Building Community: Top-down or Bottom-up? *Brookings Review* 15 (Fall):16–19. Based on a survey of large voluntary organizations that have survived in America since the nineteenth century, points to a decline in participation.

Stephens, Evelyne Huber. 1989. "Capitalist Development and Democracy in South America." *Politics and Society* 17 (June):281–352. A comprehensive overview of democracy in ten South American countries over the period since independence.

Stephens, John. 1993. "Capitalist Development and Democracy: Empirical Research on the Social Origins of Democracy," pp. 409–447 in D. Chopp, J. Hamton, and J. Roemer, eds., *The Idea of Democracy.* Cambridge, England: Cambridge University Press. A useful reference and synthesis on the links between capitalism and democracy.

Stiefel, Matthias, and Marshall Wolfe. 1994. *A Voice for the Excluded: Popular Participation in Development, Utopia or Necessity?* London: Zed Books. A report and synthesis on a series of general and country studies of participation under the UN Research Institute for Social Development during the 1970s and 1980s. Identifies various approaches, reports on individual country experiences, and speculates on developments in the 1990s.

Taub, William, ed. 1990. *The Future of Socialism: Perspectives from the Left.* New York: Monthly Review Press. Includes views by Pat Devine and others.

Therborn, Göran. 1977. "The Rule of Capital and the Rise of Democracy." *New Left Review* 103:3–41. Delves into the limits of democracy in the face of capitalism in industrial societies.

_____. 1992. "The Life and Times of Socialism." *New Left Review* 194 (July-August):17–32. A retrospective assessment of socialism in the aftermath of changes in the socialist world.

Verba, Sidney. 1993. "The Voice of the People." *PS* 26 (December):677–686. Points to the importance of democracy of citizen-initiated discourse.

Verba, Sidney, Kay Lehman Schlozman, and Henry E. Brady. 1997. "The Big Tilt: Participatory Inequality in America." *The American Prospect* 32 (May-June):74–80. Focuses on inequality in participation and its implications for American democracy.

Weffort, Francisco C. 1992. "New Democracies: Which Democracies?" Latin American Program, Woodrow Wilson Center, Working Paper 198. A pessimistic assessment of the prospects for democracy in many countries of the Third World that suffer from social and economic inequalities.

Wolfe, Alan. 1997. "Is Civil Society Obsolete?" *Brookings Review* 15 (Fall):9–12. Examines forms of civil society in an era of its declining importance.

Wolin, Sheldon S. 1993. "Democracy: Electoral and Athenian." *PS* 26 (September): 475–477. Compares Athenian democracy, in which "participation was instrumental, the means by which social groups and classes constituting the majority of inhabitants gained access to forms of power that enabled them to improve their condition by contesting the forms of power associated with wealth, birth, and education," with electoral democracy, which "allows the citizenry to 'participate,' not in power but in the rituals and festivals of power" (477).

Wood, Ellen Meiksins. 1995. *Democracy Against Capitalism: Renewing Historical Materialism*. New York and Cambridge, England: Cambridge University Press. A serious attempt at explaining how Marxism critiques capitalism. Shows how some contemporary discourse obscures analysis of capitalism and examines the concept of democracy as it emerged in Athenian Greece and in various periods of capitalism.

OTHER REFERENCES CONSULTED

The following sources are mentioned in the text to give example without listing at the end of the chapter with an annotation. The curious reader may wish to delve further into the sources.

Abraham, David. 1986. *The Collapse of the Weimar Republic: Political Economy and Crisis*. Princeton: Princeton University Press.

Almond, Gabriel, and James Coleman, eds. 1960. *The Politics of the Developing Areas*. Princeton: Princeton University Press.

Almond, Gabriel, and Sidney Verba. 1963. *The Civic Culture: Political Attitudes and Democracy in Five Nations*. Newbury Park, Calif.: Sage Publications.

Almond, Gabriel, G. Bingham Powell Jr., and Robert J. Mundt. 1993. *Comparative Politics: A Theoretical Framework*. New York: Harper Collins College Publishers.

Anderson, Perry. 1980. *Arguments Within English Marxism*. London: New Left Books.

Anglade, Christian, and Carlos Fortín. 1985 and 1990. *The State and Capital Accumulation in Latin America*. Pittsburgh: University of Pittsburgh Press.

Apter, David. 1965. *The Politics of Modernization*. Chicago: University of Chicago Press.

Aronowitz, Stanley. 1973. *False Promises: The Shaping of American Working Class Consciousness*. New York: McGraw-Hill.

Avrich, Paul. 1972. *Russian Rebels, 1600–1800*. New York: Schocken Books.

Bahro, Rudolf. 1978. *The Alternative in Eastern Europe*. London: New Left Books. Translated by David Fernbach.

Bailyn, Bernard. 1979. *The New England Merchants in the Seventeenth Century*. New York: Harper and Row.

Baran, Paul, and Paul Sweezy. 1966. *Monopoly Capital*. New York: Monthly Review Press.

Barratt Brown, Michael. 1970. *After Imperialism*. London: Merlin.

Bell, Daniel. 1960. *The End of Ideology*. Glencoe, Ill.: Free Press.

_____. 1973. *The Coming of Post-Industrial Society: A Venture in Social Forecasting*. New York: Basic Books

Bendix, Reinhard. 1964. *Nation-Building and Citizenship*. New York: Wiley.

Bettelheim, Charles. 1976–1978. *Class Struggles in the USSR*. New York: Monthly Review Press. Translated by Brian Pearce.

Bill, James A., and Robert L. Hardgrave Jr. 1973. *Comparative Politics: The Quest for Theory.* Columbus, Ohio: Merrill.

Bottomore, Tom, ed. 1983. *A Dictionary of Marxist Thought.* Cambridge, Mass.: Harvard University Press.

Bowen, Roger. 1980. *Rebellion and Democracy in Meiji Japan: A Study of Commoners in the Popular Rights Movement.* Berkeley: University of California Press.

Braverman, Harry. 1974. *Labor and Monopoly Capital.* New York: Monthly Review Press.

Bryce, James. 1921. *Modern Democracies.* New York: Macmillan.

Burgess, Philip, James Harf, and Lawrence Peterson. 1979. *International and Comparative Politics: A Handbook.* Peabody, Mass.: Allyn and Bacon.

Caldwell, Malcolm. 1977. *The Wealth of Some Nations.* London: Zed Press.

Calhoun, Craig. 1982. *The Question of Class Struggle: Social Foundations of Popular Radicalism During the Industrial Revolution.* Chicago: University of Chicago Press.

Callinicos, Alex. 1991. *The Revenge of History: Marxism and the East European Revolutions.* University Park: Pennsylvania State University Press.

Chilcote, Ronald H. 1994 (1981). *Theories of Comparative Politics: The Search for a Paradigm Revisited.* Boulder: Westview Press.

_____. 1990. *Power and the Ruling Classes in Northeast Brazil.* New York: Cambridge University Press.

Cohn, Samuel Kline, Jr. 1980. *The Laboring Classes in Renaissance Florence.* New York: Academic Press.

Conaghan, Catherine M. 1988. *Restructuring Domination: Industrialists and the State in Ecuador.* Pittsburgh: University of Pittsburgh Press.

Dahl, Robert A. 1956. *A Preface to Democratic Theory.* Chicago: University of Chicago Press.

_____. 1967. *Pluralist Democracy in the United States: Conflict and Consent.* Chicago: Rand McNally.

Dahrendorf, Ralf. 1959. *Class and Class Conflict in Industrial Society.* Stanford: Stanford University Press.

Dalton, Russell. 1988. *Citizen Politics in Western Democracies.* Chatham, N.J.: Chatham House.

Dardess, John W. 1983. *Confucianism and Autocracy: Professional Elites in the Founding of the Ming Dynasty.* Berkeley: University of California Press.

Dobb, Maurice. 1947. *Studies in the Development of Capitalism.* New York: International Publishers.

Eckstein, Harry. 1961. *A Theory of Stable Democracy.* Princeton: Center of International Affairs, Woodrow Wilson School of Public and International Affairs.

Engels, Friedrich. 1880. *Socialism, Utopian and Scientific.* New York: International Publishers. Translated by Edward Aveling.

Evans, Peter, Dietrich Rueschemeyer, and Evelyne Huber Stephens. 1985. *States Versus Markets in the World-System.* Beverly Hills, Calif.: Sage Publications.

Farnie, D. A. 1979. *The English Cotton Industry and the World Market 1815–1896.* Oxford, England: Clarendon Press.

Foner, Philip Sheldon. 1947. *History of the Labor Movement in the United States.* New York: International Publishers.

Friedrich, Carl J. 1937. *Constitutional Government and Democracy.* Boston: Ginn.

———. 1942. *The New Belief in the Common Man.* Boston: Little, Brown and Company.

Gilly, Adolfo. 1983. *The Mexican Revolution.* London: New Left Books.

Ginzburg, Carlo. 1980. *The Cheese and the Worms: The Cosmos of a Sixteenth-Century Miller.* Baltimore: Johns Hopkins University Press.

Gordon, David M., Richard Edwards, and Michael Reich. 1982. *Segmented Work, Divided Workers: The Historical Transformation of Labor in the United States.* New York: Cambridge University Press.

Gramsci, Antonio. 1977. *Selections from Political Writings 1910–1920.* Minneapolis: University of Minnesota Press.

Halévy, Elie. 1951. *Imperialism and the Rise of Labour.* New York: Peter Smith.

Hansen, Mogens. 1991. *The Athenian Democracy in the Age of Demosthenes.* Cambridge, Mass.: Basil Blackwell.

Hartz, Louis. 1955. *The Liberal Tradition in America.* New York: Harcourt, Brace.

Haydu, Jeffrey. 1988. *Between Craft and Class: Skilled Workers and Factory Politics in the United States and Britain, 1890–1922.* Berkeley: University of California Press.

Hill, Christopher. 1961. *The Century of Revolution 1603–1714.* Edinburgh: T. Nelson.

———. 1972. *The World Turned Upside Down: Radical Ideas During the English Revolution.* New York: Viking Press.

Hobsbawm, Eric J. 1959. *Primitive Rebels.* New York: W. W. Norton.

———. 1969. *Bandits.* London: Weidenfeld and Nicolson.

———. 1987. *The Age of Empire, 1875–1914.* New York: Pantheon Books.

Huntington, Samuel. 1968. *Political Order in Changing Societies.* New Haven: Yale University Press.

Jones, R. J. Barry. 1995. *Globalisation and Interdependence in the International Political Economy.* London and New York: Pinter Publishers.

Kaase, Max, and Kenneth Newton. 1995. *Beliefs in Government.* New York: Oxford University Press.

Kagan, Donald. 1991. *Pericles of Athens and the Birth of Democracy.* New York: Free Press.

Kagarlitsky, Boris. 1988. *The Thinking Reed: Intellectuals and the Soviet State, 1917 to the Present.* London and New York: Verso.

Katzenstein, Peter. 1985. *Small States in World Markets: Industrial Policy in Europe.* Ithaca, N.Y.: Cornell University Press.

Katznelson, Ira, and Aristide Zolberg, eds. 1986. *Working-Class Formation: Nineteenth-Century Patterns in Western Europe and the United States.* Princeton: Princeton University Press.

Kautsky, Karl. 1910 (1892). *Class Struggle (Erfurt Program).* Chicago: C. H. Kerr.

Kesselman, Mark, and Joel Krieger. 1992. *European Politics in Transition.* Lexington, Mass.: D. C. Heath.

Kraus, Richard Curt. 1981. *Class Conflict in Chinese Socialism.* New York: Columbia University Press.

Lippit, Victor, ed. 1996. *Radical Political Economy: Explorations in Alternative Economic Analysis.* Armonk, N.Y.: M. E. Sharpe.

Lipset, Seymour Martin. 1960. *Political Man.* Garden City, N.Y.: Doubleday.

Love, Joseph. 1996. *Crafting the Third World: Theorizing Underdevelopment in Rumania and Brazil.* Stanford: Stanford University Press.

Lukács, Georg. 1923. *History and Class Consciousness.* Cambridge, Mass.: MIT Press. Translated by Rodney Livingstone.

Mahon, James E., Jr. 1996. *Mobile Capital and Latin American Development.* University Park: Pennsylvania State University Press.

Marcuse, Herbert. 1964. *One-Dimensional Man.* Boston: Beacon Press.

Markovits, Andrei S., and Mark Silverstein. 1988. *The Politics of Scandal: Power and Process in Liberal Democracies.* New York: Holmes and Meier.

McNally, David. 1988. *Political Economy and the Rise of Capitalism: A Reinterpretation.* Berkeley: University of California Press.

Melman, Seymour. 1971. *The War Economy of the United States.* New York: St. Martin's Press.

Migdal, Joel. 1988. *Strong Societies and Weak States: State-Society Relations and State Capabilities in the Third World.* Princeton: Princeton University Press.

Mousnier, Roland. 1970. *Peasant Uprisings in Seventeenth-Century France, Russia, and China.* New York: Harper and Row. Translated by Brian Pearce.

Mummery, A. F. 1956 (1889). *The Physiology of Industry.* New York: Kelley and Millman. Originally published in London by J. Murray.

Oberman, Heiko Augustinus. 1981. *Masters of the Reformation: The Emergence of a New Intellectual Climate in Europe.* New York, Cambridge University Press.

Organski A. F. K. 1965. *Stages of Political Development.* New York: Alfred A. Knopf.

Paige, Jeffrey. 1975. *Agrarian Revolution: Social Movements and Export Agriculture in the Underdeveloped World.* New York: Free Press.

_____. 1997. *Coffee and Power: Revolution and the Rise of Democracy in Central America.* New York: Cambridge University Press.

Palmer, R. R. 1959–1964. *The Age of the Democratic Revolution: A Political History of Europe and America, 1760–1800.* Princeton: Princeton University Press.

Panitch, Leo. 1976. *Social Democracy and Industrial Militancy: The Labour Party, the Trade Unions and Incomes Policy, 1945–1974.* New York: Cambridge University Press.

Polanyi, Karl. 1944. *The Great Transformation.* Boston: Beacon Press.

Rodney, Walter. 1974. *How Europe Underdeveloped Africa.* London: Bogle L'Ouverture.

Rostow, W. W. 1960. *Stages of Economic Growth.* Cambridge, England: Cambridge University Press.

Rothstein, Robert L. 1977. *The Weak in the World of the Strong: The Developing Countries in the International System.* New York: Columbia University Press.

Schumpeter, J. A. 1936 (1911). *The Theory of Economic Development: An Inquiry into Profits, Capital, Credit, Interest, and the Business Cycle.* Cambridge, Mass.: Harvard University Press.

_____. 1939. *Business Cycles: A Theoretical, Historical, and Statistical Analysis of the Capitalist Process.* New York: McGraw Book Company.

_____. 1942. *Capitalism, Socialism, and Democracy.* 2d ed. New York: Harper and Brothers.

_____. 1954. *History of Economic Analysis.* New York: Oxford University Press.

Scott, James C. 1976. *The Moral Economy of the Peasant: Rebellion and Subsistence in Southeast Asia.* New Haven: Yale University Press.

————. 1985. *Weapons of the Weak: Everyday Forms of Peasant Resistance*. New Haven: Yale University Press.

Sen, Amartya. 1999. *Development as Freedom*. New York: Alfred A. Knopf.

Senghaas, Dieter. 1985. *The European Experience: A Historical Critique of Development Theory*. Dover, N.H.: Berg.

Sewell, William. 1980. *Work and Revolution in France: The Language of Labor from the Old Regime to 1848*. New York: Cambridge University Press.

Shanin, Teodor. 1986. *The Roots of Otherness: Russia's Turn of Century*. New Haven: Yale University Press.

Shorter, Edward, and Charles Tilly. 1974. *Strikes in France 1830–1968*. New York: Cambridge University Press.

Sinclair, R. K. 1988. *Democracy and Participation in Athens*. New York: Cambridge University Press.

Sirianni, Carmen. 1982. *Workers Control and Socialist Democracy: The Soviet Experience*. London: New Left Books.

Smith, Peter. 1979. *Labyrinths of Power: Political Recruitment in Twentieth-Century Mexico*. Princeton: Princeton University Press.

Smith, Rogers M. 1997. *Civic Ideals: Conflicting Visions of Citizenship in U.S. History*. New Haven: Yale University Press.

Strange, Susan. 1994. *States and Markets*. New York: Basil Blackwell.

Tocqueville, Alexis de. 1873. *Democracy in America*. 5th ed. Boston: John Allyn.

Toffler, Alvin. 1980. *The Third Wave*. New York: Morrow.

Trapeznikov, S. P. 1976. *Leninism and the Agrarian and Peasant Question*. Moscow: Progress Publishers.

Venturi, Franco. 1966. *Roots of Revolution: A History of the Populist and Socialist Movements in Nineteenth-Century Russia*. New York: Grosset and Dunlap. Translated by Francis Haskell.

Verba, Sidney, Kay Lehman Schlozman, and Henry Brady. 1995. *Voice and Equality: Civic Voluntarism and American Politics*. Cambridge, Mass.: Harvard University Press.

Vidal, Gore. 1987. *Empire*. New York: Random House.

Walton, John. 1984. *Reluctant Rebels: Comparative Studies of Revolution and Underdevelopment*. New York: Columbia University Press.

Williams, William Appleman. 1980. *Empire as a Way of Life*. London and New York: Oxford University Press.

Winn, Peter. 1986. *Weavers of Revolution: The Yarur Workers and Chile's Road to Socialism*. New York: Oxford University Press.

Wolfe, Alan. 1989. *Whose Keeper? Social Science and Moral Obligation*. Berkeley: University of California Press.

Wrigley, E. A., and R. S. Schofield. 1981. *The Population History of England, 1541–1871: A Reconstruction*. Cambridge, Mass.: Harvard University Press.

Zeitlin, Maurice. 1967. *Revolutionary Politics and the Cuban Working Class*. Princeton: Princeton University Press.

Zeitlin, Maurice, and Richard Earl Ratcliff. 1988. *Landlords and Capitalists: The Dominant Class of Chile*. Princeton: Princeton University Press.

Zunz, Olivier. 1982. *The Changing Face of Inequality: Urbanization, Industrial Development, and Immigrants in Detroit, 1880–1920*. Chicago: University of Chicago Press.

INDEX